HISTORY, SCRIPTURE AND AUTHORITY
IN THE CAROLINGIAN EMPIRE

A British Academy Monograph

The British Academy has a scheme for the selective publication of monographs arising from its British Academy Postdoctoral Fellowships, British Academy Newton International Fellowships and British Academy / Wolfson Fellowships. Its purpose is to assist individual scholars by providing a prestigious publishing opportunity to showcase works of excellence.

Graeme Ward is an Associate Member of the Faculty of History, University of Oxford. His research examines the intellectual culture of early medieval western Europe. Between 2018 and 2021 he held a British Academy Postdoctoral Fellowship at Oxford, and between 2013 and 2017 he was based at the Institute for Medieval Research in Vienna. He has published articles and has edited collected volumes on various aspects of Carolingian history.

HISTORY, SCRIPTURE AND AUTHORITY IN THE CAROLINGIAN EMPIRE

Frechulf of Lisieux

Graeme Ward

Published for THE BRITISH ACADEMY
by OXFORD UNIVERSITY PRESS

Oxford University Press, Great Clarendon Street, Oxford OX2 6DP

First edition published 2022

British Library Cataloguing in Publication Data
Data available

Library of Congress Cataloging in Publication Data
Data available

Typeset in the offices of The British Academy
by Portia Taylor
Printed in Great Britain by
TJ Books Ltd, Padstow, Cornwall

ISBN 978–0–19–726728–8

Contents

Acknowledgements

Writing this book has been a protracted and often difficult process, so it is a great pleasure (and great relief) finally to be able to thank the many people and institutions who have made it possible and kept me going throughout.

This book began life in 2010 as a PhD thesis. As a doctoral student, Frechulf's *Histories* were an ideal topic: a meaty text, readily available in a splendid critical edition, and little historiography to contend with. More fortunate still, my doctorate was funded through a HERA joint research project, Cultural Memory and the Resources of the Past, which allowed me to work alongside a superb team of early medievalists from Cambridge, Leeds, Utrecht and Vienna. That early experience of working with European colleagues was formative and directly led me to spend a number of happy, largely Frechulf-free years working on, or in tandem with, similarly international and collaborative projects at the Institut für Mittelalterforschung in Vienna. I was supported variously by an Ernst Mach Stipendium, a Leverhulme Study Abroad Studentship, the SFB-Project Visions of Community, and the OeAW. I returned to the UK in 2018 to take up a British Academy Postdoctoral Fellowship. The bulk of the rewriting took place over the past two years, whenever I was able to peel myself away from ongoing work on another overlooked Carolingian, Amalarius.

Two people in particular have been instrumental in this book's gestation. First and foremost, I owe a huge debt of gratitude to my doctoral supervisor, Rosamond McKitterick. I have benefitted immeasurably from her unfailing encouragement, support and generosity, both during and after my PhD. While Rosamond guided me through the first stages of my journey, Julia Smith, my mentor at Oxford, helped push me to get the revised manuscript over the line, reading almost every chapter along the way. That Julia taught me at Glasgow as an undergraduate and master's student, and spurred me on to apply for one of the advertised spots on the HERA project, makes it doubly satisfying to thank her here.

Many others have aided me in various ways. Stuart Airlie – together with Julia Smith – first fuelled my interest in the early Middle Ages. My thesis examiners, Mayke de Jong and Christopher Kelly, offered sage advice on how to go about transforming the thesis into a book. I am grateful to Walter Pohl and Max Diesenberger for hosting and supporting me at the IMAFO. I have been fortunate enough to have been able to work on (and off of) this project at the Cambridge University Library, the Universitätsbibliothek in Vienna and the Bodleian at Oxford. Many thanks are also due to the publications team at the British Academy: Portia Taylor for her patience and the occasional, and much needed, prod; the anonymous reviewer for useful and positive feedback; Hamish Scott, who offered wise counsel at the outset; and Gillian Clark for her model mentorship.

The various periods of research, writing, procrastinating and rewriting that have gone into this book have rarely been lonely, and for that I count myself lucky; this has even been the case in the challenging months of lockdown, thanks not least to Miriam Driessen, with whom most of the final stages were completed during daily online writing sessions. Between Cambridge, Vienna and Oxford, I have enjoyed countless fruitful discussions and necessary distractions with many wonderful friends and colleagues – too many to adequately record here, but I hope they know who they are. I want to give special thanks to Anna Dorofeeva, Sarah Greer, Victoria Leonard, Ingrid Rembold, Ed Roberts, Danica Summerlin and Robin Whelan, who read various chapter drafts, and provided generous and constructive feedback. Among the many others I have pestered with questions, I should single out Jacob Currie, Rob Gallagher, Cinzia Grifoni, Anya Raisharma, Giorgia Vocino, and Neil Wright, who all have helped me make sense of Frechulf's occasionally unfriendly Latin. Michael Allen supplied me with a pdf of Bertha Schelle's dissertation at the beginning of my doctorate, and more recently Sam Ottewill-Soulsby kindly shared a forthcoming essay with me. Elisabeth Mégier, whose work on historiography and exegesis I have learned much from, gifted me a copy of her book. Outside of academia, Christina suffered through the writing process almost as much as I did: she'll be glad to know that, at long last, it's done.

Last but by no means least, I want to thank my parents. My academic life has given them plenty of opportunity for travel, though less so recently. Although this book may be far less enjoyable than coffee and cake in Vienna's Innere Stadt, I hope it nevertheless brightens up their bookcase: it is to them I dedicate it.

List of Abbreviations

Augustine, *DCD*	Augustine, *De civitate Dei*, eds B. Dombart & A. Kalb, CCSL 47–8 (Brepols: Turnhout, 1955).
Chron.	Eusebius-Jerome, *Chronicon*, ed. Rudolf Helm, *Eusebius Werke*, vol. 7: *Die Chronik des Hieronymus/Hieronymi Chronicon*, Die griechischen christlichen Schriftsteller der ersten Jahrhunderte 47, 2nd edn (Berlin: Akademie-Verlag, 1956).
Bede, *DTR*	Bede, *De temporum ratione*, ed. Charles W. Jones, CCSL 123B (Turnhout: Brepols, 1977); trans. Wallis = Faith Wallis (trans.), *Bede: On the Reckoning of Time* (Liverpool: LUP, 1999).
CCM	Corpus Consuetudinum Monasticarum (Siegburg: F. Schmitt, 1963–).
CCCM	Corpus Christianorum, Continuatio Medievalis (Turnhout: Brepols, 1966–).
CCSL	Corpus Christianorum, Series Latina (Turnhout: Brepols, 1952–).
CSEL	Corpus Scriptorum Ecclesiasticorum Latinorum (Vienna: Hoelder–Pichler–Tempsky, 1866–).
CUA Press	Catholic University of America Press
CUP	Cambridge University Press
DA	*Deutsches Archiv für Erforschung des Mittelalters.*
EME	*Early Medieval Europe.*
Epist.	Frechulf of Lisieux, *Epistola ad Hrabanum Maurum de pentateucho commentando*, ed. Michael I. Allen, *Frechulfi Lexoviensis episcopi opera omnia*, CCCM 169 A (Turnhout: Brepols, 2002), pp. 3–7.
Hist.	Frechulf of Lisieux, *Historiarum libri XII*, ed. Michael I. Allen, *Frechulfi Lexoviensis episcopi opera omnia*, CCCM 169 A (Turnhout: Brepols, 2002), pp. 9-724 ; trans. Lake = Justin

	Lake, Prologues to Ancient and Medieval History: A Reader (Toronto: University of Toronto Press, 2013).
Hrab. *Epist.*	Hrabanus Maurus, *Epistolae*, ed. Ernst Dümmler, MGH *Epp.* V (Berlin: Weidmann, 1899), 381–516.
Hrab. *Exp.*	Hrabanus Maurus, *Expositio in Matthaeum*, ed. Bengt Löfstedt, CCCM 174, 2 vols (Turnhout: Brepols, 2000).
HUP	Harvard University Press.
Jerome, *DVI*	Jerome, *De viris illustribus*, ed. E. C. Richardson, *Hieronymus, Liber de viris illustribus. Gennadius, De virus illustribus* (Leipzig: J. C, Hinrichs, 1896), trans. Halton = Thomas P. Halton (trans.), *Saint Jerome: On Illustrious Men*, The Fathers of the Church 100 (Washington, DC: CUA Press, 1999).
LCL	Loeb Classical Library.
LUP	Liverpool University Press.
MGH	Monumenta Germaniae Historica.
Auct. Ant.	*Auctores Antiquissimi*, 15 vols. (Berlin: Weidmann, 1877–1919).
Capit.	*Capitularia, legum sectio* II, *Capitularia regum Francorum*, ed. Alfred Boretius & Victor Krause, 2 vols. (Hanover: Hahn, 1883–97).
Capit. Episc.	*Capitula episcoporum* I–IV, eds Peter Brommer, Rudolf Pokorny & Martina Stratmann (Hanover: Hahn, 1984–2005).
Conc.	*Concilia, Legum Sectio* III, *Concilia*: II, ed. Albert Werminghoff (Hanover: Hahn, 1906–8); III, ed. Wilfried Hartmann (Hanover: Hahn, 1984).
Epp.	*Epistolae* III–VII, (=*Epistolae merowingici et karolini aevi* (Hanover: Hahn, 1892–1939).
Fontes Iuris	*Fontes Iuris Germanici Antiqui in usum scholarum separatim editi.*
SRG	*Scriptores Rerum Germanicarum in usum scholarum separatim editi*, 63 vols. (Hanover: Hahn, 1871–1987).
SRM	*Scriptores rerum Merovingicarum*, 7 vols (Hanover: Hahn, 1885–1920).
SS	*Scriptores in folio*, 30 vols (Hanover: Hahn, 1824–1924).
MUP	Manchester University Press.
OUP	Oxford University Press.
Oros.	Orosius, *Historiae adversum paganos*, ed. Marie-Pierre Arnaud-Lindet, *Orose: Histoires (contre les païens)*, 3 vols

(Paris, Les Belles Lettres, 1990–1); trans. Fear = A. T. Fear (trans.), *Orosius: Seven Books of History against the Pagans* (Liverpool: LUP, 2010).

PL   *Patrologiae Cursus Completus, Series Latina*, ed. J.-P. Migne, 221 vols. (Paris, 1841–64).

Prolegomena   Michael I. Allen, *Prolegomena*, in *Frechulfi Lexoviensis episcopi opera omnia*, CCCM 169 (Turnhout: Brepols, 2002).

Prol. Veg.   Frechulf of Lisieux, *Prologus ad Karolum Calvum regem in libellos Flavii Vegeti Renati de re militari nuper emendatos*, ed. Michael I. Allen, *Frechulfi Lexoviensis episcopi opera omnia*, CCCM 169 A (Turnhout: Brepols, 2002), 72–59.

Settimane   Settimane di studio del Centro italiano di studi sull'alto Medioevo (Spoleto, 1953–).

Synopsis of the *Histories*

Part I: Creation to Christ

Book	No. of Chapters	Pages in CCCM edition	Summary of Contents	Relative Chronology (BC)[1]
1	57	28–86	The earliest eras of human history, including the world's creation, its destruction by the Flood and then its repopulation by Noah's descendants up until Abraham; close focus throughout on how to understand historically a range of difficult passages in Genesis (cc.1–21).	? – c. 2000
2	30	91–154	From the birth of Abraham through to Moses and the Exodus, concluding with the construction of the First Temple; Jewish history synchronised (often apologetically so) with legendary events and figures from Greek pre-history. Extended chapters on the origins of the Scythians, that is, the Goths (I.2.25) and the Trojan War (I.2.26), the latter of which includes the debated origins of the Franks.	c. 2000– c. 1000
3	19	158–206	From the First Temple to the construction of the Second Temple, between which the establishment of kingdoms of Judah and Israel, and	c. 1000– c. 538

[1] Dates relating to the Old Testament, so far as they can be known, are drawn from Michael D. Coogan, *The Old Testament: A Historical and Literary Introduction to the Hebrew Scriptures* (New York and Oxford, OUP, 2006), 550–57.

Part II: Christ's Birth to the Seventh Century

Dramatis personae

Key Carolingians

Frechulf, bishop of Lisieux (c. 824–50/2) and creator of the *Histories*.

Hrabanus Maurus: abbot of Fulda (822–42) and later archbishop of Mainz (847–56). Prolific exegete and a friend of Frechulf, stemming from their shared experiences as monks at Fulda.

Helisachar (died before 840): imperial chancellor until 819; thereafter, abbot of St Riquier and of St Aubin, Angers. Helisachar was an important player at the Carolingian court throughout the 820s and was the dedicatee of Part I of the *Histories*.

Judith of Bavaria (died 843): Bavarian elite and, from 1819, Carolingian empress. Wife of Louis the Pious (reigned 814–40) and mother of the future West Frankish king, Charles the Bald. Judith, another central figure at the Carolingian court, was the dedicatee of Part II of the *Histories*.

Charles the Bald (died 877): in c. 830, while still a boy, he was evoked in dedicatory preface to Part II; in the late 830s or early 840s, when king of west Francia, he was the recipient of Frechulf's edition of Vegetius's *Epitoma*.

Frechulf's (Select) Authorities

Flavius Josephus (died c. 100): author of the *Jewish War* and *Jewish Antiquities*, two Hellenistic histories of the Jewish world which had been translated into Latin by the mid-sixth century.

Eusebius of Caesarea (died 339/40): eastern Roman bishop, historian and exegete, whose *Chronicle* and *Ecclesiastical History*—read in the early medieval west in their Latin respective translations and continuations by Jerome and Rufinus of Aquileia—fundamentally shaped Christian perceptions of the past and were central to Frechulf's project.

Vegetius (flourished fourth century): author of the *Epitoma rei militaris*, a fourth-century military handbook which Frechulf edited and dedicated to Charles the Bald.

Jerome of Stridon (died 420): priest, translator and exegete. His Latin translation and continuation of Eusebius's *Chronicle* together with his catalogue of Christian authorities, the *De viris illustribus* ('On Illustrious Men'), were key sources for Frechulf.

Paulus Orosius (flourished c. 417): Spanish priest and pupil of Augustine. His *Seven Books of Histories against the Pagans* supplied an abundance of material throughout all twelve books of Frechulf's *Histories*.

Augustine (died 430): bishop of Hippo and prodigious author and exegete. Frechulf was a careful reader of Augustine's magnum opus, *De civitate Dei* ('On the City of God'); as a result, Augustine's influence has been considered decisive in shaping the *Histories*.

Cassiodorus (died 585): retired senator and founder of the school of Vivarium. He produced a handbook from Christian study (the *Institutions*) and sponsored the Latin translation and compilation of three fifth-century Greek continuators of Eusebius's *Ecclesiastical History*, Socrates, Sozomen and Theoderet: the resulting text, known as the *Historia ecclesiastica tripartita* ('The Tripartite History'), was one of Frechulf's main sources for Christian imperial history between Constantine and Theodosius II.

Jordanes (flourished mid-sixth century): sixth-century Constantinopolitan author; Frechulf was keen reader of both his *Romana* ('Roman history') and *Getica* ('Gothic history').

Bede (died 735): monk at Wearmouth–Jarrow in Northumbria, exegete and historian. The world chronicle that comprised c. 66 of his *De temporum ratione* ('On the Reckoning of Time') was used throughout the *Histories*, especially towards the end.

Introduction

Framework of this Study

Why was history written and read in the early Middle Ages? Within the vast amount of academic literature that has been devoted to addressing this fundamental question, a dominant trend has emerged in recent decades: history-writing was, above all, a political act.[1] Understood from this perspective, historical narratives were written not simply to record major events but to justify or challenge them. Histories and chronicles are now primarily understood as participants in, rather than mere transmitters of, episodes of dynastic change, succession, conquest, rebellion and its suppression. Historiography was thus a medium through which power, authority and legitimacy were either communicated or contested. The political force and relevance of history have been uncovered not only in the representation of contemporary or near contemporary episodes; accounts of the distant past too have been understood in the light of present-day struggles over power and status.

This book sets out to challenge this paradigm, not by rejecting the study of power and politics but by prioritising the intellectual contexts and institutional settings in which historical knowledge not only was created but also was consumed. It does so with specific reference to the Carolingian empire, a loose territorial unit symbolically born into existence when Charlemagne (ruled 774–814) was crowned emperor in Rome in 800 after decades of bloody conquest and expansionism. The empire endured in various forms over the course of the ninth century under the leadership of Charlemagne's successors until the death of Charles the Fat in 888.[2] In tandem with, and arguably as a consequence of, the establishment of Carolingian dynastic authority, the later eighth and especially ninth centuries witnessed a dramatic rise in the production and preservation of written knowledge in ecclesiastical centres of learning spread across western Europe. In monastic and cathedral churches all across this expansive area, from

[1] Justin Lake, 'Current Approaches to Medieval Historiography', *History Compass*, 13(3) (2015): 89–109 at 92–5; see also Justin Lake, 'Authorial Intention in Medieval Historiography', *History Compass*, 12(4) (2014): 344–60 at 352–3.

[2] Marios Costambeys, Matthew Innes and Simon MacLean, *The Carolingian World* (Cambridge: CUP, 2011) and Stuart Airlie, *Making and Unmaking the Carolingians, 751–888* (London: Bloomsbury, 2020).

Saxony to Catalonia, considerable effort was invested in copying, studying and even cataloguing texts, especially those perceived as possessing a special, authoritative, status. At the epicentre of this textual boom stood the various books of the Old and New Testaments together with the writings of the *sancti patres*, the church fathers, a vast and varied body of literature produced during an earlier era of Christian empire. Taken together, the patristic heritage of Latin Late Antiquity, which roughly speaking stretched from the second century through to the death of Gregory the Great (died 604), became the collective bedrock of all medieval intellectual culture. The Carolingian age played a decisive role in shaping the medieval patristic canon.[3]

The processes by which a patristic canon came into being were gradual and piecemeal, and significantly predated the Carolingians.[4] The perception of a recognised corpus had taken shape in the fourth century (if not earlier), and over the course of fifth, sixth, seventh and eighth centuries the canon variously expanded and contracted as new authorities were approved and incorporated and others condemned or rejected. The Carolingian church thus inherited many hundreds of years' worth of creative experiments in the production and definition of authoritative knowledge originally undertaken in the Roman Empire as well as in the post-imperial western kingdoms of Ostrogothic Italy, Vandal North Africa, Visigothic Iberia, Britain and Ireland, and Merovingian Gaul. Far from being mere passive recipients, Carolingian ecclesiastics made a profound contribution to this process of inheritance. In copying old texts, the language and grammar of corrupted exemplars were corrected in line with new standards, and older forms of the written word were replaced by what is now known as Caroline minuscule, a neat, well-regulated script that was employed throughout the empire and lasted long after it. Furthermore, the patristic canon—as a canon—was intensively scrutinised, its constituent elements compared and contrasted, and intricate compilations of patristic knowledge were fashioned to address myriad problems

---

[3] This is one aspect of what was traditionally referred to as the 'Carolingian Renaissance', a topic with an enormous bibliography. For context, see: Giles Brown, 'Introduction: The Carolingian Renaissance', in *Carolingian Culture: Emulation and Innovation*, ed. Rosamond McKitterick (Cambridge: CUP, 1994), 1–51; John Contreni, 'The Carolingian Renaissance: Education and Literary Culture', in *The New Cambridge Medieval History, Vol. II, c.700–c.900*, ed. Rosamond McKitterick (Cambridge: CUP, 1997), 709–57; Rosamund, McKitterick, 'The Carolingian Renaissance and the Culture of Learning', in *Charlemagne: Empire and Society*, ed. Joanna Story (Manchester: MUP, 2005), 151–66; Phillipe Depreux, 'Ambitions et limites des réformes culturelles à l'époque Carolingienne', *Revue historique*, 304 (2002): 721–53.

[4] François Dolbeau, 'La formation du Canon des Pères, du IVᵉ au VIᵉ siècle', in *Les réceptions des Pères de l'Église au Moyen Âge: le devenir de la tradition ecclésiale*, eds Nicole Bériou, Rainer Berndt and Michel Fédou, Archa verbi. Subsidia 10, 2 vols (Münster: Aschendorff, 2013), vol. 1, 17–39; Stéphane Gioanni, 'Les listes d'auteurs «à recevoir» et «à ne pas recevoir» dans la formation du canon patristique: le *decretum gelasianum* et les origines de la «censure» ecclésiastique', in *Compétition et sacré au haut Moyen Âge: entre mediation et exclusion*, eds Philippe Depreux, François Bourgard and Régine le Jan (Turnhout: Brepols, 2015), 17–28.

of biblical interpretation, devotion and worship, ecclesiastical organisation and office-holding, and the morals and norms of all modes of Christian life, from the expected comportment of the laity to the rigours of monastic existence. Stemming from this intense, empire-wide activity, the Latin patristic canon, as it was perceived throughout the Middle Ages, is now to a large extent considered to have been the creation of the later eighth and ninth centuries.[5]

It is against this backdrop that the present study unfolds. This monograph, which is a revised version of my 2014 doctoral dissertation, takes as its focus the work of a single ninth-century historian, Frechulf of Lisieux, and examines his text not, first and foremost, as a historiographical response to Carolingian politics and power, but rather as a rich cultural artefact that illuminates the role of history and historiography within the intellectual culture of ninth-century western Europe, centred as it was on the interpretation of the Bible and the study of the Latin patristic canon.[6]

'The Books from the Beginning of the World': Frechulf's *Histories*

Frechulf and his work lie at the centre of this monograph. Frechulf was bishop of the north-western see of Lisieux (in modern-day Normandy), a position he took up c. 824/825 and held until 850/852. Before entering the episcopate, he was likely trained at Fulda, where he formed a lasting friendship with the monastery's prominent abbot, Hrabanus Maurus. As a bishop, Frechulf not only was a key regional player, but also was involved in the ecclesiastical politics of the Carolingian empire and enjoyed connections with the imperial court circle of the reigning emperor, Louis the Pious (ruled 814–40). The next sections of this introduction will look in more detail at Frechulf's biography, his associations and their implications for the interpretation of his extant writings. First, I shall briefly introduce his principal text.

Frechulf completed his *Twelve Books of Histories* around 830.[7] This work comprised a sweeping account of rulers, *regna* and memorable deeds, which

---

[5] Conrad Leyser, 'Late Antiquity and the Medieval West', in *A Companion to Late Antiquity*, ed. Philip Rousseau (Chichester: John Wiley, 2009), 29–42 at 32-3; Bernice Martha Kaczynski, 'The Authority of the Fathers: Patristic Texts in Early Medieval Libraries and Scriptoria', *Journal of Medieval Latin*, 16 (2006): 1–27; Willemien Otten, 'The Texture of Tradition: The Role of the Church Fathers in Carolingian Theology', in *The Reception of the Church Fathers in the West: From the Carolingians to the Maurists*, ed. Irena Backus, 2 vols (Leiden: Brill, 2001), vol. I, 3-50. For the wider medieval picture, see Nicole Bériou, Rainer Berndt and Michel Fédou (eds), *Les réceptions des Pères de l'Église au Moyen Âge: le devenir de la tradition ecclésiale*, Archa verbi. Subsidia 10, 2 vols (Münster: Aschendorff, 2013). On Carolingian minuscule, see David Ganz, 'Early Caroline: France and Germany', in *The Oxford Handbook of Latin Palaeography*, eds Frank T. Coulson and Robert G. Babcock (Oxford: OUP, 2020), 237–61.

[6] Celia Chazelle and Burton van Name Edwards, 'Introduction: The Study of the Bible and Carolingian Culture', in *The Study of the Bible in the Carolingian Era*, eds Celia Chazelle and Burton van Name Edwards, Medieval Church Studies 3 (Turnhout: Brepols, 2003), 1–16.

[7] *Hist.*, pp. 17–724.

stretched from the world's creation through to the seventh century. On the whole, the *Histories* were fashioned from excerpts from a wide array of late antique narratives, which were carefully compiled together into a new, expansive whole that runs to some 700 pages in the modern critical edition and comprises over 138,000 words. Frechulf's grand narrative was conceived in two separate but conceptually linked volumes (labelled throughout this book as Parts I and II). Part I, split into seven books, covered the period between the creation of Adam and the birth of Jesus Christ. It was dedicated to Helisachar, an ecclesiastical magnate and prominent member of the imperial entourage of Louis the Pious. Sometime after completing Part I, Frechulf began work on his second volume, which he arranged in five books and dedicated to the Empress Judith, wife of Louis the Pious, purportedly for the education of her young son Charles. Part II's narrative picked up where the first left off and took the story forward from Christ's Nativity through to the death of Pope Gregory the Great and the establishment of post-imperial kingdoms in Gaul and Italy. A synopsis of the structure and contents of the *Histories*, as well as an overview of the principal actors and textual authorities that will be encountered throughout what follows, can be found at the front of this book.

Around a decade after its completion, Frechulf offered a neat summary of his *Histories*. In the late 830s or early 840s, he produced a 'corrected' edition of Vegetius's *Epitoma rei militaris*, a Roman military handbook first written in the late fourth century, which he gifted to this same Charles, now no longer a six-year-old boy but the king of western Francia (840–77).[8] In the accompanying letter of dedication, Frechulf offered a retrospective precis of his *Histories*, inviting his exalted royal dedicatee to cast his mind back to those:

> books from the beginning of the world through to the [establishment of] kingdoms of the Franks in Gaul, compiled by my insignificant self from the histories of sacred and secular authors, in which are contained those things that seem worthy of memory and which occur repeatedly in each part of the world or in the more eminent kingdoms, as well as how each of the gentile kingdoms began and how, either through carelessness or idleness, they perished.[9]

Writing to Judith, Frechulf underscored the role that the reading of history ought to play in the instruction of a young prince; to Charles, he restated the link

---

[8] *Prolegomena*, 25*–53*. The preface has been dated variously to 838, 840 or 843/853; Michael Allen favoured the date of 842. See further Michael D. Reeve, 'The Transmission of Vegetius's *Epitoma rei militaris*', *Aevum*, 74 (2000): 243–354 and Christopher T. Allmand, *The De re militari of Vegetius: The Reception, Transmission and Legacy of a Roman Text in the Middle Ages* (Cambridge: CUP, 2011).

[9] *Prol. Veg.*, p. 729: 'Igitur post libros ab inicio mundi usque ad regna Francorum in Galliis a paruitate mea congestos ex agiografphorum siue gentilium historiis—in quibus continentur quaeque uidentur uel frequentantur digna in singulis partibus orbis uel in eminentioribus regnis memoria, seu quomodo initia sumendo inchoauerunt uel qua desidia uel incuria singularum regna gentium defecerunt—cui operi si regia maiestas adriserit, utiliter subnectendos hos censeo fore thomos.'

between erudition and rulership. Read in tandem, his *Histories* and Vegetius's *Epitoma* would help 'rulers safeguard themselves and their men from harm, should divine grace grant it'.[10]

The education of one young ruler, however, was neither the only nor even the primary purpose that guided Frechulf in his endeavours. The high-profile dedications of Frechulf's work, while often the aspect that catches the eyes of modern scholars, were but one part of the careful study of received knowledge which connects Frechulf, directly and indirectly, to other learned ecclesiastics of the period, labouring away in the service of God as well as kings. Maurus, abbot of Fulda and archbishop of Mainz (died 856) and Bishop Hartgar of Liège (died 855) for example, also dedicated copies of Vegetius to Carolingian rulers and high-ranking aristocrats.[11] Within the imperial culture of the ninth century, there was real interest in the writings of Roman antiquity.[12] Yet this paled in comparison to the central role played by the writings of Christian antiquity. The creation and dissemination of the *Histories* testify to this.

Frechulf's was 'the richest and longest example of Carolingian historical writing', and was one of the most influential, insofar as can be gauged by the text's transmission and reception.[13] Parts I and II circulated separately as well as together: in total forty-one manuscripts survive from across much of western Europe, most of which, it should be noted, contain only the text of Part I; at least a further fourteen medieval copies are known to have been lost.[14] Already within Frechulf's lifetime it is possible to catch glimpses of the *Histories'* diffusion in the Carolingian empire. The earliest complete witness, in which Parts I and II were stitched together as a single tome (or 'pandect'), was most likely produced at Lisieux under Frechulf's supervision. By 875 it had been transported to the abbey library at St Gall in modern-day Switzerland, where it is still preserved today.[15] Within Frechulf's lifetime, another 'pandect' was available at Reichenau, St Gall's monastic neighbour on Lake Constance. Only a fragment of this codex is extant, but parts of it were transcribed by Walahfrid Strabo, who served at the imperial court as Charles the Bald's 'tutor' before becoming abbot of Reichenau (838–49),

---

[10] *Prol. Veg.*, p. 729: 'Quibus inspectis cum superioribus libris, si diuina permiserit gratia, principes sua suorumque incommoda praecauere poterint.'

[11] Hrab. *Epist.*, no. 57, pp. 514–15 and Ernst Dümmler, 'De procinctu Romanae milicia', *Zeitschrift für deutsches Alterthum*, 15 (1872): 443–51; Paul J. Kershaw, 'Eberhard of Friuli, a Carolingian Lay Intellectual', in *Lay Intellectuals in the Carolingian World*, eds Patrick Wormald and Janet L. Nelson (Cambridge: CUP, 2007), 77–105.

[12] See, for example, Sinéad O'Sullivan, 'Glossing Vergil and Pagan Learning in the Carolingian Age', *Speculum*, 93(1) (2018): 132–65.

[13] Michael I. Allen, 'Frechulf of Lisieux', in *The Oxford Guide to the Historical Reception of Augustine*, eds Karla Pollmann and Willemien Otten, 3 vols (Oxford: OUP, 2013), vol. 2, 1010–11, at 1010.

[14] For an extensive survey, see *Prolegomena*, 55*–179*.

[15] St. Gallen, Stiftsbibliothek, Cod. Sang. 622, on which see *Prolegomena*, 58*–78*. See also Michael I. Allen, 'Bede and Frechulf at Medieval St Gallen', in *Beda Venerabilis: Historian, Monk and Northumbrian*, eds L. A. J. R. Houwen and A. A. MacDonald (Groningen: E. Forsten, 1996), 61–80.

where he took an interest in the *Histories*.[16] A copy of Part I of the *Histories* was also counted amongst the rich holdings of the monastic library at Lorsch in the Middle Rhine Valley (c. 860), and the codex itself was produced at the monastery of Saint-Vaast, Arras.[17] A further ninth-century fragment from a text of Part II produced at an unidentified scriptorium in northern Francia hints at an even wider ninth-century distribution.[18]

One attempt to measure the relative influence of historical narratives in the Middle Ages considered any work that has been transmitted in more than thirty manuscripts to have been 'un succès grand'.[19] For comparison, the only examples of Carolingian history writing that rival the *Histories'* rate of survival are Einhard's *Life of Charlemagne* (123 manuscripts), the *Royal Frankish Annals* (thirty-nine) and Regino of Prüm's *Chronicle* (thirty).[20] Yet Frechulf's 'great success' appears all the more remarkable because the *Histories* were compiled at Lisieux, an otherwise obscure episcopal church in Neustria (northern modern-day France). While the libraries and intellectual cultures of the prominent centres where copies of the *Histories* ended up—St Gall, Reichenau and Lorsch—can be partially reconstructed and investigated in the light of detailed contemporary catalogues and a wealth of extant narratives, charters and codices, Lisieux presents a notably more enigmatic case.[21] Were it not for the survival of Frechulf's work, neither this bishop nor his bishopric would figure at all in modern accounts of the cultural history of the Carolingian age. And even with the impressive evidence that Frechulf's writings provide, there have been very few detailed considerations of their significance.[22]

---

[16]　*Prolegomena*, 79*–82*; Richard Corradini, 'Approaches to History: Walahfrid's Parallel Universe', in *Historiography and Identity III: Carolingian Approaches*, eds Rutger Kramer, Helmut Reimitz and Graeme Ward (Turnhout: Brepols, 2021), 155–97, esp. 176–81; compare Wesley M. Stevens, *Rhetoric and Reckoning in the Ninth Century: The Vademecum of Walahfrid Strabo* (Turnhout: Brepols, 2018), 70–1.

[17]　*Prolegomena*, 147*–8*; Angelika Häse, *Mittelalterliche Bücherverzeichnisse aus Kloster Lorsch: Einleitung, Edition und Kommentar* (Weisbaden: Harrassowitz, 2002), p. 165: 'Historia Frehculfi [sic], libri VII in uno codice'.

[18]　*Prolegomena*, 98*–9*.

[19]　Bernard Guenée, *Histoire et culture historique dans l'Occident médiéval* (Paris: Aubier, 1980), 250–5.

[20]　For the manuscript transmission of Einhard, see Matthias M. Tischler, *Einharts Vita Karoli: Studien zur Entstehung, überlieferung und Rezeption*, 2 vols (Hanover: Harrassowitz, 2001); for Regino, see Wolf-Rüdiger Schleidgen, *Die Überlieferungsgeschichte der Chronik des Regino von Prüm* (Mainz: Selbstverlag der Gesellschaft für Mittelrheinische Kirchengeschichte, 1977).

[21]　See, for example, Bernard Bischoff, *Die Abtei Lorsch im Spiegel ihrer Handschriften* (Lorsch: Heimat- und Kulturverein Lorsch mit Unterstützing der Stadt Lorsch, 1989); Walter Berschin, *Eremus und Insula. St. Gallen und die Reichenau im Mittealter. Modell einer lateinischen Literaturlandschaft* (Wiesbaden: Ludwig Reichert, 1987); Anna A. Grotans, *Reading in Medieval St Gall* (Cambridge: CUP, 2006).

[22]　Theses: Bertha Schelle, 'Frechulf von Lisieux: Untersuchungen zu Leben und Werk' (PhD dissertation, University of Munich, 1952), and Michael I. Allen, 'History in the Carolingian Renewal: Frechulf of Lisieux (fl. 830), his Work and Influence' (unpublished PhD dissertation, University of Toronto, 1994). Dedicated studies: Werner Goez, 'Zur Weltchronik des Bischofs Frechulf von Lisieux', in *Festgabe für Paul Kirn zum 70. Geburtstag, dargebracht von Freunden und Schülern*, ed. Ekkehard Kaufmann (Berlin: E. Schmidt, 1961), 93–110; Chester F. Natunewicz, 'Freculphus of Lisieux, his *Chronicle* and a Mont St Michel Manuscript', *Sacris Erudiri*, 17 (1966): 90–134; Raffaele Savigni, 'Storia universale e storia ecclesiastica nel *Chronicon* di Freculfo di Lisieux', *Studi medievali*, 28 (1987):

Indeed, the various ways that Frechulf can be connected to the wider trends that energised the Carolingian church in the late eighth and ninth centuries have not yet been fully explored. Before turning to these trends, it will first be helpful to say more about Frechulf and his world.

'On the Western Shore of the Ocean': Frechulf's Lisieux

Soon after assuming episcopal office, perhaps in late 824 or early 825, Frechulf wrote to Hrabanus Maurus, the recently elected abbot of Fulda (822–42), imploring that books be sent out to Lisieux, located far away 'on the western shore of the ocean'.[23] Pastoral concerns prompted this request: the community for which he was now responsible was 'hungry for the words of salvation' but had not yet come to realise it. To begin to build up his flock's spiritual appetite, Frechulf needed resources, but these, he discovered, were sorely lacking. In his new episcopal see (*episcopium*), neither the books of the Old and New Testaments nor their patristic exegesis were to be found. It was thus imperative that Hrabanus compile commentaries on the Pentateuch, the first five books of the Christian Bible, and send them to Lisieux. This Hrabanus duly did in five separate instalments.[24] Two context-related topics emerge from this exchange: the state of Lisieux, and Frechulf's background and career. I deal with each in turn.

Frechulf's depiction of Lisieux as bereft of the basic resources needed to administer pastoral care was likely exaggerated, but nevertheless begs the question: what sort of situation did Frechulf find himself in? A paucity of written sources and material culture makes it difficult to say much at all about Lisieux. Under the metropolitan leadership of Rouen, Lisieux was one of the *civitates* of the Roman administrative province of *Lugdunensis Secunda*, along with Bayeux, Avranches, Évreux, Séez and Coutances. By the sixth century, this administrative province had been transformed into an ecclesiastical one, which would later become the archiepiscopal diocese of Rouen.[25] Although this area of north-western Francia would emerge as part of the territory of the dukes of Normandy in the tenth and eleventh centuries, in the Carolingian period it appears somewhat peripheral, lying beyond the major ecclesiastical centres and *scriptoria* on the Seine (for example, St Denis, St Germain-des-Prés, Rouen and Fontenelle) and the Loire (for example, Tours and Orléans) and thus beyond the scope of most of the surviving

155–92; Nikolaus Staubach, '*Christiana tempora*: Augustin und das Ende der alten Geschichte in der Weltchronik Frechulfs von Lisieux', *Frühmittelalterliche Studien*, 29 (1995): 167–206; Michael I. Allen, 'Fréculf de Lisieux: l'histoire de l'antiquité comme témoignage de l'actualité', *Tabularia*, 8 (2008): 59–79.
[23] *Epist.*, p. 5: 'in occiduo litore Oceani'.
[24] Hrab. *Epist.*, nos. 8–12, pp. 393–400. Sita Steckel, *Kulturen des Lehrens im Früh- und Hochmittelalter. Autorität, Wissenskonzepte und Netzwerke von Gelehrten* (Cologne: Böhlau, 2011), 432–4.
[25] *Notitia Galliarum*, ed. Theodor E. Mommsen, MGH *Auct. Ant.* IX, (Berlin: Weidmann, 1892), pp. 552–612 at 586; Jill Harries, 'Church and State in the Notitia Galliarum', *Journal of Roman Studies*, 68 (1978): 26–43.

sources.[26] Detailed studies of the various regions of the Carolingian world have contributed enormously to the modern understanding of the social and political dynamics of the period.[27] In the absence of sufficient documentation, a comparable investigation into ninth-century Normandy would be difficult, to say the least.[28] Before Frechulf, for example, the only bishop of Lisieux about whom more than a name is known is Aetherius, who was the subject of a colourful anecdote in the *Histories* of Gregory of Tours. Around 583, Aetherius was briefly expelled from Lisieux following a conspiracy orchestrated by a lustful but learned priest from Le Mans on whom Aetherius had unwisely taken pity.[29] The name of one bishop before Aetherius is recorded in the subscription lists attached to sixth-century Frankish church councils; after Aetherius, three subsequent names are preserved. The last named bishop was Hincho, who witnessed a charter in 660.[30] The extant

---

[26] On Rouen, see Felice Lifshitz, *The Norman Conquest of Pious Neustria: Historiographic Discourse and Saintly Relics, 684–1090* (Toronto: Pontifical Institute of Mediaeval Studies, 1995) and Jacques Le Maho, 'Die erzbischöfliche Pfalz von Rouen', in *Splendor palatii: Neue Forschungen zu Paderborn und anderen Pfalzen der Karolingerzeit*, eds L. Fenske, J. Jarnut and M. Wemhoff (Göttingen: Vandenhoeck and Ruprecht, 2011),193–210; Jacques Le Maho, 'Francs et Normands avant 911: es dessous d'une réécriture', in *911–2011: penser les mondes normands médiévaux: actes du colloque international de Caen et Cerisy (29 septembre–2 octobre 2011)*, eds David Bates and Pierre Bauduin (Caen: Presses Universitaires de Caen, 2016), 29–52; Janet L. Nelson, 'Normandy's Early History since *Normandy Before 1066*', in *Normandy and its Neighbours, 900–1250: Essays for David Bates*, eds David Crouch and Kathleen Thompson (Turnhout: Brepols, 2011), 3–15. On Neustria in general, see Hartmut Atsma (ed.), *La Neustrie. Les pays au nord de la Loire 650 à 850. Colloque historique international*, 2 vols (Sigmaringen: Thorbecke, 1989); Rosamond McKitterick, *The Frankish Kingdoms under the Carolingians, 751–987* (London: Longman, 1983), 228–40; Rosamond McKitterick, 'Postérité et transmission des œvres historiographiques carolingiennes dans des mondes normands', in *L'Historiographie médiévale normande et ses sources antiques (X–XIIᵉ siècle)*, eds Pierre Bauduin and Marie-Agnès Lucas-Avenel (Caen: Presses Universitaires de Caen, 2014), 25–39.

[27] Regional Studies: Julia M. H. Smith, *Provience and Empire: Brittany and the Carolingians* (Cambridge: CUP, 1992); Matthew Innes, *State and Society in the Early Middle Ages: The Middle Rhein Valley, 400–1000* (Cambridge: CUP, 2000); Hans J. Hummer, *Politics and Power in Early Medieval Europe: Alsace and the Frankish Realm, 600–1000* (Cambridge: CUP, 2005); Marios J. Costambeys, *Power and Patronage in Early Medieval Italy: Local Society, Italian Politics, and the Abbey of Farfa, c. 700–900* (Cambridge: CUP, 2007); Ingrid Rembold, *Conquest and Christianization: Saxony and the Carolingian World, 772–888* (Cambridge: CUP, 2018); Cullen J. Chandler, *Carolingian Catalonia: Politics, Culture, and Identity in an Imperial Province, 778–987* (Cambridge: CUP, 2019).

[28] See, for example, Elisabeth Deniaux, Claude Lorren, Pierre Bauduin and Thomas Jarry (eds), *La Normandie avant les Normands de la conquête romaine à l'arrivée des Vikings* (Rennes: Ouest-France, 2002).

[29] Gregory of Tours, *Libri historiarum X*, VI. 36, ed. Bruno Krusch and Wilhelm Levison, *MGH SRM* 1:1, 2nd edn (Hanover: Hahn, 1951), pp. 306–8.

[30] Council of Orleans (538), ed. *Concilia Galliae a. 511–695*, Charles de Clercq, CCSL 148 A (Turnhout: Brepols, 1963), p. 129: 'Theodobaudus in Christi nominee ecclesiae Lixivi episcopus consensi'; Council of Orleans (541), p. 145: 'Edebius presbyter missus a domno meo Theudobaudo episcopo Lixivine ecclesiae subscripsi'; Council of Orleans (549), p. 159: 'Theudobaudis episcipus ecclesiae Lixoviensis subscripsi'; Council of Paris (614), p. 281: 'Ex civitate Loxovia Chamnegisilus episcopus and p. 281: 'Ex civitate Loxovias Launomundus episcopus'; Council of Chalon-sur-Saône (647–53), p. 309: 'Launobodis episcopus ecclesie Lixogensis subscripsi'; on Hincho, see Louis Duchesne, *Fastes épiscopaux de l'ancienne Gaule*, 3 vols (Paris, Thorin & fils, 1894–1915), vol. 2, 237. On these councils, see Odette Pontal, *Die Synoden im Merowingerreich* (Paderborn: Ferdinand Schöningh, 1986), 78–101, 182–8, 193–7.

lists of bishops (so-called *Fastes épiscopaux*) of the episcopal churches within the metropolitan diocese of Rouen are late and patchy, generally displaying extended gaps between the late seventh century and well into the reign of Louis the Pious.[31] Lisieux is especially poorly served by this evidence. The list compiled in the twelfth century by Robert of Torigni at Mont Saint-Michel began its series of bishops of Lisieux with Aetherius, jumped to Frechulf, then progressed to Roger, who was bishop in the late tenth and early eleventh centuries.[32] Factoring in individuals of whom Robert of Torigni was unaware (including Frechulf's direct successor, Hairard—attested between 853 and 876), we are still left with the names of only eight bishops over the course of half a millennium.

It is unclear what such a scrappy record signifies. Read together with Frechulf's letter to Hrabanus, it might imply a breakdown of local ecclesiastical order. Had Frechulf taken charge of a community in Francia's 'wild west' that had lain unoccupied for more than a century and half?[33] Had the local community been functioning, albeit without an ordained bishop? Or have the names of intervening leaders simply been lost, leaving twelfth-century compilers such as Robert of Torigni little to work with? It seems implausible that the community was abandoned entirely. Later writers such as Hincmar of Rheims occasionally presented the earlier eighth century as a time when bishoprics and ecclesiastical land were seized and doled out to secular lords, and this offers one possible context: ecclesiastical organisation was seriously disrupted in this part of Neustria at the time of Charles Martel, and it was not until the reign of Louis the Pious that it could be restored.[34] On the other hand, the notion that things had broken down so dramatically in the early eighth century that they needed to be fixed by early Carolingian reformers has been effectively challenged.[35] As part of this re-evaluation, the *fastes* épiscopaux have been shown in general to be unreliable evidence of any widescale collapse.[36] Pushing back to the 820s the resolution of the supposed traumas of the 720s and 730s, traumas which themselves have been fundamentally questioned, raises more problems than it solves.

Another possible, partly related, context that sheds some light on the situation in Lisieux was the gradual, piecemeal crystallisation of an ecclesiastical hierarchy within Francia, which was first stimulated by the actions of Boniface in the 740s and continued throughout the long reign of Charlemagne (768–814). Central to

---

[31] Duchesne, *Fastes épiscopaux*, vol. 2, 200–41; Jacques Dubois, 'Les listes épiscopales témoins de l'organisation ecclésiastique', *Revue d'histoire de l'église de France*, 62 (1976): 9–23.

[32] Paris BNF lat. 6042, fol. 1v. Robert of Torigni was himself a reader of Frechulf: see *Prolegomena*, 99*–107*.

[33] The phrase is from Steckel, *Kulturen*, 432.

[34] Allen, 'History in the Carolingian Renewal', 35–6.

[35] Gregory I. Halfond, *Archaeology of Frankish Church Councils, AD 511–768* (Leiden: Brill, 2010), 198–211; Paul Fouracre, *The Age of Charles Martel* (Harlow: Longman, 2000), 122–37.

[36] Halfond, *Archaeology*, 202–3; Fouracre, *Charles Martel*, 136–7.

this hierarchy was the subordination of suffragan bishops to a new conception of metropolitan authority.[37] The example of Rouen can be understood within this framework. At Boniface's bequest, Archbishop Grimo of Rouen was confirmed by Pope Zacharias in 744, and when Charlemagne drew up his will in 811, Rouen was counted amongst the metropolitan sees of the Frankish empire.[38] In 802, when Charlemagne sent out instructions for *missi* (royal agents), one version was sent to Archbishop Magenaud of Rouen and Count Madelgaud. Their assigned *missaticum* ('administrative district') included Lisieux, Bayeux, Coutances, Avranches and Évreux.[39]

At the very least this suggests that Lisieux was within the orbit of Carolingian authority before Frechulf entered the scene. The bishopric had not languished for a century and a half: the external evidence is simply too threadbare to read Frechulf's appeal to Hrabanus as a literal reflection of Lisieux's decrepit state. The *Deeds of the Abbots of Fontenelle*, written between 833 and 843 at St Wandrille, record that sometime before becoming abbot in 789, a certain Gervoldus was installed by Charlemagne as bishop of Évreux, one of Lisieux's neighbouring sees, after having served as chaplain to Bertrada, the king's mother.[40] The source states, furthermore, that there was a bishop before Gervoldus. This incidental detail about one episcopal career may not be much to go on, but it can be considered a further indication that this part of Neustria had not lain neglected since the late seventh century. Our view is merely obscured by the absence of evidence. But the example of Gervoldus also raises important biographical questions. What is

---

[37] Rosamond McKitterick, *Charlemagne: The Formation of a European Identity* (Cambridge: CUP, 2008), 299–305; Steffen Patzold, 'Eine Hierarchie im Wandel: die Ausbildung einer Metropolitanordnung im Frankenreich des 8. und 9. Jahrhunderts', in *Hiérarchie et stratification sociale dans l'Occident médiéval 400–1100*, eds Dominique Iogna-Prat, François Bougard and Régine Le Jan (Turnhout: Brepols, 2008), 161–84; Halfond, *Archaeology*, 207. In general, see Daniel Carlo Pangerl, *Die Metropolitanverfassung des karolingischen Frankenreiches* (Hanover: Hansche Buchhandlung, 2011).

[38] Boniface, *Epistolae*, ed. Michael Tangl, *Die Briefe des heilgen Bonifatius und Lullus*, MGH *Epp. Sel.* 1 (Berlin: Weidmann, 1916), pp. 102–8. Charlemagne's will: Einhard, *Vita Karoli*, ed. Oswald Holder-Egger, MGH *SRG* 25 (Hanover: Hahn, 1911), pp. 1–41; English trans. by David Ganz, *Two Lives of Charlemagne* (Harmondsworth: Penguin, 2008), 17–44, at 37–41, c. 33; Matthew Innes, 'Charlemagne's Will: Piety, Politics and Imperial Succession', *English Historical Review*, 112 (1997): 833–55, esp. 852.

[39] *Capitularia missorum specialia*, ed. Alfred Boretius, MGH *Capit.* 1 (Hanover: Hahn, 1883), no. 34, p. 100: 'In Cenomanico, Hoxonense, Livino, Baiocasim, Constantino, Abrincadin, Ebrecino et Madricinse, et de illa parte Sequanae Rodomense Magenardus episcopus et Madelgaudus.' For context, see McKitterick, *Charlemagne*, 213, 256–63; Willhelm Alfred Eckhardt, 'Die *Capitularia missorum specialia* von 802', *DA*, 12 (1956): 498–516.

[40] *Gesta fontanellensis coenobii*, c. 12, ed. Pascal Pradié, *Chronique des abbés de Fontenelle (Saint-Wandrille)* (Paris: Les Belles Lettres, 1999), pp. 134–7; on the *Gesta*, see Ian N. Wood, 'Saint-Wandrille and its Hagiography', in *Church and Chronicle in the Middle Ages: Essays Presented to John Taylor*, eds Ian N. Wood and Graham A. Loud (London: Bloomsbury, 1991), 1–14. See also Rudolf Schieffer, 'Karl der Große und die Einsetzung der Bischöfe im Frankenreich', *DA*, 63 (2007): 451–68 and Jinty Nelson, 'Charlemagne and the Bishops', in *Religious Franks: Religion and Power in the Frankish Kingdoms: Studies in Honour of Mayke de Jong*, eds Dorine van Espelo, Bram van den Hoven van Genderen, Rob Meens, Janneke Raaijmakers, Irene van Renswoude, and Carine van Rhijn (Manchester: MUP, 2016), 350–69.

known about Frechulf's career before and after entering the Neustrian episcopate? Did he also owe his own appointment to royal favour?

Tuus Hrabanus: Frechulf's Background and Career

For most of the twentieth century, it was accepted that Frechulf was trained at court under Helisachar, Louis the Pious's imperial chancellor between 814 and 819, before acting as a *missus dominicus*. Like Gervoldus, it seemed Frechulf was awarded a bishopric as a result of royal service. While this might make sense of Frechulf's reference to Helisachar as his 'venerable teacher' in the dedicatory prologue to Part I, it leaves unexplained the epistolary exchange with the abbot of Fulda, Hrabanus Maurus, which displays a warmth and closeness that goes beyond the rhetorical conventions of letter writing.[41] Frechulf addressed his petition to the 'venerable abbot Maurus and fellow priest (*consacerdos*)', employing Hrabanus's *agnomen* ('nickname') and stressing their shared status of ordination. Hrabanus in turn referred to Frechulf as a 'venerable father', his 'holy brother' and 'the most beloved of the bishops'.[42] He ended the last in his series of prefatory letters with the valediction: 'Farewell, holy brother, and be ever mindful of your Maurus in your sacred prayers'.[43] When in 829 Hrabanus sent a commentary on the Books of Kings to Hilduin, imperial chaplain and abbot of St Denis, he had to clarify that the name Maurus was given to him by his teacher, Alcuin of York (died 804).[44] Knowledge of Hrabanus's *agnomen* was not always taken for granted. That it was in Frechulf's case suggests the men were already well enough acquainted.

In seeking to account for this, Johannes Trithemius first mooted in the late fifteenth century that Frechulf was educated as a monk at Fulda under Hrabanus, but this notion was already being called into question in the eighteenth century.[45]

---

[41] On Carolingian letters (and their survival), see generally Martin Gravel, 'Les lettres de autres: correspondances et réseaux en filigrane des grandes collections carolingiennes', *Le Moyen Âge*, 126(2) (2020): 243–71; Michael I. Allen, 'Writing to Bishops in the Letter-Book of Lupus of Ferrières', in *Écriture et genre épistolaires: IVᵉ-XIᵉ siècle*, eds Thomas Deswarte, Klaus Herbers and Hélène Sirantoine (Madrid: Casa de Velàzquez, 2018), 59–68; John van Engen, 'Letters, the Lettered Voice, and Public Culture in the Carolingian Era', in *Scrivere e leggere nell'alto Medioevo*, Settimane 59, 2 vols (Spoleto: Centro italiano di studi sull'alto Medioevo, 2012), vol. 1, 403–26.

[42] For example, Hrab. *Epist.*, no. 8, pp. 393 (*reverentissimo atque sanctissimo patri*) and 394 (*frater sanctissime*), no. 9, p. 395 (*dilectissime antestitum*), no. 10, p. 397 (*sanctae frater, sancte pater*), no. 11, p. 398 (*sanctae frater Frechulfe, venerande pater*), no. 12, p. 399 (*sancta frater*).

[43] Hrab. *Epist.*, no. 12, p. 400: 'Vale, sancte pater, Maurique tui in sacris orationibus semper memor esto.'

[44] Hrab. *Epist.*, no. 14, p. 402: 'M litteram Mauri nomen exprimentem, quod meus magister beatae memoriae Albinus mihi indidit, prenotare curavi'. Cf. Bruno Judic, 'Grégoire le Grand, Alcuin, Raban et le surnom de Maur', in *Raban Maur et son temps*, eds Philippe Depreux, Stépane Lebecq, Michel Perrin, and Olivier Szerwiniack (Turnhout: Brepols, 2010), 31–48.

[45] Jean Mabillon, *Annales ordinis s. Benedicti*, 6 vols (Paris, Charles Robustel, 1703–39), vol. 2, 534–5: 'Freculfum monachum Ordinis nostri vocat cum Trithemio Bellarminus; quamquam de monastica eius professione nihil certum hactenus nobis occurrit. Ipse Freculfus praeceptorem suum appellat Helisacarem abbatem, qui eidem auctor fuit, ut libros duos chronicorum componeret'. Remy Ceillier,

An alternative scenario was that Frechulf and Hrabanus were both educated together under Alcuin, either at Tours or at Aachen. While Hrabanus was a pupil of Alcuin and studied under him c. 798 and again c. 802/3, there is no evidence that Frechulf ever did.[46] Frechulf's possible monastic background was therefore dropped entirely in favour of emphasising his relationship with Helisachar.[47] Michael Allen, however, made a forceful and convincing case for putting Frechulf back at Fulda. He identified the later bishop of Lisieux as the 'Frehhulf' who was counted amongst the monastery's monks in 822 and witnessed a number of charters between 817 and mid-July 824, but who was no longer found in the monastic register drawn up in 825/6.[48]

Allen's argument has been accepted, though some uncertainties remain. Frechulf has been listed amongst the pupils of Hrabanus, along with Otfrid of Wissembourg, Walahfrid Strabo and Lupus of Ferrières. He may, however, have been roughly coeval with Hrabanus, not the generation below.[49] He writes not as a former pupil, but as an equal: he 'humbly requests (*humiliter deposcimus*)' but also 'faithfully orders (*fiducialiter impero*)' the abbot of Fulda to produce commentaries for him.[50] Moreover, the precise circumstances or even mechanisms by which Frechulf was plucked from Fulda and transferred to Lisieux remain obscure. That Fulda was an important Carolingian monastery would suggest imperial

---

Histoire générale des auteurs sacrés et ecclésiastiques, nouvelle edition, 14 vols (Paris, Louis Vivès, 1858–63), vol. 12, p. 417, thought Hrabanus described the demands of the Rule of Benedict 'comme étrangère à Fréculphe quant à la pratique'. See further p. 29, n. 4 below.

[46] Dieter Schaller, 'Der junge *Rabe* am Hof Karls des Großen (Theodulf. Carm. 27)', in *Festschrift Bernhard Bischoff. Zu seinem 65. Geburtstag dargebracht von Freunden, Kollegen und Schülern*, eds Johanne Autenrieth and Franz Brunhölzl (Stuttgart: Hiersemann, 1971), 123–41; Eckhard Freise, 'Zum Geburtsjahr des Hrabanus Maurus', in *Hrabanus Maurus: Lehrer, Abt und Bischof*, eds Raymund Kottje and Harald Zimmermann (Wiesbaden: Steiner, 1982), 18–74, at 60–1.

[47] Schelle, 'Frechulf von Lisieux', 6–11. Followed by Wilhelm Wattenbach and Wilhelm Levison, *Deutschlands Geschichtsquellen im Mittelalter. Vorzeit und Karolinger*, Part 3: *Die Karolinger vom Tode Karls des Grossen bis zum Vertrag von Verdun*, revised by Heinz Löwe (Weimar: Hermann Böhlaus Nachfolger, 1957), 350–1; Natunewicz, 'Frechulphus', 100–1; Savigni, 'Storia universale', 160–1; Staubach, '*Christiana tempora*', 174; Steckel, *Kulturen des Lehrens*, 432; Thomas F. X. Noble, *Images, Iconoclasm and the Carolingians* (Philadelphia, PA: University of Philadelphia Press, 2009), 352. Compare Josef Adamek, *Vom römischen Endreich der mittelalterlichen Bibelerklärung* (Würzburg: Triltsch, 1938), 69, who referred to Frechulf as 'Rhabans Schulfreund'.

[48] *Prolegomena*, 12*–15*. On Fulda in the Carolingian period, see Janneke Raaijmakers, *The Making of the Monastic Community of Fulda, c. 744–c.900* (Cambridge: CUP, 2012). Baturich of Regensburg has been considered as a comparable example of a Fuldan monk turned bishop: Allen, 'History in the Carolingian Renewal', 26; compare Stephan Freund, *Von Agilolfingern zu den Karolingern: Bayerns Bischöfe zwischen Kirchenorganisation, Reichsintegration und karolingischer Reform (700–847)* (Munich: Beck, 2004), 258–67, who rejected the assumption that Baturich ever was a monk at Fulda.

[49] Michel Sot, 'Introduction', in *Raban Maur et son temps*, eds Philippe Depreux, Stéphane Lebecq, Michel J.-L. Perrin and Olivier Szerwiniack (Turnhout: Brepols, 2010), 9–17, at 9 and 13. In this same volume, see also Philippe Depreux, 'Raban, l'abbé, l'archevêque. Le champ d'action d'un grand ecclésiastique dans la société carolingienne', 49–61, at 55 and Geneviève Bührer-Thierry, 'Raban Maur et l'épiscopat de son temps', 63–76, at 65–6 and Magali Coumert, 'Raban Maur et les Germains', 137–53, at 142,148–9 and 152.

[50] Steckel, *Kulturen*, 321.

involvement, but that does not explain why Frechulf in particular was chosen for a post so far from home. An unrecorded period of time spent at court during his monastic upbringing may help to account for the decision to transplant Frechulf from an eastern Frankish monastery to a north-western episcopal see, and also may help explain the prior relationship he seems to have had with Helisachar, even if this was not as his pupil as such. During this stay, Frechulf also may have gained exposure to the spoken, proto-Romance language of western Francia, which differed from the early Germanic dialect of the eastern lands and would presumably have been essential for discharging his pastoral and administrative duties.[51] At the very least, Frechulf's example reinforces Steffen Patzold's recent observation that the 'Carolingian world was mobile'.[52]

Whether or not he owed his position to the regime, his subsequent activities as bishop of Lisieux mainly can be observed in the service of Carolingian politics. Soon after taking up office, Frechulf was sent to Rome as an imperial envoy in the context of a dispute between the papacy and Constantinople over the worship of images; at a council held in Paris in early November 825, he was called in to relay his experiences '*viva voce*'.[53] Several years later, Frechulf was present at another council in Paris, one of four major assemblies convened across the empire in 829 to discuss the state of the Carolingian *ecclesia*.[54] He was amongst the bishops who witnessed the deposition of Archbishop Ebbo of Rheims on 4 March 835 following a major rebellion against Louis the Pious in 833;[55] after being detained in Fulda, Ebbo was carted almost 500 miles westwards to Lisieux to be kept temporarily under Frechulf's watchful eye, before being sent on to Fleury, some 140 miles to the south-east.[56] After the tripartite division of the Carolingian empire in 843 into

---

[51] Michel Banniard, 'Language and Communication in Carolingian Europe', in *The New Cambridge Medieval History, Vol. 2, c. 700–c.900*, ed. Rosamond McKitterick (Cambridge: CUP, 1995), 695–708. I am grateful to Ed Roberts for this suggestion.

[52] Steffen Patzold, 'Verortung in einer mobilen Welt: Zum Zusammenhang zwischen Kirchenzehnt und der Einhegung von Mobilität im Karolingerreich', *Historische Zeitschrift*, 308 (2019): 285–312, at 289; see also 293–4 on language issues associated with mobility.

[53] Council of Paris (825), ed. Albert Werminghoff, MGH *Conc.* II/2, (Hanover: Hahn, 1908), pp. 473–551, at p. 482. *Prolegomena*, 11*–12*; Noble, *Images*, 263–85; Joshua M. O'Brien, 'Locating Authorities in Carolingian Debates on Image Veneration: The Case of Agobard of Lyon's *De picturis et imaginibus*', *Journal of Theological Studies*, 62 (2011): 176–206 at 202–5.

[54] Council of Paris (829), MGH *Conc.* II/2, pp. 605–80, at pp. 606 (subscription) and 608 ('we, unworthy bishops, who gathered together at Paris from the dioceses of Rheims, as well as Sens, Tours, and Rouen').

[55] On 833, Mayke de Jong, *The Penitential State: Authority and Atonement in the Age of Louis the Pious, 814–840* (Cambridge: CUP, 2009) and Courtney Booker, *Past Convictions: The Penance of Louis the Pious and the Decline of the Carolingians* (Philadelphia, PA: University of Pennsylvania Press, 2009) are indispensable.

[56] Council of Thionville (835), MGH *Conc.* II/2, pp. 701–3 and *Narratio clericorum Remensium* (840), ed. Albert Werminghoff, MGH *Conc.* II/2, p. 808: 'Finito autem concilio, reductus est sub arta custodia ad eundem sancti scilicet Bonifacii monasterium; post aliquantum vero temporis conmendatus est similiter ad custodiendum Freculfo Lexoviensi episcopo, inde etiam Bosoni abbati in monasterium sancti Benedicti, sub cuius manu exulabat, quando dominus imperator viam totius ingressus est

western, eastern and middle kingdoms, Frechulf's name can be found amongst the subscription lists of a few more ecclesiastical assemblies in the western realm of Charles the Bald. At Germigny in September/October 843, he attested a charter affirming the rights and liberties of the abbey of Curbion (near Blois);[57] he was at a council overseen by Archbishop Wenilo of Sens sometime between 843 and 845 concerning the relocation of the monastery of Saint-Rémy from Sens to Vareilles;[58] and his name crops up in a synod held in Paris in 846 or 847 concerning the governance of the monastic community at Corbie.[59] His final such appearance was as one of twenty-two west Frankish archbishops and bishops who in 850 banded together (perhaps in Anjou) to challenge the perceived transgressions of the Breton ruler Nominoë.[60]

Beyond synodal participation, Frechulf played a starring role in an account of the translation of the relics of the seventh-century saints Ragnobert and Zeno from Bayeux to a newly built church just outside Lisieux. The text was written in two phases, the first of which was at the behest of Archbishop Paul of Rouen sometime between 856 and 858, although it narrates events set in 846 and 847/849.[61] Frechulf features as a *venerabilis episcopus* and *religiossimus praesul*, who instructs the protagonist Herveus to go to Bayeux and dig up the bodies of the saints. Later, Frechulf congregated with two other bishops, Batfrid of Bayeux and Ansegaudus of Avranches, and together the three *praesules* consecrated each of the church's three new altars.[62] (Ansegaudus, incidentally, is the first known bishop of Avranches since the late seventh century: there is a pattern here.)

Frechulf's subscription in 850 was his last recorded appearance as bishop of Lisieux, an office he held for the best part of three decades. By April 853, his successor Hairard had taken over.[63] Exactly when Frechulf died is unclear, but nevertheless it can be documented with more precision than often is possible for early medieval churchmen. From around 838 to 855, successive ninth-century bishops of the cathedral church at Würzburg maintained a necrology, that is, a list of deceased ecclesiastics and other notables whose souls the community was to pray for.[64] During the episcopacy of Gozbald (842–55), 'the death of Bishop

---

carnis.' *Prolegomena*, 13*.
[57] Synod of Germigny (843), ed. Wilfried Hartmann, MGH *Conc.* III (Hanover: Hahn, 1984), no. 1, pp. 1–6, at 6.
[58] Synod in Sens (843–5), MGH *Conc.* III, no. 10, pp. 56–60, at 60.
[59] Synod of Paris (846/7), MGH *Conc.* III, no. 13, pp. 140–8, at 148.
[60] Synod of Anjou (?) (850), MGH *Conc.* III, no. 20, pp. 202–6, at 204.
[61] *Historia translationis corporum ss. Ragnoberti et Zenonis*, ed. Olivier Larue, 'La Translation de corps de saint Regnobert et de saint Zénon', *Bulletin de la Société des Antiquaires de Normandie*, 51 (1952): 215–64. On the source, see Christophe Maneuvrier, 'Le récit de la translation des reliques de saint Regnobert: histoire d'une éphémère fondation monastique effectuée aux portes de Lisieux sous l'épiscopat de Fréculf', *Tabularia*, 5 (2005): 1–11.
[62] *Historia translationis*, pp. 223–4 and 229–231.
[63] Synod of Soissons (853), MGH *Conc.* III, no. 27, pp. 253–93, at 278.
[64] Edition in Ernst Dümmler, 'Karolingische Miscellen', *Forschungen zur Deutschen Geschichte*, 6

Frechulf' was noted, and was dated to 8 October. The year this happened must have fallen between 850 and 855, though perhaps this can be narrowed down to before 853, assuming Hairard had already been ordained as bishop by the end of 852 and Frechulf was dead before his successor took over. Notably, Frechulf was the only west Frankish bishop inscribed on this necrology, which otherwise reflects an area centred on the archdiocese of Mainz and its important abbey, Fulda: this is further evidence of his roots in this region of the Carolingian world.[65]

The few details of Frechulf's biography which can be cobbled together underscore aspects of the ninth-century church that serve to frame my analysis of his *Histories*. As a bishop in charge of a community of clerics and the people of his diocese, Frechulf's concerns were local and pastoral. As a bishop, Frechulf was also plugged into a larger framework of ecclesiastical politics, as his occasional involvement in assemblies and synods convened in Neustria over the course of his twenty-five-year tenure reveals. His writings, however, are the most striking evidence connecting Frechulf, his bishopric and the wider Carolingian *ecclesia*. Although compiled at Lisieux, both volumes of his *Histories* depended upon the circulation of texts from centres such as Fulda. Both volumes were dedicated to high-ranking figures at the imperial court and sent to prominent abbeys with close ties to the ruling dynasty; likewise, his edition of Vegetius was sent to Charles the Bald. Together, these dedications illuminate the channels of power and networks of knowledge through which Carolingian imperial Christianity operated. Frechulf's career and literary output furthermore capture some of the impressive ways that texts, people and ideas moved throughout the Carolingian empire. The *Histories*, in other words, can and should be understood as being more than just an example of Carolingian history-writing. Yet, it is primarily as a historian that Frechulf has been judged and often found wanting.

Out of Place? Frechulf and Carolingian Historiography

The Carolingian period witnessed 'a veritable explosion of history-writing ... with all kinds of new genres developed and older forms reconfigured and adapted to record contemporary history'.[66] Within this creative burst of historiographical activity, it

---

(1866): 115–29, at 115–17; Rainer Leng, 'Ein Würzburger Necrolog aus dem 9. Jahrhundert', *DA*, 63 (2007): 1–40, who reproduced the text at 23–6.

[65] Leng, 'Ein Würzburger Necrolog', 25 (text) and 34 (analysis); see also Allen, 'History in the Carolingian Renewal', 64–5. Similarly, Frechulf was unusual for being a principal correspondent of Hrabanus Maurus who was not based within the province of Mainz, which again is explained by (and further attests to) his links to Fulda: Bührer-Thierry, 'Raban Maur', 65–9.

[66] McKitterick, *Charlemagne*, 36. Generally on Carolingian historiography: Matthew Innes and Rosamond McKitterick, 'The Writing of History', in *Carolingian Culture: Emulation and Innovation*, ed. Rosamond McKitterick (Cambridge: CUP, 1994), 193–220; Rosamond McKitterick, *History and Memory in the Carolingian World* (Cambridge: CUP, 2004); Rosamond McKitterick, *Perceptions of the Past in the Early Middle Ages* (Notre Dame, IL: University of Notre Dame Press, 2006). See also Hans-

has been argued that 'the most dramatic developments ... were concentrated in the reign of Louis the Pious'.[67] Frechulf's *Histories*, compiled in later 820s, were clearly a product of this vibrant age, yet they sit somewhat uneasily amongst the better studied examples of historical writing, geared as they were towards recording 'contemporary history'. It is these contemporary narratives—chronicles and annals, biographies of emperors, bishops and saints, but also charters and conciliar acta— which commonly function as the historian's bread and butter, providing a staple diet of facts, events and dates with which to reconstruct narratives and analyse political actions. To be sure, vital work has been done in the past few decades to highlight how narratives of all shapes and sizes can be sophisticated creations that defy simple readings. Yet, despite their biases, distortions and complexities, narratives covering the recent past still speak directly to students of the Carolingian centuries, since they deal directly with, or allude to, eighth- and ninth-century actors and episodes. Frechulf's is an ostensibly more enigmatic text. Ending as it does in the seventh century, long before the Carolingian family had even entered onto the political stage, it is not obviously a 'ninth-century narrative'.[68]

Even within the context of Carolingian histories of the world, Frechulf's narrative stands out on account of its complete lack of coverage of the Carolingian period. Frechulf's work is usually categorised as a universal history or world chronicle, since its narrative embraces human history from its inception and traces humanity's growth and development across the earth over a vast span of time.[69] Classifying sources into clearly defined genres and subgenres is inherently problematic. Many of the labels now commonly employed reflect nineteenth- century categories, not early medieval ones.[70] Moreover, neatly defined genres

---

Werner Goetz, 'Vergangenheitswahrnehmung, Vergangenheitsgebrauch und Geschichtssymbolismus in der Geschichtsschreibung der Karolingerzeit', in *Ideologie e pratiche del reimpiego nell'alto medioevo*, Settimane 46 (Spoleto: Centro italiano di studi sull'alto medioevo, 1999), 177–225.

[67] Innes and McKitterick, 'Writing of History', 203. Janet Nelson, 'History-Writing at the Courts of Louis the Pious and Charles the Bald', in *Historiographie im frühen Mittelalter*, eds Anton Scharer and Georg Scheibelreiter (Vienna: Oldenbourg, 1994), 435–42 is also fundamental here.

[68] De Jong, *Penitential State*, ch. 2 on 'ninth-century narratives' for the reign of Louis the Pious.

[69] On this genre, see Anna-Dorothee von den Brincken, *Studien zur lateinischen Weltchronistik bis in das Zeitalter Ottos von Freising* (Münster: Michael Triltsch, 1957); Karl Heinrich Krüger, *Die Universalchroniken* (Turnhout: Brepols, 1976); Hans-Werner Goetz, 'On the Universality of Universal History', in *L'historiographie médiévale en Europe: actes du colloque organisé par la Fondation européenne de la science au Centre de recherches historiques et juridiques de l'Université Paris I du 29 mars au 1er avril 1989*, ed. Jean-Philippe Genet (Paris: Presses du CNRS, 1991), 247–61; Michael I. Allen, 'Universal History 300–1000: Origins and Western Developments', in *Historiography in the Middle Ages*, ed. Deborah Mauskopf Deliyannis (Leiden: Brill, 2003), 17–42; Ian Wood, 'Universal Chronicles in the Early Medieval West', *Medieval Worlds*, 1 (2015): 47–60. For a comparative perspective, see Andrew Marsham, 'Universal Histories in Christendom and the Islamic World, c.700–c.1400', in *The Oxford History of Historical Writing, Vol. 2: 400–1400*, eds Sarah Foot and Chase F. Robinson (Oxford: OUP, 2012), 431–56; and for a later period, see the essays collected in Michael Campopiano and Henry Bainton (eds), *Universal Chronicles in the High Middle Ages* (Woodbridge: York Medieval Press, 2017).

[70] Wood, 'Universal Chronicles'; Edward Roberts, *Flodoard of Rheims and the Writing of History in the Tenth Century* (Cambridge: CUP, 2019), 78–83 on genre and annals.

create fixed boundaries between different sources that often overlap and bleed into one another. That said, there are a number of histories that were composed between the mid-eighth and early-tenth centuries that are usually grouped together under the rubric 'universal chronicles'.[71] It is in relation to this (admittedly) heterogenous collection of sources that Frechulf has tended to be assessed, and unfavourably so. His *Histories* have been considered alongside Ado of Vienne (wrote c. 870) and Regino of Prüm (wrote c. 908), both of whose chronicles are valued since they shed light on late ninth-century events.[72] For this reason, François Louis Ganshof, in a classic overview of Frankish historical writing, considered Ado and Regino to be valuable for students of 'la monarchie franque'. His views on Frechulf were very different: the *Histories* were not at all fit for this purpose, since they said very little about the Merovingian kings and nothing at all about the Carolingians.[73]

That Frechulf had relatively little to say about the Frankish past cannot be doubted. In Part I, he offered a remarkable note about the origins of the Franks, stating that, while some authorities claim the Franks descended from the Trojans, others held that, along with the Goths and other 'Germanic nations (*nationes Theotistae*)', they came 'from *Scanza*, the womb of nations', to which 'the idiom of their language bears witness. For, as some relate, there is an island in that region which to this day is called Francia.'[74] To this Frechulf added: 'with God's favour, we

[71] In general, see Hervé Inglebert, 'Les conceptions historiographiques de la totalité du passé à l'époque carolingienne (750–910)', in *Rerum gestarum scriptor: histoire et historiographie au Moyen Âge*, eds Magali Coumert, Marie-Céline Isaïa, Klaus Krönert and Sumi Shimahara (Paris: Presses de l'Université Paris-Sorbonne, 2012), 77–86 and McKitterick, *Perceptions of the Past*, 7–33. For recent studies of particular chronicles, see Sören Kaschke, 'Enhancing Bede: the *Chronicon universale* to 741', in *Historiography and Identity III: Carolingian Approaches*, eds Rutger Kramer, Helmut Reimitz and Graeme Ward (Turnhout: Brepols, 2021), 201–29; Rutger Kramer, 'A Crowning Achievement: Carolingian Imperial Identity in the *Chronicon Moisiacense*', in *Historiography and Identity III: Carolingian Approaches*, eds Rutger Kramer, Helmut Reimitz and Graeme Ward (Turnhout: Brepols, 2021), 231–69; and Sukanya Raisharma, 'Much Ado about Nothing: A Localizing Universal *Chronicon*', in *Historiography and Identity III: Carolingian Approaches*, eds Rutger Kramer, Helmut Reimitz and Graeme Ward (Turnhout: Brepols, 2021), 271–90.
[72] On Regino, see Simon MacLean, *History and Politics in Late Carolingian and Ottonian Europe: The Chronicle of Regino of Prüm and Adalbert of Magdeburg* (Manchester: MUP, 2009); Stuart Airlie, '"Sad Stories of the Death of Kings": Narrative Patterns and Structures of Authority in Regino of Prüm's *Chronicon*', in *Narrative and History in the Early Medieval West*, eds Elizabeth M. Tyler and Ross Balzaretti (Turnhout: Brepols, 2006), 105–31; Charles West, 'Knowledge of the Past and the Judgement of History in Tenth-Century Trier: Regino of Prüm and the Lost Manuscript of Bishop Adventius of Metz', *EME* 24(2) (2016): 137–59; for a comparison between Frechulf and Regino, see Geoffrey Koziol, 'The Future of History after Empire', in *Using and Not Using the Past after the Carolingian Empire, c.900–c.1050*, eds Sarah Greer, Alice Hicklin and Stefan Esders (London: Routledge, 2020), 15–35. On Ado, see—in addition to Raisharma, 'Much Ado'—Nathanaël Nimmegeers, *Évêques entre Bourgogne et Provence (Vᵉ–XIᵉ siècle): la province ecclésiastique de Vienne au haut Moyen Âge* (Rennes: Presses Universitaires de Rennes, 2014), 159–62.
[73] François Louis Ganshof, 'L'historiographie dans la monarchie franque sous les Merovingiens et les Carolingiens', in *La storiografia altomedievale*, Settimane 17 (Spoleto, Centro italiano di studi sull'alto Medioevo, 1970), 631–85, at 663–4.
[74] See further Matthew Innes, 'Teutons or Trojans? The Carolingians and the Germanic Past', in *The Uses of the Past in the Early Middle Ages*, eds Yitzhak Hen and Matthew Innes (Cambridge: CUP, 2000),

wish to say more about this people in a subsequent work'.[75] Despite this assertion, when he turned to this *sequens opus*, that is Part II of the *Histories*, the Franks still played a relatively minor role.[76] On the whole, Frechulf's was not a Frankish history, and should not be judged as one.

Ganshof, however, did not completely write off the *Histories*. He conceded that, because the work was 'in every sense of the word a compilation', Frechulf's tome 'reveals the richness of the libraries utilised by the author'.[77] This is undoubtedly the case: almost all of Frechulf's *Histories* were copied directly or paraphrased from earlier historical texts. Ado and Regino themselves built their chronicles upon excerpts from older sources, and indeed most early medieval histories are to some extent compilations.[78] But Ado and Regino also offered original contributions, which built upon 'compiled' sections, extending their narratives of the past to within sight of their respective presents. Primarily, it has been these 'original' additions with which scholars have concerned themselves. At least in part this was a result of the critical editions in which sources were accessed. The nineteenth-century editors of the *Monumenta Germaniae Historica* (MGH), for instance, had specific criteria in mind for deciding what works to print. Typically, they 'selected [texts] for the light they could shed on past realities'.[79] When Georg Pertz edited Ado of Vienne's *Chronicon* for the MGH in 1829, he omitted the vast majority of it; only the unique passages about the local history of Vienne and other materials useful for studying the eighth and ninth centuries were printed.[80] In Frechulf's case, only the prefaces that accompanied Parts I and II of his *Histories* were published in the MGH. They were edited by Ernst Dümmler as examples of letters and Latin verse, thus shorn of their original historiographical context.[81] That Frechulf's text was not found within the relevant volumes of the MGH devoted to Carolingian chroniclers and annalists was an implicit statement about its perceived historical value.

227-49. and Coumert, 'Raban Maur et les Germains'. See also Frederic Clark, *The First Pagan Historian: The Fortunes of a Fraud from Antiquity to the Enlightenment* (New York: OUP, 2020), 92–3 (whence my translation draws).

[75] *Hist.*, I.2.26 [173/4], p. 148: 'Domino autem annuente de his in sequenti opere plenius enarrare cupimus'.

[76] I return briefly to the Franks in Chapter 5: a fuller study would be worthwhile.

[77] Ganshof, 'L'historiographie', 663.

[78] See below, Chapter 1.

[79] Walter Pohl, 'History in Fragments: Montecassino's Politics of Memory', *EME*, 10(3) (2003): 343–74, at 348. See also Helmut Reimitz, 'Histories of Carolingian Historiography: An Introduction', in *Historiography and Identity III: Carolingian Approaches*, eds Rutger Kramer, Helmut Reimitz and Graeme Ward (Turnhout: Brepols, 2021), 1–35 at 7–11.

[80] Ado of Vienne, *Chronicon*, ed. Georg Pertz, MGH SS 2 (Hanover: Hahn, 1829), pp. 315–23.

[81] *Epistolae variorum*, ed. Ernst Dümmler, MGH *Epp.* V (Berlin: Weidmann, 1899), nos. 13–14, pp. 317–20; MGH *Poetae* II (Berlin: Weidmann, 1884), pp. 669–70.

Editing the *Histories*

To begin to appreciate the *Histories*' worth, a critical edition was essential. Up until the beginning of the twenty-first century, historians were dependent upon J. P. Migne's *Patrologia Latina* text of 1851, which reproduced Melchior von Neuß's edition, published in Cologne in 1539.[82] The deficiencies of this edition had long been recognised. The work of rectifying its faults began with Emil Grunauer, who in 1864 published his doctoral dissertation on Frechulf's sources.[83] Chester Natunewicz, who too wrote his dissertation on Frechulf's *Histories* in 1957, began the work of creating a critical edition, and he was well aware of the difficulties that lay ahead: 'the task will be an enormous one, perhaps even greater than that which Freculphus [sic] himself ... faced'.[84] In 1990 the edition was far from complete and Natunewicz passed the torch onto Michael Allen, when he began his own doctoral research on the *Histories*, which he completed in 1994.[85] The fruits of this long editorial process appeared in 2002, when Allen's landmark edition of Frechulf's corpus was published in the medieval series of the Corpus Christianorum.

Equipped with Allen's exquisite edition, readers can now easily comprehend the organisation and structure of the *Histories* and, using the *apparatus criticus*, discern with crystal clarity the various sources from which Frechulf derived the bulk of his material throughout Part I and Part II. This, however, does not represent the last word. Rather, as Rosamond McKitterick has written:

> ... establishing on what sources a particular author drew is only the first and essential step in assessing the implications of selection, rearrangement, incorporation, and new emphases accorded those same sources in their new contexts. ... The entire text of each history needs to be assessed, for it is this that can best offer insights into the intellectual world of the early medieval historical writers and compilers and their perspective on, and knowledge of, the past. The text created can help us to understand the motives for the selection of particular themes and information. It can reveal the consequent varying perceptions of the past.[86]

Such an approach lies at the heart of this book. Frechulf's text, ostensibly lacking 'contemporary' or 'original' material, is nevertheless still wholly novel and individual, as a result of every decision that was made regarding what to include and where to put it: compiling of this sort was always an active and dynamic process.[87]

---

[82] On this edition, see *Prolegomena*, 85*-7*; Natunewicz, 'Freculphus of Lisieux', 96–8.
[83] Emil Grunauer, 'De Fontibus Historiae Freculpi Episcopi Lixoviensis' (doctoral dissertation, University of Zurich, 1864).
[84] Natunewicz, 'Freculphus of Lisieux', 130.
[85] *Prolegomena*, 5*.
[86] McKitterick, *Perceptions of the Past*, 4.
[87] See also Helmut Reimitz, 'The Social Logic of Historiographical Compendia in the Carolingian Period', in *Configuration du texte en histoire*, ed. Osamu Kano (Nagoya: Graduate School of Letters, 2012), 17–28.

Appreciating the structure, themes and emphases of a work is not only integral to understanding a text as a text, that is, as a literary source, but also offers insights into the concerns of the culture and society within which it was produced. In short, my interpretation is shaped by the commonplace assumption that texts should be read in context. But what sort of context should the *Histories* be situated within?

Approaching the *Histories*

One of the most fruitful approaches adopted in recent decades when analysing historiographical texts is to identity what Christina Pössel has termed a '"key context", that is, an event or circumstance, political or personal, that provided the work's specific motivation and which can thus help us to decode it'.[88] As stated at the outset of this introduction, the study of early medieval historiography has focused on questions of politics; consequently, 'key contexts' have been located in moments of heightened political and social tension, and crises of all sorts have been seen as engendering the production of histories.[89] Framing a source as a response or reaction to a particular moment or set of moments can help focus analysis, since it limits the range of possible meanings that can be unpacked from it. More broadly, political contexts help infuse narratives with contemporary meaning and agency, transforming them from neutral or detached accounts of events into actors with real stakes in the events they narrate. Modern historians, after all, want the sources they study to matter.

This sort of analysis has been fruitfully applied to cases in which the authors of texts are known, since their hopes and frustrations, ambitions and anxieties can be read into their writings: scholarship on historians such as Nithard (died 844), Hincmar of Rheims (died 882), Regino and, later, Flodoard of Rheims (died 966) has amply demonstrated the value and effectiveness of this approach.[90] Anonymous

---

[88] Christina Pössel, 'The Consolation of Community: Innovation and Ideas of History in Ratpert's *Casus Sancti Galli*', *Journal of Ecclesiastical History*, 65(1) (2014): 1–24, at 2.

[89] See, for instance, Hans-Werner Goetz, 'Historical Writing, Historical Thinking and Historical Consciousness in the Middle Ages', *Revista Dialogos Mediterrânicos*, 2 (2012): 110–28, at 127: 'most chronicles were not written in the heyday of their institution. Quite on the contrary, they were written in times of crisis, when it was necessary to recollect the former status (whether with justification or invented) and to legitimize these claims.'

[90] Nithard: Janet Nelson, 'Public Histories and Private History in the Work of Nithard', *Speculum*, 60(2) (1985): 251–93 [repr. in her *Politics and Ritual in Early Medieval Europe* (London: Hambledon Continuum, 1986), 196–237]; Stuart Airlie, 'The World, the Text and the Carolingian: Royal, Aristocratic and Masculine Identities in Nithard's *Histories*', in *Lay Intellectuals in the Carolingian World*, eds Patrick Wormald and Janet L. Nelson (Cambridge: CUP, 2007), 51–76; repr. in his *Power and its Problems in Carolingian Europe* (Farnham: Ashgate, 2012), item IX; Dana M. Polanichka and Alex Cilley, 'The Very Personal History of Nithard: Family and Honour in the Carolingian world', *EME*, 22(2) (2014): 171–200. Hincmar: Janet Nelson, 'Hincmar's Life in his Historical Writings', in *Hincmar of Rheims: Life and Work*, eds Rachel Stone and Charles West (Manchester: MUP, 2015), 44–59; Regino: MacLean, 'Insinuation, Censorship and the Struggle for late Carolingian Lotharingia in Regino of Prüm's *Chronicle*', *English Historical Review*, 124 (2009): 1–28; West, 'Knowledge about the

works and compilations, especially when examined in their manuscript contexts, have also received critical scrutiny, both for what they can reveal about perceptions of the past but also the politics of the present. Helmut Reimitz's exhaustive study of the writing and rewriting of Frankish history between Gregory of Tours and the mid-ninth century perhaps now best exemplifies this approach. Reimitz's main focus was early medieval ethnicity. Underpinning his reading of the Frankish annals of later eighth and ninth centuries is a careful excavation of 'a politics of identity', that is, the 'Carolingian instrumentalization of Frankish identity'.[91] The rise and consolidation of Carolingian power is thus retold in terms of the mutating discourse of ethnicity, with anonymous annalists playing a main role in shaping debates and agendas. Regardless of form or authorship, consensus now holds that medieval historiography was often 'an act of political engagement'.[92]

I take a different path in this book. This is not because I consider Frechulf to have been a politically disinterested scholar, labouring away in his *scriptorium* oblivious to the outside world. The rough outlines of his biography that I sketched above confirm that this was not the case. Yet identifying the points at which Frechulf's career as a plugged-in bishop and the compilation of his *Histories* intersected is less straightforward. The events of 829/30, for instance, could be taken as a 'key context'. Much has been made of the dedication of Part II to the Empress Judith. This dedication, it has been argued, must have reached Judith in 829 or early 830 at the latest, since otherwise the praise it lavished upon her would have been impolitic: in April 830, a rebellion was launched against the emperor by his two eldest sons, Lothar I and Pippin of Aquitaine, during the course of which Judith was seized and forcibly sent into cloistered confinement in the nunnery of Sainte Radegund at Poitiers.[93] A catalyst for this revolt, moreover, was thought to have been the alteration to Louis' succession plans, first established in 817 in what is today known as the *Ordinatio imperii*. With this document, the imperial inheritance was divided up between Lothar, Louis the German and Pippin of Aquitaine, Louis' sons with Ermengard, his first wife who died in 818; in 829, their six-year-old sibling obtained his slice, which amounted to portions of land around Alemannia, Rhaetia and Burgundy.[94] That Charles received land in the region

---

Past'. Flodoard: Roberts, *Flodoard*.

[91] Helmut Reimitz, *History, Frankish Identity and the Framing of Western Ethnicity, 550–850* (Cambridge: CUP, 2015), 406–9. See also McKitterick, *History and Identity*.

[92] The phrase is from Simon MacLean, 'Recycling the Franks in the Twelfth-Century England: Regino of Prüm, the Monks of Durham, and the Alexandrine Schism', *Speculum*, 87(3) (2012): 649–81, at 649.

[93] *Prolegomena*, 16*–17*. For the events, De Jong, *Penitential State*, 38–44 and 185–213.

[94] Sören Kaschke, 'Die Teilungsprojekte der Zeit Ludwigs des Frommen', in *La productivité d'une crise: le règne de Louis le Pieux (814–840) et la transformation de l'Empire Carolingien = Produktivität einer Krise: die Regierungszeit Ludwigs des Frommen (814–840) und die Transformation des karolingischen Imperiums*, eds Philippe Depreux and Stefan Esders (Ostfildern: Thorbecke, 2018), 87–128, at 95–6, with further literature.

from where his mother's powerful family hailed was likely no coincidence,[95] and it has been argued that this endowment also lay behind the gifting of the *Histories'* second volume.[96] Further evidence for this is found in the prologue itself: when Frechulf implored Judith to bear in mind the example of Bathsheba, mother of King Solomon, and use the work to educate her cherished son, the implication was that he hoped Charles would one day succeed his father, ahead of his brothers, just like his scriptural forerunner.[97]

There are two problems here: the first is historiographical; the second pertains specifically to Frechulf. In part, the argument that the *Histories* were completed by early 830 depends on the assumption that the rebellion of 830 was an attempt to preserve the 817 status quo against the undue influence of the Empress Judith and her family. Although the alteration of Louis' succession plans may have played some role in the decision of Lothar and Pippin to take up arms against their father, recent scholarship has convincingly demonstrated that it was far less significant than once thought, even to the point of being negligible.[98] Furthermore, that Frechulf targeted Judith and Charles for praise because he could see which ways the political winds were blowing also involves attributing a degree of foresight to him that is not strictly necessary. Flattering royalty with Old Testament comparisons was par for the course when it came to praising rulers. As Elizabeth Ward has already pointed out, it 'would be unwise to infer from Frechulf's hyperbole that Charles was to exclude his elder brothers in the manner of Solomon and become his father's heir'.[99] If the traditional reading of the rebellion of 830 is removed, and

---

[95] On Judith's family, see Regine Le Jan, 'Aux frontières de l'idéel, le modèle familial en question?', in *La productivité d'une crise: le règne de Louis le Pieux (814–840) et la transformation de l'Empire Carolingien = Produktivität einer Krise: die Regierungszeit Ludwigs des Frommen (814–840) und die Transformation des karolingischen Imperiums*, eds Philippe Depreux and Stefan Esders (Ostfildern: Thorbecke, 2018), 273–88 at 278–81; Mayke de Jong, 'Queens and Beauty in the Early Medieval West: Balthild, Theodelinda, Judith', in *Agire da donna: Modelli e pratiche di rappresentazione (secoli VI–X); Atti del convegno (Padova, 18–19 febbraio 2005)*, ed. Cristina La Rocca (Turnhout: Brepols, 2007), 235–48 at 244–6.

[96] *Prolegomena*, 16*–17*, 26*; Airlie, *Making and Unmaking*, 110.

[97] *Prolegomena*, 16*–17*; 'Fréculf', p. 68; Philippe, Depreux, 'L'actualité de Fréculf de Lisieux: à propos de l'édition critique de son œvre', *Tabularia*, 4 (2004): 53–60, at 55. More emphatically: Nikolaus Staubach, *Das Herrscherrbild Karls de Kahlen: Formen und Funktionen monarchischer Repräsentation im früheren Mittelalter*, Teil I (Münster: University of Münster, 1982), 72–4. Broadly on Solomonic imagery, see Paul Kershaw, *Peaceful Kings: Peace, Power and the Early Medieval Political Imagination* (Oxford: OUP, 2011). See further Chapter 6, below.

[98] For a summary, see Constambeys, Innes and MacLean, *Carolingian World*, 214–18; De Jong, *Penitential State*, 41; Nelson, *Charles*, 87. The decisive critique of the older—especially German-language—historiography is Steffen Patzold, 'Eine "Loyal Palastrebellion" der "Reichseinheitspartei": Zur "Divisio imperii" von 817 und zu den Ursachen des Aufstandes gegen Ludwig den Frommen im Jahre 830', *Frühmittelalterliche Studien*, 40 (2006): 43–77. Compare Airlie, *Making and Unmaking*, 138–46.

[99] Elizabeth Ward, 'Caesar's Wife: The Career of the Empress Judith', in *Charlemagne's Heir: New Perspectives on the Reign of Louis the Pious (814–840)*, eds Peter Godman and Roger Collins (Oxford: Clarendon Press, 1990), 205–27, at 224–5.

the extent of Frechulf's political prognostics questioned, then 829/30 appears less immediate as a 'key context' than it previously has done.[100]

That Frechulf dedicated Part II to Judith for political reasons seems probable. Books were high-value objects, in terms of both their material and spiritual value, and therefore they were dedicated to rulers and other elites for many different reasons, such as to acknowledge hierarchical relationships, offer thanks for patronage, demonstrate political loyalty, and maintain horizontal social relations between peers over the vast extent of the empire; Frechulf's correspondence with his monastic brother Hrabanus Maurus and his dedications of Part I to Helisachar (another imperial bigwig) and later of Vegetius's *Epitoma* to Charles the Bald attest to the different functions of book giving.[101] My point of departure, however, is that I understand dedications to represent only one stage in the gestation of a work, and likely one of the last. We can recover something of Frechulf's savvy and his knowledge of the rules of the game from his prologues, but to gain a better understanding of what spurred him on to produce his monumental compilation, and to account for the fact that it found so many readers beyond those specified in his prefaces, we have to place the *Histories* in their intellectual context. As stated above, I take this context to be the study of scripture and the writings of the church fathers.[102]

In addition to making the intellectual context my starting point, I have also reoriented my basic categories of comparison. Reading the *Histories* in the light of other universal chronicles such as those by Ado or Regino, or other narrative texts such as the Royal Frankish Annals, tends to emphasise Frechulf's idiosyncrasies, even deficiencies as a historian. The apparent oddness of Frechulf's work, however, begins to dissolve when it is approached not primarily as an example of Carolingian historiography, but rather as one particular consequence of the deep, ubiquitous early ninth-century engagement with the received writings of Christian antiquity. To this end, Frechulf's letter to Hrabanus Maurus at the outset of his episcopacy offers a more meaningful 'key context' than the fraught politics of 829/30. There is much more to be uncovered about the methods and practices that underlay the construction of Frechulf's compilation, the understanding of textual authority upon which it was built, and its overall organisation and specific emphases by comparing it with the biblical exegesis of Hrabanus Maurus rather than with the

---

[100] According to De Jong, 'Exegesis for an Empress', Hrabanus Maurus dedicated biblical commentaries to Judith either in late 830 or 831 as a way of showing support *after* the rebellion: this could also apply to Frechulf.

[101] I return to this in Chapter 6.

[102] Compare Matthew Innes, '"He Never Even Allowed his White Teeth to be Bared in Laughter": The Politics of Humour in the Carolingian Renaissance', in *Humour, History and Politics in Late Antiquity and the Early Middle Ages*, ed. Guy Halsall (Cambridge: CUP, 2002), 131–56, esp. 136, and Justin Lake, *Richer of Saint-Rémi: The Methods and Mentality of a Tenth-Century Historian* (Washington, DC: CUA Press, 2013), both of whom make cases for prioritising non-political contexts.

universal chroniclers with whom he tends to be lumped. Hrabanus, like Frechulf, dedicated his exegesis to the great and the good of the realm: to kings and queens, churchmen and courtiers.[103] In 855/6 Hrabanus himself compiled excerpts from Vegetius's *Epitoma rei militaris* and sent them to Lothar II, Charles the Bald's nephew. Most tellingly, however, Frechulf's and Hrabanus's works have been subjected in the past to very similar criticism, namely that as 'mere compilations' of earlier works they are of little historical value.

Comparing Frechulf with Hrabanus is by no means novel, and this is not surprising in the light of their correspondence. In her dissertation of 1952, Bertha Schelle came to the conclusion that Frechulf had more in common with Hrabanus than any of the narrative sources that he read. For Schelle, this was delivered as a stinging critique of Frechulf's abilities as a historian, and was informed by the predominant view of the twentieth century that Hrabanus Maurus was nothing but a passive recipient of patristic knowledge.[104] By contrast, I begin my study with this comparison. In a similar vein, my basic premise is not radically different from Ganshof's above-quoted criticism, it is just differently accented: the *Histories* have a wealth to offer if they are examined with books and libraries, rather than politics and power, in mind.

Frechulf, the Fathers and the Authority of Augustine

Frechulf marshalled an extraordinary range of texts in the process of compiling his *Histories*. Although his project is distinguished by the quantity of sources employed, it is important to make clear at the outset that his most frequently used sources were widely diffused in the Carolingian period, often surviving in hundreds of medieval manuscripts; likewise, they were well attested in the extant ninth-century library catalogues, and were drawn upon by contemporary biblical exegetes, compilers of conciliar sources, hagiographers and writers of didactic literature. Frechulf's 'resources of the past' comprised the core foundations of collective historical memory and, moreover, reflected the general understanding of Christianity as history.[105]

History was both written and read in the Carolingian empire, yet there is an imbalance in the extent to which these activities have been explored.[106] The

---

[103] Mayke de Jong, 'The Empire as *Ecclesia*: Hrabanus Maurus and Biblical *Historia* for Rulers', in *The Uses of the Past in the Early Middle Ages*, eds Yitzhak Hen and Matthew Innes (Cambridge: CUP, 2000), 191–226, together with her 'Exegesis for an Empress', in *Medieval Transformations: Texts, Power and Gifts in Context*, eds Esther Cohen and Mayke de Jong (Leiden: Brill, 2001), 69–100, are essential.

[104] Schelle, 'Frechulf von Lisieux', esp. 147–50.

[105] Walter Pohl and Ian N. Wood, 'Introduction: Cultural Memory and the Resources of the Past', in *The Resources of the Past in Early Medieval Europe*, eds Clemens Gantner, Rosamond McKitterick and Sven Meeder (Cambridge: CUP, 2015), 1–14.

[106] David Ganz, review of McKitterick, *History and Identity*: https://reviews.history.ac.uk/review/474; but see West, 'Knowledge about the Past'.

accumulated evidence from the eighth and ninth centuries reveals that more effort was expended in copying, studying and utilising existing historiographical narratives than in generating new ones. Yet it is primarily these new narratives that have been edited, translated and analysed by historians of the Carolingian period, because they contain the data on contemporary politics that they crave. Frechulf is such a revealing case study because he sits at the intersection between reading and writing and permits both activities to be investigated simultaneously. Far from being the stale compiler that he was assumed to have been, his dual roles as reader/writer meant he shaped a fundamentally novel account of the human past that not one of his main sources had told independently of any other: in this respect, he very much produced something new. He was still, however, a compiler, whose novel production was the result of a close reading and interpretation of authoritative histories and chronicles. The status of these narratives is key, since this allows us to take Frechulf as an (admittedly eminent and exceptionally glossy) representative of what was surely a common activity in the ecclesiastical centres of learning where such sources were stored and consulted. The main narrative sources which formed the core of Frechulf's project were those that were regularly used by monks and clerics to learn about the foundations of their religion's past, to discover the role of God's providence in human history, to contextualise scripture and the writings of the church fathers, and to learn about chronology and geography. Taking the time to engage with the *Histories* may leave one wondering what Frechulf thought about the rise of the Carolingian dynasty, the reign of Charlemagne or even more recent events; what can be appreciated instead was what, for educated churchmen, would have been considered almost general, textbook knowledge about the overall shape and meaning of the Christian past. To give one example of this, modern studies of Carolingian historiography rarely dwell on the significance of Genesis 49:10, but the fulfilment of this prophecy— covered in detail by Frechulf—captured a fundamental tenet of Christianity.

The context of compilation, furthermore, builds directly upon what is by far the most influential reading of the source. In a brilliant essay from 1995, Nikolaus Staubach made Frechulf's reception of St Augustine's *On the City of God* the foundation of his bold reassessment of the *Histories*. Within the hallowed canon of the church fathers, Augustine has always been a towering figure, whose influence was felt throughout the whole Middle Ages and whose reception has been intensively studied.[107] Since at least the nineteenth century it has been known that Frechulf utilised the *City of God*, but it was long assumed that he had failed

---

[107] Karla Pollmann and Willemien Otten (eds), *The Oxford Guide to the Historical Reception of Augustine*, 3 vols (Oxford: OUP, 2013); Allan Fitzgerald and John C. Cavadini (eds), *Augustine Through the Ages: An Encyclopedia* (Grand Rapids, MI: William B. Eerdmans, 1999); Conrad, Leyser, 'Augustine in the Latin West, 430–ca. 900', *A Companion to Augustine*, ed. Mark Vessey (Chichester: John Wiley, 2012), 450–64.

to grasp the sophisticated vision of history articulated by the bishop of Hippo in his magnum opus. Frechulf was thus added to a long list of medieval ecclesiastics who misunderstood Augustine, a list which was headed by Augustine's own pupil, Orosius. Staubach, by contrast, argued that Frechulf in fact got Augustine right: the whole structure of the *Histories*, even their peculiarly early end point, could be explained in the light of the bishop of Lisieux's reception of *De civitate Dei*.[108]

Staubach's thesis has influenced all subsequent scholarship on Frechulf. Even after the publication of Allen's edition, Staubach's remains the most compelling analysis of the *Histories* as a whole; Allen himself has further emphasised Frechulf's 'authentically Augustinian' understanding of history.[109] There are problems with this interpretation, however. For Frechulf to have written his *Histories* along Augustinian lines, he would have had to have read *On the City of God* as scholars do today, as a work with its own self-contained 'theology of history' (*Geschichtstheologie*). For modern students, the contours of that theology have been laid out many times, most influentially by Robert Markus, but the extent to which it would have been recognisable to a Carolingian intellectual is a moot point.[110] Augustine's authority in the early Middle Ages was more obviously tied to his interpretations of the Bible.[111] When his writings and ideas were debated in the ninth century, it was furthermore in the context of issues such as double predestination and the eucharist, issues central to life and death in the Carolingian period (and beyond).[112] *Geschichtstheologie*, by contrast, was not a contemporary category. Regarding Frechulf's work more specifically, putting so much emphasis on Augustine fails to do justice to the many other texts of which Frechulf made use when compiling his *Histories*. It serves furthermore to

---

[108] Staubach, '*Christiana tempora*'. Staubach's study was part of series of articles on the medieval reception of Augustine: the overall framing was stated in Nikolaus Staubach, 'Quattuor modis intellegi potest hierusalem: Augustins *Civitas Dei* und der vierfache Schriftsinn', in *Alvarium: Festschrift für Christian Gnilka*, eds Wilhelm Blümer, Rainer Henke and Markus Mülke, Jahrbuch für Antike und Christentum Ergänzungsband 33 (Münster: Aschendorff, 2002), 345–58 at 357–8.

[109] Allen, 'Universal History', 39; 'Frechulf of Lisieux', 1010–11; *Prolegomena*, 201*.

[110] Robert A. Markus, *Saeculum: History and Society in the Theology of St Augustine*, rev. edn (Cambridge: CUP, 1988).

[111] Bernice Martha Kaczynski, 'Reading and Writing Augustine in Medieval St Gall', in *Insignis sophiae arcator: essays in Honour of Michael W. Herren on his 65th Birthday*, eds Gernot R. Wieland, Carin Ruff and Ross G. Arthur, Publications of the Journal of Medieval Latin 6 (Turnhout: Brepols, 2006), 107–23. See also Henry Mayr-Harting, 'Augustine of Hippo, Chelles, and the Carolingian Renaissance: Cologne Cathedral Manuscript 63', *Frühmittelalterliche Studien*, 45 (2011): 51–75.

[112] Matthew Bryan Gillis, *Heresy and Dissent in the Carolingian Empire: The Case of Gottschalk of Orbais* (Oxford: OUP, 2017); Warren Pezé, *Le virus de l'erreur. La controverse carolingienne sur la double prédestination: Essai d'histoire sociale* (Turnhout: Brepols, 2017); Pierre Chambert-Protat, Jérémy Delmulle, Warren Pezé and Jeremy C. Thompson (eds), *La controverse carolingienne sur la prédestination: histoire, textes, manuscrits: actes du colloque international de Paris des 11 et 12 octobre 2013* (Turnhout: Brepols, 2018). See, however, Sophia Mösch, *Augustine and the Art of Ruling in the Carolingian Imperial Period: Political Discourse in Alcuin of York and Hincmar of Rheims* (Abingdon: Routledge, 2020).

make the bishop of Lisieux exceptional for parsing the meaning and pursuing the implications of Augustine's famed tome, and this exceptionality reflects modern assumptions about Augustine's pre-eminence within the Latin patristic canon.[113] Echoing Staubach, Tom Noble has written that 'Frec[h]ulf's was the most important reception of Augustine's conception of history before Otto of Freising in the twelfth century.'[114] I argue instead that for Frechulf, Augustine was just one authority amongst many and that the *Histories* make most sense when analysed in the light of a plurality of authorities.

The Present Study

The following six chapters offer an in-depth and contextualised investigation of Frechulf's vast historical compendium. The first two expand upon some of the basic points that I have briefly sketched out above. Chapter 1 grounds the *Histories* in the transmission, reception and ordering of authoritative knowledge, a context characteristic of but by no means unique to the Carolingian age; Chapter 2 proceeds to unpack the exegetical dimensions of the bishop of Lisieux's approach to history-writing, especially as seen in his first book, which runs from Adam to Abraham. Chapters 3–5 then treat the remainder of the *Histories'* two volumes. The chronological structure of Frechulf's compilation paces this monograph, since it is only by following the order of the narrative which the author laid out that the key emphases and inner tensions of his work manifest themselves. In the absence of any published translation, this has the added effect of allowing Anglophone readers to follow Frechulf's narrative alongside my critical analysis of it. This portion of the study culminates in a new interpretation of the *Histories'* controversial seventh-century ending. In the final chapter, I take a step back from the inner workings of Frechulf's opus in order to examine the thorny topics of audience, purpose and use. Frechulf's ecclesiastical career and the scholarship he produced undoubtedly offer valuable insights into, for instance, the working of Carolingian political patronage; yet it is the Carolingian culture of exegesis and its attendant stresses on patristic authority that takes us closer to answering the question with which I began this introduction, namely why history was written and read in the early Middle Ages.

---

[113] For example, Johannes van Oort, *Jerusalem and Babylon: A Study into Augustine's City of God and the Sources of his Doctrine of the Two Cities* (Leiden: Brill, 1991), 2: 'In Augustine Western patristic theology, and possibly even the whole of the patristic period, reaches its undisputed zenith.'
[114] Noble, *Images*, 353.

1

Frechulf and the Carolingian Culture of Compilation

Introduction

Frechulf's *Histories* are a compendium of older historiographical narratives. In the nineteenth and twentieth centuries, this was considered a problem to overcome, since 'originality' was privileged as a metric for assessing the value of historical evidence. In recent decades, a significant amount of scholarship has been devoted to showing how the compilation of knowledge was always a dynamic and creative process, which was practised widely in pre-modern societies. Building on this work, the first chapter of this monograph argues that compilation not only generated important and original texts but was ubiquitous to all aspects of Carolingian intellectual culture. Far from being a hinderance to appreciating Frechulf's achievement, this crucial context establishes an essential milieu in which his work was produced. Seen from this perspective, the *Histories* no longer appear as an idiosyncratic work of Carolingian historiography, but as an innovative example of Carolingian intellectual culture. I begin with Frechulf's first extant source, a letter sent from Lisieux to Fulda, petitioning Hrabanus Maurus to send him an exegesis of the Pentateuch, in which some of the core concerns of this chapter are introduced.

Writing from Lisieux

Soon after Frechulf became bishop of Lisieux in 824/5, he addressed a letter to Hrabanus Maurus, his former monastic 'holy brother' and now abbot of Fulda.[1] Writing far away, 'on the western shore of the ocean', Frechulf explained how he

---

[1] *Prolegomena*, 19*. Frechulf appears as Hrabanus's *sancte frater* in Hrab. *Epist.*, no. 8, p. 394, 9, no. 11, p. 398, 8, and no. 12, p. 399, 21; he is addressed as *dilectissime antestitum Frechulfe* ('Frechulf, most beloved of the bishops') in no. 9, p. 395, 28.

had found himself in pastorally dire straits. Upon taking up office, he discovered that the people under his spiritual care were hungry 'for the word of salvation', although they themselves had not come to realise this.[2] Lacking the necessary resources, however, he felt wholly ill-equipped to satisfy their needs. To this end, he requested that 'the venerable abbot Maurus' compose a series of commentaries on the Pentateuch, the first five books of the Christian Old Testament. These commentaries, Frechulf made clear, were to follow a set design: Hrabanus was to explicate each of the books of the *Legislator*, with particular reference to pre-existing interpretations. Frechulf, pre-emptively countering any objections, justified his petition:

> You might try to excuse yourself from undertaking a task of such great difficulty and enormous effort, and endeavour to respond to my request by asking why I do not invest my own energy into scrutinising those books from which I order this commentary to be made and collect those things which are pleasing to procure. To this [I say], let the vigilance of your charity be extended, since, even if the insignificance of our blunt sense were to flourish, no abundance of books is available to us for this to be accomplished: in the episcopal see entrusted to us, I have not found the canonical books of the New and Old Testaments, much less expositions of them.[3]

There are grounds for being wary of taking at face value Frechulf's claim that, at the outset of his episcopacy, Lisieux was wholly lacking resources. It is upon such statements that traditional accounts of the Carolingian renaissance have been built, since they depict a moribund and decrepit church in need of revitalisation. Instead, it may be that, by stressing the total absence of books that were key to any Christian community—the Bible and its commentary—Frechulf was deploying exaggerated language in order to goad Hrabanus into action; he may even have included an oblique reference to the *Rule of Benedict*, designed to remind Hrabanus of their shared background at Fulda and to stress that, now in Lisieux, he was far removed from the demands that the *Rule* placed on the nightly reading of the 'Old and New Testaments' together with 'their [patristic] expositions'.[4]

---

[2] *Epist.*, p. 5, 3/9: 'Nouit, mi dilectissime, tuae caritatis beniuolentia in occiduo litore Oceani, quamuis nullis suffragantibus meritis, pastoralem me suscepisse curam, ubi populum famem passum uerbi salutaris repperi, sed minime suam sentientem inediam. Non enim spiritales esuriendo desiderabat dapes, quarum suauitatis gustum necdum expertus erat, quem primum lacte alendum, non solido censui cibo.'

[3] *Epist.*, p. 9, 32/40: 'Ergo si aliquas excusationis praetendere temptaueris occasiones ne tantae molis opus ingentisque laboris subeas, et respondere niteris cur non proprio sudore eos legendo perlustro libros ex quibus haec fieri mando et quaeque libuerint decerpendo colligam, ad haec uestrae caritatis uigilantia intendat, quoniam nulla nobis librorum copia ut haec facere possimus subpeditat, etiamsi paruitas obtunsi sensus nostri uigeret, dum in episcopio nostrae paruitati commisso nec ipsos noui ueterisque testamenti canonicos repperi libros, multo minus horum expositiones.'

[4] Compare *Epist.*, p. 6, 38/40: 'nec ipsos noui ueterisque testamenti canonicos repperi libros, multo

Less speculative points can be gleaned from the letter. Firstly, for a bishop such as Frechulf, scripture and its exegesis were the essential tools of the trade. His perception of Christian leadership and instruction was predicated upon the Bible and commentaries written to expound it. What Frechulf had in mind here was a canon of texts deemed to be authoritative. Second, irrespective of the state in which he found the library at Lisieux, Frechulf was able to use his connections to get his hands on resources.[5] Hrabanus, for example, responded positively to the request for books: he sent to Lisieux commentaries on the Pentateuch in five separate instalments, each of which came with an accompanying letter of dedication.[6] Texts evidently could circulate across the Carolingian empire, and the *Histories* themselves testify to this point. Not only was the text disseminated from Lisieux after it was produced, but the work's material composition was also the result of the movement of texts. One of the most distinctive aspects of the source is that it was a compilation, built upon a vast array of excerpts from earlier works of historiography. Even accounting for possible exaggeration in his bleak assessment of the state of his new see, the sheer number of resources which Frechulf was able to consult and utilise while compiling his *Histories* suggests that Lisieux either quickly came to possess an extraordinarily well-stocked library, or—through its bishop—became part of an intellectual network through which books could circulate. This latter point can indeed be appreciated in material terms: Michael Allen's detailed scrutiny of the textual traditions of Frechulf's sources suggests that several exemplars stemmed from Hrabanus's Fulda or Helisachar's St Riquier.[7]

---

minus horum expositiones' with *Regula Benedicti*, c. 9, 8, ed. Rudolf Hanslik, CSEL 75 (Vienna, Hoelder-Pichler-Tempsky, 1960), p. 55: 'Codices autem legantur in vigiliis divinae auctoritatis tam veteris testamenti quam novi; sed et expositiones earum quae a nominates et orthodoxis catholicis patribus factae sunt.' Hrabanus made explicit mention of the rule in a later letter, sent with his commentary on Leviticus: Hrab. *Epist.*, no. 10, p. 396.

[5] On the circulation of texts, see Philippe Depreux, 'Büchersuche und Büchertausch im Zeitalter der karolingischen Renaissance am Beispiel des Briefwechsels des Lupus von Ferriès', *Archiv für Kulturgeschichte*, 76 (1994): 267–84. See also John J. Contreni, 'Carolingian Biblical Studies', in *Carolingian Essays: Andrew W. Mellon Lectures in Early Christian Studies*, ed. U.-R. Blumenthal (Washington, DC, CUA Press, 1983), 71–98, esp. 83–94; repr. in his *Carolingian Learning, Masters and Manuscripts* (Aldershot, Variorum, 1992), item V; Mark Stansbury, 'Early-Medieval Biblical Commentaries, their Writers and Readers', *Frühmittelalterliche Studien*, 33 (1999): 49–82, at 80.

[6] All edited by Ernst Dümmler, MGH *Epp.* V, nos. 7–12, pp. 391–400. See also Hrab. *Epist.*, no. 27, p. 441, 29/31: sometime between 838 and 842, Hrabanus told Humbert, bishop of Würzburg, that Frechulf still had the exemplars of the Pentateuch commentaries: 'Priorum vero librorum commentarios, hoc est Pentatheuci Moysi, quos petente sancto viro Freculfo, non sine labore edidi, iam sibi ad rescribendum transmisi; quos cum recepero, exemplar eorum tibi scriptum destinabo' ('But the commentaries of the prior books [of the Old Testament], that is the Pentateuch of Moyses—which I prepared with great effort at the request of the holy man, Frechulf—I have sent to him to be copied. When I get them back, I shall send the exemplars of them to you to be copied'); and also Rudolf of Fulda, *Miracula sanctorum in fuldenses ecclesias translatorum*, c. 15, ed. Georg Waitz, MGH SS 15/1 (Hanover: Hahn, 1887), pp. 328–341, at 340 (ll. 35–7).

[7] *Prolegomena*, 17*; Allen, 'Fréculf', 72–3.

All modern commentators have taken note of the fact that Frechulf created a historiographical compendium. His *Histories* have been described as 'a pure compilation', 'a work of tessellation' ('Mosaikarbeit', 'Mosaiktext') or as a 'Text-Collage'.[8] Although recognised since the nineteenth century, the work's 'compilatory character' has been perceived with ambivalence at best.[9] Frechulf's skill at weaving together his sources often has been credited, yet equally prevalent in the secondary literature is the assumption that compilation is inferior to original composition, and thus is less valuable as historical evidence.[10] Staubach, for instance, acknowledged Frechulf's 'feat of transforming his vast mass of excerpts into a fine and readable text', but he devoted far more attention to demonstrating that the *Histories* transcended their composite nature. Frechulf's real achievement was to fashion a theologically sophisticated narrative, *despite* choosing to do so via compilation, 'seemingly so inauspicious a mode of representation'.[11]

This chapter demonstrates that, far from being an unfortunate feature to be worked around, compilation should be treated as a key component of Frechulf's work, which not only captures its essence but also shines light on the intellectual culture that gave rise to it. Frechulf may not have narrated events we now think of as being central to Carolingian history, but the very means by which he crafted his text speaks to the sort of work that Carolingian ecclesiastics dedicated enormous amounts of time, energy and resources to producing. Tellingly this work, even when undertaken by known intellectuals, has often suffered from the same critical apathy that resulted in the *Histories* being long overlooked or undervalued. Negative perceptions of Hrabanus Maurus, Frechulf's monastic *frater* and correspondent, can be taken as emblematic of this indifference. Ernst Robert Curtius dismissed the abbot of Fulda as a 'dreary compiler' whose explicit embrace of patristic authority was taken to signal a lack of any 'intellectual independence'. Hrabanus, like many others of his era, 'offered nothing but tradition and excerpts. They confined themselves … to a more or less intelligent extracting and copying, a "transcribing", of Antiquity'.[12] The ways in which Hrabanus and other Carolingian intellectuals acted not as passive receivers but as active moulders and appliers of patristic tradition has been underscored frequently over the past two decades. Frechulf, whose work closely aligns with theirs, ought to be understood in

---

[8] Goez, 'Zur Weltchronick', 93; Max Manitius, *Geschichte der lateinischen Literatur des Mittelalters, I: Von Justinian bis zur Mitte des 10. Jahrhunderts* (Munich, Beck, 1911), 665; Staubach, '*Christiana tempora*', 170; Steffen Patzold, *Episcopus: Wissen über Bischöfe im Frankenreich des späten 8. bis frühen 10. Jahrhunderts* (Ostfildern, Thorbecke, 2008), 175.

[9] Phrase from Staubach, '*Christiana tempora*', 170.

[10] Natunewicz, 'Frechulphus', 120.

[11] Staubach, '*Christiana tempora*', 169–70, 174–5 and 204.

[12] Ernst Robert Curtius, *European Literature and the Latin Middle Ages*, trans. Willard R. Trask (Princeton, NJ, Princeton University Press, 1953), 85 and 527. On this seminal work, see Stephen Jaeger, 'Ernst Robert Curtius: A Medievalist's Contempt for the Middle Ages', *Viator*, 47(2) (2016): 367–80.

similarly positive terms. Furthermore, the context of compilation also allows the Carolingian period itself to be set in a wider comparative framework.

Compiling: a Wider View

That Frechulf's *Histories* took the form of a compilation is not unusual. Most surviving medieval histories and chronicles were, to varying different degrees, compilations.[13] Yet my contention, as sketched in the introduction and which I develop here, is that in order to make sense of the *Histories* it is vital to understand them in relation to a more diverse body of material. It requires no great imaginative leap to arrive at this approach. It follows on from the basic observation that the techniques associated with compilation—selecting, excerpting, paraphrasing, condensing and organising material from other sources—were not at all unique to history-writing. One could go so far as to say that, in the ancient and medieval worlds, the process of gathering together, compressing and ordering what had been written down in the past was a ubiquitous means of preserving, construing and canonising knowledge.[14] For this reason, 'compilation' is best understood not as a specific type or genre of text, but rather as an analytical way of working with texts.

The evidence from the Carolingian period exemplifies this point. Biblical commentaries, homiliaries, penitentials, martyrologies, canonical and other legal collections, normative codes for religious life, priests' handbooks, as well as histories and chronicles were all predicated upon compiled knowledge; once the large and diverse range of manuscripts lumped under the heading 'miscellanies' are factored in, this list will expand considerably.[15] The sources from which this knowledge was

---

[13] Lake, 'Current Approaches', 96; Gert Melville, 'Le problème des connaisances historique au Moyen Âge: compilation et transmission des textes', in *L'historiographie médiévale en Europe. Actes du colloque organisé par la Fondation Européenne de la Science au Centre de Recherches Historiques et Juridiques de l'Université Paris I du 29 mars au 1ᵉʳ avril 1989*, ed. Jean-Philippe Genet (Paris: Presses du CNRS, 1991), 21–41.

[14] See, for example, Stephan Dusil, Gerald Schwedler and Raphael Schwitter (eds), *Exzerpieren - Kompilieren - Tradieren: Transformationen des Wissens zwischen Spätantike und Frühmittelalter* (Berlin, De Gruyter, 2016); Carmen Cardelle de Hartmann, 'Überlieferungsprozesse: Sammeln, Auswählen, Kanonisieren: eine Einführung', *Mittellateinisches Jahrbuch*, 53 (2018): 1–10.

[15] On sermons, see Maximilian Diesenberger, Yitzhak Hen and Marianne Pollheimer (eds), *Sermo doctorum: Compilers, Preachers, and their Audiences in the Early Medieval West* (Turnhout: Brepols, 2013). For important methodological reflections on miscellanies, see Anna Dorofeeva, 'Miscellanies, Christian Reform and Early Medieval Encyclopaedism: A Re-consideration of the Pre-bestiary Latin *Physiologus* Manuscripts', *Historical Research*, 90 (2017): 665–82. See further, Anna Dorofeeva, 'What is a Vademecum? The Social Logic of Early Medieval Compilation', in *The Art of Compilation: Manuscripts and Networks in the Early Medieval Latin West*, eds Anna Dorofeeva and Michael Kelly (Binghamton, NY: Gracchi Books, forthcoming 2022) and 'Reading Early Medieval Miscellanies', in *Scribes and the Presentation of Texts (From Antiquity to c. 1550). Proceedings of the 20th Colloquium of the Comité international de paléographie latine*, eds C.W. Dutschke and B. A. Shailor (Turnhout: Brepols, forthcoming 2021). Recent work on priests' handbooks has also shed valuable light on the production of compilations: see articles in Steffen Patzold and Carine van Rhijn (eds), *Men in the Middle: Local Priests in Early Medieval Europe* (Berlin, De Gruyter, 2016); Steffen Patzold, *Presbyter:*

extracted were overwhelmingly biblical and patristic. This is significant, because it was scripture and the church fathers that Carolingian kings, bishops and abbots enjoined communities of monks and clerics to copy, study and internalise;[16] these are the authoritative texts that can be found in abundance in the thousands of surviving codices from the ninth century, and which were prominently listed in the extant library catalogues from the period. The making of new written products from recycled resources thus can be linked to, and perhaps even taken as a consequence of, the religious reforms of the later eighth and ninth centuries.

Before turning to this Carolingian context, I first want to make it clear that, although I consider the work of ninth-century intellectuals to be distinct in terms of some of the compilations that they made, the period cannot be viewed in isolation from longer term trends of knowledge creation. As is often the case, these sorts of trends are characterised more by continuity than by change. To illustrate this, Ann Blair's seminal book *Too Much to Know: Managing Scholarly Information before the Modern Age* is a good place to begin.[17] Blair's focus was early modern reference works, defined as 'large collection[s] of textual information designed to be consulted rather than read through'.[18] She situated her study in a wide comparative framework that stretched back to the ancient world (and took into account pre-modern Islamic and Chinese contexts too).[19] This allowed her to trace the lineage of early modern 'techniques of text management' back to classical antiquity, when the two core methods of 'summarizing and compiling' were 'developed most effectively'. These two techniques were then 'bequeathed to the Latin Middle Ages directly'.[20]

Experts of the periods that fall within the vast expanse of time surveyed by Blair have looked more closely at different cultures of compilation and identified particularities that help nuance and enrich her panorama. Jason König and Tim Whitmarsh's edited volume, *Ordering Knowledge in the Roman Empire*, examined a range of ancient 'texts that follow a broadly "compilatory" aesthetic, accumulating information in often enormous bulk'.[21] As they explain in their programmatic introduction, the sort of 'knowledge-ordering' and 'knowledge-bearing texts' that their edited collection explored were shaped by imperial, Roman ways of thinking. Roman knowledge practices are considered to have

Moral, Mobilität und die Kirchenorganisation im Karolingerreich (Stuttgart, Anton Hiersemann, 2020).
[16] Classic statements: *Admonitio Generalis*, eds Hubert Mordek, Klaus Zechiel-Eckes and Michael Glatthaar, *Die Admonitio Generalis Karls des Großen*, MGH *Fontes iuris* 16 (Hanover: Hahnsche Buchhandlung, 2012) and *Epistola de colendis*, MGH *Capit.* 1, n. 29, p. 79.
[17] Ann Blair, *Too Much to Know: Managing Scholarly Information before the Modern Age* (New Haven, CT, and London: Yale University Press, 2010).
[18] Blair, *Too Much to Know*, 269, n. 1.
[19] Blair, *Too Much to Know*, 11–61.
[20] Blair, *Too Much to Know*, 20; cf. 21, 22, 46.
[21] Jason König and Tim Whitmarsh, 'Ordering Knowledge', in *Ordering Knowledge in the Roman Empire*, eds Jason König and Tim Whitmarsh (Cambridge: CUP, 2007), 3–39, at 3.

been intensified in Late Antiquity, stimulated in part by cultural and material factors, namely Christianity and the codex as a writing technology.[22] Compiled and compressed texts 'arguably [became] part of the defining literary aesthetic' of the fourth, fifth, and sixth centuries.[23] Genres associated with this aesthetic include epitomes, florilegia, commentaries, scholia, *catenae* ('chains' of excerpts) and *centones* (poems which recast the words of classical authors to tell new Christian stories). During the Merovingian centuries, even if the evidence is less abundant than for earlier or later periods, a comparable picture emerges.[24] In the eastern Roman Empire in the tenth century, there was a pronounced effort to collect and systematise knowledge.[25] Despite the quantity of surviving sources, the place of the Carolingian period in this narrative has not fully been appreciated. Blair herself treated the early medieval Middle Ages very cursorily, as her survey was geared towards the later twelfth and thirteenth centuries, a critical juncture in western European intellectual history, when the basic 'techniques of text management' were sharpened and refined to deal with an ever-increasing bulk of information.[26] This reflects a prominent viewpoint that the thirteenth century marked a watershed moment both in the production of scholarly compilations and in the history of the book.[27]

The extent to which thirteenth-century practices were 'new' has been contested.[28] One of the more obviously novel changes that happened around this time is to be found not in the practice, but in the lexicon of compilation: before c.1200, the Latin word *compilatio* generally did not mean 'compilation', but instead

---

[22] Marietta Horster and Christiane Reitz, 'Handbooks, Epitomes, and Florilegia', in *A Companion to Late Antique Literature*, eds Scott C. MacGill and Edward Jay Watts (New York: John Wiley, 2018), 431–50; Marco Formisano, 'Towards an Aesthetic Paradigm of Late Antiquity', *Antiquité tardive*, 15 (2007): 277–84; Scott Fizgerald Johnson, *Greek Literature in Late Antiquity: Dynamism, Didacticism, Classicism* (Aldershot, Ashgate, 2006), 56–7. With a focus on Information Technology, see Matthew R. Crawford, *The Eusebian Canon Tables: Ordering Textual Knowledge in Late Antiquity* (Oxford: OUP, 2019) and Andrew M. Riggsby, *Mosaics of Knowledge: Representing Information in the Roman World* (Oxford: OUP, 2019), esp. 216–22.

[23] Quote from Johnson, *Greek Literature*, 56.

[24] For a survey of the evidence, see Ian Wood, 'The Problem of Late Merovingian Culture', in *Exzerpieren – Kompilieren – Tradieren: Transformationen des Wissens zwischen Spätantike und Frühmittelalter*, eds Stephan Dusil, Gerald Schwedler and Raphael Schwitter (Berlin: De Gruyter, 2016), 199–222.

[25] András Németh, *The Excerpta Constantiniana and the Byzantine Appropriation of the Past* (Cambridge: CUP, 2018).

[26] Blair, *Too Much to Know*, 33.

[27] Malcolm Parkes, 'The Influence of the Concepts of *Ordinatio* and *Compilatio* on the Development of the Book', in *Medieval Learning and Literature: Essays Presented to Richard William Hunt*, eds J. J. G. Alexander and M. T. Gibson (Oxford: Clarendon Press, 1976), 115–41. See, however, Richard R. Rouse and Mary A. Rouse, '*Ordinatio* and *Compilatio* Revisited', in *Ad litteram: Authoritative Texts and their Medieval Readers*, eds Mark D. Jordan and Kent Emery Jr (Notre Dame, IL: Notre Dame University Press, 1992), 113–34.

[28] Adam J. Kosto, '*Statim invenire ante*: Finding Aids and Research Tools in Pre-Scholastic Legal and Administrative Manuscripts', *Scriptorium*, 70(2) (2016): 285–309. Rouse and Rouse, '*Ordinatio* and *Compilatio*' are emphatic that 'the activity of compiling … did not begin with the thirteenth century' (120).

had a negative connotation. A *compilator* was not a 'compiler', but a 'plunderer'; to *compilare* was to pillage another's property.[29] Bernard Guenée also noted this shift within the context of medieval historiographical compilations, and also made it clear this was a discursive shift rather than a practical one. What changed around 1200 was not the act of compilation, but rather the words used to express it.[30] Between the fourth and twelfth centuries, there was a range of expressions that Latin compilers could employ to describe what they were doing. Over the course of these 800 years, some of the most frequently used terms had already been employed in what was ostensibly the first work of Christian historiography, Eusebius's *Ecclesiastical History*. Readers of Rufinus's Latin translation would have learned that Eusebius gathered together excerpts, 'as if plucking flowers from the learned fields of teachers', and then attempted 'by means of a historical composition to make of them a single body'.[31] Turning to Frechulf's vocabulary of compilation not only confirms that early medieval compilers drew on the same descriptive language as their more ancient predecessors, but also helps us to appreciate what was distinctive about the early Middle Ages.

Frechulf's Language of Compilation

The process of compilation was not a solitary one. In what follows, I attribute authorial and editorial decisions to 'Frechulf', but this is partly out of convenience. Frechulf would not have worked alone, but with a team of scribes and assistants. The precise working methods of Carolingian compilers is difficult to know, and the various stages that would be involved in making a compilation can usually only be guessed at. It is likely that they would have included marking up relevant passages in source texts, making notes of selected passages on scraps of parchment or wax tablets, ordering and editing excerpts to make them fit together, and copying them out onto parchment. Only occasionally can we catch glimpses of scholars at work.[32] Florus of Lyon's enormous compilation of Augustinian exegesis of the Pauline epistles is one such case, since the end product can be studied alongside

[29] Neil Hathaway, '*Compilatio*: From Plagiarism to Compiling', *Viator*, 20 (1989): 19–44.
[30] Bernard Guenée, 'L'historien et la compilation du XIIIe siècle', *Journal des Savants*, (1985): 119–35.
[31] Eusebius-Rufinus, *Historia ecclesiastica*, Pref., eds Eduard Schwartz and Theodor Mommsen, *Eusebius Werke*, vol. 2: *Die Kirchengeschicte*, Die griechischen christlichen Schriftsteller der ersten drei Jahrhunderte 6, 3 vols (Liepzig: J.C. Hinrichs, 1903–9), 2nd end (Berlin: Akademie Verlag, 1999), p. 9: 'quaecumque igitur proposito operi convenire credidimus, ex his, quae illi sparsim memoraverant, eligentes ac velut e rationabilibus campis doctorum flosculos decerpentes historica narratione in unum corpus redigere et coagmentare temptavimus, satis abundeque gratum putantes, etsi non omnium, nobilissimorum certe salvatoris nostri apostolorum successiones celebrioribus quibusque ecclesiis traditas in unum colligere atque in ordinem modumque digerere.' Translation adapted from Jeremy M. Schott, *The History of the Church: A New Translation* (Oakland, CA: University of California Press, 2019), 40.
[32] See essays in Mariken Teeuwen and Irene van Renswoude (eds), *The Annotated Book in the Early Middle Ages: Practices of Reading and Writing* (Turnhout: Brepols, 2018). See further recent work on the controversy of double predestination: Pezé, *Le virus de l'erreur*, esp. chapters 5–7.

an annotated source text. Louis Holtz's seminal study presented a maximalist reading of authorial control: Florus both masterminded and micromanaged the production of his Augustinian *Expositio*.[33] It is not clear whether Frechulf was as attentive a reader as Florus; the occasional instance of duplicated excerpts suggests he was not quite as rigorous in controlling his scribes' handiwork.[34]

Frechulf was explicit that his work was a compilation, or rather a compendium: he spoke of his *Histories* variously as an *opus conpendii* ('a work of abridgement'), and *opus conpendiosum* and an *opusculum conpendiosum* ('a compendious little work').[35] A clear statement of how he went about fashioning this 'compendious work' can be found in the Prologue to Part I, a text to which we shall return often in the first three chapters of this monograph, and then again more critically in Chapter 6. Helisachar, Frechulf explained, had commanded him 'to hunt through the volumes of the ancients ... and gather together all that pertained to the truth of history'. The key verb in this sentence is *colligere* ('to collect' as well as 'to bring together' or 'assemble'), which in effect meant 'to compile' and was very frequently used by compilers to speak of compilation before the twelfth century: this was the main verb used already by Eusebius-Rufinus.[36] Throughout the *Histories*, Frechulf employed a number of other words that evoke the stages involved in making a compilation: he searched through his sources (*perscrutari, indagare*),[37] selected passages (*eligere*) from which to make excerpts (*excerpere, decerpere*),[38] and then inserted them (*inserere*).[39] Two further verbs, *perstringere* ('to touch upon', or 'describe briefly') and *adnotare* ('to make note of'), capture the selective concision of Frechulf's *opus conpendiosum* and thus are also synonymous with compilation.[40] Lastly, Frechulf also employed figurative language that stemmed

---

[33] Louis Holtz, 'Le ms. Lyon, B.M. 484 (414) et la méthode de travail de Florus', *Revue bénédictine*, 119 (2009): 270–315. See further Shari Boodts, 'Les sermons d'Augustin', in *Les douze compilations pauliennes de Florus de Lyon*, eds Pierre Chambert-Protat, Franz Dolveck and Camille Gerzaguet (Rome, École française de Rome, 2017), 197–211.

[34] For some examples of duplicated or overlapping passages, see: *Hist.*, I.3.12 [73/9], pp. 178–9, I.3.17 [195/205], pp. 196–7 and I.4.7 [17/24], p. 222; I.4.19 [18/48], pp. 237–9 and I.4.28 [14/43], pp. 265–7; II.3.14 [77/90], pp. 591–2 and II.3.21 [7/20], pp. 608–9. Compare *Hist.* I.3.10 and 11, where the respective *capitula* reflect the content of I.3.12 [5/20], pp. 175–6.

[35] *Hist.*, II.3.16 [104.5], p. 601; II.4.4 [30.1], p. 622, II.4.16 [39.40], p. 645.

[36] *Hist.*, I.Prol. [14.15], p. 18; compare the verb *congere*: II.Prol. [22], p. 436; *Prol. Veg.* [29], p. 729; Guenée, 'L'historien', 121.

[37] *Perscrutari*: *Hist.*, I.Prol.[13.14], p. 18 ('perscrutando diligenter volumina antiquorum'). *Indagare*: *Hist.*, I.1.57 [18/20], p. 84.

[38] *Eligere*: *Hist.*, I.Prol., p. 20. *Excerpere*: *Hist.* I.7.2 [26.27], p. 370 ('Haec de Iosepphi excerpsimus dictis'); II.2.23 [90], p. 549 ('de qua pauca excerpsimus nos'). *Decerpere*: I.2.27 [1/5], p. 52 ('ex Iosepphi atque Hieronomi libris decerpere libuit'); I.2.Prol. [19/21], p. 85; I.2.26 (capitula), p. 90; I.2.17 [101/103], p. 115; I.3.11 [129.130], p. 181; II.1.1 [1/5], p. 440 ('In prioribus libris ... ex multorum opusculis ... decerpere curavi quaeque utilia parvitati meae sunt visa et legentibus profutura').

[39] *Hist.*, I.Prol., p. 20; I.1.10, p. 38; I.2.Prol, pp. 85 and 86; I.2.17, p. 119.

[40] *Perstringere*: *Hist.*, I.1.1, p. 28; I.1.25 [3.4], p. 50; II.1.2 [5.6], p. 441: 'ut in prioribus libando perstrinximus libris'; II.2.16 [67/9], p. 533; II.5.27 [21.22], p. 724. *Pestringere* can also mean to 'bind together tightly', that is, 'compile'. See Hrabanus Maurus, *Epist.* 20, p. 426, 13: 'Ego autem hoc opus

from a literary topos that likened compilation to gathering flowers. This topos can already be found in classical Latin sources and appears through the Middle Ages.[41] (It was from this language that the comparatively modern genre of the florilegium derived, but the metaphor was not restricted to texts now classified as florilegia.) Frechulf began the very first chapter of his *Histories* by describing his work as 'summarising (*perstringere*) in succinct prose a certain sequence of times from the studies of noble writers of both divine and secular histories, selecting a few florets from their many volumes, as if from the blooms of various flowery meadows'.[42]

Seen from a diachronic perspective, Frechulf's vocabulary is not unusual: it had been part of the Latin lexicon of compilation for hundreds of years and would continue to be used long after the ninth century. Much more, however, can be learned through synchronic comparison, and the most revealing place to begin is with the letter sent from Lisieux to Fulda c. 824/5. When Frechulf addressed his exegetical request to Hrabanus, he drew on the very same vocabulary that he later used in relation to his own project. He asked Hrabanus to produce an *opus conpendiosum*. This was to be 'gathered together by searching through the works of earlier investigators (*ut priorum perscrutando conferatis tractatorum labores*)' of the Pentateuch, which Frechulf's own 'hunt through the volumes of ancients (*perscrutando ... volumina antiquorum*)' obviously echoed; the verb *conferre* exists in the same semantic field as *colligere*. While Frechulf plucked florets of historiography, Hrabanus was to pick at his sources as if he were a bee, 'plucking sweet flowers from beautiful, blossoming meadows and collecting them together in the beehive'; his compendium of commentary was to be offered as 'sweet-smelling honeycomb'.[43] Historiography and exegesis shared a common language of scholarly practice.

---

meum tribus libellis perstrinxi', where the meaning seems to be closest to 'compile' ('I have compiled my work in three books'). *Adnotare*: I.Prol. [29.30], p. 19 and [54.55], p. 20; I.3.17, p. 156; II.2.22 [5/9], p. 545; II.3.1 [1/8], p. 558; II.3.7 [57/60], p. 568; II.3.10 [13/18], p. 580; II.4.18 [20/23], p. 648. Compare Bede, *Historia ecclesiastica*, V. 25, ed. and trans. Bertram Colgrave and R. A. B. Mynors, *Bede's Ecclesiastical History of the English People* (Oxford: OUP, 1969), pp. 566–7: 'I have made it my business to make brief extracts (*adnotare*) from the works of venerable fathers on the holy scriptures.'

[41] On this metaphor, see Jacqueline Hamesse, 'La vocaubulaire des florilèges médiévau', in *Méthodes et instruments du travail intellectuel au Moyen Âge. Etudes sur le vocabulaire*, ed. Olga Weijers (Turnhout: Brepols, 1990), 209–30; Gert Melville, 'Zur *Flores-Metaphorik* in der mittelalterlichen Geschichsschreibung: Ausdruck eines Formungsprinzips', *Historisches Jahrbuch*, 90 (1970): 65–80; Tore Janson, *Latin Prose Prefaces: Studies in Literary Conventions* (Stockholm: Almqvist and Wiksell, 1964), 151–4 (Frechulf at 153). On early medieval florilegia, see also Mary Garrison, 'The Collectanea and Medieval Florilegia', in *Collectanea Pseudo-Bedae*, eds Martha Bayless and Michael Lapidge (Dublin, Dublin Institute for Advances Studies, 1998), 42–83, esp. 43–8; Rosamund McKitterick, *The Frankish Church and the Carolingian Reforms, 789–895* (London: Royal Historical Society, 1977), pp. 155–83.

[42] *Hist.*, I.1.1 [1/5], p. 28: 'Dum aliquam temporum seriem commatico sermone ex nobilium studiis tam diuinarum scriptorum historiarum quamque saecularium et ex pluribus eorum paucos libando flosculos libris ceu ex diuersorum uernantium pratorum floribus perstringere curare ...'

[43] *Epist.*, pp. 5–6: 'Qui scilicet Legislatoris libri, humiliter deposcimus ut ita uestro succincte delucidentur studio ut priorum perscrutando conferatis tractatorum labores et uelut ex pratis uernantibus amoenisque flores mellifluos carpendo apum more in aluiarium congestos, nobis fauum cum melle odorifero porrigere non neglegatis.'

Sources of Authority

The parallels between Frechulf's and Hrabanus's projects can be taken further. Frechulf expected Hrabanus to make known the names of the authorities from which his *opus conpendiosum* was assembled. This was to be achieved via marginal signs, placed next to an excerpted passage. For example, AUG in the margin would signal to the reader that the associated passage stemmed from Augustine.[44] When no authority could be found to provide commentary on a given passage, Hrabanus was asked to trust that the Holy Spirit—which, Frechulf made clear, had spoken to men in the past, still spoke to them and would continue in the future to do so—would inspire him to supply his own interpretation. This was to be marked by the letter M, in connection with the first letter of Hrabanus's nickname, 'Maurus'. This would allow readers 'to rejoice equally in [Hrabanus's] own gift as well in the gifts of more eminent men'.[45] (This comment, it should be noted, essentially slices through the rhetoric of humility, as it effectively aligns Hrabanus with the church fathers.[46]) Pleasingly, Hrabanus's first reply reveals that he had received and fulfilled Frechulf's request:

> For I did as you asked, and, as far as it was possible, I have read through the books of the holy fathers, in which I judged that something concerning the *sententiae* of the Law had been expressed; and, as it seemed to me to be sufficient, I have inserted each [excerpted *sententia*] in a fitting place and have noted down on the page the names [of those who wrote them]. But if the grace of God deemed it worthy for my undeserving self to explain anything, I have likewise inserted at the relevant place a note with my nickname [that is, Maurus], so that the reader may know which opinion is held by the tradition of the fathers, and which is held by our smallness, which although [expressed] in rustic speech, nevertheless I believe that [the reader] should discover something explained in the catholic sense.[47]

---

[44] Sita Steckel, 'Von Buchstaben und Geist: pragmatische und symbolische Dimensionen der Autorensiglen (*nomina auctorum*) bei Hrabanus Maurus', in *Karolingische Klöster: Wissenstransfer und kulturelle Innovation*, eds Julia Becker, Tino Licht and Stefan Weinfurter (Berlin: De Gruyter, 2015), 89–130.

[45] *Epist.*, p. 7, 19/28: 'Eo itaque modo opus hoc conpendiosum fieri flagitamus ut primum sensus litterae ac deinde spiritalis intellegentiae accurate succisa prolixitate pandatur, et singulorum nomina auctorum in fronte notentur pagellae ex quibus praesentes decerpseritis sententias. Insuper praecamur obnixe ut quicquid spiritus sanctus, qui loquebatur olim in uiris Deo deditis et adhuc loquitur et loquetur, uestro beniuolo et deuoto inspirauerit animo, sub nullo reticeatis silentio, sed littera praenominis uestri prima seorsum adnotetis, ut eminentius etiam de proprio gaudere ualeamus pariter dono.'

[46] Compare Bede's perception of himself as being more than his humility topoi might suggest: Roger Ray, 'Who Did Bede Think He Was?', in *Innovation and Tradition in the Writings of the Venerable Bede*, ed. Scott DeGregorio (Morgantown, WV: West Virginia University Press, 2006), 11–35.

[47] Hrab. *Epist.*, no. 8, p. 394, 1/7: 'Feci enim sicut postulasti, et sanctorum patrum libros, in quibus rebar aliquid de sententiis legis expressum esse, quantum licuit perlegi et singula secundum oportunitatem loci, prout mihi satis esse videbatur, inserui, eorum nominibus ante in pagina prenotatis. Si quid vero gratia divina indigno mihi elucidare dignata est, in locis necessariis simul cum nota agnominis mei interposui, quatinus sciret lector, quę ex patrum traditione haberet, et quę ex parvitate nostra, licet sermone rustico, tamen ut credo sensu catholico exposita inveniret.' See also no. 9, p. 395, 31/4; no. 10,

Frechulf's letter presupposed a knowledge of Hrabanus's approach to biblical commentary.[48] Hrabanus set out this approach clearly in his exegesis of the Gospel of Matthew, which he prepared c. 821/2, so before Frechulf entered the episcopate, when presumably he was still at Fulda. In a dedication to Haistulf, archbishop of Mainz, Hrabanus explained that he had examined works by 'Cyprian and Eusebius, Hilary, Ambrose, Jerome, Augustine, Fulgentius, Victorinus, Fortunatianus, Orosius, Leo, Gregory of Nazianzus, Gregory [the Great], John Chrysostom and the other fathers, whose names are written in the book of life'.[49] Hrabanus declined to note the names of his sources within the body of the text, but rather decided it would be convenient (*commodum*) to note 'the first letters of the names at the side [of the page]', in order to flag up which passages were borrowed from whom.[50]

This approach to exegesis was not unique to Hrabanus. A similar procedure can be observed in Claudius of Turin's *Genesis Commentary*, a text written c. 811 and of which Frechulf made extensive use in the very first book of his *Histories*. Claudius wrote in his preface that:

> After studying and investigating opinions on historical events taken from mystical treasure troves of learned men, I abridged them in a brief compendium of one codex. The reader does not read my words. Instead, he reads theirs again. I have collected their words like beautiful flowers from many meadows, so my treatise is

---

p. 396, 28/35; no. 11, p. 398, 8/18; no. 12, p. 399, 8/11. The expression *Feci enim sicut postulasti*, which comes up quite often in Hrabanus's correspondence, shows not only a humility topos in use but also scholarly networks in action: see Contreni, 'Biblical studies', 85 and n. 47.

[48] *Prolegomena*, 19*–20*. On Hrabanus's working methods: Philippe le Maître, 'Les méthodes exégétiques de Raban Maur', in *Haut Moyen-Age: culture, éducation et société. Études offertes à Pierre Riché* , eds Claude Lepelley and Michel Sot (Nanterre: Éditions Publidix, 1990), 343–52; Marc-Aeilko Aris, '*Nostrum est citare testes*: Anmerkungen zum Wissenschaftsverständnis des Hrabanus Maurus', in *Kloster Fulda in der Welt der Karolinger und Ottonen*, ed. Gangolf Schrimpf, Fuldaer Studien 7 (Frankfurt: J. Knecht, 1996), 437–64; and Caroline Chevalier-Royet, 'Entre tradition et innovation: Raban Maur, un érudit carolingien face à ses sources', in *Érudition et culture savante: de l'Antiquité à l'époque moderne*, eds François Brizay and Véronique Sarraz (Rennes: Presses Universitaires de Rennes, 2015), 53–70. More generally on Hrabanus's commentaries, see the series of important articles by Mayke de Jong: 'Old Law and New-Found Power: Hrabanus Maurus and the Old Testament', in *Centres of Learning: Learning and Location in Pre-Modern Europe and the Near East*, Jan Willem Drijvers and Alasdair A. MacDonald (Leiden: Brill, 1995), 161–76; De Jong, 'Empire as *Ecclesia*'. Useful also is Oliver Berggötz, 'Hrabanus Maurus und seine Bedeutung für das Bibliothekswesen der Karolingerzeit: zugleich ein Beitrag zur Geschichte der Klosterbibliothek Fulda', *Bibliothek und Wissenschaft*, 27 (1994): 1–48.

[49] Hrab. *Exp.*, Praef. [49/56], pp. 2–3: 'Adgregatis igitur hinc inde insignissimis sacrae lectionis atque dignissimis artificibus, quid in opusculis suis in beati Matthaei uerbis senserint, quid dixerint, diligentius inspicere curaui; Cyprianum dico atque Eusebium, Hilarium, Ambrosium, Hieronimum, Augustinum, Fulgentium, Victorinum, Fortunatianum, Orosium, Leonem, Gregorium Nazanzenum, Gregorium papam Romanum, Iohannemque Crisostomum et ceteros patres, quorum nomina sunt scripta in libro uitae'. For a discussion, see Owen M. Phelan, 'The Carolingian Renewal in Early Medieval Europe through Hrabanus Maurus's *Commentary on Matthew*', *Traditio*, 75 (2020): 143–75, esp. 149–61.

[50] Hrab. *Exp.*, Praef. [62/67], p. 3: 'Quorum uidelicet quia operosum erat uocabula interserere per singula et quid a quo auctore sit dictum nominatim ostendere, commodum duxi eminus e latere primas nominum litteras inprimere per que has uiritim, ubi cuiusque patrum incipiat, ubi sermo, quem transtuli, desinat, intimare, sollicitus per omnia, ne maiorum dicta furari et haec quasi mea propria componere dicar'.

a work of theirs. And so no one will think me presumptuous and rash because I took arms from the cabinet of another, I have indicated the name of each learned authority by placing letters in the margin, just as the blessed priest Bede did. But his work is difficult at times and cannot be understood by everyone.[51]

The importance of Bede's working methods are made explicit in Claudius's prologue. They are also implicitly clear from Hrabanus's: a considerable amount of the prologue to his Matthew commentary was copied verbatim from the prologue to Bede's exposition of Luke; crucially, the borrowed passages dealt with Bede's comments on his use of sources.[52]

In the prologue to Part I, Frechulf also showed that sources were on his mind. It is implied that Helisachar had urged Frechulf to do precisely what Frechulf had expected of Hrabanus. His response suggests he took a different approach:

> I have not, as you previously advised me, included in every instance the names of the authors from whom I gathered the material collected in these seven books, since in those cases where they were in agreement I took the meaning that I had chosen and tried to phrase it more concisely. In those cases where certain authors (whether Christian or pagan) differed from the rest, however, I decided to mention their names and reproduce their opinions as found in their books. I implore whoever desires to read this, therefore, not to impute anything that may displease him to the presumptuousness of my weakness, but instead to my obedience, and not to make rash criticism before carefully reading the authors from whom we have excerpted.[53]

---

[51] Claudius of Turin, *Epistolae*, ed. Ernst Dümmler, MGH *Epp.* IV (Berlin: Weidmann, 1895), no. 1, p. 592, 11/17: 'Has autem rerum gestarum sententias de mysticis thesauris sapientium inquirendo et investigando in unum codicem conpendio brevitatis coartavi, in quibus l[ector] non mea legit, sed illorum relegit, quorum ego verba quae illi dixerunt veluti speciosos flores ex diversis pratis in unum collegi et meae litterae ipsorum expositio est. Et ne ab aliquibus praesumptor et temerarius diiudicarer, quod [ab] alieno armario sumpserim tela, uniuscuiusque doctoris nomen cum suis characteribus, sicut et beatus fecit presbiter Beda, subter in paginis adnotavi. Sed [eius] opusculum quibusdam in locis operosum est, et non ab omnibus eum intelligibilem arbitror.' Trans. in Michael M. Gorman, 'The Commentary of Genesis on Claudius of Turin and Biblical Studies under Louis the Pious', *Speculum*, 72 (1997): 279–329, at 287. For similar expressions, see Claudius, *Epistolae*, no. 2, pp. 594, 6/16 and 595, 15/23; no. 7, p. 603, 6/11; no. 9, p. 607, 26/36.

[52] See Hrab. *Exp.*, Praef. [59/71], p. 3. Compare Bede, *In Lucae evangelium expositio*, ed. David Hurst, CCCM 120 (Turnhout: Brepols, 1960), p. 7. See Aris, '*Nostrum est citare testes*', 442–3. On Bede's commentary, see Arthur G. Holder, 'Bede and the New Testament', in *The Companion to Bede*, ed. Scott DeGregorio (Cambridge: CUP, 2010), 142–55, at 147; Stansbury, 'Biblical Commentaries', 72–5; Bernice Martha Kaczynski, 'Bede's Commentaries on Luke and Mark and the Formation of a Patristic Canon', in *Anglo-Latin and its Heritage: Essays in Honour of A. G. Riff on his 64th Birthday*, eds Siân Echard and Gernot R. Wieland, Publications of the Journal of Medieval Latin 4 (Turnhout: Brepols, 2001), 17–26; Michael M. Gorman, 'Source Marks and Chapter Divisions in Bede's Commentary on Luke', *Revue bénédictine*, 112 (2002): 246–90.

[53] *Hist.*, I.Prol. [51/61], p. 20: 'Igitur nomina auctorum ex quibus ea collegi quae in septem libris conclusi idcirco non ubique inserui ut praemonuisti, quoniam in his in quibus concordare uidebantur sensum quem elegeram defloraui et sub breuitate dictare studui. Eorum autem nomina adnotare decreui, nostrorum seu gentilium, sententiasque illorum adsumpsi ut in suis habentur libris, qui uariando a ceteris exorbitare uidentur. Obsecro itaque legere uolentem, non praesumptioni reputet meae inbecillitatis si quid in his ei displicuerit libris, sed oboedientiae, nec temere reprehendat antequam curiosius eos legat auctores ex quibus haec decerpsimus.' Trans. Lake, 112.

Frechulf tied his *Histories* to past authorities in a way that chimes with Hrabanus and Claudius, although he was more explicit about the fact that his compendium involved more than simply compiling direct excerpts: source extracts were often silently spliced together and paraphrased or reworked as Frechulf saw fit.

It would be unwise to draw too many sharp contrasts between Frechulf's handling of his sources on the one hand, and Hrabanus's or Claudius's on the other. The latter were not rigorous in marking up borrowed passages: they integrated extracts silently, often after having subjected them to editing. If these scholars employed comparable methods, the form and focus of their respective compilations were nevertheless different. Exegetical compilations such as Hrabanus's and Claudius's were ordered around the chapters and verses of whatever biblical book they were analysing, whereas Frechulf's compilation took the form of a historical narrative, a *narratio rei gestae*: much more on this in the next chapter. A further difference ostensibly lies in the nature of the sources from which these respective compendia were drawn. Hrabanus worked with the writings of the *sancti patres*, the 'holy fathers': this was underlined in each of the five letters he sent to Frechulf.[54] On the whole, these were the usual patristic subjects, distinguished authorities such as Ambrose, Jerome, Augustine and Gregory the Great, whose commentaries, homilies and letters formed the patristic canon upon which most Carolingian texual scholarship was built. Frechulf's source base, by contrast, was 'the *volumina antiquorum*': the histories and chronicles of the ancients. Yet salient points of contact still can be found: Hrabanus Maurus also worked with historiographical texts, though far less intensively; and the usual patristic subjects, as historical actors and authors, were embedded into Frechulf's narrative. These will be explored further in later chapters. Here I want to make two interrelated points: that Frechulf's sources were also perceived as holy, and that they too were part of the patristic canon.

History and the Holy

In scrutinising the 'volumes of the ancients', Frechulf recognised two broad categories of authors: Christian and non-Christian, 'our authors and those of the pagans (*nostri sive gentiles … scriptores*)'.[55] Frechulf made very little direct use of 'pagan' historiography. The names of Roman historians, such as Sallust, Tacitus and Justin, as well as a selection of statements from ancient Hellenistic writers, can be found scattered throughout Part I. But they were all incorporated indirectly through Frechulf's other sources.[56] Rather, the vast majority of the material that

---

[54] For example, Hrab. *Epist.*, no. 11, p. 398: '… studui preceptis tuis parere et sanctorum partum sententias ad hoc undique colligere'.

[55] *Hist.*, I.Prol. [17/21], p. 18 and [54/7], p. 20.

[56] See *Hist.*, I.1.10, pp. 37-9; I.1.25 [14/28], pp. 50-1; I.2.4 [24/38], p. 96; I.2.5 [24/35], p. 98; I.2.10

fed into the *Histories* was extracted from Christian authors. Frechulf drew on the best part of thirty separate texts, some only once or twice, others much more frequently and intensively. I refer to these more heavily utilised texts as Frechulf's 'core resources', and they include: the *Chronicle* of Eusebius-Jerome; Augustine's *On the City of God*; Orosius's *Histories against the Pagans*; the Latin translations of Josephus's *Jewish Antiquities* and *Jewish War*, which although not Christian were nevertheless read as part of the Christian canon; the five-book Christianised abbreviation of Josephus's *Jewish War* ascribed to Hegesippus; Rufinus's fifth-century Latin translation and continuation of Eusebius's *Ecclesiastical History*; Cassiodorus-Epiphanius's *Tripartite History*; Jerome's *On Illustrious Men*; Jordanes' *Romana and Getica*; and Bede's *Greater Chronicle*, which formed chapter 66 of his *De temporum ratione*.[57] In addition to referring to Christian authors as 'ours' (*nostri*)', Frechulf's also applied a more peculiar term: *hagiographi*.[58] There has been some disagreement over how to translate this word. Justin Lake has interpreted the phrase in question as 'the authors of saints' lives and pagan writers';[59] Elisabeth Mégier preferred 'the writings of biblical ... and pagan authors'.[60] Neither of these renderings are quite accurate or fully satisfying, ironically on account of being too precise in their evocation of distinct sorts of texts.[61] Frechulf made limited use of what we today call hagiography, that is stories about the lives of Christian holy men and women; likewise, his direct engagement with scripture also was conspicuously limited. The term can only denote Christian historians. Why might he have chosen it?

In the Middle Ages, the Latin word *hagiographa* was used most frequently to define a subset of Old Testament books.[62] Isidore of Seville grouped these authors in the third category of Old Testament texts, after the Law and the Prophets, and, as was his wont, unpacked the meaning of the word: *hagiographa* was derived from Greek, and in Latin meant *sancta scribentium*, that is, 'those writing about holy things', or the 'holy writings'.[63] While it seems unlikely that the bishop of Lisieux

---

[29/43], pp. 104–5; I.2.17 [101/25], pp. 115–6; I.3.4 [9/32], pp. 163–4; I.3.17 [52/68], pp. 190–1.

[57] *Prolegomena*, 199*–219* provides commentary on the major sources and see pp. 276*–331* for a very useful *index scriptorum*. For editions and translations, see the bibliography.

[58] *Hist.*, I.Prol. [13/16], p. 18: 'iussisti ut perscrutando diligenter uolumina antiquorum, seu agiographorum siue etiam gentilium scriptorium ...'; II.1.1 [1/5], p. 440: 'In prioribus libris ... ex multorum opusculis agiograforum seu gentilium... decerpere curaui ...'; *Prol. Veg.* [28/30], p. 729: 'Igitur post libros ab inicio mundi usque ad regna Francorum in Galliis a paruitate mea congestos ex agiografphorum siue gentilium historiis ...'.

[59] Lake, *Prologues*, 111.

[60] Mégier, 'L'histoire biblique', 1064.

[61] Compare Henri de Lubac, *Medieval Exegesis: The Four Senses of Scripture* vol. 1, translated by Mark Sebanc (Grand Rapids, MI: William B. Eerdmans, 1999), 4.

[62] Jerome, *Prologus in libro Regum*, ed. Robert Weber, *Biblia Sacra: iuxta Vulgatam* (Stuttgart, Deutsche Bibelgesellschaft, 1969), p. 365; Cassiodorus, *Institutiones*, I.6, ed. R. A. B. Mynors (Oxford: Clarendon Press, 1937), pp. 25–7. Jerome and Cassiodorus differ in who they count amongst this group.

[63] Isidore of Seville, *Etymologiae*, VI.1.7, ed. W. M. Lindsay, 2 vols (Oxford: Clarendon Press, 1911):

had this particular subsection of biblical texts in mind, Isidore's etymological explanation nevertheless shines some light on what Frechulf's word-choice conveyed.[64] His *hagiographi* were not the Old Testament *Hagiographa*, but in their own way they were still holy.[65] Inspiration, the special quality by which texts were believed to be imbued with sacred significance, was not exclusive to the scriptural canon, as Frechulf's comment in his letter to Hrabanus about the workings of the Holy Spirit amongst people in the past, present and future indicates. Many of Frechulf's main authorities were themselves also reckoned amongst the *sancti patres*. The attribution of holiness, moreover, cannot be disentangled from the close relationship between scripture and historiography that Frechulf's work articulates. Frechulf did not consider 'the volumes of the pagans and those who wrote about holy matters' to be part of the canon of scripture, but nevertheless viewed them in relation to it.[66] His historiographical compendium was not only built on notions of textual authority but also on textual holiness: in examining his *Histories*, this aspect needs to be kept in mind.

History as Canon

The association between Christian history and scripture significantly predated the Carolingian age, and, at least since the sixth century, Frechulf's source base had been viewed as a corpus. What I label Frechulf's 'core resources', those which comprise the lion's share of his *Histories*, were all recommended by Cassiodorus in his *Institutiones*, a manual for biblical study to be used by students at his southern Italian monastery, Vivarium.[67] The first book of the *Institutiones* was devoted to 'divine learning'. After guiding readers through the various books of the Old and New Testaments and their key patristic commentaries, Cassiodorus urged that his budding scholars familiarise themselves with 'Christian histories', as part of their overall engagement with 'Christian studies':

'Tertius [est] ordo Hagiographorum, id est sancta scribentium, in quo sunt libri nouem'. English translation by Stephen A. Barney, W. J. Lewis, J. A. Beach and Oliver Berghof, *The Etymologies of Isidore of Seville* (Cambridge: CUP, 2006), 135.

[64] Other ninth-century authors seem to have used the word in its biblical sense: see Claudius of Turin, *Epistolae*, no. 11, p. 609, 19; Hrab. *Epist.*, no. 17, p. 421, 30; Council of Aachen (836), II. 31, ed. Albert Werminghoff, MGH Conc. II/2 (Hanover: Hahn, 1908), pp. 704–67, at p. 758, I. 39.

[65] Compare Albert Blaise, *Dictionnaire Latin-Français des auteurs du Moyen-Age*, CCCM Lexicon Latinitatis medii aevi (Turnhout: Brepols, 1975), 29: *agiographa*, 'écrivain d'une inspiration surnaturelle' and 433: *hagiographus*, 'théologien'. The latter is also given in J. F. Niermeyer and C. van de Kieft, *Mediae Latinitatis lexicon minus* (Leiden: Brill, 2002), vol. 1, 627.

[66] Savigni, 'Storia universale', 163.

[67] Mark Vessey, 'Introduction', in *Cassiodorus: Institutions of Divine and Secular Learning and On the Soul* (Liverpool, LUP, 2004), 1–101. See also Robert A. H. Evans, '"Instructing Readers' Minds in Heavenly Matters": Carolingian History Writing and Christian Education', in *Churches and Education*, eds Morwenna Ludlow, Charlotte Methuen and Andrew Spicer, *Studies in Church History*, 55 (2019): 56–71.

> Since they tell of the history of the Church and describe changes happening through
> different periods, they inevitably instruct the minds of readers in heavenly matters.
> For these historians insist that nothing happens by chance or because of the weak
> powers of the gods as the pagan [historians] did; instead they truly strive to attach
> all events to the providential guidance of the Creator.[68]

Cassiodorus's Christian histories were the Latin Josephus, Eusebius-Rufinus,
the *Tripartite History*, Orosius, Marcellinus Comes, Eusebius-Jerome, Prosper
of Aquitaine's *Chronicle*, and Jerome's *On Illustrious Men* and its continuation
by Gennadius of Marseilles. The placement of these authors after the Bible is
revealing: in Mark Vessey's words, these texts followed on from 'the commentators
on Scripture, as adjuncts to a correct appreciation of the one truly reliable
narrative of past, present and future, which is the sacred history intimated, and
partly revealed, by the Bible'.[69]

The ways that history and scripture converge in Frechulf's compendium will
be the focus of the next chapter. The point that I want to underline here is that
Christian historiography, as prescribed by Cassiodorus in the sixth century and
then intensively studied by Frechulf in the ninth, can be fruitfully thought of as
a canon, as a coherent and accepted body of authoritative texts central to elite
intellectual life. That said, the connection between Cassiodorus and Frechulf was
indirect: there is no evidence that the bishop of Lisieux read the *Institutiones*. A
direct link, however, is not necessary. Cassiodorus's handbook represents one
stage in the gradual development of a recognised corpus of orthodox knowledge,
a process that was already underway at least from the fourth century but which
reached a high point in the Carolingian period. As Conrad Leyser has noted, the
'Carolingians were largely (although not solely) responsible for the construction of
the Latin patristic tradition'.[70] Rosamond McKitterick, moreover, has demonstrated
that Christian historiography was also part of this tradition.[71] Frechulf's core
resources were copied throughout the Carolingian realm, and excerpts from them
can be found in a range of other sources, such as biblical commentaries, conciliar
reports, letters and hagiographies.[72] When, in the course of the ninth century,

---

[68]   Cassiodorus, *Institutiones*, I.17.1, p. 55: 'qui cum res ecclesiasticas referant, et vicissitudines
accidentes per tempora diversa describant, necesse est ut sensus legentium rebus caelestibus semper
erudiant, quando nihil ad fortuitos casus, nihil ad deorum potestates infirmas, ut gentiles fecerunt, sed
arbitrio Creatoris applicare veraciter universa contendunt.' Trans. James W. Halporn, *Cassiodorus*, 149.
[69]   Vessey, 'Introduction', 58.
[70]   Leyser, 'Late Antiquity', 32.
[71]   McKitterick, *History and Memory*, 218–64; more broadly, Rosamond McKitterick, *The Carolingians
and the Written Word* (Cambridge: CUP, 1989), 164–210.
[72]   Frechulf's core resources, for example, were used by two historians at Rheims in the ninth and tenth
centuries: see Céline Ménager, 'Écrire l'histoire de Constantin à l'époque carolingienne. Valeur historique
de la *Vita Helenae* d'Almanne d'Hautville', in *Rerum gestarum scriptor: histoire et historiographie au
Moyen Âge*, eds Magali Coumert, Marie-Céline Isaïa, Klaus Krönert and Sumi Shimahara (Paris: Presses
de l'Université Paris-Sorbonne, 2012), 303–12 and Roberts, *Flodoard*, esp. ch. 4.

major ecclesiastical institutions began to organise and catalogue the extensive collections of authoritative knowledge that they had amassed, we find specific histories and chronicles listed prominently alongside scripture and the writings of the church fathers.[73]

Appreciating that Frechulf's chosen sources were part of an accepted corpus of historiography, and that historiography was viewed in relation to scripture, forms an important foundation of this monograph. As we shall see in subsequent chapters, one of Frechulf's most striking achievements was to mould excerpts from the Christian historiographical canon into an expansive narrative that highlighted the basic framework of history generated through biblical exegesis. Indeed, a characteristic feature of a canon is that its various components are complementary and viewed in relation to one another: they tell different aspects of the same story. For the remainder of this chapter, however, I want to examine the implications this has for understanding what sort of compilation Frechulf produced. More to the point, I want to suggest that, even if compiling was not distinctly Carolingian, the *Histories* represented a distinctively Carolingian approach to compilation.

Frechulf and the Carolingian Culture of Compilation

Ann Blair's survey of pre-modern reference texts posited two main reasons for making compilations: as a means either to manage an over-abundance of information, or 'to palliate the scarcity of books'.[74] For the Carolingian evidence under consideration, neither of these explanatory poles are quite satisfactory. Hrabanus, while still master of the school at Fulda, dedicated his commentary on Matthew to Haistulf of Mainz, the archbishop of the ecclesiastical province within which Fulda lay, with the hope that his superior would deem it suitable for use amongst 'the brothers placed under [his] control'. A new commentary such as this was not desperately needed, but came about rather because it would be convenient (*commodum*) to 'collect the thoughts and opinions of many [authorities] into a single [volume], so that the impoverished reader, who does not have [access to] an abundance of books or for whom it is not possible to explore the deep meanings of the fathers, may at least find their needs satisfied'.[75] Yet Hrabanus's preface reveals

---

[73] See Johanna Jebe, 'Bücherverzeichnisse als Quellen der Wissensorganisation: Ordnungspraktiken und Wissenordnungen in den karolingerzeitlichen Klöstern Lorsch und St Gallen', in *Die Bibliothek – The Library – La Bibliothèque: Denkräume und Wissensordnungen*, eds Andreas Speer and Lars Reuke, Miscellanea Mediaevalia 41 (Berlin: De Gruyter, 2020), 3–28. At St Riquier, where Helisachar, the dedicatee of Part I, was abbot, history books were listed under the subsection 'De libris antiquorum qui de gestis regum vel situ terrarium scripserunt': see Hariulf, *Chronicon Centulense*, 3, 3, ed. Ferdinand Lot, *Chronique de l'abbaye de Saint-Riquier (Ve siècle-1004)* (Paris: Alphonse Picard et fils, 1894), pp. 86-94, at p. 93. Frechulf's *volumina antiquorum* may echo these *libri antiquorum*.

[74] Blair, *Too Much to Know*, 34.

[75] Hrab. *Exp.*, Praef. [11/16], p. 1: '... non quasi pernecessarium, cum multi me scriptores in illo uestigio praecesserint, sed quasi magis commodum, cum plurimorum sensus ac sententias in unum

another side to the story. The initial impetus, he explained, responded to local needs: some monks at Fulda, with whom he was reading Matthew, grumbled that they lacked a single, detailed, commentary on the first Gospel; in response, the schoolmaster began gathering together from his monastery's rich patristic holdings all the relevant material he could find to elucidate the text of the first Gospel in its entirety. Hrabanus may have offered up his commentary to Haistulf for the benefit of the resource-starved reader (*lector pauperculus*) and it would clearly have served an important function for such a person, seeing as it conveyed many books' worth of wisdom within a single codex. (This may also have been an expression of charity and humility: the wealth of Fulda's library is given over to the poor.) Clearly, Hrabanus's text was predicated upon the availability of a substantial body of commentaries and homilies written by the church fathers. The approach and rationale behind Hrabanus's commentary seem to me less about palliating scarcity, than digesting and repurposing the received writings of Christian antiquity for the benefit of contemporary study and practice. While not pretending to be comprehensive or encyclopaedic, the result was to collect in one place a wide selection of material, taken from many different sources, all of which pertained to Matthew's Gospel.

Two key features here were convenience (*commodum*) and usefulness (*utilitas*).[76] By compressing a wealth of learning into a single, practical, compendium, underequipped readers would be well served, though of course so too would students and scholars of Matthew at wealthier institutions, as it would save them the need to dig through whatever undigested material they had at their disposal to find relevant patristic commentary on whatever gospel verse they were studying, be that, for example, in the context of the performance of the daily liturgy or in the preparation of a sermon.[77] *Commodum* and *utilitas* are concepts which speak first and foremost, though by no means exclusively, to ecclesiastical audiences, for whom scripture and its authoritative exegesis were central. These key words appear throughout the many other commentaries Hrabanus dedicated, both to high-ranking ecclesiastics and members of the Carolingian dynasty itself. In the letters he sent to Frechulf, he explained how, for each of the books of the Pentateuch, he had gathered together the words of the holy fathers into a single volume (*in unum volumen*) and that he hoped his offerings would be useful, both for Frechulf himself and for those under his pastoral care.[78] When Hrabanus

---

contraxerim, ut lector pauperculus, qui copiam librorum non habet aut cui in pluribus scrutari profundos sensus patrum non licet, saltem in isto sufficientiam suae indigentiae inueniat'. (In requesting exegesis of the Pentateuch, Frechulf presented himself as having no 'abundance of books' (*copia librorum*): see n. 3, above.)

[76] Hrab. *Exp.*, Praef. [93/95], p. 4: 'Omnia uero ad utilitatem fratrum et ad commoditatem legentium parare sategimus, optantes, ut ad plurimorum peruveniant profectum.'

[77] Phelan, 'Carolingian Renewal'.

[78] See, for example, Hrab. *Epist.*, no. 9, p. 395, 31/7: 'Feci enim, sicut in tua epistola mihi iussisti et

dedicated his Kings commentary to Louis the Pious's arch-chaplain Hilduin in c. 829, he stated not only that he collected the words of the holy fathers in one volume, but also that this was 'for the convenience of the reader' (*ob commoditatem legentis*).[79] Indeed, the impulse to compile and arrange authoritative knowledge into coherent, practical, compendia stamps Hrabanus's oeuvre.[80]

John Contreni has observed that 'the one-volume anthology of patristic commentaries became the dominant form of exegesis in the 820s and 830s'.[81] As the patristic tradition underpinned Carolingian religious thought and practice, it becomes easy enough to appreciate why such anthologies, which rendered many codices' worth of disparate material into single, coherent volumes, became desirable. The more that emphasis was placed on copying orthodox and patristic texts, the greater the need became not only to facilitate access to, but also to organise, this growing mass of knowledge. Compilations such as Hrabanus's, which collected together diverse patristic statements on a given book of the Bible, can be viewed in the same light as the emergence of library catalogues, through which institutions classified their 'spiritual capital'. Similar goals evidently lay behind other compilations from the period.

---

collegi undique de sanctorum patrum dictis in unum volumen singularum sententiarum exsolutiones et, ubi minus antiquorum invenire potui, explanationes nostras iuxta eorum sensus similtudinem, prout divina gratia me posse concessit, inserui expositiones. Unde deprecor, ut, si confectum opus dignum duxeris, tam tuis quam aliorum utilitatibus illud accommodes et communiter secundum caritatis regulam cum proximis tuis utaris bono quod tibi agnoscis munere conlatum esse divino. (For I did, as you ordered in your letter, and I collected into one volume the explanations [drawn] widely from the words of the holy fathers … , when I was unable to find ancient expositions, I inserted my own expositions, which, as far as divine grace allows me, are close to the sense of the Fathers. Whence I beg, that should you consider the work that I have put together to be worthy of being composed, you might apply it to your advantage as well the advantages of others; and according to the rule of charity you should put it to good use communally with your neighbours, because you should recognise that it has been gathered together for you, in the service of God.)'

[79] Hrab. *Epist.*, no. 14, p. 402: 'Aestimo enim, si illud relegeritis, per omnia vobis non displicere, cum cognoveritis me ad hoc laborare velle, ut sanctorum patrum dicta, quae de predicto libro exposita in pluribus exemplaribus dispersa sunt, in unum ob commoditatem legentis colligerem, quatenus quid quisque eorum in sententiis diversis historiae regum per singula loca senserit, pariter et secundum ordinem a nobis dispositum repperiret. (… for the convenience of the reader, I have gathered together in one volume the words of the holy fathers, which have been explained regarding the above-mentioned book, have been dispersed across a number of codices …)'. Compare no. 28, p. 443: 'habeatque satis commodum compendium, quando id, quod in multis codicibus patrum scrutari debuit, in unum reppererit collectum: nec iam sibi laborare necesse esse inquirendo, ubi aliorum labore quieti suae invenerit consultum. (And may this be considered a sufficiently convenient compendium, when one might find collected together in a single [codex], that which had to be examined thoroughly in many codices of the Fathers: it is not now necessary to devote one's own labour to investigating, when, at one's own convenience he/she will find authoritative pronouncements as a result of the labour of others.)'

[80] Chevalier-Royet, 'Entre tradition et innovation'; Maria Rissel, *Rezeption antiker und patristischer Wissenschaft bei Hrabanus Maurus: Studien zur karolingischen Geistesgeschichte*, Lateinische Sprache und Literatur des Mittelalters 7 (Bern: Peter Lang, 1976).

[81] John J. Contreni, 'The Patristic Legacy to c. 1000', in *The New Cambridge History of the Bible: From 600 to 1450*, eds Richard Marsden and E. Ann Matter (Cambridge: CUP, 2012), 505–35, at 530.

Smaragdus of Saint-Mihiel's *Expositio libri comitis* (written c. 812) was an exegesis of the lectionary (the book of Gospel readings for celebrating Mass), which keyed relevant patristic excerpts to the scriptural readings of the liturgical year.[82] Smaragdus stated in his prologue that he produced 'a single book from many (*ex multis unum*)' and that he viewed himself equally as an 'excerptor and epitomizer (*pariter derivator, pariterque ... breviator*)' of the writings of the 'great fathers'.[83] Either a handful of years later, or significantly earlier as M.A. Claussen has recently argued, Benedict of Aniane undertook an ambitious project, the importance of which has only recently begun to be appreciated.[84] Benedict studied all the monastic rules known to him, with the aim of showing how this disparate corpus harmonised with the rule of his namesake, Benedict of Nursia (died 547), which was increasingly becoming the central document of Carolingian monasticism.[85] Benedict explained in the prologue to his *Concordia regularum* ('The Concordance of Rules') that:

> on account of those who, even while holding these opinions [concerning the harmony of monastic rules], do not know in what places agreement between rules occurs, I decided to amalgamate all the sententiae from sources that are acknowledged to harmonize with the rule of Benedict, so that one unified book, having been collected from many, should exist, but in such a fashion that the sententiae of blessed Benedict should take precedence, to which the others can be consequently connected.[86]

Smaragdus and Benedict both made clear their aim to condense knowledge gleaned from many sources into a single text; they also sought to show the overall

---

[82] Smaragdus, *Expositio libri comitis*, PL 102, cols 13C–552D. See Fidel Rädle, *Studien zu Smaragd von Saint-Mihiel* (Munich: W. Frink, 1974) and Matthew D. Ponesse, 'Standing Distant from the Fathers: Smaragdus of Saint-Mihiel and the Reception of Early Medieval Learning', *Traditio*, 67 (2012): 71–99. There are also useful comments in Daniel Sheerin, 'Interpreting Scripture in and through Liturgy: Exegesis of Mass Propers in the Middle Ages', in *Jewish Biblical Interpretation and Cultural Exchange: Comparative Exegesis in Context*, eds Natalie B. Dohrmann and David Stern (Philadelphia, PA: University of Pennsylvania Press, 2008), 161–81 at 169–70.

[83] Smaragdus, *Expositio libri comitis*, PL 102, col. 13C. Smaragdus, like Hrabanus, named the various authorities he used: '... de magnorum tractatibus prolatisque sermonibus Patrum, id est Hilarii, Hieronymi, Ambrosii, Augustini, Cypriani, Cyrilli, Gregorii, Victoris, Fulgentii, Ioannis Chrysostomi, Cassiodori, Eucherii, Tychonii, Isidori, Figuli, Bedae, Primasii et de caute legendis, Pelagii et Origenis'.

[84] M. A. Claussen, 'Benedict of Aniane as Teacher', in *Discovery and Distinction in the Early Middle Ages: Studies in Honour of John J. Contreni*, eds Cullen J. Chandler and Steven A. Stofferahn (Kalamazoo, MI, Western Michigan University, 2013), 73–87 and 'Reims, Bibliotèque Carnegie, 806: A Little-known Manuscript of Benedict of Aniane's *Concordia Regularum*', *EME*, 23(1) (2015): 1–42. See also Renie S. Choy, *Intercessory Prayer and the Monastic Ideal in the Time of the Carolingian Reforms* (Oxford: OUP, 2016), 11–14.

[85] Albrect Diem, 'The Carolingians and the *Regula Benedicti*', in *Religious Franks: Religion and Power in the Frankish Kingdoms: Studies in Honour of Mayke de Jong*, eds Rob Meens, Dorine van Espelo, Bram van den Hoven dan Genderen, Janneke Raaijmakers, Irene van Renswoude, and Carine van Rhijn (Manchester: MUP, 2016), 243–61.

[86] Benedict of Aniane, *Concordia regularum*, ed. Pierre Bonnerue, CCCM 168A (Turnhout: Brepols, 1999), 3–4; trans., Claussen, 'A Little-known Manuscript', 5.

coherence of the sources they chose to investigate. Convenience and utility were central, but there was also an implied stress on intertextual harmony. Within the masses of transmitted material—be it on the lessons of the Gospels or monastic rules—there was internal logic that careful study could reveal.

These were not objective works of scholarship: creating compilations of authoritative knowledge often meant suppressing divergence and difference. Selection as well as exclusion are inherent to the process of compilation. What is essential to highlight here, however, is how neatly Frechulf's own project can be slotted in not only with the likes of Hrabanus and Claudius, but also Smaragdus and Benedict. As subsequent chapters will demonstrate, Frechulf's compilation of historiography was not designed simply to present a digest of world history, but to show how a plurality of narratives all conveyed the same unifying Christian story. Put simply, Frechulf did for the Christian historiographical canon what other compilers did for scriptural exegesis, monastic rules and the Gospel pericopes.

The Practice of Compilation

The last point I want to make in this chapter pertains to the organisation of compilations. For compilations to be 'convenient' and 'useful', received material had to be chopped up, processed and reassembled in such a way as to promote usability. Even if composed of 'old' knowledge, compendia were nevertheless inherently novel in the way they organised and arranged their source material. The new structures into which received knowledge was inserted ensured that compilations were more than the sum of their parts. More to the point, the *Histories* and the other sorts of texts mentioned in this chapter were predicated upon the expectation that they would be consulted and read. These analytical anthologies were practical not only because they compressed many texts into one, but also because they were organised so as to allow users to locate and retrieve information, which they could then absorb and apply in other contexts. All this depended on the specific form of the codex.

Frechulf produced his own compendium in two parts (*opera*), within which material was portioned up into smaller organisational units: books (*libri*) and then smaller still, chapters (*capitula*). Each book was prefaced with a list of its *capitula*, that is, headings that consisted of short summaries of the contents of each chapter. Throughout each book, chapters were then marked out (for example, *capitulum X*, or sometimes just the Latin numeral), often set apart from the text in the margin. The contents of a chapter could easily be grasped via its chapter heading, and then the chapter itself could be located without too much trouble.[87] Chapter headings exist in St Gall 622, the earliest extant pandect of the *Histories*, which, as Michael

---

[87] In St Gall 622, capitula numbers of Book 1 of Part II are rubricated until c. 15.

Allen has demonstrated, reached the Bodensee from Lisieux itself: these were not later additions, but were integral to Frechulf's designs.[88]

The presence of *capitula* is not in itself surprising. In eighth-century Northumbria, Bede produced an extensive collection of chapter headings for a number of books of the Old and New Testaments, updating those that, by this time, had long been in existence, in both Latin and Greek versions of the Bible.[89] As with the discourse of compilation that was built into medieval historiography, this method of organisation can already be found in Eusebius's *Ecclesiastical History*.[90] Carolingian scholars inherited ancient and venerable practices, but also intensified them and put them to new use, catering for sizeable and varied ecclesiastical audiences (monastic and cathedral communities, but also rural priests) as well as secular office-holders. To return again to Hrabanus Maurus's Commentary on Matthew: as Owen Phelan has recently highlighted, Hrabanus augmented the received division of Matthew into 355 short sections of text (corresponding to the divisions of the Eusebian canon table) by breaking up his commentary into eight books, each of which reflected a coherent unit of the narrative of the gospel; across these eight books, the narrative was further divided into fifty subunits: a list of these fifty chapters was then placed at the beginning of the commentary.[91] As Phelan notes, 'Hrabanus's sophisticated design makes Matthew more accessible more quickly and in multiple ways.'[92] Not all examples of organisation were quite so ambitious, but nevertheless accessibility and utility were key. The erudite abbot of Reichenau, Walahfrid Strabo, who was a student of Hrabanus Maurus, inserted chapter divisions and chapter titles into his editions of Einhard's *Vita Karoli* and Thegan's *Vita Hludowici*, in both instances doing so with the expressed intention of making it easier for readers to find what they were looking for.[93] When in 825

---

[88] *Prolegomena*, e.g. 55*, 64*-6*. The other early witness, produced at Saint-Vaast for Lorsch before 850, contains the same *capitula* for the books of Part I.

[89] The practice seems to have begun with the Gospels. See Paul Meyvaert, 'Bede's *Capitula lectionum* for the Old and New Testaments', *Revue bénédictine*, 105 (1995): 348–80 and Gorman, 'Source Marks'.

[90] The creation of chapter lists (or tables of contents) was a textual development of the third and fourth centuries: Jeremiah Coogan, 'Transforming Textuality: Porphyry, Eusebius, and Late Ancient Tables of Contents', *Studies in Late Antiquity*, 5(1) (2021): 6-27 and Crawford, *Eusebian Canon Tables*, 32–3 and literature cited there. See also Pierre Petitmengin, '*Capitula* païens et chrétiens', in *Titres et articulations du texte dans les oeuvres antiques: actes du colloque international de Chantilly, 13-15 décembre 1994*, eds Jean-Claude Fredouille, Jean-Claude Fredouille, Marie-Odile Glouet-Cazé, Philippe Hoffman, Pierre Petitmengin and Simone Deléani (Paris: Institut d'études Augustiennes, 1997), 491–507.

[91] Phelan, 'Carolingian Renewal', 149–61.

[92] Phelan, 'Carolingian Renewal', 156.

[93] Walahfrid, *Prologus in Einhardi Vitam Karoli*, ed. Oswald Holder-Egger, MGH *SRG* 25 (Hanover: Hahn, 1911) p. xxix: 'Huic opusculo ego Strabus titulos et incisiones, prout visum est congruum, inserui, ut ad singula facilior quaerenti quod placuerit elucescat accessus.' Walahfrid, *Prologus*, in Thegan, *Gesta Hludowici Imperatoris*, ed. Ernst Tremp, MGH *SRG* 64 (Hanover: Hahn, 1995), p. 168: 'Huic opusculo ego Strabo quasdam incisions et capitula inverui...ut facilius volentibus scire singular pateant titulorum compendio'; trans. Thomas F. X. Noble, *Charlemagne and Louis the Pious: The Lives by Einhard, Notker, Ermoldus, Thegan, and the Astronomer* (University Park, PA: State University of

Jonas of Orléans rewrote the life of the eighth-century holy man, Hubert of Liège, he split the text into chapters and added a chapter list.[94] If we look beyond narrative texts to the wide range of sources known as capitularies—so-called because they were organised into *capitula*—then we can further appreciate that this was a widespread means of organising, communicating and accessing knowledge.[95] The basic means by which Frechulf organised his compilation thus speaks to aspects of a wider Carolingian intellectual culture rather than to the specific context of historiography.

The organisation of the *Histories* has implications for how we envisage the work being created and used. It may be that Frechulf began the task of identifying his principal sources and marking out passages and copying them onto wax tablets or sheets of parchment while he was still a monk at Fulda, and then brought his raw resources with him when he took up his new post. Or, once at Lisieux, he used his connections with Hrabanus, his monastic frater and now abbot of Fulda, to get his hands on more texts. At some point, furthermore, he established an important relationship with Helisachar, to whom Part I was dedicated. According to this dedication, Helisachar—who was an important member of the imperial court as well as the abbot of St Riquier, an abbey with a well-stocked collection of historical texts—provided Frechulf with a copy of Eusebius-Jerome's *Chronicle*: as we shall see in Chapter 3, the *Chronicle* was central to his working methods. Whatever scenario we envisage for how the constituent parts of the *Histories* arrived at Lisieux, the arduous task of scouring source texts, marking up or extracting selected passages and then assembling such an enormous mass of texts took place there, perhaps in the *scriptorium* attached to the episcopal residence (or wherever this sort of work might have occurred). The complex yet concealed processes that lay behind the final product stemmed from an intimate knowledge of an extraordinary range of sources.

The textual make-up of the *Histories* captures the fact that, for elite intellectuals like Frechulf, their worlds were shaped by books. It is not clear whether Frechulf had in mind the sort of hypothetical 'poor reader', cut off from the world of books, to whom Hrabanus Maurus drew attention in the prologue to his *Matthew Commentary*. Presumably, he wanted the clerics within his own cathedral school or community to benefit from the fruits of what was evidently a shared labour in copying out and improving the text. We also know that in the ninth century, copies of the *Histories* were available for students at Lorsch, Reichenau and St Gall.

Pennsylvania Press, 2009), 194: 'I, Strabo, have inserted some divisions and chapter headings into this little work ... so that those who wish to know may find the individual titles easily.'

[94] Francesco Veronese, 'Jonas of Orléans', in *Great Christian Jurists and Legal Collections in the First Millennium*, ed. Philip L. Reynolds (Cambridge: CUP, 2019), 413–28, at 418.

[95] For a recent study with extensive bibliography, see Steffen Patzold, 'Capitularies in the Ottonian Realm', *EME*, 27 (2019): 112–32.

My sense of the matter is that the *Histories* would have worked best when read in conjunction with an existing and accessible collection of books, not in place of one. Firstly, weighty tomes such as Frechulf's were generally not numbered amongst the sort of books that local priests were expected to have in order to carry out their ministry.[96] Second, the inherent intertextuality of Frechulf's project implies that readers would have had access to the main sources from which the *Histories* were constructed. In the prologue to Part I, the bishop of Lisieux warned potential critics not to rush to judgement on his compendium 'before carefully reading the authors from whom we have excerpted'.[97] Frechulf's use of cross-references suggests he was not just deploying rhetorical self-defence.

Guides for further reading are scattered throughout the *Histories*.[98] For example, Frechulf offered very basic commentary on Genesis 2:9 on the literal and symbolic meanings of the 'tree of life' and the 'tree of knowledge of good and evil'. Interested readers seeking further exegesis were encouraged to 'read the books *On the City of God* by Father Augustine'. References could be a little more specific. After providing a condensed summary of the reign of Jeroboam, one of the sons of King Solomon, Frechulf noted that anyone 'desiring to know more will find it in the eighth book of Josephus['s *Antiquities*]'; readers curious to learn more about the aggression between Agesilaus of Sparta and Conon of Athens after the Peloponnesian War were told to turn to 'the third book of Orosius's *Contra paganos*'; or concerning the Council of Nicaea, Frechulf advised that:

---

[96] Priests were expected to have books to help with teaching and preaching and to ensure the liturgy was performed properly: see, for example, Haito of Basel, *Capitula*, 6, ed. Peter Brommer, MGH *Capit. Episc.* I (Hanover: Hahn, 1984), p. 211; Ghärbald of Liège, *Capitila III*, 9, ed. Peter Brommer, MGH *Capit. Episc.* I (Hanover: Hahn, 1984), pp. 39–40.

[97] *Hist.*, I.Prol. [57/61], p. 20; trans. Lake, 112.

[98] Full list: *Hist.*, I.1.5 [9/11], p. 31: 'Si quis uero de his plenius scire uoluerit, patris Augustini libros De ciuitate Dei legat'; I.3.5 [19/20], p. 166: 'in Iosephi libro VIII scire cupiens plenius inveniet'; I.4.11 [25/27], p. 227: 'Si quis enim plenius discordiam Atheniensium et bella grauia quae sunt perpessi scire uoluerit actusque Alcibiadis et exilia, librum Orosii Aduersus paganos secundum legat'; I.4.16 [20.1], p. 234: 'Sed qui haec plenius scire uoluerit, in libro tertio Horosii Contra paganos inueniet'; I.4.23 [37/42], p. 253: I.5.11 [101.2], p. 312: 'qui latius scire uoluerit, Orosii ceterorumque historiographorum libros legere curabit'; I.6.11 [50.1], p. 340: 'Ergo qui latius actus eius scire uoluerit, tertium decimum Iosepphi librum Antiquitatis historiae legere curabit'; I.6.12 [1/5], pp. 340–1: 'Quibus etiam diebus Romanos multiplices perturbauerunt calamitates, quamuis iam domini multarum uocitarentur gentium, quas succincte breuitatis gratia transcurrere statui. Sed si quis eas plenius scire uoluerit, quintum librum Horosii legat'; I.7.12 [150], p. 402: 'Si quis plenius scire uoluerit, in Iosephi XIII libro requirat'; I.7.18 [19/22], p. 422: 'Cetera uero eius opera munificenter condita omitto; scire uero cupientes ad Iosepphi uel Egesippi libros conuolare studeant, unius namque ciuitatis portum atque opera enarrabo ab eo peracta'; II.1.7 [43.4], p. 451: 'qualiter haec gesta sunt, pleniter in primo libro Eusebii Ecclesiasticae historiae continentur'; II.1.15 [3], p. 466: 'De quo deceptore Iosepphus pleniter refert'; II.3.6 [6.7], pp. 564–5: 'De qua persecutione Eusebius refert in libro sexto Ecclesiasticae historiae'; II.3.14 [117/20], p. 593: 'Quibus Eusebius Caesariensis episcopus, Ecclesiasticae scriptor historiae, dum interesset, quae in ueritate conperit et cernendo conspexit octauo historiarum et nono libris partim manifestare studuit'; compare I.4.2 [48/52], pp. 618–19: 'Igitur quibus mirabiliter modis saepius sit ereptus de manibus animam illius quaerentium, Ecclesiastica quae dicitur tripertita narrat historia, ipse etiam qui passus ordinatim in suis refert opusculis, nec non et Rufinus praedicti temporis Ecclesiasticae historiae scriptor.'

Should anyone wish to know about what went on at this council, they should, after having put aside all other works, examine thoroughly the *Ecclesiastical History* of Eusebius of Caesarea, which was translated into Latin by Rufinus, along with the histories of the three illustrious men, Sozomen, Socrates and Theodoret. But whoever desires to fuller knowledge of the acts and life of the pious ruler Constantine, should peruse only Eusebius's little works on this matter.[99]

'Guides for further reading' represent yet another practice which Carolingian scholars inherited from their ancient sources. For instance, in the context of his account of the Roman siege of Jerusalem in AD 70, Frechulf added that 'whoever wants to know more should read the Histories of Josephus'—but this was a direct quote from Rufinus's translation of Eusebius.[100] Within similar works of patristic abridgement, cross-referencing further strengthened the idea of a canon, since the works being abridged tended also to be those that were recommended to readers.

Conclusion

Within the context of early medieval exegesis, the centrality of the writings of the fathers is very well known. Using a commonly cited phrase, Silvia Cantelli once remarked that ninth-century biblical commentators produced 'exegesis of exegesis', or as John Cavadini later recast it, 'exegesis of exegetes'.[101] The writings of the holy fathers, the *sancti patres*, were invested with special qualities and great significance; the study of the Bible, as John Contreni has recently remarked, often amounted to 'the study of the interpretation of the Bible'.[102] Frechulf's *Histories* represent a parallel process. The bishop of Lisieux self-consciously compiled a history from the works of previous historiographers. This was part of the same drive to digest and process the vast quantity of patristic material that scribes were copying and preserving throughout monasteries and cathedrals of western Europe in the later-eighth and ninth centuries. Claudius of Turin had talked of drawing on 'the mystical treasure troves of learned men' and Hrabanus had very frequently stressed that he was following in the footsteps of greater men.[103] Frechulf likewise

---

[99] *Hist.*, II.3.16 [98/105], p. 601: 'Ergo qui per singula scire uoluerit quae in hoc gesta sunt concilio, omissis aliorum opusculis Ecclesiasticam Eusebii Caesariensis historiam perlegat, quae a Rufino in nostrum interpretata est eloquium, nec non trium uirorum inlustrium Historias, Sozomeni, Socratis, et Theodoriti. Actus uero et uitam huius principis Constantini, qui scire plenius desiderat, Eusebii praedicti opuscula de hoc tantum negotio perlegat.' If the last reference was to the *Vita Constanti*, Eusebius's biography of Constantine, Frechulf presumably would have known of it only indirectly though the *Historia ecclesiastica tripartita* (e.g. I.18.12, p. 76; II.1.3, p. 83; XII.4.29, p. 668. *Prolegomena*, 218*.

[100] *Hist.*, II.1.22 [24], p. 482.

[101] Silvia Cantelli, *Angelomo e la scuola esegetica di Luxeuil*, Biblioteca di Medioevo latino 1 (Spoleto, Centro italiano di studi sull'alto Medioevo, 1990), 61; John Cavadini, 'A Carolingian Hilary', in *The Study of the Bible in the Carolingian Era*, eds Celia Chazelle and Burton van Name Edwards (Turnhout: Brepols, 2003), 133–40, at 133.

[102] Contreni, 'Patristic Legacy', 531.

[103] De Jong, 'Empire as *ecclesia*', 202–3.

self-consciously rested on ancient authority, the *volumina antiquorum*, and by referring to 'the histories of holy writers', we can see not only that he adhered to written authority, but he was part of a bigger intellectual enterprise which emphasised and indeed created it. Nevertheless, Frechulf wrote history, not commentary. Before looking in greater detail at his narrative, it is important first to consider the meaning of the word *historia* and explore further how the study of history could be understood in relation to the study of the Bible.

2

The Truth of History

Introduction

Frechulf's approach to history-writing, as underscored in the previous chapter, reflects one of the key characteristics of contemporary ninth-century exegesis: the compilation of authoritative knowledge. To describe the *Histories* as a 'compilation' of older narratives does not diminish the text's value in any way, but merely forces us to look beyond the well-studied corpus of Carolingian annals and chronicles when seeking to contextualise and comprehend Frechulf's work. This chapter pushes the comparison with biblical commentary one step further, arguing that Frechulf shared not only the working methods but also the basic goals and critical language of biblical scholars.

Exegetical aspects of the *Histories* have long been noted, primarily because they can be inferred from two of the individuals within whose orbit Frechulf aligned himself: Hrabanus Maurus, the famed exegete from whom Frechulf requested a commentary on the Pentateuch upon his appointment to Lisieux in 824/5; and Helisachar, who, according to the Prologue to Part I, had commissioned Frechulf to fashion an account of human history from Adam to Christ. Bertha Schelle first picked up on the clear overlap between how Frechulf described his approach to sources and what he expected of Hrabanus, concluding that there was little to differentiate the working 'methods of the theologian and the historian'.[1] Some forty years later, Matthew Innes and Rosamond McKitterick, in their brief sketch of the *Histories*, specified that Frechulf 'was a protégé of Hraban[us] Maur[us] of Fulda, and his style of scholarship is reminiscent of Hraban[us]'s in that he created a recognizably novel synthesis'. In addition, they attributed to Helisachar a degree of influence that went beyond simply ordering the *Histories* to be written: 'The first book of Frec[h]ulf's chronicle can best be seen as linked to the great project

[1] Schelle, 'Frechulf von Lisieux', 41–2, 149–50. See also Franz Brunhölzl, *Geschichte der lateinischen Literatur des Mittelalters, I: Von Cassiodor bis zum Ausklang der karolingischen Erneuerung* (Munich: Fink, 1975), 398–9.

of collective biblical exegesis, organised by Helisachar and in which Hrabanus Maurus participated.'[2]

Hrabanus's biblical exegesis has already been outlined. Helisachar's, by contrast, requires some comment, not least because it can only be tentatively reconstructed, if not only hypothesised. While reams of commentary exist in Hrabanus's name, filling six volumes worth of columns in the *Patralogia Latina*, evidence of Helisachar's achievement is less straightforward to come by. It was first posited by Bernhard Bischoff, who discovered what he thought to be traces of an extensive exegetical enterprise, preserved within fourteen separate manuscripts.[3] These manuscripts cannot be tied explicitly to Helisachar, but were linked to him partly on account of their northern Frankish origins: in addition to serving as Louis the Pious' arch-chancellor (until August 819), Helisachar was abbot of several monasteries, including St Riquier and St Aubin, Angers. It remains unclear whether Helisachar ever oversaw such a project, although Bischoff's suggestion has often been accepted as fact: Innes and McKitterick, for example, took it on board, as have several others.[4] There are obvious problems with placing Frechulf within a larger project which may never have existed. Yet, even if that broader backdrop were discounted, the language employed by Frechulf in Part I of his *Histories*, not least in the prologue he addressed to Helisachar, draws the reader into an intellectual world oriented on the Bible and its interpretation.

In the prologue to Part I, Frechulf reflected on the overall purpose of his project. He explained that Helisachar, after having doled out tasks to others (perhaps at court?), at last turned to him, and requested that he 'hunt diligently through the volumes of the ancients ... and exert [himself] to collect briefly and clearly everything that pertains to the truth of history, from the creation of the first man up until the birth of Christ'.[5] More specifically, Frechulf stated that within this grand narrative he had been given specific instruction to dwell upon the history of the first two ages

---

[2] Innes and McKitterick, 'Writing of History', 212.

[3] Bernard Bischoff, 'Libraries and Schools in the Carolingian Revival of Learning', in his *Manuscripts and Libraries in the Age of Charlemagne*, trans. by Michael Gorman (Cambridge: CUP, 1994), 93–114, at 111–13; for the German text, 'Die Bibliothek im Dienste der Schule', in Bernhard Bischoff, *Mittelalterliche Studien: ausgewählte Aufsätze zur Schriftkunde und Literaturgeschichte* (Stuttgart: Hiersemann, 1981), vol. III, 213–33, at 231–3.

[4] Innes and McKitterick, 'Writing of History', 212 and n. 76; Michel Huglo, 'Trois livres manuscrits présentés par Helisachar', *Revue bénédictine*, 99 (1989): 272-85 and his 'D'Helisachar à Abbon de Flerury, *Revue bénédictine*, 104 (1994): 204–30; Paul-Iréné Fransen, 'Le dossier patristique d'Helisachar: le manuscript Paris BNF lat. 11574 et l'une de ses sources', *Revue bénédictine*, 111 (2001): 464–82; John J. Contreni, 'Carolingian Biblical Culture', in *Iohannes Scottus Eriugena: The Bible and Hermeneutics*, eds Gerd Van Riel, Carlos Steel and James McEvoy (Leuven: Leuven University Press, 1996), 1–23, at 9; repr. in his *Learning and Culture in Carolingian Europe: Letters, Numbers, Exegesis, and Manuscripts* (Ashgate: Farnham, 2011).

[5] *Hist.*, I.Prol. [13/17], p. 18: 'iussiti ut perscrutando diligenter uolumina antiquorum, seu agiographorum siue etiam gentilium scriptorum, quaeque pertinent ad historiae ueritatem breuiter ac lucide colligere desudarem, a conditione quidem primi hominis usque ad Christi natiuitatem Domini'.

(*saecula*) of the world, from Adam to Noah, and then from Noah to Abraham. He was to compare what previous Christian and pagan historians had written about particular people and events, while 'not neglecting to resolve the difficult problems found in the writings of the lawgiver throughout the period, insofar as it pertains to the truth of history'.[6] The phrase 'the truth of history (*veritas historiae*)' was utilised twice in quick succession, to refer both to the entirety of Part I as well as to specific interpretative issues surrounding the writings of the *Legislator*, by which Frechulf meant Genesis, the first book of the Christian Old Testament whose authorship was attributed to Moses, the author of the Divine Law. This latter concern for truth comprised the bulk of the very first book of Part I. It is within Frechulf's treatment of the pre-Abrahamic past that his *Histories* most obviously resemble biblical commentary. So pronounced and distinctive was this first book that already in the ninth century, a scribe at Reichenau listed the text in the abbey's library catalogue as: 'Frechulf's chronicle with a commentary on Genesis'.[7]

This chapter seeks to understand better the fusion of chronicle and commentary, of history and exegesis, that contemporaries evidently perceived within the *Histories*. Frechulf himself seems to have been aware, if not even to have encouraged this fusion in his use of the phrase 'the truth of history'. His central objective in Part I was to excavate historical truth from his sources, and it was with reference to historical truth that Frechulf was to resolve problematic questions in the first book of the Pentateuch. Addressing the *veritas historiae* was thus a defining facet of Part I, but the meanings and associations that this crucial expression conveyed are complex and so need to be unpacked. To do so, it is necessary to survey two broad practices of learning that shaped how ecclesiastics such as Frechulf engaged with and understood history: grammar and rhetoric on the one hand, and biblical hermeneutics on the other. Both of these contexts help place Frechulf at the surface of an ocean of knowledge that reached down into the depths of the patristic and classical Roman worlds. By considering these complementary contexts of textual interpretation, we are better placed to appreciate not only the sort of history Frechulf produced, but also the sort of historian he was. Investigating what the 'truth of history' meant to Frechulf therefore has significant implications for the overall argument of this monograph. To begin, however, it is necessary to take into account the peculiar character of the very first book of the *Histories*, in which Frechulf most often expressed his concern for historical veracity.

---

[6] *Hist.*, I.Prol. [21/4], p. 18; trans. Lake, 111–12.

[7] Paul Lehmann, *Mittelalterliche Bibliothekskatalog Deutschlands und der Schweiz* (Munich: Beck, 1918), vol 1, p. 265, l. 28: 'Frecholfi chronica I cum expositione super genesim'; and *Prolegomena*, 79*–80*. Previously it was thought that Frechulf wrote a separate commentary over and above the *Histories*: for example, Natunewicz, 'Freculphus', 107; Innes and McKitterick, 'Writing of History', 212, and n. 76: 'At Reichenau his work was copied alongside exegesis in the same manuscript'; Schelle, 'Frechulf von Lisieux', 21–3 and 42–3; Savigni, 'Storia universale', 165. In twelfth-century Rouen, it was also thought he wrote a commentary on the Pauline epistles: *Prolegomena*, 156*–7*, 165*.

'In the Beginning': History before Abraham
Book 1 of the *Histories*

The *Histories* begin with the world's creation, as recounted in the Book of Genesis. Frechulf's first book covers the first two ages of the world: 'before the universal flood' that covered the earth in the time of Noah, and then between the flood and the 'birth of Abraham and the reign of Ninus, king of the Assyrians'.[8] This book is remarkable, both within the context of Frechulf's text and early medieval history-writing as a whole. Frechulf introduced Book 2 with a prologue that restated and directly responded to the contents of the dedicatory prologue to Helisachar; this was the only book in the whole work to which a separate, distinct prologue was attached. Bracketed by paratext, Book 1 was marked out as being different.[9] This difference was in part the product of the particular resources available to early medieval readers and writers for understanding the earliest eras of human history. The historiographical texts from which Frechulf compiled the vast majority of his *Histories*—in both Parts I and II—were largely silent on the pre-Abrahamic past.[10] Frechulf explained this at the very beginning of his first chapter:

> While I was taking care to summarise a certain sequence of times in succinct prose from the studies of the noble writers of both divine and secular histories, selecting a few florets from their many volumes, as if from the blooms of various flowery meadows, so that the reader might easily recognise which of the more notable deeds were performed in particular times both of kings and kingdoms, the smallness of my weakness discovered that almost all the historians, especially of the Greeks and Romans, began their narratives of events from Ninus, son of Belus, namely from the first king over many peoples—especially, that is, disasters of war, the fall of kings and regions and the miseries of men—and, as we are informed by their statements, that wars are nothing other than a successive round of misfortunes, which they have described most exhaustively. Yet they have left untouched the ages which passed before [Ninus] as if they had no beginning, as some of those historians believed, and as if men had previously lived like dumb beasts.[11]

---

[8] *Hist.*, I.Prol. [17/20], p. 18: 'de primo saeculo, quod ante generale fuerat cataclismum, siue de secundo, quod fuit post diluuium usque ad natiuitatem Abrahae et regis Assyriorum Nini regnum'.

[9] *Hist.*, I.2.Prol., pp. 85–6.

[10] Elisabeth Mégier, 'L'histoire biblique pré-abrahamique est-elle un sujet pour les historiens? S. Jérôme, S. Augustin et les critères d'historicité dans les *historiae* de Fréculphe de Lisieux', in *Les réceptions des Pères de l'Église au Moyen Âge: le devenir de la tradition ecclésiale*, eds Rainer Berndt and Michel Fédou, Archa verbi: Yearbook for the Study of Medieval Theology 10 (Münster: Aschendorff, 2013), vol. 2, 1057–73.

[11] *Hist.*, I.1.1 [1/16], p. 28: 'Dum aliquam temporum seriem commatico sermone ex nobilium studiis tam diuinarum scriptorum historiarum quamque saecularium et ex pluribus eorum paucos libando flosculos libris ceu ex diuersorum uernantium pratorum floribus perstringere curarem, ut lector animaduertere facile ualeret quid ex celebrioribus factis in singulis tam regum quamque regnorum sit gestum temporibus, offendit meae inbecillitatis paruitas omnes paene historiographos, maxime autem Grecorum atque Latinorum, a Nino Beli filio, rege gentium multarum scilicet primo, suas gestorum inchoasse narrationes—praecipue uidelicet bellorum casus, regum regionumque destitutiones atque hominum miserias—et, ut eorum instruimur adsertionibus, nihil aliud esse bella nisi in alterutrum

Frechulf here echoed Orosius, who, at the beginning of his *Seven Books of History against the Pagans* (written c. 417), took issue with ancient, non-Christian, historians for starting their narratives of kingdoms, peoples and wars only with King Ninus of Assyria.[12] Orosius, by contrast, began his account of wars and other miseries at their root cause: original sin. Despite this assertion, Orosius in fact said very little about history before Abraham,[13] in part because he would have had to rely on the Old Testament as a source, something which he purposefully eschewed since it would have weakened his apologetic purpose.[14] Orosius wrote to convince educated Roman elites of Christianity's world-historical significance.[15] Working four hundred years later in a more fully Christianised society, Frechulf's intentions were different. He echoed Orosius's critique of classical historians, but was unencumbered by his apologetic baggage:

> Aided by the omnipotence of God and supported by the authority of divine scripture, I have taken care to begin my own narrative from the very first man himself, who, created in the shape of God on the sixth day, was the first parent and the progenitor of all mortal beings. It cannot be doubted that after the creation of man, God ceased from any new work, though not from governing his creatures. Concerning this, scripture recorded that on the seventh day God rested from all his works.[16]

Frechulf made the Bible the foundation of his narrative, which for Book 1 meant Genesis. The opening book of the *Histories*, however, was not a historiographical retelling of the first book of the Pentateuch in the manner of Josephus's *Jewish Antiquities*; Josephus, one of Frechulf's sources, served to augment and supplement material principally drawn from biblical commentary: Alcuin's *Questions on Genesis* (written in the late eighth century), Claudius of Turin's *Genesis Commentary* (written c. 811), and Augustine's *City of God*, books 15 and 16 of which were stuffed full of exegetical argument and problem solving.

---

uergentia mala, quae studiosissime descripserunt. Transacta autem retro saecula, ac uelut sine initio forent, ut quibusdam illorum placuit, et homines ritu pecorum inrationabilium prius uixisse, intacta reliquerunt.'

[12] Oros., I.1.1–4, p. 10 and also I.1.11-12, pp. 11–12. A point also made by Savigni, 'Storia universale', 165, Staubach, '*Christiana tempora*', 183 and Mégier, 'L'histoire biblique', 1062–3 and 1065–6.

[13] Oros., I.1.4, p. 10 and I.3, pp. 42–3.

[14] Oros., I.1.7–8, p. 11: 'this is why the matter in hand now demands that a few things be taken, albeit as briefly as possible, from those books which deal with the beginning of the world and which gained credibility in the past by predicting future events which came to pass. This is not because I want to insist on their authority to anyone, but because it would be worthwhile to draw attention to the common consensus which I share with everyone else'. Trans. Fear, 34.

[15] Peter Van Nuffelen, *Orosius and the Rhetoric of History* (Oxford: OUP, 2012).

[16] *Hist.*, I.1.1 [16/20], pp. 28–9: 'Igitur auxilio omnipotentis Dei fultus atque auctoritate diuinae scripturae fretus, ab ipso protoplausto exordium meae narrationis sumere curaui, qui primus parens auctorque mortalium hominum ultimus in fabrica Dei conditus est, sexta scilicet die. Post cuius namque conditionem Deum cessasse a noua operatione, non a gubernatione creaturarum, haud dubium est. Qua de re scriptura commemorat Deum requieuisse die septimo ab omnibus operibus suis.'

The distinctive sources and subject matter of Book 1 therefore invite us to consider how scripture, its exegesis and historiography, could blur in the early medieval imagination. To be sure, the relationship between history and scripture has been investigated in detail by modern historians of the central Middle Ages and by scholars of the Northumbrian monk Bede.[17] Students of the Carolingian period, however, have paid less attention to this, perhaps because, unlike Bede, none of the prominent Carolingian exegetes also wrote histories. Frechulf, by starting his narrative with the biblical story of creation and by utilising biblical commentary, compels us to examine the fundamental bond between the study of the past and the study of the Bible. To understand the bases of this bond, it is necessary first to consider the range of meaning contained within the Latin word for history: *historia*.

Historia: Between Grammar and Rhetoric

In the Middle Ages, history was not an autonomous discipline. Within the trivium, the first three of the seven liberal arts, history was counted as a part of either grammar or rhetoric.[18] It was in relation to grammar, 'the origin and foundation of the liberal arts', that Isidore of Seville, in his *Etymologies*, offered one of the few early medieval overviews of the meaning of history. Accordingly, the *Etymologies* often provide the canonical departure point for modern discussions of medieval *historia*, and for good reason.[19] Isidore's 'spree of articulated knowledge' was

---

[17] Elisabeth Mégier, *Christliche Weltgeschichte im 12. Jahrhundert: Themen, Variationen und Kontraste: Untersuchungen zu Hugo von Fleury, Ordericus Vitalis und Otto von Freising* (Frankfurt am Main: Peter Lang, 2010); Hans-Werner Goetz, 'Die "Geschichte" im Wissenschaftssytem des Mittelalters', in Franz-Joseph Schmale, *Funktion und Formen mittelalterlicher Geschichtsschreibung: Eine Einführung* (Darmstadt: Wissenschaftliche Buchgesellschaft, 1985), pp. 165–213, at 194–208. On Bede, see, for example, Roger Ray, 'Bede, the Exegete, as Historian', in *Famulus Christi: Essays in Commemoration of the Thirteenth Centenary of the Birth of the Venerable Bede*, ed. Gerald Bonner (London: SPCK, 1976), 125–40 and 'Jennifer O'Reilly, 'Islands and Idols at the Ends of the Earth: Exegesis and Conversion in Bede's *Historia Ecclesiastica*', in *Bède le Vénérable: entre tradition et postérité*, eds Stéphane Lebecq, Michel Perrin and Olivier Szerwiniak (Villeneuve d'Ascq: Université Charles-de-Gaule-Lille, 2005), 119–45.

[18] For theoretical overviews of medieval *historia*, see Arno Seifert, '*Historia* im Mittelalter', *Archiv für Begriffsgeschichte*, 21 (1977): 226–84; compare Gert Melville, 'Wozu Geschichte schreiben? Stellung und Funktion der Historie im Mittelalter', in *Formen der Geschichtsschreibung*, eds Reinhart Koselleck, Heinrich Lutz and Jörn Rüsen (Munich: Deutscher Taschenbuch Verlag, 1982), 86–146; Joachim Knape, *Historie im Mittelalter und früher Neuzeit: Begriffs- und gattungsgeschichtliche Untersuchungen im interdisziplinären Kontext*, Saecula Spiritalia 10 (Baden-Baden: Valentin Koerner, 1984), 85–9; Goetz, 'Die "Geschichte"'; Verena Epp, 'Von Spurensuchern und Zeichendeutern. Zum selbstverstännis mittelalterlicher Geschichtsschreiber', in *Von Fakten und Fiktionen: mittelalterliche Geschichtsdarstellungen und ihre kritische Aufarbeitung*, ed. Johannes Laudage (Cologne: Böhlau, 2003), 43–62; David Ganz, 'Historia: Some Lexicographical Considerations', in *Medieval Cantors and their Craft: Music, Liturgy and the Shaping of History, 800-1500*, eds Katie Anne-Marie Bugyis, A. B. Kraebel and Margot E. Fassler (York: York Medieval Press, 2017), 8–22. See also Mireille Chazan, 'La méthode critique des historiens dans les chroniques universelles médiévales', in *La méthode critique au Moyen Âge*, eds Mareille Chazan and Gilbert Dahan (Turnhout: Brepols, 2006), 223–56.

[19] Elizabeth M. Tyler and Ross Balzaretti, 'Introduction', in *Narrative and History in the Early Medieval*

a massively influential resource throughout the medieval period and acted as a cultural bridge between the ancient and medieval worlds, reframing classical learning for the benefit of a multitude of Christian audiences.[20] Frechulf can be counted amongst Isidore's many readers: as Allen notes, the *Etymologies* 'stand as a looming presence, as one would expect'.[21]

Isidore defined *historia* as:

> a narrative of events, through which those things that happened in the past are discerned. […] This discipline has to do with grammar, because whatever is worthy of remembrance is committed to writing. And for this reason, histories are called 'monuments', because they grant a remembrance of deeds that have been done.[22]

A *historia* was a narration of things that had happened (*narratio rei gestae*). History was not the past itself or the discipline devoted to studying the past, but a written text commemorating past happenings. The past was accessed and remembered through historical narratives. Isidore supplied further criteria that marked out the contours of history. In contrast to other forms of record keeping, such as day-by-day, month-by-month or year-by-year reports of events, history 'concerns itself with many years or ages'. Furthermore, while the year-by-year format of annals dealt with 'those years that our age has not known', history was concerned with 'those times that we have seen'. For Isidore, the writing of history was best practised by those who had witnessed or were involved in the events they narrated, since it allowed them to write 'without falsehood'. This in turn spoke to history's most crucial quality: veracity. Isidore wrapped up his overview by stating that 'histories are true deeds that have happened', and as such they were differentiated from two other forms of narrative: *argumenta* ('things that, even if they have not happened, nevertheless could happen') and *fabula* ('things that have not happened and cannot happen, because they are contrary to nature').[23]

Although included under the rubric of grammar, the tail end of Isidore's overview of history owed much to another of the trivium's disciplines: rhetoric.[24] In Roman

---

West, eds Elizabeth M. Tyler and Ross Balzaretti (Turnhout: Brepols, 2006), 1–9, at 4. See also Deborah Mauskopf Deliyannis, 'Introduction', in *Historiography in the Middle Ages*, ed. Deborah Mauskopf Deliyannis (Leiden: Brill, 2003), 1–13, at 3–4.

[20] Quote from John Henderson, 'The Creation of Isidore's *Etymologies or Origins*', in *The Ordering of Knowledge in the Roman Empire*, eds Jason König and Tim Whitmarsh (Cambridge: CUP, 2007), 150–74 at 153.

[21] *Prolegomena*, 212* and 310*.

[22] Isidore of Seville, *Etymologiae*, I.41: 'Historia est narratio rei gestae, per quam ea, quae in praeterito facta sunt, dinoscuntur…Haec disciplina ad Grammaticam pertinet, quia quidquid dignum memoria est litteris mandatur. Historiae autem ideo monumenta dicuntur, eo quod memoriam tribuant rerum gestarum. Series autem dicta per translationem a sertis florum invicem conprehensarum.' Trans. Barney *et al.*, *Etymologies*, 67.

[23] The above paragraph draws on Isidore, *Etymologea* I.41–4; trans. Barney *et al.*, *Etymologies*, 67.

[24] Matthew Kempshall, *Rhetoric and the Writing of History, 400–1500* (Manchester: MUP, 2011) is the best place to start for an introduction to rhetoric in the light of medieval historiography. For an in-depth Carolingian case study, see Mayke de Jong, *Epitaph for an Era: Politics and Rhetoric in the*

rhetorical handbooks, such as the pseudo-Ciceronian *Rhetorica ad Herennium* and the authentically Ciceronian *De inventione*, history was related to oratory. A *narratio* was 'an exposition of events that have occurred or are supposed to have occurred', and it was one of the six components of a rhetorical speech.[25] When it came to crafting a narrative of events designed to entertain or edify, the orator had three categories from which to choose, depending on the substance of their speech. These categories match up with those that would later be listed by Isidore in the *Etymologies*: *fabula*, *argumentum* and *historia*. In contrast to Isidore, who associated history with living memory and direct experience, Cicero glossed it as 'an account of actual occurrences remote from the recollection of our own age'.[26] Yet whether relating the recent or the distant past, a historical narration described real things that actually happened. Any narrative was expected to conform to the three key qualities of brevity, clarity and plausibility: the so-called 'virtues of narrative' (*virtutes narrandi*).[27] History needed not only to be plausible, but also true.[28]

Taken together, grammar and rhetoric provide a combined context within which the meaning of the word *historia* would have been encountered in Carolingian centres of learning, namely monasteries, cathedral schools and even royal palaces such as Aachen.[29] The study of grammar and rhetoric, however, did not simply transmit definitions of what constituted history, but also imparted practical skills needed to read and write historical narratives. Grammar and rhetoric were the tools needed to analyse, understand and compose written texts. Hrabanus Maurus, in his *De institutione clericorum* (written 819), defined grammar as 'the science of interpreting poets and historians, and of writing and speaking correctly'.[30] Regarding the writing of history, there is a fascinating discussion preserved in a late-eighth-century manuscript from Monte Cassino, which, according to David

---

Carolingian World (Cambridge: CUP, 2019).

[25] Cicero, *De inventione*, I.19.27, ed. J. Henderson, trans. H. M. Hubbell, LCL 386 (Cambridge, MA: 1949) ed. J. Henderson, trans. H. M. Hubbell, LCL 386 (Cambridge MA: HUP, 1949), pp. 54–5: 'Narratio HUP, est rerum gestarum aut ut gestarum expositio.'

[26] Cicero, *De inventione*, I.19.27, pp. 54–5; *Rhetorica ad Herennium*, I.VIII.13, trans. Harry Caplan, LCL 403 (Cambridge, MA: HUP, 1954), pp. 22–5.

[27] *Rhetorica ad Herennium*, I.IX.14 pp. 24–5: 'Tres res conuenit habere narrationem, ut breuis, ut dilucida, ut ueri similis sit'; Quintilian, *Institutio Oratorio*, IV.2.31, ed. and trans. Donald A. Russel, LCL 125 (Cambridge MA and London: HUP, 2001), pp. 234–5; Martianus Capella, *De nuptiis Philologiae et Mercurii*, V.550, ed. James Willis (Leipzig: B.G. Teubner Verlagsgesellschaft, 1983), p. 133: 'Narrationis laudes tres sunt, ut lucida sit, ut veri similis, ut brevis.'

[28] For a tenth-century case study, see Justin C. Lake, 'Truth, Plausibility, and the Virtues of Narrative at the Millennium', *Journal of Medieval History*, 35(3) (2009): 221–38.

[29] See, for example, Alcuin, *Disputatio de rhetorica et de virtutibus*, ed. and trans. Wilbur Samuel Howell, *The Rhetoric of Alcuin and Charlemagne: A Translation* (Princeton, NJ: Princeton University Press, 1941), 100–3. On this text, see Matthew Kempshall, 'The Virtues of Rhetoric: Alcuin's *Disputatio de rhetorica et de virtutibus*', *Anglo-Saxon England*, 37 (2008): 7–30.

[30] Hrabanus Maurus, *De institutione clericorum*, III.18, ed. Detlev Zimpel, p. 468: 'Grammatica est scientia interpretandi poetas atque historicos, et recte scribendi loquendique.'

Ganz, was 'clearly designed to train pupils in various genres of prose composition'.[31] The author of this text began by defining *historia* as 'an account of events worthy of memory', before noting that the three 'duties of a historian' are 'that he expounds true matters, that he writes clearly and that he writes briefly'.[32]

Truth, clarity and brevity were the classical virtues of narrative. Frechulf, in the prologue to Part I, echoes these qualities: his task was to collect briefly and clearly (*breviter et lucide*) all that pertained to the truth of history. Since these categories resemble the demands of rhetorical historiography, it is worthwhile considering Frechulf's work in the light of the general reflections on *historia* just sketched. Traces of Isidore's definition of *historia* as a 'narrative of events through which those things that happened in the past are discerned' can be found throughout the *Histories*. At one point, the myths of poets and fables were contrasted with the facts of history.[33] Frechulf's narrative of Moses' life up until he liberated the 'sons of Israel' was 'plucked from the *historia* of Josephus'; his account of the Trojan War was based upon the '*historia* of Dares [the Phrygian]'; and in the reign of the Persian king Cambyses 'the *historia* of Judith was written down'.[34] In all these cases, histories were written texts through which past events were accessed; crucially, they comprised both historiographical narratives and books of the Bible.[35] Any written representation of what happened in the past was a history, and Frechulf perceived his own work in this light too. When contrasting the scope of his own narrative with the *narrationes gestorum* of earlier Greek and Latin historians at the outset of Part I (as quoted above), he all but labelled his work a *narratio rei gestae*. His was a single narrative extracted from a plurality of *historiae*.

Frechulf's *narratio* was also concerned with memory. Isidore said that history pertains to grammar 'because whatever is worthy of remembrance (*dignum memoria*) is committed to writing', and the short text from Monte Cassino labelled *historia* as 'an account of events worthy of memory'. Frechulf understood that the historian's purpose was to transmit to future readers the record of events in writing.[36] Including events deemed 'worthy of memory (*digna memoria*)' appears

---

[31] Ganz, 'Historia', 15.

[32] *Excerpta Rhetorica*, ed. C. F. Halm, *Rhetores Latini minores* (Leipzig: Teubner, 1863), pp. 585–9, at 588: 'Historia est rerum gestarum et dignarum memoria relatio ... Historia officii sunt tria: ut vera res, ut dilucide, ut breviter exponat'. For translation and discussion, see Ganz, 'Historia', 15–16 and his 'The Astronomer's Life of Louis the Pious', in *Rome and Religion in the Medieval World: Studies in Honour of Thomas F. X. Noble*, eds Valerie L. Garver and Owen M. Phelan (Farnham: Ashgate, 2014), 129–48 at 134–5.

[33] *Hist.*, I.2.9 [8/10], p. 103 via Augustine, *DCD*, XVIII.8, p. 599.

[34] *Hist.*, I.2.17 [101], p. 115: 'Haec namque ex Iosepphi decerpsimus historia'; I.2.26 [29.30], p. 142: 'Quod ita contigisse <in> Historia Daretis atque aliorum legimus'; I.319 [1/3], p. 204: 'Cambises Cyri filius, Persarum rex secundus, annis VIII ... Sub quo Iudith historia conscribitur ...'

[35] There were also liturgical *historiae*: Graeme Ward, 'The Order of History: Liturgical Time and the Rhythms of the Past in Amalarius's *De ordine antiphonarii*', in *Writing the Early Middle Ages: Studies in Honour of Rosamond McKitterick*, eds Elina Screen and Charles West (Cambridge: CUP, 2018), 98–111.

[36] *Hist.*, II.4.16 [34/40], p. 645: 'historiographi, quorum intentio fuit ut litteris haec ad futuram

to have been a catchphrase of sorts for Frechulf, appearing in the dedicatory prologue to Part I as well as in the second prologue inserted between the first two books.[37] With this phrase, however, we are now in the realm of literary convention. Prologues, although often the most reflective parts of a text, also tend to be laden with topoi.[38] Commonplace expressions were not empty words, but nevertheless they still need to be handled with care. Frechulf's aim to write with brevity and clarity, for instance, might not have been meant as a straightforward reflection of qualities of his text, but can be taken as evidence of his knowledge of the expectations of historical narrative. Yet is this the context in which Frechulf's search for the 'truth of history' should be placed?

Writing Truth

The topos of truth permeated historiographical discourse in the early Middle Ages.[39] According to Cicero, 'history's first law', was 'that its author must not dare to tell anything but the truth' and that 'he must make bold to tell the whole truth'.[40] Einhard, an author known for his Ciceronian eloquence (or at least his professed lack of said eloquence), stressed that his *Life of Charlemagne* was concerned with true things.[41] He argued that, on account of his closeness to the king, he was particularly well suited to write an account of Charlemagne's life: 'no one could write these things more truthfully than I could'.[42] Einhard's first editor, Walahfrid Strabo, re-emphasised this point when he came to write a prologue for the *Vita*: 'Because [Einhard] was present at most of these events he attested them with the purest truth (*purissimae veritatis*)'.[43] These statements can

---

posteritatem porrigerent ...'
[37] *Hist.*, I.Prol., [29.30], p. 19; I.2. Prol [6/8 and 19], p. 85; *Prol. Veg.*, p. 729.
[38] Gertrud Simon, 'Untersuchungen zur Topik der Widmungsbriefe mittelalterlicher Geschichtsschreiber bis zum Ende des 12. Jahrhunderts', Part I: *Archiv für Diplomatik*, 4 (1958): 52–119 and Part II: *Archiv für Diplomatik*, 5 (1959): 73–153. I discuss Frechulf's prologues at greater length in Chapter 6.
[39] Lake, 'Current Approaches', 90–2 gives a helpful overview. More generally, see Ruth Morse, *Truth and Convention in the Middle Ages: Rhetoric, Representation, and Reality* (Cambridge: CUP, 1991).
[40] Cicero, *De oratore*, II.62–3, ed. H. Rackham, trans. H. M. Hubbell, LCL 386 (Cambridge, MA: HUP, 1949), pp. 242–5: 'nam quis nescit primam esse historiae legem, ne quid falsi dicere audeat? deinde ne quid veri non audeat?'
[41] Matthew S. Kempshall, 'Some Ciceronian Models for Einhard's Life of Charlemagne', *Viator*, 26 (1995): 11–37.
[42] Einhard, *Vita Karoli*, ed. Holder-Egger, p. 1: 'tamen ab huiscemodi scriptione non existimavi temperandum, quando mihi conscius eram nullum ea veracius quam me scribere posse, quibus ipse interfui quaeque praesens oculata, it dicunt, fide cognovi et utrum ab alio scriberentur necne liquido scire non potui'. Trans. by David Ganz, in *Two Lives of Charlemagne* (London: Penguin, 2008), 17.
[43] Walahfrid, *Prologus*, ed. Holder-Egger, p. xxviii; trans. Ganz, *Two Lives*, 15. See further David Ganz, 'The Preface to Einhard's *Vita Karoli*', in *Einhard. Studien zu Leben und Werk*, ed. Hermann Schefers (Darmstadt: Hessische Historiche Kommission, 1997), 299–310 and Steffen Patzold, 'Einhards erste Leser: zu Kontext und Darstellungsabsicht der *Vita Karoli*', *Viator*, 42 (2011): 33–55, esp. 41–6. See also Astronomer, *Vita Hludowici imperatoris*, Prol., ed. and trans. Ernst Tremp, MGH *SRG* 64 (Hanover: Hahn, 1995), p. 284.

be viewed from an Isidorean perspective.[44] Isidore explained that:

> History is so called from the Greek term *historein* ('inquire, observe'), that is, from 'seeing' or from 'knowing'. Indeed, among the ancients no one would write a history unless he had been present and had seen what was to be written down, for we grasp with our eyes things that occur better than what we gather with our hearing.[45]

For many medieval historians, separated from their subjects either by time or space, this ancient ideal was impossible to uphold. Unsurprisingly, it was not the sole determinant of historiographical truth. Assurances of veracity could be communicated in other ways.

Around a century before Einhard penned his celebrated *Vita Karoli*, Bede prefaced his equally celebrated *Ecclesiastical History* with a letter to the Northumbrian king, Ceolwulf, in which he pleaded his own truth-telling credentials:

> So I humbly beg the reader, if he finds anything other than truth set down in what I have written, not to impute it. For, in accordance with the true law of history (*vera lex historiae*), I have simply sought to commit to writing what I have collected from common report, for the instruction of posterity.[46]

There has been much debate about Bede's *vera lex historiae*. Roger Ray argued that Bede's appeal to the 'true law of history' was a tacit response to Isidore's emphasis on the importance of eye-witness testimony. For the most part, the *Ecclesiastical History* narrated events well before Bede's lifetime, for which he principally relied on the 'common report (*fama vulgans*)' of oral sources. Demonstrating awareness of the principles of Roman rhetoric, Bede, as a truthful historian (*verax historicus*), was able to shape this material into something profitable.[47] This sort of truth, according to Walter Goffart, was simple, even rustic; against it was contrasted the more sophisticated truths found in Bede's theological writings.[48]

Bede and Einhard both felt compelled to highlight that their respective narratives were imbued with truth, and that as narrators they were to be trusted. Einhard emphasised the privileged position he himself had in relation to his subject, and Bede justified his use of a body of sources which his readers would

[44] Ganz, 'Historia', 12–13; Kempshall, *Rhetoric*, 185.
[45] Isidore, *Etymologiae*, I.41.1–2: 'Dicta autem Graece historia ἀπὸ τοῦ ἱστορεῖν, id est a videre vel cognoscere. Apud veteres enim nemo conscribebat historiam, nisi is qui interfuisset, et ea quae conscribenda essent vidisset. Melius enim oculis quae fiunt deprehendimus, quam quae auditione colligimus. Quae enim videntur, sine mendacio proferuntur.' Trans. Barney *et al.*, *Etymologies*, 67.
[46] Bede, *Historia ecclesiastica*, Preface, Colgrave and Mynors (eds and trans.), *Bede's Ecclesiastical History of the English People*, pp. 6 and 7: 'Lectoremque suppliciter obsecro ut, siqua in his quae scripsimus aliter quam se veritas habet posita reppererit, non hoc nobis inputet, qui, quod vera lex historiae est, simpliciter ea quae fama vulgante colligemus ad instructionem posteritatis litteris mandare studuimus.'
[47] Roger Ray, 'Bede's *Vera lex historiae*', *Speculum*, 55(1) (1980): 1–21.
[48] Walter Goffart, 'Bede's *Vera lex historiae* Explained', *Anglo-Saxon England*, 34 (2005): 111–16; repr. in his *Barbarians, Maps, and Historiography* (Farnham: Ashgate, 2009), item VII.

not be able to check for themselves and verify. Frechulf's focus on the *veritas historiae*, however, is at odds with the emphases of these well-known advocates of historiographical truth. They wished to assure their readers of the content of the narratives they themselves had crafted; their truth claims thus pertained to the writing of history, for which the lessons of rhetoric most readily applied.[49] Frechulf, by contrast, worked primarily with histories whose values and verities had long been established. He was an exegete of the known, not a narrator of the new.

Frechulf's first book contains the most eye-catching material with which to examine this issue, since the underlying authority was not any mere historian or chronicler but Moses, a divinely inspired biblical author. According to Hrabanus Maurus, grammar was the 'science of interpreting historians and poets', but grammar, rhetoric and the other liberal arts were deemed essential for parsing the books of the Bible and especially those of the Old Testament, which were understood both to be history and to transcend it.[50] Of the books of the Old Testament, Genesis was an especially demanding text to grasp historically, since it dealt with topics that were hard to comprehend literally, from the creation of all life to the existence of giants and 900-year-old men. The difficult subject matter was certainly one reason why Genesis was continuously scrutinised by Christian commentators from late antiquity onwards.[51] Since Frechulf worked closely with this hermeneutic literature, it too must be considered: grammatical, rhetorical and historiographical contexts illuminate aspects of what *historia* meant to the bishop of Lisieux, but to reach a fuller understanding, scriptural exegesis must also be factored in.

Historia fundamentum est

Like narrative *historia*, biblical commentary had its own characteristic features, and in Frechulf's surviving letter to Hrabanus Maurus, we see a man familiar with the tools of the trade. For each biblical verse, Frechulf wanted Hrabanus first to outline its literal sense (*sensus litterae*), then to unpack its spiritual meaning (*spiritalis intellegentiae*).[52] In theory, there were four different ways in which scripture could be understood: literally, allegorically, anagogically and tropologically.[53] In practice,

---

[49] Kempshall, *Rhetoric*.

[50] See John J. Contreni, 'Learning for God: Education in the Carolingian Age', *The Journal of Medieval Latin*, 24 (2014): 89–130, on Christian use of non-Christian learning.

[51] For an overview, see Thomas O'Loughlin, *Teachers and Code-Breakers: The Latin Genesis Tradition, 430–800* (Turnhout: Brepols, 1998); for a later medieval focus, see also Joy A. Schroeder (ed. and trans.) *The Book of Genesis*, The Bible in Medieval Tradition (Grand Rapids, MI: William B. Eerdmans, 2015).

[52] *Epist.*, p. 6: 'Et itaque modo opus hoc conpendiosum fieri flagitamus ut primum sensus litterae ac deinde spiritalis intellegentiae accurate succisa prolixitate pandatur.'

[53] See the classic, wide-ranging study of Henri du Lubac, *Medieval Exegesis: The Four Senses of Scripture*, trans. by E. M. Macierowski (Grand Rapids, MI: William B. Eerdmans, 1998–2009) vols 2–4; see esp. vol. 2.

however, there were two main levels of interpretation: literal and spiritual.[54] The spiritual interpretation of scripture, especially of the Old Testament, uncovered figures and events that prefigured Christ, the Church and the Eschaton (allegory and anagogy), while also offering moral lessons (tropology) to contemporary readers. The literal sense dealt with the surface meaning of a given scriptural passage, which could comprise analysis of its grammar and syntax as well as drawing attention to its factual truth and historical reality. For this reason, literal exegesis is also known as the historical sense of scripture. The *sensus litterae*, the 'sense of the letter', could also be expressed as *historia, historica explanatio, historica expositio* and, most significantly for my purpose, *historiae veritas*.[55] In the context of exegesis, the 'truth of history' was the historical interpretation of scripture.

The Latin expression *veritas historiae* can be found in abundance amongst the writings of Jerome of Stridon (died 420), although its roots go back further to the Greek exegete, Origen of Alexandria (died 254).[56] Jerome's Old Testament commentaries were rich in historical detail and analysis, to the extent that it was once noted that he 'was actually haunted by an historical sense'.[57] When offering historical commentary, Jerome used the expression the 'truth of history'

---

[54] De Lubac, *Medieval Exegesis*, 127.

[55] On distinctions between *littera* and *historia*, see Frances M. Young, *Biblical Exegesis and the Formation of Christian Culture* (Cambridge: CUP, 1997), 192–201. For a study of ninth-century historical vis-à-vis literal exegesis, see Elisabeth Mégier, '*Historia* and *Littera* in Carolingian Commentaries on St Matthew. Elements for an Inventory of Exegetical Vocabulary in the Medieval Latin Church', in *Producing Christian Culture: Medieval Exegesis and its Interpretative Genres*, ed. Giles E. M. Gasper (Abingdon: Routledge, 2017), 89–113. More generally of the literal sense, see Jon Whitman, 'The Literal Sense of Christian Scripture: Redefinition and Revolution', in *Interpreting Scriptures in Judaism, Christianity, and Islam: Overlapping Inquiries*, eds Mordechai Z. Cohen and Adele Berlin (Cambridge: CUP, 2016), 133–58.

[56] Aline Canellis, 'Jerome's Hermeneutics: How to Exegete the Bible?', in *Patristic Theories of Biblical Interpretation: The Latin Fathers*, ed. Tarmo Toom (Cambridge: CUP, 2016), 49–76. Concerning Origen, see de Lubac, *Medieval Exegesis*, vol. 2, 45, 47 and more generally Peter Martens, *Origen and Scripture: The Contours of the Exegetical Life* (Oxford: OUP, 2012). On Jerome's Carolingian influence, see remarks in Bernice Martha Kaczynski, 'Editions, Translation and Exegesis: The Carolingians and the Bible', in *The Gentle Voices of Teachers': Aspects of Learning in the Carolingian Age*, ed. Richard E. Sullivan (Columbus, OH: Ohio State University Press, 1995), 171-85; for a more focused study, see Janneke Raaijmakers, 'Studying Jerome in a Carolingian Monastery', in *The Annotated Book in the Early Middle Ages: Practices of Reading and Writing*, eds Mariken Teeuwen and Irene van Renswoude (Turnhout: Brepols, 2018), 621–46.

[57] Francis X. Murphy, 'St. Jerome as an Historian', in *A Monument to Saint Jerome: Essays on Some Aspects of his Life, Work and Influence*, ed. Francis X. Murphy (New York: Sheed & Ward, 1952), 115–41, at 116; see also Anna-Dorothee von den Brincken, 'Hieronymus als Exeget "secundum historiam": Von der Chronik zum Ezechiel-Kommentar', *DA*, 49 (1993): 453–78. On the literal sense in Jerome's commentaries, see Dennis Brown, *Vir trilinguis: A Study in the Biblical Exegesis of Saint Jerome* (Kampen: Kok Pharos Publishing House, 1992), 124–38; with specific reference to Isaiah, see Pierre Jay, *L'exégèse de Saint Jérôme d'après son 'Commentaire sur Isaïe'* (Paris: Études augustiennes, 1985), 127–214 (on *historia* esp. 135–42) and also Annexe IV, 419–21. As historian: Hervé Inglebert, *Les Romains chrétiens face à l'histoire de Rome: histoire, christianisme et romanités en Occident dans l'Antiquité tardive (IIIe–Ve siècles)* (Paris: Institut d'études augustiniennes, 1996), 213–15; Giuseppe Zecchini, 'Latin Historiography: Jerome, Orosius and the Western Chronicles', in *Greek and Roman Historiography in Late Antiquity: Fourth to Sixth Century A.D.*, ed. Gabriele Marasco (Leiden: Brill, 2003), 317-45, at 317-19.

in his expositions of Isaiah,[58] Jeremiah,[59] Ezekiel,[60] Daniel,[61] Amos,[62] Micah,[63] Zechariah[64] and Malachi.[65] He often coupled *veritas historiae* with the *spiritalis intellegentia*: the 'truth of history', Jerome made clear, lay the 'foundation of spiritual understanding'.[66] To uncover scripture's hidden meaning, its literal/ historical truth first had to be appreciated. Jerome often based his historical analysis on his own translation of the Hebrew Bible, what he termed the 'Hebrew Truth', but subjected verses from the Septuagint to allegorical readings.[67] History and allegory were often viewed as two parts of the same whole. For example, Ezekiel 41:24 described the Jerusalem Temple: 'And in the two doors on both sides were two little doors, which were folded within each other.' Inspired by this description, Jerome reflected on how the biblical text should be approached: 'so that we may have both the spiritual understanding in the history and the truth of history in the tropology, each of which requires the other, and if one is missing, perfect knowledge is lacking'.[68] This passage nicely encapsulates one of the key tenets of biblical exegesis as it was practised in the Latin west: to understand scripture was to understand the letter of the text as well as the spirit hidden within.[69]

---

[58] Jerome, *Commentarii in Esaiam*, Prol., ed. Marcus Adriaen, CCSL 73 (Turnhout: Brepols, 1963), p. 3 [73.4]: 'Unde post historiae veritatem, spiritaliter accipienda sunt omnia'. See also I (1.1), p. 6 [55.6]: '… sequentes historiae ueritatem sic interpretamur spiritaliter'; V (18:5–6), p. 191 [15/17]: 'ac ne putares eum de uinea dicere, et non de hominibus, uertit metaphoram in historiae ueritatem'.

[59] Jerome, *Commentarii in Hieremiam prophetam*, I (1:10), ed. Siegfried Reiter, CCSL 74 (Turnhout: Brepols, 1960), p. 7 [14].

[60] Jerome, *Commentarii in Hiezechielem*, VI (28:25), ed. Franciscus Glorie, CCSL 75 (Turnhout: Brepols, 1964), p. 246; XI (36:16–18), p. 508; XII (41:22b–26), p. 603.

[61] Jerome, *Commentariorum in Danielem*, IV (12:4), ed. Franciscus Glorie, CCSL 75A (Turhnout: Brepols, 1964), p. 938.

[62] Jerome, *Commentarii in Amos prophetam*, II (5:1.2), ed. Marcus Adriaen, CCSL 76 (Turnhout: Brepols, 1969), pp. 211–348, II, at p. 272.

[63] Jerome, *Commentarii in Michaeam prophetam*, I (2:9–10), ed. Marcus Adriaen, CCSL 76 (Turnhout: Brepols, 1969), pp. 421–524, at p. 447.

[64] Jerome, *Commentarii in Zachariam prophetam*, I (4:8–10), ed. Marcus Adriaen, CCSL 76A (Turnhout: Brepols, 1970), pp. 747–900, at pp. 781-2; I (6:1–8), p. 794.

[65] Jerome, *Commentarii in Malachiam prophetam*, I (2:10–12), ed. Marcus Adriaen, CCSL 76A (Turnhout: Brepols, 1970), pp. 901-42, at p. 922.

[66] Jerome, *Epistulae*, Ep. 129, 6, ed. Isidorus Hilberg, 3 vols, CSEL 54–55 (Vienna: Verlag der österriechischen Akademie der Wissenschaften, 1996), vol. 3, p. 173: 'aut quo auferam historiae veritatem, quae fundamentum est intelligentiae spiritalis …'. On the metaphor of 'foundation' in patristic exegesis, see de Lubac, *Medieval Exegesis*, vol. 2, 47–8 with examples. For a twelfth-century case study, see Grover A. Zinn, 'Historia fundamentum est: The Role of History in the Contemplative Life according to Hugh of St. Victor', in *Contemporary Reflections on the Medieval Christian Tradition. Essays in Honor of Ray C. Petry* ed. George H. Shriver (Durham, NC: Duke University Press, 1974), 135–58.

[67] Josef Lössl, 'A Shift in Patristic Exegesis: Hebrew Clarity and Historical Verity in Augustine, Jerome, Julian of Aeclanum and Theodore of Mopsuestia', *Augustinian Studies*, 32(2) (2001): 157–75.

[68] Jerome, *Commentariorum in Hiezechielem*, XII (41:22–6) p. 603 [1603/5]: 'ut et in historia spiritualem habeamus intelligentiam et in tropologia historiae veritatem, quorum utrumque altero indiget et si unum defuerit perfecta caret scientia'. Trans. Thomas P. Scheck, in *St Jerome: Commentary on Ezekiel* (New York: Newman Press, 2017), 485.

[69] See de Lubac, *Medieval Exegesis*, vol. 2, 47–8 for examples.

Literal/historical exegesis could take many forms. One important facet was the historical realisation of prophecy.[70] Jerome viewed the 'truth of history' and the 'faith of prophecy' in the same light.[71] Occasionally the historical interpretation was enough when prophecy was involved: as Jerome said in his commentary of Zechariah, 'when prophecy is most evident, and the proper order of history is narrated by translation, then a figurative interpretation is superfluous.'[72] In other instances, however, the historical interpretation was only the first but still significant step. Amos 5:1-2 runs as follows: 'Hear ye this word, which I take up concerning you for a lamentation. The house of Israel is fallen, and it shall rise no more. The virgin of Israel is cast down upon her land, there is none to raise her up.' Jerome first tackled the historical truth of this passage: 'so far as it pertains to the order of the letter and the undertaken truth of history, the ten tribes, which are called Israel, were led into captivity, and afterwards they never returned to their land. The virgin is called the people of Israel, not because they will remain in the purity of virginity, but because some day, like a virgin, they shall be joined to the Lord in resemblance of a virgin.'[73] Jerome here was explaining the historical truth of Amos 5:1-2 by demonstrating how the prophet's words manifested themselves historically, before going on to explain them allegorically.

The work of Jerome, together with the wider patristic canon, played a central role in the development and crystallisation of intellectual undertakings in the eighth and ninth centuries. Hrabanus Maurus integrated much of Jerome's exegesis into his own biblical commentaries. When he came to write his exposition of Ezekiel, he copied out nearly verbatim Jerome's (above-quoted) reflection on the relationship between the historical and spiritual interpretations, as prompted by Ezekiel 41:24.[74] Indeed, many of the references I have noted concerning Jerome's use of the expression *veritas historiae* appear in the works of Hrabanus.[75] By the early ninth century, there was a rich collection of Jerome's work at Fulda, which

---

[70] Jay, *Exégèse*, 376–9; see also Elisabeth Mégier, 'Christian Historical Fulfilments of Old Testament Prophecies in Latin Commentaries on the Book of Isaiah (ca. 400 to ca. 1150)', *Journal of Medieval Latin*, 17 (2007): 87–100.

[71] Jerome, *Commentarii in Hiezechielem*, XI (36:16–18), p. 508 [903.4]: 'haec iuxta historiae ueritatem, immo iuxta prophetiae fidem'.

[72] Jerome, *In Zachariam*, III (11:4.5), p. 850 [87/9]: 'ubi manifestissima prophetia est, et per translationem historiae uerus ordo narratur, superflua est tropologiae interpretatio'. This example is taken from Brown, *Vir trilingus*, 126, whose translation I have modified slightly.

[73] Jerome, *In Amos*, II (5:1.2), p. 272 [7/14]: 'Quantum ad ordinem litterae pertinet et coeptam historiae veritatem, decem tribus, quae appellantur Israel, ductae in captivitatem, nequaquam in terram suam postea sunt reversae. Virgo autem appellatur populus Israel, non quia in virginitatis permanserit puritate, sed quia quondam instar virginis sit Domino copulatus. Unde et planctum super eum propheta iubetur assumere, quod nequaquam in antiquum restituatur gradum.'

[74] Hrabanus Maurus, *Commentariorum in Ezechielem libri viginti*, PL 110, cols. 493–1084, at col. 978C. On this commentary, see Hans Butzmann, 'Der Ezechiel-Kommentar des Hrabanus Maurus und seine älteste Handschrift', *Bibliothek und Wissenschaft*, 1 (1964): 1–22.

[75] Hrabanus Maurus, *In Ezechielem*, PL 110, col. 712D, 858A, 978C; *Expositionis super Hieremiam prophetam libri viginti*, PL 111, cols. 793–1272, at col. 800C.

Hrabanus was able to exploit; if we accept the hypothesis that Frechulf was also a monk at Fulda before taking up his episcopal post at Lisieux, then such a collection may also have played a role in his own intellectual formation.[76]

Beryl Smalley, one of the leadings lights in the modern study of medieval biblical culture, was famously dismissive of Carolingian exegesis: 'To study the commentaries of [Carolingian exegetes] is simply to study their sources.'[77] Eighth- and ninth-century scholars certainly did rely heavily upon the Church Fathers, yet recent work has shown that deep meditation on patristic texts helped form a distinct and diverse culture of exegesis.[78] The language of the Fathers first entered into Carolingian intellectual discourse through earlier florilegia, but during the course of the ninth century the rich patristic legacy became—together with scripture itself—the core resource upon which nearly all elite writing and reflection were based.[79] Towards the end of his life, for example, Hrabanus referred to the 'truth of history' in his encyclopaedic *De rerum naturis* (also known as *De universo*).[80] When discussing the sky and heavens, Hrabanus wrote:

> In holy scripture, many things which can be taken as history, must also be understood spiritually, in order that faith may be had from the truth of history, and spiritual understanding may be seized by the mysteries of allegory, as we understand what the psalmist says: 'I will look at your heavens, the works of your fingers, at the moon and the stars which you set in place' (Ps. 8). Observe! Reasoned speech stands in accordance with the truth of history, since the works of heaven are of God, and the moon and stars were created and established by him.[81]

Hrabanus derived much of this from Gregory the Great's *Homiliae in Hiezechihelem prophetam*, but he exchanged Gregory's coupling of 'reasoned speech' with 'the exterior description' for the 'truth of history'. The sense remained unchanged: the exterior meaning was found on the outer surface of the text, whereas the interior contained hidden significances.[82] The message here is entirely on a par with the other

---

[76] Raaijmakers, *Monastic Community of Fulda*, 193.

[77] Beryl Smalley, *The Study of the Bible in the Middle Ages*, 2nd edn (Oxford: Blackwell, 1983), 37–8.

[78] Chazelle and Van Name Edwards (eds), *Study of the Bible.*

[79] Contreni, 'Carolingian Biblical Culture' and 'Patristic legacy'; Otten, 'The Texture of Tradition'.

[80] Toby Burrows, 'Holy Information: A New Look at Raban Maur's *De naturis rerum*', *Paregon*, 5 (1987), 28–37.

[81] Hrabanus Maurus, *De rerum naturis*, 9.4, *PL* 111, cols 9a–614B, at col. 263B: 'In Scriptura sacra plerumque et ea, quae accipi secundum historiam possunt, spiritaliter intelligenda sunt: ut et fides habeatur in veritate historiae, et spiritalis intelligentiae capiatur in mysteriis allegoria: sicut hoc quoque novimus, quod Psalmista ait: Quoniam videbo coelos opera digitorum tuorum, lunam et stellas, quos tu fundasti. Ecce enim iuxta veritatem historiae stat sermo rationis: quia et coeli opera Dei sunt, et luna ac stellae ab eo creatae atque fundatae sunt. Translation adapted from Priscilla Throop, trans., *Hrabanus Maurus: De Universo. The Peculiar Properties of Words and Their Mystical Significance*, 2 vols (Charlotte, VT: MedievalsMS, 2009), vol. 1, 284–5.

[82] Gregory the Great, *Homiliae in Hiezechielem Prophetam*, II, Hom. I, ed. Marcus Adriaen, CCSL 142 (Turnhout: Brepols, 1971), pp. 208–9: 'Ecce enim in exteriori descriptione stat sermo rationis, quia et caeli opera dei sunt, et luna ac stellae ab eo creatae atque fundatae sunt.'

examples cited: in order to fully contemplate God's work, the historical veracity of the Bible ought to be accepted before seeking to unlock its deeper meanings.

There were no fixed rules concerning how to balance historical vis-à-vis spiritual interpretation. Ultimately, it was at the discretion of the exegete. In his *Genesis Commentary*, Claudius of Turin put equal weight on the exposition of text and mystery (that is, allegory).[83] Angelomus of Luxeuil, who, 'sometime before 833', also produced a Genesis commentary, explained in his prologue that:

> in certain places, while always explaining the historical meaning [*veritatem hystoriae*], we have tried to insert allegorical and moral interpretations, so that, as I have already explained, historical interpretations might confirm the truth of what happened and confirm the faith in what is recounted, allegorical interpretation might reveal the secrets of divine allegories, and moral interpretation might lead to an improved life. The reader should not be burdened by the historical meaning, but rather captured by the sweet allegorical and moral interpretations ...[84]

While allegorical exegesis was the goal for most commentators, *historia* could be an end in itself. Jerome's Matthew commentary, for example, was conceived as a *historica interpretatio*, although a few sprinklings of allegorical readings (*spiritalis intelligentia*) were thrown in for good measure.[85] Alcuin, in his *Questions*, explained in his preface that the questions addressed were 'mainly historical and contain a simple response'; to unpick more challenging, allegorical, questions 'would require a more thorough investigation and a longer work'.[86] Towards the end of the text, Alcuin asserted that 'the foundations of history first must be laid down, so that the roof of allegory might fittingly be placed over it'.[87] Writing in the

---

[83] Claudius of Turin, *Commentarri in Genesim*, Prol., ed. Ernst Dümmler, MGH *Epp.* IV (Berlin: Weidmann, 1895), pp. 590–3, at 592: 'ipsumque Geneseos lib[rum] hystorica et allegorica expositione ad calcem usque perduxi. Ita tamen inter textum et mysterium tanta libratione pensando, ut utramque partem neque nim[is] discussionis pondus deprimeret neuqe rursum torpor incuriae vacuam reliquisset'.

[84] Angelomus of Luxeuil, *Commentarius in Genesin*, in *Epistolae variorum*, ed. Ernst Dümmler, MGH *Epp.* V (Berlin: Weidmann, 1895), no. 5, p. 622, 7/14: 'Sed antequam ysagogen ad calcem perveniat, notandum est, quod in quibusdam locis veritatem videlicet hystoriae semper pandens, spiritalem moralemque intellegentiam inserere nisi sumus, inibi scilicet, ubi predixisti, ut hystoria veritatem factorum ac fidem relationis inculcet, et spiritalis intellegentia ad caelestium figurarum secreta perducat, et moralis persuasio ad meliorationem vitae invitet, ne solummodo hystoria pressus, sed spiritalis immo moralisque dulcedine captus lector excusationis invenire possit anfractus, sed ex hoc cum ambrosios coeperit decerpere gustus, magis libenter campos doctorum satagat lustrare ovans latissimos. Vale'. See Michael Gorman, 'The Commentary on Genesis of Angelomus of Luxeuil and Biblical Studies under Lothar', *Studi medievali*, 40 (1999): 559–631 ('sometime before 833': 562); translation at 605.

[85] Jerome, *Commentarii in Matheum*, Praef., eds David Hurst and Marcus Adriaen, CCSL 77 (Turnhout: Brepols, 1969), pp. 4–5.

[86] Alcuin, *Interrogationes et responsiones in Genesin*, Pref., *PL* 100, clos. 515–66, at col. 517B; trans. from Michael Fox, 'Alcuin the Exegete: The Evidence of the *Quaestiones in Genesim*', in Celia Chazelle and Burton van Name Edwards (eds), *The Study of the Bible in the Carolingian Era*, Medieval Church Studies 3 (Turnhout: Brepols, 2003), 39–60 at 41.

[87] Alcuin, *Interrogationes*, Int. 231, col. 559 C: 'Sed prius historiae fundamenta ponenda sunt, ut aptius

860s, Christian of Stavelot was a firm upholder of the central importance of the historical level of interpretation above all others:

> I have striven to follow the historical sense more than the spiritual, because it seems to me irrational to seek the spiritual understanding in a book and ignore thoroughly the historical, when the historical understanding is the foundation of all others. This understanding should first be sought out and embraced. Without it one is not able fully to move on to any other [sense].[88]

In championing the *sensus historicus*, Christian of Stavelot was unusual: most Carolingian exegetes, and most of the patristic exegesis which fed into eighth- and ninth-century commentaries, considered the *spiritalis intellegentia*, even if balanced against the literal sense, to be the ultimate goal of biblical study.[89] Frechulf himself, as far as can be judged from the letters that Hrabanus sent to Lisieux prefacing his expositions of the each of the books of the Pentateuch, sought out allegorical exegesis of the 'books of the Lawgiver'.[90] Curiously, Hrabanus's commentary on Genesis was not one of Frechulf's sources.[91] Exegesis of the first book of the Pentateuch, nevertheless, was integral to the opening book of the *Histories*: Alcuin's *Questions on Genesis* and Claudius of Turin's *Genesis Commentary*, but also Augustine's *City of God*. The remainder of this chapter considers the effect which this material had on Frechulf's account of pre-Abrahamic history.

Frechulf, the Historian, as Exegete?[92]

The *Histories'* first book corresponds to the first twenty-one chapters of Genesis, running in chronological order from the world's beginning through to the birth of Abraham's second son, Isaac. Frechulf's chapters cohere around the central figures and events from the first half of Genesis: man's creation and expulsion from paradise (cc. 1–5 = Genesis 1–3), Cain, Abel, Seth and the first seven generations of humanity (cc. 6–19 = Genesis 4–5), Noah and the Flood (cc. 20–26 = Genesis 6–9), the sons of Noah and the repopulation of the planet (cc. 27–34 = Genesis 9–10) and the life of Abraham (cc. 35–57 = Genesis 11–21). A clear narrative runs through the book, which traces the genealogy of mankind from Adam (Eve

---

allegoriae culmen priori structurae superponatur.'

[88] Christianus dictus Stabulensis, *Expositio super Librum Generationis*, ed. R. B. C. Huygens, CCCM 224 (Turnhout: Brepols, 2008), 52: 'Studui autem plus istoricum sensum sequi quam spiritalem, quia inrationabile mihi uidetur spiritalem intellegentiam in libro aliquo quaerere et istoricam penitus ignorare, cum historica fundamentum omnis intellegentiae sit et ipsa primitus quaerenda et amplexanda, et sine ipsa perfecte ad aliam non possit transiri.'

[89] Compare Smalley, *Study of the Bible*, which is about the development of litteral commentary, especially in the twelfth and thirteenth centuries.

[90] For example, Hrab. *Epist.*, no. 9, p. 395 (ll. 1–3), no. 11, p. 398 (ll. 8–11). This of course may speak to Hrabanus's preferences.

[91] *Prolegomena*, 212*.

[92] Compare Ray, 'Bede'.

is only ever alluded to) and unfolds in relation to sin, punishment and divine providence. Such themes were already present in the Old Testament and then endlessly expounded upon by medieval commentators.

Frechulf's expressed concern to address 'difficult questions in the writings of the Lawgiver' meant that this narrative was told in a distinctive way. The majority of Book 1's fifty-seven chapters were framed as answers to questions about specific verses and passages from Genesis. Exegesis by means of questions and answers was baked into Christian Old Testament commentary, as titles such as Jerome's *Hebrew Questions on Genesis,* Augustine's *Questions on the Heptateuch* and also Alcuin's *Questions on Genesis* imply.[93] This format permeated Frechulf's Christian sources and his *Histories* in turn reproduced it. Frechulf's chapters addressed fundamental questions. For instance: why, of all God's creations, was man made last? How was God able to communicate with the first humans? What was God's anger? Why was Abraham circumcised?[94] Questions served to identify people and places mentioned in Genesis, to clarify the order of events when they appeared confused, and to resolve apparent contradictions and other ostensibly contentious passages. For instance, Abraham and his brother Nachor married the two daughters of their deceased brother, Aran. The daughters' names were Melcha and Sara, yet 'in Genesis it is read *that the father of Melchae was the father of Jesca* (Gn. 11:29)'. Jesca, it was explained, was Sara's cognomen; moreover marriage 'between uncles and nieces was to have been prohibited by law'.[95] Ten chapters later it was asked how Abraham was innocent of adultery seeing as he had a child with the handmaid of his legitimate and still living wife; the answer given was that 'the evangelical law of one wife had not yet been promulgated'.[96] When a passage from Genesis was seemingly contradicted by one from Exodus, both were shown to have been true.[97] Making sense of the biblical text as a historical account of what happened corresponds precisely with the literal/historical mode of exegesis.

All of the difficult questions Frechulf addressed had long been answered, but evidently they remained relevant for Christian students and scholars to know. The example of Methuselah is a case in point. Chapter 16 began with Genesis 5:28–9 (Lamech lived 182 years, and begat a son, whom he called Noah). Frechulf then added: 'When Noah was 600 years old, there came a flood across all the earth,

[93] In general, see Gustave Bardy, 'La littérature patristique des *quaestiones et responsiones* sur l'Ecriture sainte', *Revue biblique*, 41 (1932): 210–36, 341–69, 515–37 and 42 (1933), 14–30 and 211–29 and 328–52. For the Carolingian context, see Pierre Riché, 'Instruments de travail et méthodes de l'exégète à l'époque carolingienne', in *Le Moyen Âge et la Bible*, eds Pierre Riché and Guy Lobrichon (Paris: Éditions Beauchesne, 1984), 147–61, at 158–60.

[94] *Hist.*, I.1.2 [1.2], p. 29; I.1.8 [1.2], p. 33; I.1.18, pp. 44–5; I.1.52 [1], p. 81.

[95] *Hist.*, I.1.39 [1/5], p. 71.

[96] *Hist.*, I.1.49 [1/9], p. 79.

[97] *Hist.*, I.1.47 [4], p. 78: 'Quod in utroque divina scriptura vera repperitur.'

which destroyed the whole human race except Noah, his sons and their wives, whom the Lord spared in the ark to restore humanity.'[98] In the context of the Flood, 'a most famous question ar[ose]'. The genealogical data supplied by the Septuagint version of Genesis suggested Methuselah, the grandfather of Noah, died fourteen years after the flood. How, it was asked, could this be true if he was not amongst those on the ark who were spared? Numerical error in the Greek translation of Genesis resolved the confusion, yet Frechulf did not include the faulty figures, nor did Claudius of Turin, on whose work he based his own rendering of the solution. The question continued to be *famosissima* because pre-eminent church fathers such as Jerome and Augustine had examined it 400 years earlier, before the Vulgate had eclipsed the Septuagint; it lived on not as a live chronological issue, but as an authoritative statement of scriptural inerrancy.[99]

Two important points emerge from this example: the plausibility and the sacred character of Genesis. Methuselah was understood to have lived to the biologically defying age of 969. Noah himself lived to be 950. Frechulf assured his readers that, when confronted with lives of such length, they were dealing with facts not fictions: 'if it seems incredible to anyone that the lifespan of ancient men was so long, they should take heed to the assertion of Josephus'. In the excerpt from the *Jewish Antiquities* which followed, it was explained that people were better nourished in the very distant past, and that God granted the earliest humans extra-long lives in order to help them make discoveries in astronomy and geometry.[100] Human longevity, which otherwise would have spelled disbelief, formed one part of the answer to another 'difficult question': how did Cain manage to build and populate the city Enoch (= Genesis 4:17), at a time when there only seemed to be three people alive in the world?[101] Frechulf reasoned (this time via Augustine) that, if men lived to be at least 750 years old, and that, if over the course of the 300 years separating Abraham and his grandson Jacob the Hebrew people had swelled to include 600,000 men, then is was no wonder (*mirum*) that, in the space of 800 years, Cain's family could grow large enough to construct and fill a city (and, indeed, cities) with people.[102]

A further argument was made to underline the historical reality of Enoch: 'it is believable (*credibile*) that Cain's city was commemorated [in Genesis] on account

---

[98] *Hist.*, I.1.16 [1/6], p. 43.

[99] Jerome, *Hebraicae Quaestiones in Libro Geneseos*, 5:25–7, ed. Paul de Legarde, CCSL 72 (Turnhout: Brepols, 1952), pp. 8–9; Augustine, *DCD*, XV.11, pp. 467–7. Thomas O'Loughlin, 'The Controversy over Methuselah's Death: Proto-Chronology and the Origins of the Western Concept of Inerrancy', *Recherches de théologie ancienne et médiévale*, 62 (1995): 182–225.

[100] *Hist.*, I.1.26 [1/21], p. 51–2: '... Ergo si cuilibet incredibile uidetur tantae diuturnitatis uitam antiquorum hominum fuisse, Iosephi adsertionem animaduertat ...'

[101] *Hist.*, I.1.9 [2/5], p. 34: 'Vnde quaeri potest: dum non plus eo tempore quam uiri quattuor, uel potius tres postea quam fratrem frater occidit, fuisse uiderentur in terra, quomodo Cain solus ciuitatem aedificasse dicitur?'

[102] *Hist.*, I.1.9 [26/36], pp. 35–6.

of the earthly city, which began from its very founder's disposition'.[103] Some of
the wider implications of Frechulf's description of Enoch City have recently been
teased out by Sam Ottewill-Soulsby.[104] From the description of Enoch's origins,
furthermore, stemmed Frechulf's overview of the Augustinian concept of the two
cities, of two human societies, one of the impious and one the just, which Nikolaus
Staubach unpacked in a seminal essay.[105] It is important, however, not to lose sight
of the basic exegetical purpose which Frechulf's reception of Augustine served: to
make sense of a verse from Genesis that could strain credulity and thus risked being
understood as unhistorical. Genesis was in some ways a historical narrative like any
other. It was seen by Christian exegetes to conform to the expectations of history,
namely that it be plausible and that it moreover be true. Isidore referred to Moses as
the first Christian historian; Frechulf labelled him 'the truth-telling historiographer
(*veridicus historiographus*)'.[106] That said, the source of Moses' truthfulness elevated
his narrative above the compositions of mere men. As with all of the scriptural
canon, Genesis was understood to have been the product of inspired authorship,
and so was accorded special status: 'sacred history (*sacra historia*)'.[107]

Sacred history was selective. When, for instance, Frechulf noted that Genesis
appeared to recount that there were only three people alive when Cain built a city,
he added (directly via *De civitate Dei*) that Moses, the 'writer of this sacred history
[i.e. Genesis]' did not list the names of all living people, only those necessary to
the work's 'plan', that is 'those through whom a genealogy was realised by narrating
first to Noah and then to Abraham'.[108] According to Augustine, the genealogy
represented the city of God, the community of just and pious worshippers whose
presence was occasionally noted in Genesis in amongst the impious; Frechulf
absorbed this idea directly through *De civitate Dei* and indirectly through Claudius
of Turin, a keen ninth-century reader of the bishop of Hippo.[109] Frechulf applied

---

[103] *Hist.*, I.1.9 [37.38], p. 36: 'Sed haec ciuitas Cain propter terrenam ciuitatem commemorata fuisse
credibile est, quae ab ipso constitutionis conditore initium sumpsit'. Neither Augustine nor Claudius
used the word *credibile*.

[104] Sam Ottewill-Soulsby, '"Hunting Diligently through the Volumes of the Ancients": Frechulf of
Lisieux on the First City and the End of Innocence', in *Remembering the Ancient City in the Post-
Antique World*, eds Javier Martinez Jimenez and Sam Ottewill-Soulsby (Oxford: forthcoming 2022).

[105] Staubach, '*Christiana tempora*' and Allen, 'Frechulf of Lisieux'.

[106] Isidore, *Etymologiae*, I.42.1. Trans. Barney *et al.*, *Etymologies*, 67: 'Among us Christians Moses was
the first to write a history, on creation.' *Hist.*, I.1.15 [8], p. 42.

[107] For a classic discussion of sacred vis-à-vis secular history in Augustine, see Markus, *Saeculum*,
1–21, esp. 12–15.

[108] *Hist.*, I.1.9 [5/10], pp. 34–5: 'Sed quos hoc mouet parum considerant non omnes homines qui tunc
esse potuerunt scriptorem sacrae huius historiae necesse habuisse nominare, sed eos solos quos operis
suscepti ratio postulabat, illos uidelicet per quos ad Noe ac deinde ad Abraham genealogia texendo
perduceretur.' Drawing on Augustine, *DCD*, XV.8, p. 463.

[109] On Claudius, see John Cavadini, 'Claudius of Turin and the Augustinian Tradition', *Proceedings of
the PMR Conference*, vol. 11 (Villanova: Villanova University, 1986), 43–50; Allen, 'Universal History',
39–40; Cristina Ricci, 'Claudius of Turin', in *The Oxford Guide to the Historical Reception of Augustine*,
eds Karla Pollmann and Willemien Otten, 3 vols (Oxford: OUP, 2013), vol. 2, 798–800.

the 'city of God' as a historical concept that threaded together his narrative, running first from Adam to Noah, then Noah to Abraham, and then onwards to Christ. For example, after God struck down the Tower of Babel and confounded humanity through the division of tongues (Genesis 11:9), the language of the first men was preserved in the house of Heber, a descendant of Noah's eldest son Seth. From Heber the language came to be called Hebrew; it was passed onto Abraham and then the patriarchs, through whom 'it poured forth into the people of God'. Not all descendants of Heber nor Abraham, however, inherited this language, but 'only those who appeared to pertain to the city of God, from whom Christ was born in the flesh (*secundum carnem*)'.[110] In the next chapter, the text's sacred and selective character was described more explicitly: Moses was selective, because to be exhaustive, 'would be exceedingly long, and would exhibit more historical accuracy than prophetic foresight. The writer of Sacred Scripture, therefore—or, rather, the Spirit of God acting through him—is concerned only with those events which both compose an account of the past and also foretell the future, and only with those which pertain to the City of God'.[111]

For Augustine, the city of God was above all a figurative and eschatological concept: the symbol of the Christian *ecclesia* and the shadow of what was to come at the end of time; the heavenly kingdom, where the saved would dwell for eternity.[112] The *civitas Dei* was the object both of historical and spiritual commentary. Frechulf, when summarising the parallel paths of the two cities, was clearly aware of the city of God's eschatological significance.[113] Yet for the most part, he stuck rigidly to the historical level and carefully worked around passages in Augustine and Claudius that dealt with the *spiritalis intellegentia*. A single example will suffice: Augustine understood the account of Noah's ark in Genesis to be a representation of reality, while also 'a symbol of ... the city of God, that is the Church'; he argued emphatically that the narrative ought to be taken both as historical fact and as a prefiguration of the *ecclesia* to come.[114] Frechulf devoted four chapters to the ark, all of which he extracted from Claudius's *Genesis Commentary*, who had already digested many insights from Augustine's tome. He was concerned only with the ark

---

[110] *Hist.*, I.1.32 [22/27], pp. 63–4: 'Quae per successiones peruenit ad Abraham, ac sic per patriarchas qui ex styrpe Abraham sunt propagati profusa est in populum Dei. Attamen nec Heber nec ipse pater Abraham in omnem progeniem suam hanc diffundere ualuerunt, sed in eos qui ad ciuitatem Dei pertinere uidebantur, de quibus secundum carnem natus est et Christus.' See also *Hist.*, I.1.15 [11/15], pp. 42–3: 'Sic namque Matheus non primogenitos tantum adsumens in cathalogo generationis Christi, sed eos ex quibus natiuitas Domini secundum carnem ducebatur.'

[111] *Hist.*, I.1.33 [15/19], p. 64; Augustine, *DCD*, XVI.2, p. 500. English trans. R. W. Dyson, *The City of God against the Pagans* (Cambridge: CUP, 1993), 697–8.

[112] The literature is vast: Gerard O'Daly, *Augustine's City of God: A Readers Guide* (Oxford: OUP, 1999), 53–66 and van Oort, *Jerusalem and Babylon* are helpful starting places.

[113] *Hist.*, I.1.9 [49/52], p. 36: '... ac deinceps per uniuersum orbem in membris eius haec ciuitas sancta fecundius aedificatur et ad ciues suos, angelos scilicet Dei, quotidie colligitur, quorum praesidiis in hac peregrinatione iugiter suffragatur'.

[114] Augustine, *DCD*, XV.27, pp. 495 and 497.

as an actual, physical, object, which, like the lifespans of the earliest humans, was hard to grasp historically. It was not to be thought beyond belief (*inpossibile*) that a ship of such a size once existed, on which so many different species of animal could fit.[115] Frechulf's sources offered him ample opportunity to move beyond history and to consider the ark as foreshadowing Christ and the *ecclesia*. After presenting the facts 'according to history (*iuxta historiam*)', Claudius had 'extended the sails of the spiritual understanding' and offered an exhaustive list of the ark's many mystical meanings.[116] Frechulf, by contrast, eschewed allegory.[117] Frechulf tapped into exegesis as a source of sacred knowledge, but only insofar as it reflected the historical level of truth. By contrast, a later Carolingian chronicler, Ado of Vienne, was perfectly content to maintain the allegory of his exegetical excerpts when discussing the ark, and something similar can be observed in Bede's *Greater Chronicle*. What distinguished Frechulf, therefore, was not simply the exegetical quality of his work, since exegesis was ubiquitous to medieval Christian culture; what was distinctive, rather, was his steadfast focus on the *veritas historiae*.[118]

One exception proves the rule. Chapter 17 centred on Genesis 4:23–4, in which Lamech, a descendant of Cain, confessed to his wives that he killed a man: 'Sevenfold vengeance shall be taken for Cain, but for Lamech seventy times sevenfold.' The sevenfold vengeances against Cain, it was explained, 'were paid back by the waters of the Flood, since all Cain's progeny'—down to Lamech, in the seventh generation from Adam—'was annihilated by it'. 'It is to be believed (*credibile*)', Frechulf added, 'that Lamech the murderer was counted amongst those who were to perish'.[119] But what about the seventy-seven vengeances on Lamech?

> According to the truth of history, seventy-seven generations are discovered from Adam to Christ, in which the sin of Lamech [= Luke 3:23–38], that is, the sin of the whole world, was fulfilled by the shedding of Christ's blood. Indeed, seventy-seven vengeances were established in the Jewish people on account of the murder

---

[115] *Hist.*, I.1.21–4, pp. 47–9.

[116] Claudius, *Commentarii in Genesim, PL* 50, cols. 929D–932C. Compare *Hist.*, I.1.23 [13/16], p. 49.

[117] Where appropriate, Frechulf utilised Claudius, but at I.1.8 he inserted extracts from Augustine's *DCD* which interpreted God's warning to Cain about sacrifice (Gn. 4:7) in the light of sin and repentance, while Claudius (drawing on Augustine's *Conra faustum*) focused on the typological comparison between Cain and Abel as Jews and Christians. Later on, Frechulf inserted Alcuin's 165th, 166th and 168th *quaestiones* in three sequential chapters (I.1.44–6, pp. 76–7); he ignored quaestio 167, which asked: 'Quid igitur in illo mystico signo de posteritate generis sui Abrahae intelligendum erat?' (*PL* 100, col. 536D). Compare *Hist.*, I.1.5 [1/3], p. 30: 'Erat utique in paradiso corporaliter lignum quod nuncupatur uitae, sicut et petra quae percussa aquas praebuit in heremo populo Dei, quamuis significarent mystice Christum.' Frechulf of course knew the language of mystical commentary.

[118] For example, Ado, *Chronicon, PL* 123, cols. 29B–33A: 'In hac secunda aetate sacrae litterae continent, praeter veritatem historicam, fidem et sacramentis plenam Patrum obedientiam ...' See further Elisabeth Mégier, 'Karolingische Weltchronistik zwischen Historiographie und Exegese: Frechulf von Lisieux und Ado von Vienne', in *Diligens scrutator sacri eloquii. Beiträge zur Exegese- und Theologiegeschichte des Mittelalters. Festgabe für Rainer Berndt SJ zum 65. Geburtstag*, eds Matthias M. Tischler, Hanns Peter Neuheuser and Ralf M. W. Stammberger (Münster: Aschendorff, 2016), 37–52.

[119] *Hist.*, I.1.17 [8/10], p. 44: 'Inter reliquos perituros ipsum homicidam Lamech repperisse credibile est.'

of Christ, in accordance with that Gospel [= Matthew 18:21–2] in which the apostle Peter was told that if anyone should offend his brother, they ought to be forgiven not only seven times, but seventy-seven times: that is to say, after the seventy-seven vengeances have been established, the returning Jewish people will be received with the indulgence of Christ.[120]

The last lines of this passage drift towards allegory and eschatology, by looking out to the end of history. Yet it otherwise speaks to the core problem of this chapter, since in it we see 'the truth of history' in action.[121] Here *veritas* was predicated upon the authority of scripture; historical truth was bound up not simply with the accuracy of Genesis as a narrative of events, but as testament to what would happen in the future. Cain's curse was undone by the Flood; Lamech's by the coming of Christ. Constructed retrospectively by Christian exegetes, the later realisation of prophecy became integral to Moses' status as a 'truth-telling historiographer'. The New Testament resolution of the seventy-seven-fold vengeances against Lamech can be compared to Frechulf's reception of Augustine: the city of God denoted the sacred genealogy that connected Adam, Noah and Abraham, and ultimately it was from this line that Christ was born in the flesh (*secundum carnem*). History, after all, was the stuff of the flesh. To read scripture literally was also to read it *corporaliter*. Its mystical, spiritual meaning, the purview of most biblical commentary, lay outside Frechulf's remit.

Conclusion

Frechulf's *Histories* exist at the nexus of historiography and exegesis. Frechulf, an educated churchman and a keen reader of the canon of Christian history-writing, was clearly familiar with the topoi of historians and the basic tenets of rhetorical narrative. Above all in Book 1, he also displayed his knowledge of the art of exegesis. Rhetorical *historia* and exegesis most obviously intersect at the concept of truth: Frechulf made it clear at several different moments that Genesis was believable, perhaps in line with the rhetorical demands of verisimilitude. Be that as it may, the 'truth of history' was undoubtedly a technical term of biblical hermeneutics. To what end did he apply it? As a historian dipping his toes into commentary? Or as an exegete applying his critical mind to historiography?

Frechulf's first book, as he encapsulated it, 'contain[ed] in part (*partim*) the truth of history from the origin of the world through to the birth of Abraham'. It

---

[120] *Hist.*, I.1.17 [12/20], p. 44: 'Secundum historiae tamen ueritatem ab Adam usque ad Christum LXXVII generationes inueniuntur, in quibus peccatum Lamech, id est totius mundi, sanguinis Christi effusione solutum est. Siquidem et in populo Iudaeorum propter interfectionem Christi LXXVII uindictae sunt statutae, iuxta illud euangelium in quo dictum est Petro apostolo non solum septies, sed etiam septuagies septies si poenituerit fratri remittendum: Iudaeum scilicet reuertentem post LXXVII uindictas statutas recipiendum ad indulgentiam Christi.'

[121] Claudius of Turin, Frechulf's source, stated only 'secundum historiam': *PL* 50, col. 924B.

'encompassed two ages' and, to boot, tackled a number of difficult questions relating to interpretation of Genesis, 'insofar as it pertains to the narrative of [the] events (*quantum adtinet ad rei gestae narrationem*)'.[122] Frechulf employed two variations of this latter phrase to describe his explicitly exegetical tasks. He 'took care to elucidate, in accordance with the traditions of venerable authors, questions which seemed difficult in the writings of the truth-telling Lawgiver, insofar as it pertains to the plan of [the] history (*quantum ad historiae rationem*)'.[123] Last but not least, textual difficulties in Genesis were also worked out, 'insofar as it pertains to the truth of [the] history (*quantum adtinet ad historiae veritatem*)'.[124] History's truth and plan (*veritas* and *ratio*) were equated with the narrative of Genesis. Besides paralleling Isidore's definition of *historia* as a *narratio rei gestae*, these phrases derive from the toolkit of exegetes and denote the historical interpretation of scripture, specifically here the first book of the Christian Bible. Each instance of *historia* might best be translated with a definite article, since it reflects a specific book, indeed even specific passages or episodes within that book: the truth of *the* narrative contained within Genesis. Here the phrase clearly aligns with the use of scriptural exegesis.

Frechulf's focus on the 'writings of the Lawgiver', however, was always subordinated to a less textually precise search for truth. Book 1, as just noted, 'contain[ed] the truth of history' from Adam to Abraham; looking ahead to the rest of Part I, he added that 'in the subsequent [six] books, we strive to investigate the truth of history according to the goal of our study'.[125] This goal, crisply expressed in the prologue to Helisachar, was to 'hunt diligently through the volumes of the ancients and collect briefly and clearly all that pertains to the truth of history, from the creation of the first man through to the birth of the Lord Christ'.[126] Did the meaning and force of the phrase *veritas historiae* change when it was applied to the writings of the Lawgiver and when it was applied to all history between Adam and Christ, as transmitted by the *volumina antiquorum*?[127] To answer these questions, a careful examination of the remainder of Frechulf's first volume of *Histories* is necessary, which is the subject of the next chapter.

To conclude this chapter, let me return briefly to Hrabanus Maurus. In his handbook on clerical instruction (*De institutione clericorum*), Hrabanus explained that all priests must possess a thorough grasp of scripture, as well as having 'an abundance of knowledge, rectitude of life and a full education'. 'For one may not neglect', he continued, 'any of those things, with which [those who administer

---

[122] *Hist.*, I.1.57 [14/20], p. 84.
[123] *Hist.*, I.2.Prol. [8/11], p. 85: 'Insuper etiam quae difficilia uidentur in ueridici Legislatoris scriptis, quantum ad historiae rationem adtinet, elucidare secundum traditiones uenerabilium curaui auctorum.'
[124] *Hist.*, I.Prol. [21/24], p. 18.
[125] *Hist.*, I.1.57 [18/20], p. 84: 'In sequentibus uero libris historiae ueritatem secundum propositum studii nostri indagare curabimus.'
[126] *Hist.*, I.Prol. [13/17], p. 18.
[127] Mégier, 'Frechulf und Ado', 38–43 argues it did.

the church] ought to instruct either themselves or their subjects'. These things comprised 'the knowledge of the sacred scriptures, the pure truth of histories (*pura veritas historiarum*), the modes of figurative speech, the meaning of mystical things and the utility of all disciplines'.[128] In this context the 'pure truth of histories' seemingly relates to the historical interpretation of scripture. For Hrabanus, moreover, exegesis was not simply an intellectual genre, but a mode of thought that guided the lives of educated Christians.

Several chapters later Hrabanus highlighted that historiography could be brought to bear on the interpretation of the Bible.[129] In his exegesis, Hrabanus put this into practice. He began his commentary on the Old Testament Book of Judith with a historical overview of the Assyrian and Median kingdoms, so as to set this biblical story in its proper context.[130] This was done:

> so that the diligent reader, coming across any notice gathered briefly by us in this work of the kings of the Assyrians and Medes, may be better prepared to track down the truth of history (*paratius historiae indagare possit veritatem*), having discerned the succession of the kings, to which the order of the narrative of the above mentioned kings especially agrees.[131]

Frechulf, part of the same cultural and intellectual milieu as Hrabanus, employed similar technical language: his own purpose in the first part of his *Histories* was also to 'track down the truth of history'.[132] Establishing the order of past events and the succession of kings and kingdoms was for him likewise crucial. This was not done in order to frame an interpretation of a single biblical book, but rather to comprehend the whole sequence of the past between Adam and Christ. Frechulf's use of exegetical sources in his first book is distinctive, but, as we shall now see, the discourse of contemporary biblical scholarship and its broad aims continued to shape his analysis of authoritative Christian history-writing.

---

[128] Hrabanus, *De institutione clericorum*, III.1, p. 435.

[129] Hrabanus, *De institutione clericorum*, III.17, pp. 464 (drawing on Augustine, *De doctrina christiana*, II. 42; ed. and trans. R. P. H. Green, p. 55).

[130] Hrabanus Maurus, *Expositio in Librum Judith*, PL 109, cols. 539–92C, at cols. 541C–543B.

[131] Hrabanus, *Judith*, PL 109, col. 543C: 'Haec autem ideo posuimus, ut lector diligens aliquam notitiam regum Assyriorum atque Medorum in praedicto opere breviter a nobis succinctam inveniens, paratius agnitis regum successionibus historiae indagare possit veritatem, cui maxime praedictorum regum ordo narrationis conveniat'. Compare Hrab. *Epist.*, no. 19, pp. 424–5, 30/2; trans. De Jong, 'Empire as Ecclesia', 217.

[132] *Hist.*, I.1.57 [18/20], p. 84.

3

Reframing Eusebius-Jerome's *Chronicle*

'As if Depicted on a Concise Chart'

Angelomus of Luxeuil began his commentary on Genesis (written in the early 830s), a text encountered briefly in the previous chapter, by reflecting on the qualities that marked out Moses as an exceptional authority:

> And how can we accord him confidence that what he said was true, unless because what happened in the past is often confirmed by what happened in the future, and what happens in the future by what happened in the past, as it is proved in the Book of Daniel and is shown in this book [that is, Genesis]? The man Moses wrote about the time when there was no man, when he says, *In the beginning God created heaven and earth* (Gen. 1:1). For just as a man wrote about that time when there was no man, he also wrote about future events, in a time when there was man, which were afterwards confirmed as fulfilled in truth, as is declared in the blessing of the patriarch Jacob , on which he himself says, *The sceptre shall not be taken from Judah* (Gen. 49:10), etcetera, which was foretold as a prefiguration of Christ, but already they are believed to have been fulfilled in truth. For if he had not said the truth about the future, no one would have been willing to believe what he wrote about the past, which was certain.[1]

For Angelomus, accepting Moses' truthfulness concerning the past was predicated upon his knowledge about the future, since what he predicted was confirmed by events which happened long after he wrote. Truth and history were thus intimately bound up with the inspired, prophetic powers of biblical authors. Angelomus

---

[1] Angelomus, *Commentarius in Genesin*, PL 115, col. 111D–112B: 'Et quomodo ei fidem accommodare possumus, vera dixisse, nisi quia futuris saepe probantur praeterita, et praeteritis futura, sicut in Daniele comprobatur, et in hoc libro ostenditur? Denique de illo tempore Moyses scripsit homo, quando non erat homo, cum ait: In principio creavit Deus coelum et terrant. Sicut enim de illo tempore scripsit homo, quando non erat homo; ita etiam futura scripsit eo tempore, quando erat homo, quae postea expleta comprobantur in veritate, sicut in patriarchae Jacob benedictione declaratur, juxta quod ipse ait dicens: Non auferetur sceptrum de Juda, etc., quae in figura Christi praedicta fuerant; sed jam in veritate creduntur completa. Si enim de futuro verum non dixisset, de praeterito, quod certum scripserit, nemo credere voluisset.' Translation adapted from Gorman, 'Angelomus', appendix 1, pp. 606-7.

drew attention to the penultimate chapter of Genesis, in which the patriarch Jacob blessed his twelve children. In particular, he singled out the prophecy Jacob uttered to his son Judah (49:10), which was of foundational importance for the Christian interpretation of the Bible since it was believed to predict Christ's birth. In addition to Moses, Angelomus also highlighted Daniel's prophetic foresight, which likewise was celebrated by Christian exegetes insofar as it related to the Nativity, a pivotal moment within Christianity. 'None of the prophets', Jerome had stressed in his seminal *Daniel Commentary* (written c. 407), 'had spoken with such clarity concerning Christ. For not only did [Daniel] assert that [Christ] would come, a prediction common to the other prophets as well, but also he showed the time at which he would come.'[2]

Besides reiterating the exegetical resonances underpinning Frechulf's pursuit of the 'the truth of history', Angelomus' words help frame this current chapter, which, moving beyond Frechulf's treatment of pre-Abrahamic history, examines the next six books of Part I. Both of the prophecies to which Angelomus alluded— Genesis 49:10 and those found in the Book of Daniel—are vital for understanding the overall story that propelled the first part of the *Histories*. In the dedicatory prologue addressed to Helisachar, Frechulf set out the broad contours of this narrative. Having covered pre-Abrahamic history, he was next instructed:

> to keep a careful count of years through the kings of the Assyrians, the Medes and the Persians, and the Greeks, down to the monarchy of Octavian Caesar (the peoples to whom the empire of the Assyrians was transferred in succeeding ages) and, in the case of the people of God, through the patriarchs, judges, kings and priests, and then kings again, and to note whatever deeds were worthy of memory in each part of the world. And I was to show how certain things are eternally/endlessly repeated during each era, when and where they took place, who was ruling at the time in the most important kingdoms, and who ruled over the people of God. In addition, you prompted me to bring together and arrange in an abbreviated form the history of the Jews from the destruction of the Temple at Jerusalem until the birth of our lord Christ, since these events appear confused on account of the disasters that befell them.[3]

---

[2] Jerome, *In Danielem*, Prol. [14/16], p. 772: 'in praeftione commoneo, nullum prophetarum tam aperte dixisse de Christo: non enim solum scribit eum esse uenturum, quod est commune cum ceteris, sed quo tempore uenturus sit docet.' Translation by Gleason L. Archer, which is based upon the PL edition: http://www.tertullian.org/fathers/jerome_daniel_02_text.htm. Compare Augustine, *DCD*, XVIII.34, p. 628. On Jerome's Daniel commentary, see Régis Coutray, *Prophète des temps derniers: Jérôme commente Daniel* (Paris: Beauchesne, 2009) and 'La réception du "Commentaire sur Daniel" de Jérôme dans l'Occident médiéval chrétien (VII–XII siècle), *Sacris Erudiri*, 44 (2005): 117–87.

[3] *Hist.*, I.Prol. [24/37], pp. 18–19: 'inde autem per reges Assyriorum, Medorum, atque Persarum, siue Grecorum, et usque Octouiani Caesaris monarchiam, ad quas gentes Assyriorum diriuando regnum per succedentia peruenit tempora, in populo autem Dei per patriarchas, iudices, reges ac sacerdotes, iterum que reges, numerum custodire annorum cautius obseruarem, et ea quae gesta in singulis mundi partibus et memoria sunt digna adnotarem, ut quaeque inmortaliter per singula frequentantur tempora, quando uel ubi fuerint, qui tunc etiam imperauerint in eminentioribus regnis uel qui populo praefuerint Dei ostenderem. Insuper a destructione templi Hierosolimitani usque ad Domini natiuitatem Christi,

Frechulf restated much of this material in the additional prologue he inserted between the first two books of Part I.[4] He was to take heed of the sequence of years (*numerus/series annorum*) running through history, in relation to the pre-eminent kingdoms of the ancient world as well as 'the people of God', that is, the Hebrews. Within this chronological framework, Frechulf was to chart the rise, fall and transformation of kingdoms, while also drawing attention to the achievements of renowned individuals and recording memorable deeds. To help with this monumental undertaking, Helisachar presented Frechulf with material support, in the form of a text that was to serve as the template for the construction of Part I of the *Histories*. 'All these things', Frechulf reminded his *praeceptor*, 'you showed me … as though depicted on a concise chart, and leaving me no opportunity to refuse, you ordered me to get to work quickly'.[5] Pleasingly, this 'concise chart' or, as Michael Allen translated it, 'compendious table', on which so much was compressed can be identified: the *Chronicle* of Eusebius-Jerome.[6]

Writing in Greek in the first decades of the fourth century, Eusebius, bishop of Caesarea, produced his now-lost two-volume *Chronological Canons*. The first volume, known as the *Chronography*, consisted of a large collection of synchronised regnal lists and snippets from historical texts. The second part, the *Canons*, was based on the data contained within the first and it proved to be a source of enormous and long-lasting importance, both in the eastern and the western ends of the Christian Roman world.[7] In the west, this was due to Jerome's Latin translation, elaboration and continuation, carried out c. 380.[8] Jerome rendered

---

quaeque in populo gesta sunt Iudaeorum, quoniam confusa propter calamitates quae eis acciderunt esse uidentur, ordinando summatim colligere instigasti.' Translation adapted from Lake, *Prologues*, 112.
[4] *Hist.*, I.2.Prol. [12/27], pp. 85–6.
[5] *Hist.*, I.Prol. [37/40], p. 19: 'Haec quidem omnia ceu picta breui in tabula meae ostendens paruitati nullam excusationis occasionem reliquisti, sed otius operam dare imperasti.' Translation adapted from Lake, *Prologues*, p. 112.
[6] *Prolegomena*, 16*. *Chron.*; all translations from Eusebius-Jerome are based on the collaborative 2005 English translation available at: https://www.tertullian.org/fathers/jerome_chronicle_00_eintro.htm.
[7] Armenian version: Eusebius, *Die Chronik aus dem Armenischen Übersetzung, mit textkritischem Commentar*, ed. Josef Karst, *Eusebius Werke*, vol. 5 (Leipzig: J.C. Hinrichs, 1911); for the Syriac reception, see Witold Witakowski, 'The *Chronicle* of Eusebius: Its Type and Continuation in Syriac Historiography', *Aram*, 12 (2000): 419–37; for the Greek reception, William Adler, 'Eusebius' *Chronicle* and its Legacy', in *Eusebius, Christianity and Judaism*, eds Harold W. Attridge and Gohei Hata (Detroit, MI: Wayne State University Press, 1992), 467–91.
[8] For recent treatments, see Christopher Kelly, 'The Shape of the Past: Eusebius of Caesarea and Old Testament History', in *Unclassical Traditions, Volume I. Alternatives to the Classical Past in Late Antiquity*, eds. Christopher Kelly, Richard Flower and Michael Stuart Williams (Cambridge Classical Journal, Proceedings of the Cambridge Philological Society, Supplementary Volume 34, 2010), 13–27; Anthony Grafton and Megan Hale Williams, *Christianity and the Transformation of the Book: Origen, Eusebius, and the Library of Caesarea* (Cambridge, MA: HUP, 2006), 133–77; Mark Vessey, 'Reinventing History: Jerome's *Chronicle* and the Writing of the Post-Roman West', in *From the Tetrarchs to the Theodosians: Later Roman History and Culture, 284–450 CE*, eds Scott McGill, Cristiana Sogno and Edward Watts (Cambridge: CUP, 2010), 265–89. Richard W. Burgess, 'Jerome Explained: An Introduction to his Chronicle and a Guide to its Use', *Ancient History Bulletin*, 16 (2002): 1–32 [repr. in his *Chronicles, Consuls, and Coins: Historiography and History in the Later Roman Empire* (Farnham: Ashgate, 2011)]

into Latin the Greek original, which extended to 325, while also peppering it with supplementary notes concerning Roman history and literature; he attached, moreover, his own original continuation from 325 to 378. For the many medieval readers of the *Chronicle*, it should be noted, there was no Eusebius independent from Jerome. For this reason, when discussing the authority and authorship of the *Chronicle*, the combined name Eusebius-Jerome is commonly used.

The structure of Eusebius-Jerome is unique, and unusual Latin vocabulary, coined by the sixteenth-century chronologist Joseph Scaliger, is still employed to describe it.[9] The past was represented in a graphic, tabular form and began with the birth of Abraham in the reign of King Ninus of the Assyrians.[10] Throughout its carefully regulated pages, different kingdoms were given their own columns—the *fila regnorum* or *fila annorum*—and each column named the successive rulers of a given realm and counted the years they ruled. The spaces between these columns—the *spatia historica*—recorded the deeds and achievements of various peoples and powers. As the *Chronicle* progressed, columns variously sprang up and disappeared as new kingdoms arose and old powers perished. Until construction of the Second Temple in Jerusalem (521 BC), columns and events were presented across double-page spreads, with biblical history presented on the left-hand page and secular on the right; afterwards, when the historical record of scripture dried up and all history became extra-biblical, the format switched to a single-page layout. From that point on, the listed ruling nations gradually thinned out. After the death of Cleopatra (30 BC), only Jewish and Roman columns were left; following the destruction of the Second Temple by Titus and Vespasian in AD 70, the Roman *filum* alone remained, visually illustrating the empire's perceived global dominance.

Far from the Latin prose of the classical Roman world, Eusebius-Jerome's *Chronicle* marked a radical shift in both the content and form of historiography. This 'concise chart' fused the disparate histories of various realms into an expansive yet unified Christian whole. It amounted to 'something like a comprehensive political, religious, and cultural history of the ancient world, one that served until the sixteenth century as the richest single source of information for anyone interested in the history of human culture'.[11] Throughout the Middle Ages it was the foundation upon which almost all knowledge of the chronology of Mediterranean antiquity was based. Jerome himself never referred to the *Chronicle* as a *brevis tabula* as Frechulf was later to do, but he did employ very similar imagery when describing his own efforts to produce compact compilations. For instance, he

---

is helpful although written with ancient historians in mind.

[9] Burgess, 'Jerome Explained': On Scaliger: Anthony Grafton, *Joseph Scaliger: A Study in the History of Classical Scholarship, Vol. 2: Historical Chronology* (Oxford: Clarendon Press, 1993), 514–36 and 569–91.

[10] Eusebius drew inspiration from Origen's *Hexapla*: Grafton and Williams, *Transformation of the Book*, esp. 170.

[11] Grafton and Williams, *Transformation of the Book*, 137–40.

likened his psalm commentary to the work of cartographers, who 'depict the locations of lands and cities *in brevi tabella* and attempt to display the most distant regions upon a small space'.[12] Frechulf's allusion to the *Chronicle—ceu picta brevi in tabula*—resembles Jerome's characterisation of maps of the world and encapsulates how he viewed the *Chronicle*: as a map of history, in which past events were located and dated within space and time.

The central role that Eusebius-Jerome played in the making of Part I of Frechulf's *Histories* has by no means gone unnoticed. In 1952, Bertha Schelle had already identified the *Chronicle* as Frechulf's 'principal source (*Hauptquelle*)', but Michael Allen has above all laid the groundwork for what follows. A cursory glance at the *index auctorum* at the back of the *Prolegomena* to Allen's edition reveals the sheer extent of Frechulf's borrowings from the *Chronicle*.[13] Allen, moreover, made the essential connection between the *Chronicle* and the 'compendious table' that Helisachar was said to have supplied to Frechulf, and has also underscored Eusebius-Jerome's contribution to shaping the bishop of Lisieux's sense of chronology, which I shall build upon below.[14] Expanding the compressed, tabulated form of the *Chronicle* into a richly detailed narrative stands out as one of the most striking of Frechulf's achievements. His critical engagement with the *Chronicle* does not account for everything that he did in Part I, yet it helps understand crucial aspects of his narrative from Abraham to Christ, not least its structure, principal themes and exegetical inflections. To begin, however, it is important to survey the late antique and early medieval reception of *Chronicle*, as well as the text's manuscript transmission. By appreciating the reactions and responses of earlier authors and compilers, we are better placed to assess Frechulf's.

Eusebius-Jerome's *Chronicle*: Transmission and Reception

Only relatively recently have modern scholars begun to take Eusebius-Jerome's *Chronicle* seriously as a sophisticated literary text.[15] Robert Markus, in his classic study of Augustine, assumed that the *Chronicle*, or at least the chronographic genre it represented, 'can scarcely be called "history"'. It was a way of meeting a

[12] Jerome, *Commentarioli in Psalmos*, Prol., ed. Germanus Morin, CCSL 72 (Turnhout: Brepols,1959), 177–8: 'quod solent ii facere, qui in breui tabella terrarum et urbium situs pingunt, et latissimas regiones in modico spatio conantur ostendere'. Jerome elsewhere used this same phrase but in different contexts. Exegesis: *Commentarius in Ecclesiasten* 12:1, ed. Marcus Adriaen, CCSL 72 (Turnhout: Brepols), pp. 247–361, at XII: 1, p. 349; *Commentariorum in Esaiam* 18 (66:22), ed. Marcus Adriaen, CCSL 73A (Turnhout: Brepols, 1963), 796; *Commentariorum in Hiezechielem libri XIV*, 9 (30: 1–19), ed. Franciscus Glorie, CCSL 75 (Turnhout: Brepols, 1964), 423. Letters: *Epistulae*, Ep. 60, 7, ed. Isidorus Hilberg, 3 vols, CSEL 54–56 (Vienna: Verlag der österreichischen Akademie der Wissenschaften, 1996), vol. 1, p. 556; Ep. 73, 5, ed. Hilberg, vol. 2, p. 17; Ep. 123, 12, ed. Hilberg, vol. 3, p. 87.
[13] *Prolegomena*, 292*–306*.
[14] *Prolegomena*, 16*, 208*–210*; 'Universal History', 9–41; 'Complementary Notes', 736–9.
[15] J. N. D. Kelly, *Jerome: His Life, Writings, and Controversies* (London: Duckworth, 1975), 72–5; there are more examples in Burgess, 'Jerome Explained', 1, 6–7.

need for elementary Christian orientation in a predominantly pagan world, rather than of catering for a desire to know about the past.[16] There has since been a huge amount of work on chronicles which has revised this view, much of it specifically on Eusebius-Jerome.[17] The *Chronicle*'s sharp, sophisticated, apologetic emphases have now been laid bare and its status as Christian literature affirmed.[18] Its various influences on subsequent historiography, moreover, continue to be underlined. Eusebius-Jerome formed the foundation of a vast range of historical works throughout the Middle Ages and beyond, and the extent to which the *Chronicle* shaped subsequent history-writing can scarcely be overstated.[19] Later chroniclers often made the *Chronicle* their starting point, thus harnessing their own works to its 'great streams of divine time'.[20] Jerome himself jump started this process by not only translating, but also augmenting Eusebius's original Greek text with a great many notices on Roman history, as well as appending his own continuation, marked simply with: 'up to this point Eusebius of Pampilius, companion of the martyrs wrote this history, to which we ourselves add the following'.[21] In the fifth century, Hydatius and the so-called 'Chronicler of 452' followed Jerome in appending their own continuations onto the combined stalk of Eusebius-Jerome, signalling where their own contributions began.[22] There was scope, moreover, for re-imagining the shape of the *Chronicle* rather than simply continuing it. Prosper of Aquitaine wrote several continuations (to 433, 445, 451, then 455), which were attached to the core Eusebius-Jerome stalk; he also produced a streamlined, epitomised version of the *Chronicle*, in which its multiple columns were collapsed into one, and the chronology was extended back to Adam.[23] Eusebius-Jerome

---

[16] Markus, *Saeculum*, 4.

[17] In general, see Richard W. Burgess and Michael Kulikowski, *Mosaics of Time: The Latin Chronicle Traditions from the First Century BC to the Sixth Century AD* (Turnhout: Brepols, 2013).

[18] Kelly, 'Shape of the Past'; Vessey, 'Reinventing History'; Madeline McMahon, 'Polemic in Translation: Jerome's Fashioning of History in the *Chronicle*', in *Historiography and Identity I: Ancient and Early Christian Narratives of Community*, eds Helmut Reimitz and Veronika Wieser (Turnhout: Brepols, 2019), 219–45.

[19] Von den Brincken, *Studien*, 65: 'Sie ist nicht nur eine unter vielen Vorlagen, sondern das Fundament der gesamten nachfolgenden Chronistik'; Mireille Chazan, 'La *Chronique* de Jérôme: source, modèle ou autorité?', in *Apprendre, produire, se conduire: le modèle au Moyen Âge. XLVᵉ Congrès de la SHMESP (Nancy-Metz, 22 mai–25 mai 2014)* (Paris: Éditions de la Sorbonne, 2015), 261–74.

[20] Andrew H. Merrills, *History and Geography in Late Antiquity* (Cambridge: CUP, 2005), 22.

[21] *Chron.*, p. 231 [12/13]: 'Huc usque historiam scribit Eusebius Pamphili martyris contubernalis. Cui nos ista subiecimus'.

[22] Hydatius, *Chronicle*, ed. R. W. Burgess, *The Chronicle of Hydatius and the Consularia Constantinopolitana: Two Contemporary Accounts of the Final Years of the Roman Empire* (Oxford: OUP, 1993), 71; *Chronicle of 452*, ed. Richard Burgess, 'The Gallic Chronicle of 452: A New Critical Edition with a Brief Introduction', in *Society and Culture in Late Antique Gaul: Revisiting the Sources*, eds Ralph W. Mathisen and Danuta Shanzer (Aldershot: Ashgate, 2001), pp. 52–84, at 67.

[23] Prosper, *Chronicle*, ed. Theodor Mommsen, MGH SS Auct. Ant. 9 (Berlin: Weidmann, 1892), pp. 385–485. Steven Muhlberger, *The Fifth-century Chroniclers: Prosper, Hydatius, and the Gallic Chronicler of 452* (Leeds: F. Cairns, 1990), 48–135; Mark Humphries, 'Chronicle and Chronology: Prosper of Aquitaine, his Methods and the Development of Early Medieval Chronography', *EME*, 5(2)

also was central to the efforts of two Frankish historians in the sixth and seventh centuries, Gregory of Tours and the so-called Chronicle of Fredegar.[24]

Two later figures proved to be especially seminal: Isidore of Seville and the Northumbrian monk Bede. Isidore wrote a so-called *Lesser Chronicle*, which marked the climax to Book 5 of his *Etymologies* (completed 627/8).[25] He also wrote a *Greater Chronicle*, the first redaction of which was written under the Visigothic king Sisebut in 615/16, and the second under King Swinthila in 626.[26] In both texts, the prominence of Eusebius-Jerome is clear. Several chapters before the *Lesser Chronicle* in the *Etymologies*, Isidore wrote:

> 'Chronicle' (*chronica*) is the Greek term for what is called a 'succession of times' (*series temporum*) in Latin. Among the Greeks Eusebius, Bishop of Caesarea, compiled such a work, and the priest Jerome translated it into Latin. χρόνος in Greek means 'time' in Latin.[27]

The prologue to the *Greater Chronicle* began by noting that after Julius Africanus, 'Eusebius of Caesarea and Jerome of sacred memory published the complex history of the chronological canons, simultaneously ordered by kingdoms and times'.[28] Isidore here showed his familiarity with Eusebius-Jerome's distinctive layout, yet he himself followed the path of Prosper by collapsing the multiple, parallel columns into a single channel of sequential material. Isidore, however, was himself an innovator, leaving an influential mark on the genre: he introduced the Augustinian 'ages of the world (*aetates mundi*)' as a mechanism for ordering time, which divided the whole course of history into six periods or ages which

---

(1996): 155–75; Robert Markus, 'Chronicle and Theology: Prosper of Aquitaine', in *The Inheritance of Historiography 350–900*, eds Christopher Holdsworth and T. P. Wiseman (Liverpool: LUP, 1986), 31–43. The continuation begins: 'Hucusque Hieronimus presbyter ordinem praecentium digessit annorum: nos quae consecuta sint adicere curavimus' (ed. Mommsen, p. 460); epitome begins: 'Quibus et generationes ab Adam ad Abraham et a passione Domini omnes consules et quae consecuta sint … (p. 385).

[24] Reimitz, *History*; Justin Lake, 'Rethinking Fredegar's Prologue', *The Journal of Medieval Latin*, 25 (2015): 1–28.

[25] Isidore, *Etymologiae*, V. 39; trans. Barney *et al.*, *Etymologies*, 130–3, pp. 130–3. Isidore did not call this a lesser chronicle, but *De descriptione temporum*, 'a description of historical periods'.

[26] Both redactions are edited by Jose Carlos Martin in *Isidori Hispalensis chronica*, CCSL 112 (Turnhout: Brepols, 2003). See Sam Koon and Jamie Wood, 'The *Chronica Maiora* of Isidore of Seville: An Introduction and Translation', *e-Spania* 6 (2008), available online at: http://e-spania.revues.org/15552 [last accessed 2 June 2019] For a discussion of this complicated text, see Martin's edition along with Jamie Wood, *The Politics of Identity in Visigothic Spain: Religion and Power in the Histories of Isidore of Seville* (Leiden: Brill, 2012), 70–2. On the *Chronicle*, see also Paul M. Bassett, 'The Use of History in the *Chronicon* of Isidore of Seville', *History and Theory*, 15 (1976): 278–92.

[27] Isidore, *Etymologies*, V. 28: 'Chronica Graece dicitur quae Latine temporum series appellatur, qualem apud Graecos Eusebius Caesariensis episcopus edidit, et Hieronymus presbyter in Latinam linguam conuertit'. Trans., p. 125. See Henderson, *The Medieval World of Isidore of Seville: Truth from Words* (Cambridge: CUP, 2007), 75, 80 and 93–8, and Wood, *Politics of Identity*, ch. 3.

[28] Isidore, *Chronica*, p. 4: 'Dehinc Eusebius Caesariensis atque sanctae memoriae Hieronymus chronicorum canonum multiplicem ediderunt historiam regnis simul ac temporibus ordinatam'; trans. adapted from Koon and Wood.

corresponded to the six ages of human development, from the infancy of the first age to the sixth age, beginning with the birth of Christ and lasting until the world's end.[29]

Around a century later, Bede made his contribution to chronicle writing. Bede was a reader of Isidore and, like the archbishop of Seville, wrote two chronicles which are framed around 'ages of the world' and similarly are labelled by modern scholars *Lesser* and *Greater*.[30] Of the two, the *Chronica maiora*—which formed chapter 66 of his *De temporum ratione* ('On the Reckoning of Time'), completed c. 725—was considerably fuller and had greater impact upon future chronicles. Beyond the *aetates mundi*, Bede offered an important new take on world chronology. He made frequent and substantial use of Eusebius-Jerome's *Chronicle*, but also wondered why Jerome had 'translated the book of chronicles (*librum Chronicorum*), [though] did not wish to pass to the Latins the truth he had learned from the Hebrews'.[31] Bede here put his finger on a perceived discrepancy in Jerome's transmitted corpus. Jerome's Latin rendition of Eusebius predated his biblical translations. As a result, this earlier work retained the chronologies derived from the Septuagint, chronologies which the publication of his Vulgate would reset. Bede aimed to rectify this perceived wrong by supplying his chronicle with figures reflecting the Hebrew Truth.

Bede's *Greater Chronicle* exerted considerable influence in the Carolingian period, arguably to a greater degree than his now better-known *Ecclesiastical History*.[32] Bede provided the backbone for a number of so-called 'world chronicles' produced between the eighth and tenth centuries.[33] With the exception of Regino

---

[29] Isidore, *Etymologiae*, V.38–9; compare Augustine, *DCD*, XVI.43, p. 550 and XXII.30, pp. 865–6. Wood, *Politics of Identity*, 121–8, emphasising Isidore's innovativeness.

[30] *Chronica minora*: Bede, *De temporibus*, ed. Charles W. Jones, CCSL 123 C (Turnhout: Brepols, 1980), pp. 585–611; trans. by Calvin B. Kendall and Faith Wallis, *Bede: On the Nature of Things and On Times* (Liverpool: LUP, 2010), 107–31. *Chronica maiora*: Bede, DTR., c. 66; trans. Wallis, 157–237.

[31] Bede, *Letter to Plegwin*, ed. Charles. W. Jones, in *Bedae Venerabilis Opera: Opera Didascalica 3*, CCSL 123C (Turnhout: Brepols, 1980), c. 12, p. 623; trans. Wallis, 411.

[32] Rosamond McKitterick, 'Carolingian Historiography', in *Wilhelm Levison (1876–1947): Ein jüdisches Forscherleben zwischen wissenschaftlicher Anerkennung und politischem Exil*, eds Matthias Becher and Yitzhak Hen, Bonner historische Forschungen 63 (Siegburg: Franz Schmitt, 2010), 93–112, at 101; see also Ildar H. Garipzanov, 'The Carolingian Abbreviation of Bede's World Chronicle and Carolingian Imperial "Genealogy"', *Hortus Artium Medievalium*, 11 (2005): 291–8. More generally see Joshua A. Westgard, 'Bede and the Continent in the Carolingian Age and Beyond', in *The Cambridge Companion to Bede*, ed. Scott DeGregorio (Cambridge: CUP, 2010), 201–15, at 206–10 and Joyce Hill, 'Carolingian Perspectives on the Authority of Bede', in *Innovation and Tradition in the Writings of the Venerable Bede*, ed. Scott DeGregorio (Morgantown, WV: West Virginia University Press, 2006), 227–49.

[33] *Chronicon universale*: Kaschke, 'Enhancing Bede'. Claudius of Turin: Michael I. Allen, 'The *Chronicle* of Claudius of Turin', in *After Rome's Fall: Narrators and Sources of Early Medieval History. Essays Presented to Walter Goffart*, ed. Alexander Callander Murray (Toronto: University of Toronto Press, 1998), 287–319 and C. Philipp E. Nothaft, 'Chronologically Confused: Claudius of Turin and the Date of Christ's Passion', in *Late Antique Calendrical Thought and its Reception in the Early Middle Ages*, eds Immo Warntjes and Dáibhí Ó Cróinín (Turnhout: Brepols, 2017), 265–92. Chronicle of Moissac: Rutger Kramer, 'A Crowning Achievement' and his 'The Bede Goes On: Pastoral Eschatology in the Prologue

of Prüm, each of these chronicles was structured in relation to the six ages of
the world and took into account the chronology of the Vulgate.[34] As a result of
the model that Bede's *De temporum ratione* transmitted, the 'six-age paradigm' in
particular became 'virtually an obligatory feature in subsequent medieval efforts
to chart human history'.[35]

Frechulf utilised Isidore and Bede but, unlike almost all other Carolingian
world chroniclers with whom he typically is compared, he did not model his
Histories on the six ages of the world.[36] In Book 1, the first two ages played an
important role in breaking up and binding together different periods of the pre-
Abrahamic past, though only the second age was connected to the metaphor of
the human life cycle.[37] Much later, at the outset of Part II, Frechulf excerpted a
passage from Bede's *Greater Chronicle* regarding the inception of the sixth age.[38]
In between, however, there was no attempt to integrate the *aetates mundi* in any
sustained way.[39] And with the exception of a single figure (drawn from Bede's
De temporum ratione) reflecting the Hebrew Truth of Jerome's Vulgate, Frechulf
routinely followed Eusebius-Jerome's Septuagint-based chronology.[40] Rather than
expanding on chapter 66 of *De temporum ratione*, Frechulf went back to the font
of the chronicle tradition. He made Eusebius-Jerome his starting point.

Before exploring how Frechulf utilised the 'concise chart', it is helpful briefly
to consider the form of the *Chronicle* he had at his disposal. Any attempt to
situate Frechulf within the reception history of Eusebius-Jerome must also take
into account the complex issue of its manuscript tradition. The *Chronicle* has an
intricate textual history.[41] Remarkably, there is a full copy and several fragments
extant from the fifth century, perhaps produced within decades of Jerome's death.[42]

---

to the Chronicle of Moissac (Paris BN lat. 4886)', in *Cultures of Eschatology II: Time, Death and Afterlife
in Medieval Christian, Islamic and Buddhist Communities*, eds Veronika Wieser, Vincent Eltschinger and
Johann Heiss (Berlin: De Gruyter, 2020), 698-730. Ado: Raisharma, 'Much Ado about Nothing'.

[34] Richard Landes, 'Lest the Millennium be Fulfilled: Apocalyptic Expectations and the Pattern of
Western Chronography 100-800 CE', in *The Use and Abuse of Eschatology in the Middle Ages*, eds
Werner Verbeke, Daniel Verhelst and Andries Welkenhuysen, Mediaevalia Lovaniensia Series 1,
Studia 15 (Leuven: Leuven University Press, 1988),137-211, at 178-81 on 'the Bedan Carolingians'.

[35] Allen, 'Universal History', 38. See further Elisabeth Mégier, 'Le temps des Ages du monde, de saint
Augustin a Hugues de Fleury (en passant par Isidore de Seville, Bede le Vénérable, Adon de Vienne
et Fréculphe de Lisieux)', in *Le sens du temps: actes du VIIᵉ Congrès du Comité international de latin
médiéval, Lyon, 10–13.09.2014*, eds Pascale Bourgain, Jean-Yves Tilliette and Jan M. Ziolkowski
(Geneva: Droz, 2017), 581–600.

[36] Staubach, '*Christiana tempora*', 181.

[37] *Hist.*, I.1.25 [1/4], p. 50 and I.1.35 [19/21], p. 67: '... Quam aetatem pueritiam nominant'.

[38] *Hist.*, II.1.2 [40/2], p. 442.

[39] Allen, 'Universal History', 40; Staubach, '*Christiana tempora*', 181; Schelle, 'Frechulf von Lisieux', 141.

[40] *Hist.*, I.1.35 [10/18], p. 67 together with Allen, 'Complementary Notes', 731–2.

[41] Alden A. Mosshammer, *The Chronicle of Eusebius and the Greek Chronographic Tradition* (Lewisburg,
PA: Bucknell University Press, 1979), 29–83 provides an excellent overview.

[42] Mosshammer, *Chronicle of Eusebius*, 67; Alden A. Mosshammer, 'Two Fragments of Jerome's
Chronicle', *Rheinisches Museum für Philologie*, 124 (1981): 66–80 at 75.

The layout of the text, as presented in Rudolf Helm's critical edition, corresponds to these early exemplars. But between the fifth and ninth centuries, the content and organisation of the *Chronicle* were subject to change. For example, a gorgeous, colour-coded codex copied in the early ninth century contained an *Exordium*, a supplementary narrative first written in the early sixth century that traced human history, primarily through the genealogical material in Genesis, from Adam to Abraham.[43] A number of codices demonstrate more radical structural changes by doing away with the double-spread format.[44] One of these, London BL Add. Ms. 16974 (ninth century, north-eastern France) is for our purposes significant.[45] Firstly, this is because the *Histories* share distinctive textual variants with the text of the *Chronicle* it transmits. Second, this codex is an example of what Ian Wood has termed a 'chain of chronicles', in which the Chronicle of 452, Prosper (to 455 AD), then the chronicle of Marius of Avenches (to 581) follow on in succession from Eusebius-Jerome. [46] Frechulf drew on three of these four works, and his excerpts from Marius are particularly tantalising since this chronicle survives exclusively in the British Library manuscript.[47] Frechulf's exemplar, although textually related to this particular 'chain of chronicles', was not identical to it. Frechulf's copy, for example, seems to have preserved the older double-page layout characteristic of the ancient copies of the *Chronicle*.[48] If nothing else, the *Histories* further confirm the complexity of the early medieval manuscript tradition of Eusebius-Jerome while also attesting to the impressively rich range of chronicle sources accessible at Lisieux, which clearly was no provincial backwater. Moving now from the uncertainty of exemplars to the actual ways Frechulf employed Eusebius-Jerome, it is possible to reach less rocky ground.

---

[43]   Leiden, Universiteitsbibliotheek, MS Scaliger 14 [http://hdl.handle.net/1887.1/item:1678556]. On this manuscript, see Rosamond McKitterick, 'Glossaries and Other Innovations in Carolingian Book Production', in *Turning over a New Leaf: Change and Development in the Medieval Book* (Leiden: University of Leiden Press, 2012), 21–76, at 33–7. The text of *Exordium* (fols. 7v–14v) is printed in *Eusebi Chronicorum Libri Duo*, ed. Alfred Schöne, 2 vols (Berlin: Weidmann, 1999), 3rd ed, vol. 1, appendix 2, pp. 41–9 and in *PL* 27, cols. 61–76. Short discussions in Alfred Schöne, *Die Weltchronik des Eusebius in ihrer Bearbeitung durch Hieronymus* (Berlin: Weidmann, 1900), 276 and Allen, 'Universal History', 23–4.
[44]   For example, Bern, Burgerbibliothek, Cod. 219 (late 7th century) [https://www.e-codices.unifr.ch/en/list/one/bbb/0219)] and Lucca Bibl. Capit. 490 (c. 800). On the Lucca codex, see Alden A. Mosshammer, 'Lucca Bibl. Capit. 490 and the Manuscript Tradition of Hieronymus' (Eusebius') Chronicle', *California Studies in Classical Antiquity*, 8 (1975): 203–40 and Rosamond McKitterick, 'Transformations of the Roman Past and Roman Identity in the Early Middle Ages', in *The Resources of the Past in Early Medieval Europe*, eds Rosamond McKitterick, Sven Meeder and Clemens Gantner (Cambridge: CUP, 2015), 225–44, at 241–4.
[45]   *Prolegomena*, 208*–210*.
[46]   Ian N. Wood, 'Chains of Chronicles: The Example of London, British Library ms. add. 16974', in *Zwischen Niederschrift und Wiederschrift: Hagiographie und Historiographie im Spannungsfeld von Kompendienüberlieferung und Editionstechnik*, eds Richard Corradini, Max Diesenberger and Meta Niederkorn-Bruck (Vienna: Austrian Academy of Science Press, 2010), 67–77.
[47]   Wood, 'Chains of Chronicles', 70; *Prolegomena*, 208*–9* and 214*.
[48]   Allen, 'Complementary Notes', 738, n. 17.

Frechulf's Use of Eusebius-Jerome: Structure and Chronology

Already in her 1952 dissertation, Betha Schelle had touched upon the basic function Eusebius-Jerome served for Frechulf in Part I. The *Chronicle* supplied the basic textual architecture for the *Histories*. Like the structure of a German half-timbered building or *Fachwerkbau* (to use Schelle's metaphor) the *Chronicle* offered a basic framework of dates and events; excerpts from Frechulf's richer narrative sources were added to the framework, filling out its bare details to create a fuller, more rounded, whole. Schelle's observation, however, was offered as critique: Frechulf's dependence on what was regarded as the simplistic scheme of *Chronicle* came at the expense of articulating a more conceptually robust approach to the past.[49] Raffaele Savigni and Michael Allen reiterated Schelle's core observation, but in much more positive terms.[50] The extent and importance of Frechulf's engagement with the *Chronicle*, however, can be taken further.

I. Secular Chronology: translatio imperii

When sketching the shape of history between Abraham and Christ, Frechulf explained his plan to extract 'from the works of wise authors' a *series annorum* of Jewish and gentile history and 'those things which antiquity deemed worthy of memory'.[51] This was done to show that:

> although the order of the years is observed in the kingdom of the Assyrians and their successors, nevertheless inserted alongside them in their proper place are those things celebrated in the records of the ancients, which through immortal memory are always repeated, whether the causes of wars or the origins and transformations of kingdoms, indeed even those who flourished by their virtue or the greatest devotion to wisdom.[52]

Frechulf not only echoed the specific language of the *Chronicle*, but by stating he will place notices of historical events 'alongside (*ex latere*)' the *ordo annorum* through the reigns of the Assyrian rulers and those who inherited their power, he also evoked its layout. In most early manuscripts—though not the subgroup group that BL Add. Ms. 16974 represents—the *Chronicle*'s left-most column was reserved for the rulers of the pre-eminent secular kingdoms. At the beginning, this space

---

[49] Schelle, 'Frechulf', 85, 92, 99, 140–4.
[50] Savigni, 'Storia universale', 172; Allen, *Prolegomena*, 16* and 208* and 'Universal History', 39.
[51] *Hist.*, I.2.Prol. [19], p. 85: '... ea quae putavit digna antiquitas memoria, ex opusculis auctorum prudentium libando Domino annuente decerpere conabor'; *Chron.*, Eus. Praef., p. 19: 'et si qua alia digna memoria putavit antiquitas. Quae universa in suis locis cum summa brevitate ponemus.'
[52] *Hist.*, I.2.Prol. [21/27], pp. 85–6: 'ita uidelicet ut quamuis ordo annorum in regno custodiatur Assyriorum seu in succedentibus, tamen ea quae celebriora in antiquorum habentur monumentis et inmortali memoria per omnia frequentantur tempora, seu bellorum casus siue exordia mutationesque regnorum, quique etiam uirtute aut summo sapientiae studio uiguerunt, suis quippe congruis ex latere inserantur locis'.

was occupied by the Assyrian Empire, but then as time passed it was taken over by the Medes, then Persians, then the successors of Alexander the Great (largely in the form of Ptolemaic rulers of Egypt), and then finally the Romans.[53] These kingdoms have an important place in medieval perceptions of the past (as well as in modern perceptions of the medieval mindset): they are often known as the 'four world monarchies' (a term made possible by counting the Medes and Persians as a single kingdom), and the transfer of rulership from one to the other is known by the Latin phrase *translatio imperii*.[54]

Clear traces of this idea are found in the *Histories*. When first addressing Helisachar, Frechulf says that he has obeyed his instructions to 'count the years through the kings of the Assyrians, of the Medes and Persians, of the Greeks, and right up to the monarchy of Octavian Caesar, to peoples to which the kingdom of the Assyrians devolved successively through the passing ages'.[55] Throughout Part I, these *eminentiora regna* appear regularly at the beginnings of chapters, functioning as framing devices. This is particularly obvious in Book 2, in which almost every chapter is situated in the successive reigns of Assyrian rulers, from the 53-year long reign of Ninus, the first Assyrian king, down to 'Eupales, the thirtieth [king] of the Assyrians, [who ruled for] 38 years'.[56] Midway through Book 3, the Assyrian kingdom came to an end, 1240 years after its foundation; pre-eminent power now resided with the Medes.[57] Frechulf copied the relevant note from Eusebius-Jerome which explained this, and mirroring the change in the *Chronicle*'s left-most column, the names and regnal years of Median kings now begin each chapter.[58] The pattern is repeated when the Persian king Cyrus defeated the Medes, and again when the Persian kingdom was destroyed and its *imperium* transferred to Alexander the Great and his Ptolemaic successors.[59] The Roman Empire of Augustus was the final point in the overall schema and marked the conclusion to Part I.

The succession of secular rulership was important. Structurally, rulers framed individual chapters or, as material became more abundant, groups of chapters.

---

[53] *Chron.*, pp. 20a, 83a, 103a, 124, 156.

[54] Werner Goez, *Translatio Imperii: ein Beitrag zur Geschichte des Geschichtsdenkens und der politischen Theorien im Mittelalter und in der fruhen Neuzeit* (Tübingen: Mohr, 1958).

[55] *Hist.*, I.Prol., p. 18 and I.2.Prol., p. 85.

[56] *Hist.*, I.2.30 [1.2], p. 153.

[57] *Hist.*, I.3.9 [18/27], p. 171.

[58] *Hist.*, I.3.10 [1], p. 172 and the first line of each chapter until I.3.17 [1], p. 188.

[59] *Hist.*, I.3.18 [1/4], p. 197: 'Cyrus Persa Medorum destruxit imperium quod steterat per annos circiter CCLVIII, subversoque rege Astiage, auunculo suo, primus Persis regnauit ann. scilicet XXX. Qualiter enim Medorum ad Persas uenerit regnum pandendum reor'; I.4.25 [20/4], p. 258: 'Quamuis enim Alexandrinorum regum, id est Aegyptiorum, persequi annorum numerum regumque successiones hinc iam usque ad Caesaris Octouiani monarchiam decreuerim, tamen quas principes Alexandri partes orbis obtinuerunt innotescere curabo.' See also Allen, 'Complementary Notes', 733. Compare I.5.11 [112/115], pp. 312–13 where the end of Macedon and Carthage—which is part of Orosius's scheme of world monarchies, not Eusebius-Jerome's—is mentioned in terms of Rome's rise to dominance.

Almost every chapter of Book 2 is introduced by a new Assyrian ruler, while the first three chapters of Book 4 concern events that took place in the reign of the third Persian ruler, Darius I. The first of these chapters began with material gleaned from Eusebius-Jerome: 'Darius, son of Hystaspes, was the third Persian [king] and ruled for thirty-six years.'[60] Frechulf then turned to Orosius to provide an account of the king's famous military exploits: his conquests in the east, and then his humiliating defeat at the hands of the Athenians at Marathon.[61] The time of Darius, however, was also when the Romans rejected kingship and established the consuls. Eusebius-Jerome first synchronised the two events, and Frechulf followed suit, beginning the next chapter by stating that 'at the very same time (*eodem tempore*), the Romans had their first consuls, Brutus and Collatinus, after the expulsion of [their] kings.'[62] The third chapter concerned the Carthaginian king Himelcho, a ruler not mentioned in Eusebius-Jerome. Orosius, however, provided both the relevant information and the temporal link, conveniently (for Frechulf) ending his section with the note that 'these things happened in the times of Darius.'[63]

II. *Sacred Chronology:* populus Dei

While the transformation of the left-most column of the *Chronicle* was reflected throughout different chapters of Part I, the organisation of the chapters into a system of books depended on events from sacred history. Books, more so than the chapters they contained, were 'the most important structuring element' of the *Histories*.[64] By looking at how Frechulf parcelled excerpted text into defined, delineated, books, we can begin to see the overall structure within which his narrative flowed. Despite its remarkably different form, the inspiration behind Frechulf's system of books also lay with Eusebius-Jerome's chronological tables.

The *Chronicle* was a storehouse of facts about the ancient world, but it was also suffused with a bewildering array of numbers, which Jerome himself acknowledged could confuse readers.[65] Some figures, however, were more important than others, and the counted decades from Abraham's birth were especially so. From the very first page of the *Chronicle*, they were marked with an underlined numeral, and these years *ab Abraham nato* exist outside the left-most *filum regnorum*, occupying their own distinct space. The corresponding year of each kingdom on the page also was underscored, to facilitate reference across the kingdoms displayed on a given page and to lock all history into the rhythms of Christian time.

---

[60] *Hist.*, I.4.1 [1.2], p. 211.
[61] *Hist.*, I.4.1 [3/28], pp. 211–12.
[62] *Hist.*, I.4.2 [1/2], pp. 212.
[63] *Hist.*, I.4.3, p. 215; Oros., IV.6.15, p. 22.
[64] Staubach, '*Christiana tempora*', 175; see also Von den Brincken, *Studien*, 123.
[65] *Chron.*, Eus. Praef., p. 18.

Other significant moments in biblical history were also marked out. When compiling his *Chronicle*, Eusebius suggested a division of Hebrew history into four temporal blocks (*quattuor tempora*): 'from Abraham up to Moses, from Moses up to the first construction of the Temple, and the construction of the First Temple up to its rebuilding, and from the Temple's rebuilding up to the advent of Christ.'[66] These divisions were marked out in various ways: for example, by the use of enlarged text, chronological counts and notices about the fulfilment prophecy.[67] Christian intellectuals perceived Abraham, Moses, the two Temples and Christ's Incarnation as key moments in the history of man's redemption, from the special relationship the Jews enjoyed with God, down to the arrival of God's son on earth, whose teachings opened up the possibility of universal salvation. Frechulf's engagement with Eusebius-Jerome shaped the contours of his own narrative, and as a result these key moments were likewise emphasised in the *Histories*.[68]

To demonstrate this, it is helpful to begin at the conclusions to each book where Frechulf explains the moments at which he opted to punctuate his narrative. With a dash of literary zest, he concluded that Book 2:

> contains the *series temporum* from the birth of Abraham through to the construction of the Temple. I have chosen to divide this into two blocks—from the first year of [God's] covenant [with Abraham] until the Exodus from Egypt, and then [from the Exodus] until the building of the Temple—so that the reader can retain more easily the deeds which are narrated in each period. Now, worn out after the immense effort of so long a journey and seeking somewhere to rest, we arrive finally at the Temple of the Lord, as the sun is setting and already great shadows are advancing from the mountains. Having arrived at our desired station, we set here the end of the second book of our work.[69]

---

[66] *Chron.*, pp. 16–17: 'Nunc illud in cura est, ut etiam Hebraeorum annos in quatuor tempora dividamus, ab Abraham usque ad Moysen, a Moyse usque ad primam aedificationem templi, a prima aedificatione templi usque ad secundam instaurationem eius, ab instauratione eius usque ad adventum [Christi Domini].' See Roderich Schmidt, '*Aetates mundi*: die Weltalter als Gliederungsprinzip der Geschichte, *Zeitschrift für Kirchengeschichte*, 67 (1956): 288–317, at 304–5; with reference to Frechulf, Hans-Werner Goetz, 'Historiographisches Zeitbewußtsein im frühen Mittelalter: Zum Umgang mit der Zeit in der karolingerischen Geschichtsschreibung', in *Historiographie im frühen Mittelalter*, eds Anton Scharer and Georg Scheibelreiter, Veröffentlichen des Instituts für Österreichishe Geschichtsforschung 32 (Vienna, Oldenbourg,1994), 158–78, at 167–8.

[67] *Chron.*, pp. 23a–23b (Abraham and the Covenant); p. 43a (Exodus); pp. 70a–70b (First Temple); pp. 105a–105b (Second Temple); pp. 169, 173–4 (birth of Christ).

[68] Allen, 'History in the Carolingian Renewal', 70–72. See also Savigni, 'Storia universale', 172–3: Frechulf marks the 'tappe fondamentali della storia della salvezza'; these 'momenti epocali' underline his 'ecclesiological perspective'. Although not marked by Frechulf as 'Ages of the World', Savigni saw parallels between his and the Augustinian scheme.

[69] *Hist.*, I.2.30 [22/31], p. 154: 'Continet autem libellus iste annorum seriem a natiuitate Abrahae usque ad aedificationem templi, quam diuidere malui, id est ab anno primo repromissionis usque ad exitum Israhel de Aegypto, inde autem usque ad aedificationem templi, ut lector facilius retinere ualeat ea quae in temporibus singulorum gesta narrantur. Nunc autem post inmensum tanti itineris laborem fessi, diuerticula petentes, dum sol occiduas tendit in horas, prolixae iam e montibus procedunt umbrae, tandem ad Domini uenimus templum: optata statione potiti hinc metam secundi nostri

Frechulf's second book thus covered the first two of Eusebius's fourfold divisions of time. Immediately before the book's conclusion, a series of tallies were inserted that linked together these important junctures, as well as tying them back to pre-Abrahamic history: 480 years were counted 'from Moses and the Exodus of Israel from Egypt up to Salomon and the construction of the Temple', 1447 years between the Exodus and the Flood, 2242 between the Flood and Adam; taken together, 4169 years were counted from Adam until building work on the Temple began. This total, Frechulf makes clear, was gleaned 'from the *Chronicle* of Eusebius and [its] affirmation by Jerome'.[70]

Within the body of Book 2, moreover, God's covenant with Abraham and then the Exodus were used as dating clauses in the opening lines of each chapter.[71] I.2.10, for example, begins: 'Balaeus, ninth [king] of the Assyrians [ruled] for fifty-two years. This was 263 years since the birth of Abraham, but 188 since the covenant'.[72] Frechulf generated these numbers from the data found in the *Chronicle*. For the first figure, he simply synchronised the underlined year *ab Abrahame* (260) with the first year of Balaeus, which occurred three years later. For the latter figure, Frechulf subtracted seventy-five (Abraham's age when the covenant was made) from 263.[73] Eusebius's second division of Hebrew history, from Moses to Solomon, was signalled by the Exodus of the Israelites from Egypt, and this event becomes Frechulf's next 'sacred watershed'.[74] From this point, the years since the Jews' departure from Egypt join Assyrian monarchs in heralding the beginning of each chapter so as to mark the passage of time. This figure is calculated by subtracting the date of the Exodus—given in Eusebius-Jerome as 505 years *ab Abrahame*—from the relevant date.[75] For example, the accession of Belocus, the eighteenth Assyrian king, happened seventy-seven years after the Exodus. Frechulf could see that the king's reign began 582 years *ab Abrahame*, from which he subtracted 505.[76] The arithmetic involved is far from complex, but the results rather pleasingly show the historian actively engaged with the *Chronicle*, and it is possible to imagine him working with Eusebius-Jerome spread out before him.

The restoration of the Temple, following its destruction by Nebuchadnezzar, marks the end of Book 3 and reflects the third of Eusebius's divisions.[77] Throughout

---

operis inponimus libri.'
[70] *Hist.*, I.2.30 [12/14], p. 154: 'Hanc annorum namque supputationem iuxta Eusebii Chronicam atque Hieronimi adsertionem coaptare curauimus.'
[71] Covenant: *Hist.*, I.2.4 [1.2], p. 95; I.2.8–17, pp. 101–11; Exodus: *Hist.*, I.2.19-30, pp. 121–53.
[72] *Hist.*, I.2.10 [1.2], p. 103: 'Igitur Assyriorum nonus Baleus, ann. LII. A natiuitate Abrahae CCLXIII, repromissionis uero CLXXXVIII erat annus.'
[73] *Chron.*, p. 23a: 'Abraham cum LXXV esset annorum, divino dignus habetur adloquio et ea repromissione, quae ad eum facta est.'
[74] Allen, 'Complementary Notes', 736.
[75] *Chron.*, p. 43a; *Chron.*, Eus. Praef., p. 17 [3/6].
[76] *Hist.*, I.2.19 [2/3], p. 121–2; *Chron.*, p. 47a.
[77] Allen, 'Complementary Notes', 737.

the book, chapters typically open by synchronising the reigns of successive Assyrian and then Median kings with years elapsed since the completion of the Temple.[78] Various different expressions can be found—*a perfectione templi, a conditione templi, ab aedificatione templi*—but the calculations are consistent and produce clean results. Construction work on the Temple was completed 991 years *ab nato Abrahame*, and this figure was simply subtracted from the relevant regnal year. One example will suffice. Chapter 10 was organised around the reign of Arbaces, the first king of the Medes. The *Chronicle* showed that his reign began 1197 years from the birth of Abraham. Subtracting 991, we are left with 206 years *a constructione templi.*[79] Frechulf then wrapped things up by stating that Book 3 extended 'from the initial construction of the Temple under Solomon up to its reconstruction under Darius', and in total 'contained 512 years according to some [that is, Eusebius-Jerome], but 440 according to Josephus'.[80] The significance of the Temple's construction was furthermore underscored via comments about prophecy and scriptural authority. Work on the Temple began in the second year of the reign of Darius, when the Jews' seventy-year-long Babylonian exile had come to an end, 'just as the prophets had predicted (*sicut per prophetas praedicta fuerat*)' and as the prophet Zacharias also confirmed.[81] For text and numbers alike Frechulf depended on the *Chronicle*.

The fourth and final of Eusebius's divisions, from the Second Temple to the Nativity, occupied the remaining four books of Part I. In dating events from secular history in relation to the Second Temple, Frechulf ran into trouble. The *Chronicle* showed that restoration began in the second year of the reign of Darius and was completed four years later, 1501 years from the birth of Abraham.[82] Frechulf, however, seems initially to have followed Josephus, who dated it to the ninth year of Darius's reign, 1504 years *ab Abrahame*.[83] Yet most of the counts did not even work from this figure. Alexander's destruction of the Persian kingdom was stated to have happened 181 years after the Temple's restoration, and then the conclusion to Book 4, set seven years later at Alexander's death, brought the total to 186. As the Persian *regnum* fell 1687 years *ab Abraham* this established the Temple's restoration to the 1506th year since Abraham's birth, agreeing with neither Eusebius-Jerome nor Josephus.[84]

---

[78] *Hist.*, I.3.5–17, pp. 165, 167, 168, 169, 170, 172, 175, 181, 183, 184, 185, 188.

[79] *Hist.*, I.3.10 [1.2], p. 172.

[80] *Hist.*, I.3.19 [37/41], p. 206: Hic namque finis tertii nostri operis erit libri, qui continet in se a prima aedificatione templi sub Salomone usque ad secundam reaedificationem sub Dario, secundum quosdam quingentos XII annos, iuxta uero Iosepphi adsertionem quadringentos quadraginta.

[81] *Hist.*, I.3.19 [23/36], pp. 205–6.

[82] *Chron.*, p. 106.

[83] *Hist.*, I.3.19 [31/35], pp. 205–6: 'in the second year [of Darius's] reign the building [of the Temple] is begun by Zerubbabel and Jeshua, and the work was completed by them in four years. Josephus said the Temple was completed in seven years by the aforementioned men, which is the ninth year of Darius, when Hagai and Zachariah, as well as one of the twelve called Angelus (Malachi), were prophesising amongst the Jews'. Compare Allen, 'Complementary Notes', 738.

[84] *Hist.*, I.4.21 [133.134], p. 251 and I.4.28 [86/89], p. 269. Allen, 'Complementary Notes', 737–9.

Confusion is compounded at the Nativity, the end point of Part I and the ultimate event of Eusebius-Jerome's *quattor tempora*. Frechulf brought Book 7 to an end with a series of counts that situated Christ's birth in relation to the other moments of sacred history he had covered. Yet more so than any of the other counts, this final 'fanfare of datings' engendered perplexing results:[85]

> And so … we reach the birth of our Lord, Jesus Christ, son of man and God, which was celebrated in Bethlehem of Juda, just as it was announced in advance by the prophets, proclaimed by the angels, guided by a star and testified by the priests and teachers of the Law. One may see that from the rebuilding of the Temple, which was completed under Darius, to [the Nativity], there were 515 years; from Solomon and the first construction of the Temple, there were 1027 years; from Moses and the exodus of the Israelites from Egypt, 1506 years; from Abraham and kingdom of Ninus and Semiramis, 2011 years; and indeed from the Flood, 2921 years; from Adam, however, 5129 years.[86]

Similar counts were to be found in Eusebius-Jerome, as well as in Prosper, yet they were not keyed to Christ's Nativity, but rather to the fifteenth regnal year of the Roman emperor Tiberius (designated XV Tiberius).[87] In contrast to his sources, Frechulf chose a different moment to stress and as a result had to emend the known figures to make them fit for purpose. This could have been simple enough: there were twenty-nine years' difference between the total years separating the respective births of Abraham and Christ on the one hand, and the birth of Abraham and XV Tiberius on the other. Frechulf, however, subtracted thirty-three from the pre-existing tallies. Confusion may have arisen because Prosper had favoured dating the passion to XV Tiberius, whereas Eusebius-Jerome placed it at XVIII Tiberius.[88] If Frechulf took Prosper's note on board while working under the assumption that thirty-three was the age at which Christ was crucified, there is some logic in his deductions.[89] That said, error evidently crept into

---

[85] Allen, 'Complementary Notes', 733.

[86] *Hist.*, I.7.19 [45/53], pp. 431–2: 'Igitur, ut praemissimus, ad Domini nostri Iesu Christi natiuitatem, hominis Deique filii, peruenimus, quae, ut a prophetis praenuntiabatur, angelis praedicantibus, stella duce, ac sacerdotibus legumque doctoribus protestantibus, in Bethleem Iudae celebrata est: anno uidelicet a reaedificatione templi quae sub Dario rege facta est DXV; a Salomone autem et a prima aedificatione templi anni I XXVII; a Moyse et egressu Israhelis ex Aegypto anno millesimo DVI; ab Abraham et regno Nini et Semiramidis anni II XI; a diluuio quippe anni II DCCCCXXI; ab Adam uero V CXXVIIII.'

[87] *Chron.*, pp. 173–4 and Eus. Praef., p. 10 [6.7]; Prosper, *Chronicle*, cc. 380–6, p. 409.

[88] Prosper, *Chronicle*, c. 388, pp. 409–10; Muhlberger, *Fifth-century Chroniclers*, 65.

[89] See Allen, 'Complementary Notes', 733, and earlier, Savigni, 'Storia universale', 170, n. 52. Prosper, *Chronicle*, 388, pp. 409–10: 'Quidam ferunt anno XVIII Tiberii Jesum Christum passum, et argumentum huius rei ex evangelio adsumunt Iohannis, in quo post XV annum Tiberii Caesaris triennio dominus praedicasse intellegatur. Sed quia usitatior traditio habet dominum nostrum XV anno Tiberii Caesaris duobus Geminis consulibus crucifixum, nos sine praeiudicio alterius opinionis successiones sequentium consulum a supra scriptis consulibus ordiemur, manente adnotatione temporum quae cuiusque imperium habuit.' For comment, see Humphries, 'Chronicle and Chronology', 159–60.

Frechulf's final two calculations leading to the final sum of 5129, 'a unique and many times compromised result'. [90]

The most common world chronologies reckoned Christ's Nativity to have occurred either after 5199 years (according to the Septuagint chronology), 3952 (according to the Vulgate) or 5500 (corresponding to what is termed the Alexandrian era) from the world's creation. These totals were all theoretically known to Frechulf through his various sources, which makes his divergence from them all the more baffling. [91] He was not done there. The bishop then added: 'according to Genesis and the calculation of [Julius] Africanus, a further 129 years are discovered'. [92] Does this mean that Frechulf's total should be increased to 5258, or that the extra 129 years ought to be shaved off, leaving 5000? Interpreting this ostensible muddle is not easy. Michael Allen, who has done the bulk of the spadework on this problem, in the end thought that 'Frechulf's computations to the Incarnation almost seem to amount to a willful paradox, or even a derision'. [93] These 'additional 129' years, however, may be less chronologically significant than they appear. A very small number of manuscripts of Prosper's *Chronicle* count 5360 (rather than 5228) years from the creation to XV Tiberius. [94] In one of these manuscripts the exact note about Genesis and Africanus can be found, and here the 129 years were added to make up for a shortfall: if added up individually, the various counts resulted in a total of 5321 years between Adam and XV Tiberius, which the additional 129 brought up the stated 5360. [95] This additional note may have been added because Frechulf knew of more than one text of Prosper, which would further testify to the range and diversity of the chronological sources he was able to draw upon.

History: Sacred and Secular

Eusebius-Jerome's *Chronicle* provided Frechulf with a model: it was a source of chronology, but also structure. This is most clear in the conclusions to Books 2, 3 and 7, which reflect both of Eusebius's chronological emphases: Abraham and the Covenant, Moses and the Exodus, the two Temples and finally the Nativity. The bishop of Lisieux reiterated these moments, but also reframed them so as to match

---

[90] For the workings, see Allen, 'Complementary Notes', 733–5.

[91] Jordanes, *Romana*, c. 85, ed. Theodor Mommsen, MGH *Auct. Ant.* 5,1 (Berlin: Weidmann, 1882), pp. 9–10 preserves the world's age according to the Alexandrian era.

[92] *Hist.*, I.7.19 [54.55], p. 432: 'Secundum Geneseos igitur scripturam et Africani supputationem amplius inveniuntur anni CXXVIIII.'

[93] Allen, 'Complementary Notes', 735.

[94] These are BAV Reg. lat. 2077, fol. (6th/7th C), Paris BNF lat. 4871 (11th C) and Berlin Phillips 1879 (16th C).

[95] Berlin, Phillipps 1879, fol. 13v: 2027 (Abraham to XV Tiberius) + 942 (Flood to Abraham) + 2242 (Adam to Flood) = 5231. The MS, however, states: 'Sunt ergo omnes anni ab adam usque in annum quintumdecimum tiberii cesaris anni 5360.' (5231+ 129 = 5360.)

both the chronological extent of his own text, which had, unlike the *Chronicle*, a clear break at Christ's birth, and his work's very different form, which consisted of a detailed narrative organised into books and chapters. Frechulf was both a reader and an interpreter of the *Chronicle*. He made key aspects of its representation of time and history even more conspicuous.

Thus far, I have looked more or less separately at the two juxtaposed narrative strands running through Part I: the earthly empires of Assyria, Media and Persia, Greece and Rome on the one hand, and the people of God, on the other.[96] Eusebius-Jerome's *Chronicle*, at least at first, displayed a divide between biblical and classical history. Up until the completion of the Second Temple, Old Testament history dominated the left page, whereas pagan history occupied the right of each double-spread.[97] After the rebuilding of the Temple, however, all history appears on one page. Jewish and gentile events became increasingly intermingled.[98] History, moreover, became detached from the sacred. Those who predicted the Second Temple were the 'last of the prophets', and shortly afterwards it was pronounced that 'hitherto the divine scriptures of the Hebrews contain annals of time: those things which happened among them after these things, we provide from the book of Maccabees, and Josephus, and from the writings of Africanus, which thereafter continued the universal history until the Roman period'.[99]

This 500-year stretch of time between the Second Temple and Christ— Eusebius's fourth segment of Hebrew history—corresponds to Books 4–7 of the *Histories*. Helisachar, we are told in the prologue to Part I, had asked Frechulf to pay particular attention to Jewish history during this period, which 'appeared confused on account of the calamities that befell [the Jewish people]'.[100] For the remainder of this chapter, I too shall pay close attention to this period. Here we can see clearly how *translatio imperii* was guided by God, and that all history worked towards a single preordained moment: the Nativity.

---

[96] *Hist.*, I.Prol. [24/29], pp. 18–19; I.2.Prol. [12/22], p. 85.
[97] See Kelly, 'Shape of the Past', 15, 22; Croke, 'Origins of the Christian World Chronicle', in History and Historians in Late Antiquity, eds Brian Croke and Alanna M. Emmett (Oxford: Pergamon, 1983), 116–31 at 125; Mosshammer, *Chronicle*, 71. Muhlberger, *Fifth-century Chroniclers*, 21 noted that, when Jerome translated the *Chronicle*, he ignored the sacred/secular divide, and added notes from Roman history into the page for salvation history.
[98] *Chron.*, p. 106 onwards.
[99] *Chron.*, p. 113 [7/13]: 'Hucusque Hebraeorum divinae scripturae annales temporum continent. Ea vero, quae post haec aput eos gesta sunt, exhibebimus de libro Macchabaeorum et Iosephi et Africani scriptis, qui deinceps universam historiam usque ad Romana tempora persecuti sunt'. See also Augustine, *DCD*, XVIII.45, pp. 641–2.
[100] *Hist.*, I.Prol. [33/7], p. 19: 'Insuper a destructione templi Hierosolimitani usque ad Domini natiuitatem Christi, quaeque in populo gesta sunt Iudaeorum, quoniam confusa propter calamitates quae eis acciderunt esse uidentur, ordinando summatim colligere instigasti.'

Intertextuality: Josephus and Orosius

There was much ground to cover between the conclusion to Book 3, when the rebuilding of the Temple was announced by the 'the last prophets', and the Nativity at the end of Book 7. The narrative was teleological: structurally and theologically, the conclusion to Part I was predetermined and Frechulf consciously worked towards it. Eusebius-Jerome was employed less frequently as a source of information. Often it was drawn on for commemorating Latin writers, and Frechulf tended to group together excerpts and place them at the ends of chapters.[101] It nevertheless continued to provide chronological orientation. Frechulf's chapter on Socrates and Plato, for example, was culled largely from Augustine but was synchronised to the reign of the ninth Persian monarch, Artaxerxes Memnon: information from *City of God* was thus used to expand the compressed, but chronologically ordered, record of the *Chronicle*.[102] Instead, the majority of the second half of Part I consists of excerpts from Frechulf's richer narrative sources: the Latin translations of Josephus's *Jewish Antiquities* and *Jewish War* (as well as Hegesippus's five-book reworking of the *Jewish War*) and Orosius's *Histories against the Pagans*. Significantly, these two texts narrated very different topics: Josephus focused extensively on this history of ancient Israel, about which Orosius had little to say.[103] In Books 4–7, Frechulf sought to make these two authoritative texts speak to one another. His account of the deeds of Alexander the Great serves to illustrate this.

I.4.22 begins with an excerpt from Orosius, detailing Alexander's wars in Greece, and then his push east against the Persian ruler Darius III (ruled 336–330 BC). After Alexander's victory at Issus in 333 BC, Darius regrouped and prepared to fight back. Whilst this took place, Alexander 'went to Syria', where 'out of the many kings who came to meet him of their own free will wearing fillets on their heads, he made alliances, deposed others, and yet others he executed'.[104] At this moment, Frechulf switched to Josephus's *Antiquities*, to tell a tale entirely absent from Orosius. During his journey to Syria, Alexander paid a visit to Jerusalem. Upon entering the city, he prostrated himself before the high priest Iaddus and his entourage. When Parmenion, one of Alexander's generals, asked him about this, the king explained: 'it is not [Iaddus] I have honoured but God, at whose command he performs his priestly duties'. It transpired that God had visited Alexander in a dream, advising him to march on Asia and leading him to believe that 'with divine help (*diuino*

---

[101] *Hist.*, I.5.5 [47/50], p. 289; I.5.7 [228/31], p. 300; I.5.9 [48/50], p. 304; I.5.11 [103/10], p. 312; I.6.6 [12.13], p. 327; I.6.10 [47.8], p. 338; I.6.13 [126/36], p. 350; I.6.17 [113/22], p. 360; I.7.13 [47/63], p. 405; I.7.19 [1/44], pp. 429–31. In the last case, most of the chapter was derived from Eusebius-Jerome where notes from the *Chronicle*, pp. 163–70 were gathered together.
[102] *Hist.*, I.4.14, pp. 230–2.
[103] Oros., I.8, pp. 49–52; 1.9, pp. 52–3; III.7.6, pp. 147–8; VI.6.1–4, pp. 178–9.
[104] *Hist.*, I.4.22 [1/42], pp. 246–8; Oros., III.16.1–11, pp. 163–6; trans. Fear, 134. Compare *Chron.*, p. 123.

iuuamine)' he would ultimately crush the Persians. Alexander then proceeded to offer a sacrifice at the Temple, after which the Book of Daniel was shown to him, 'in which it was written that one of the Greeks would destroy the power of the Persians' and 'he judged that he himself was the one whom scripture signified'.[105] Frechulf seamlessly switched back to Orosius. Departing from Jerusalem, Alexander 'proceeded to other cities', capturing Tyre, Syria, Rhodes and Egypt. After a trip to the temple of Jupiter Hammon, Alexander fought and defeated Darius at Tarsus (or Gaugamela, as the battle is now known): 'after holding an empire for so many years, [the Persians] now patiently accepted the yoke of slavery'.[106]

While Frechulf preserved Orosius's resolutely negative account of the unheroic brutality of Alexander's conquests, his emphasis overall lay elsewhere.[107] The chapter ends by placing Darius's downfall within Frechulf's own Eusebius-Jerome-indebted framework: the Alexandrian realm replaced the Persian kingdom (as it did in the *Chronicle*'s left-most column), Alexander's regnal years were counted, and the beginning of his world monarchy (*monarchia orbis*) was placed '181 years from the reconstruction of the Temple'. Frechulf's use of Josephus, moreover, injected his lengthy excerpt from the *Histories against the Pagans* with a heavy dose of divine providence. The scene in which Alexander reads and interprets the Book of Daniel has the effect of foretelling his ultimate victory over Darius, casting it as the fulfilment of prophecy. This prophetic aspect was wholly missing from Orosius, Frechulf's main narrative source for the battle. It takes on even greater force because in the last chapters of Book 3, Frechulf stressed on three separate occasions that 'no Christian can doubt … what was predicted by the holy Daniel', that Daniel wrote 'truthfully (*veraciter*)', and that events reported by him 'undoubtedly took place', not least what he wrote 'about kingdom of the Greeks and Persians and other things of which he earned foreknowledge through God's guidance'.[108] I return to Daniel below.

Frechulf could merge excerpts from Josephus and Orosius, but more often than not, chapters in the latter half of Part I alternated between these two texts. Running alongside Alexander's smashing of the Persians and the beginning of the third 'world monarchy' was the consolidation of Roman power in Italy. Book 4 ends as follows:

> Here, where we observe the end of the Persian kingdom and when Italy has been subjected to slavery by the Romans, I have decided to end this present book, which

---

[105] *Hist.*, I.4.22 [43/71], pp. 248–9.
[106] *Hist.*, I.4.22 [94.95], pp. 249–50: 'patienterque Persae post imperium tot annorum iugum servitutis acceperint'; trans. Fear, 135.
[107] Compare Yann Coz, 'Quelques interprétations des *Historiae adversus paganos* d'Orose au IXème siècle', *The Journal of Medieval Latin*, 17 (2007): 286–99, at 293–4.
[108] *Hist.*, I.3.17 [154/7], p. 194; I.3.18 [92.3], p. 201 and I.3.18 [103/6], p. 201: 'Sub quo ea quae Danihel in suis reliquit scriptis contigisse haud dubium est, id est de his quae ab invidis perpessus, ac ea quae de regno Grecorum seu Persarum et ceteris, quae Domino monente praescire meruit.'

contains within itself 186 years, from the rebuilding of the Temple up to the death of Alexander the Great.[109]

The book, in fact, extends beyond Alexander's death to his successors; the penultimate chapter, taken from Josephus, deals with Ptolemy's takeover of Jerusalem, after which he brought back to Egypt with him many Jews as captives.[110] Book 5 then begins with Judaea under Ptolemaic power, and traces Jewish history as caught between Egypt and Seleucid Syria, leading up to Antiochus IV Epiphanes, the villain of the Book of Maccabees. Interspersed with this Jewish narrative is Rome's expansion into the Mediterranean, primarily as told through Rome's wars against the Carthaginians, but also against the Macedonians.[111] The separation between Jewish and Roman material is very clear: chapters 1, 4, 6, 8 and 10 deal with the former, chapters 2, 3, 5, 7, 9 and 11 with the latter. The first chapter of Book 5, for example, focused on the Greek translation of the Hebrew scriptures, ordered by the Alexandrian ruler Ptolemy Philadelphus; the next chapter began by noting that 'while these things [that is, the creation of the Septuagint] took place in Judaea and Egypt under Ptolemy, the Romans sent the consul Appius Claudius to help the Mamertines'.[112] These events in the Mediterranean, which led towards the First Punic war, Frechulf gleaned from Orosius; Eusebius-Jerome showed that they occurred around the same time as the creation of the Septuagint.[113]

Frechulf concluded Book 5 by noting: 'Now, however, when we reveal the contamination and ravaging of the Temple, and the destruction of two most powerful kingdoms, Macedon and Carthage, we set the end of this volume.'[114] Book 6 sees the same series of parallel narratives, with chapters alternating between Jewish and Roman history.[115] Of particular interest here is this book's conclusion, which Staubach considered insignificant in terms of theme and thus labelled it 'makeshift (*eine Verlegenheitsschlüß*)'.[116] What is not mentioned, either

---

[109] *Hist.*, I.4.28 [86/9], p. 269: 'Hic uero, ubi Persarum regni finem ostendimus Italiamque Romanorum seruitio subiectam, finem praesentis statui inponere libri, qui continet in se a reaedificatione templi usque ad interitum Alexandri Magni annos circiter CLXXXVI.'
[110] *Hist.*, I.4.27, pp. 263–4.
[111] *Hist.*, I.5.2, 5, 7, 9, 11.
[112] *Hist.*, I.5.2 [1/3], p. 280: 'Dum haec quae praemisimus sub Ptholomeo in Iudaea atque Aegypto ita se haberent, Romani Appium Claudium consulem Mamertinis auxilia ...' Comparable examples are: I.5.9 [1], p. 302: 'apud Romanos vero hisdem diebus'; I.5.11 [1], p. 308: 'Quo in tempore apud Romanos'; I.6.15 [1], p. 352: 'Interea apud Romanos haec gerebantur'; I.7.2 [1.2], p. 369: 'His atque aliis ita gestis, interea Crassus Gabinii successor ducatum Syriae suscepit'; I.7.3 [1], p. 370: 'Igitur eo tempore apud Romanos haec agebantur'; I.7.9 [101.2], p. 391: 'Sed quae praemissimus dum apud Romanos gererentur, haec interim in Iudaea acta sunt quae sequntur'; I.7.14 [1/3], p. 406: 'Igitur dum in Iudaea res ita se agerent ut partim retulimus, ordo deposcit ut ad seriem rei gestae Romanorum revertamur.'
[113] *Chron.*, p. 129.
[114] *Hist.*, I.5.11 [122/5], p. 313: 'Nunc uero ubi contaminationem atque uastationem templi ostendimus, duo que regna potentissima, Macedonum scilicet atque Karthaginiense, defecisse, finem etiam huius uoluminis inponere decreuimus.'
[115] *Hist.*, I.6.1, 2, 7, 11, 14 for Jewish history and I.6.3, 4, 5, 7, 8, 9, 10, 12, 13, 15, 16, 17 for Roman.
[116] Staubach, '*Christiana tempora*', 181.

in Staubach's article or Allen's edition, is how much this simultaneously echoed and altered the conclusion to one of Orosius's books.[117] Orosius completed his fifth book with the following words: I quote the Latin first so as to facilitate comparison:

> Quamobrem huic nunc quinto uolumini iam finem fecerim, ut bella ciuilia externis ubique permixta, uel quae dicta sunt, uel etiam quae sequuntur, quia sic sibi serie temporum et malis sequacibus cohaeserunt, libri saltem termino separentur.[118]

> (I shall, therefore, now put an end to my fifth volume, so that the civil wars, everywhere mixed in with foreign wars, that I have talked about and which will follow on in my account, because they cling together through the passing of time, evil following on from evil, may at least be separated from each other by the end of this book.)

Frechulf, on the other hand, wrote:

> Nam sexto <u>uolumini finem</u> inponere decreui, <u>ut bella</u> tam Romanorum, <u>ciuilia</u> et <u>externis ubique permixta</u>, quamque etiam Iudaeorum, <u>quae dicta sunt uel etiam quae sequuntur, quia sic sibi</u> continuatim <u>serie temporum et malis sequacibus cohaeserunt, libri saltim termino separentur.</u>[119]

> (For I have decided to set [here] the end of the sixth volume, so that the civil wars of the Romans, everywhere mixed in with foreign wars, as well those of the Jews ...)

This clear adaptation of Orosius casts Frechulf's aims into sharper relief. Here Orosius's pessimistic perception of the pre-Christian past is not only retained, but enhanced, bringing Jewish history into the fray. With Book 7, these two strands begin increasingly to intertwine and overlap. In the first chapter of Book 7, Rome quite literally enters into Judean affairs: during the internal conflict between Aristobulus and his supporters and Hyrcanus, Antipater and their supporters, Pompey, attacking on the Sabbath took control of Jerusalem and set foot within the Temple. Antipater, father of Herod the Great, then became allied to the Romans, and we can see Frechulf linking his Jewish and Roman narratives. At I.7.10, Frechulf excerpted from Pseudo-Hegesippus: 'And indeed because King Ptolemy of Egypt had broken faith, he was pressed hard by Caesar himself in very severe battles, as we mentioned above (*ut praemissimus*)'.[120] Readers of the *Histories* were referred back to the previous chapter, taken from Orosius, in which Caesar punished Ptolemy for his treachery after he had been restored to power. These details were not related in either Josephus or Hegesippus. Through linking together these texts, Frechulf created a unified and essentially novel narrative.

---

[117] Compare Staubach, '*Christiana tempora*', 181, n. 54.
[118] Oros., V.24.21, p. 153; trans. Fear, 260.
[119] *Hist.*, I.6.17 [123/27], p. 361. Underlined text = direct borrowing from Orosius.
[120] *Hist.*, I.7.10 [12.13], p. 391.

Calamitates Iudaeorum

This overview hardly does justice to the richness of Frechulf's narrative. Indeed, by combining excerpts from Orosius and Josephus/Pseudo-Hegesippus, Frechulf produced the fullest single historical account of the ancient world in the early Middle Ages. There are two central themes that run through these latter books of Part I, however, which require attention: the 'calamities of the Jews', and the rise of Rome, understood in relation to the previous world monarchies. In the reign of Herod the Great, as we shall see, the two collide.

The story of the Jews' calamitous past was a long one, the writing of which had already begun with Josephus, who after the destruction of the Second Temple by Titus and Vespasian in AD 70, looked back to the past to help explain the woes of the present.[121] Like many other Christian writers, Frechulf's use of Josephus was seriously skewed: Josephus's historical writings contained much of interest for Christian historians and exegetes throughout the Middle Ages, but this often involved a substantial dose of misrepresentation.[122] The various disasters that were inflicted upon the Jews were repeatedly shown to be their own doing. To an extent this narrative was to be found in Josephus, but Christian writers, above all Eusebius, reset its trajectory, homing it in on Christ and salvation history. Jewish history in Book 5 offers a useful approach to this process. Of the eleven chapters of this book, chapters 1, 4, 6, 8 and 10 all centred around the Jews, who were caught between Ptolemaic and Seleucid power. The narrative ends with the despoiling of the Temple and the draconian, brutal measures imposed upon the Jewish people by Antiochus IV Epiphanes.

In effect, the book sought to describe the events leading up to the actions of Antiochus Epiphanes. As well as describing the shifts and struggles for power between the rulers of Alexandria and Syria, Frechulf looked at the internal instability which brought the Jews into the notorious Syrian ruler's sights. The first occurs in I.5.4, which deals with the high priest Onias II and his uncle Joseph the Tobiad. On the death of Joseph, we are told that his eldest sons turned against Hyrcanus, his youngest. This fallout was driven by the elder brothers' envy (*excitati invidiae*) of Hyrcanus, who had earned the goodwill of Ptolemy Evergetes in Alexandria. The majority of the Jews supported the elder brothers, as did the high priest, Simon II. Outnumbered and beaten back, Hyrcanus retreated to Jordan, and eventually founded Tyre.[123]

---

[121] On Josephus, see essays in *A Companion to Josephus in his World*, eds Honora Howell Chapman and Zuleika Rodgers (Chichester: Wiley Blackwell, 2016).

[122] Rosamond McKitterick and Graeme Ward, 'Knowledge of the History of the Jews in the Early Middle Ages', in *Barbarians and Jews: Jews and Judaism in the Early Medieval West*, eds Yitzhak Hen and Thomas F. X. Noble (Turnhout: Brepols, 2018), 231–56.

[123] *Hist.*, I.5.10 [23/34], pp. 286–7. Compare *Chron.*, p. 138.

Further fracturing occurred when the high priest Onias III died, who was the son of Simon II. Antiochus Epiphanes gave the priesthood to Jesus (also called Jason), brother of Onias III, but then, Jesus having angered Antiochus, his brother Onias (also called Menelaus), was bestowed with the office. Jesus then rose against his brother, and again two hostile camps formed. Menelaus and those who had supported him went to Antiochus, seeking to relinquish their country's laws to adhere to the *mores Grecorum*.[124] Then, Frechulf writes:

> These seditions, which were carried out shamefully amongst the aforementioned brothers [that is, Jason and Menelaus] on account of the ambition and dignity of the high priesthood and on account of the dissensions which cruelly took place between Hyrcanus ... and his brothers, therefore sprouted the greatest seeds of disasters amongst the Jewish people. While provoking the arms of foreigners against them, they tore their own entrails to pieces; some called on Seleucus [IV] and his princes, others summoned Antiochus, his successor, to the desolation of the Temple and the betrayal of the [Jewish] people ...[125]

The remainder of this chapter narrated how Antiochus Epiphanes, returning from his campaign in Egypt, marched on Jerusalem and took the city, plundering the Temple and ruthlessly oppressing the Jewish people and their religion.

Significantly, while Frechulf's account of Antiochus Epiphanes' despoiling of the Temple drew primarily upon Josephus, his interjection regarding Jewish *seditions* and the calamities they 'sprouted' echoed the phrasing of Eusebius-Jerome's *Chronicle*.[126] Throughout Book 5, it is clear that Frechulf read the *Jewish Antiquities* with the *Chronicle*'s framework in mind. Each of the chapters devoted to Jewish history begins by introducing a new Alexandrian ruler (Ptolemy Philadephus, Ptolemy Evergetes, Ptolemy Philopater, Ptolemy Epiphanes then Ptolemy Philometor), and each new reign is synchronised against the years elapsed since the reconstruction of the Temple.[127] Frechulf, furthermore, keyed excerpts from Josephus to the *Chronicle*, meaning that events do not follow the order of Josephus's narrative.[128] The *Chronicle* of Eusebius-Jerome thus shaped

---

[124] *Hist.*, I.5.4 [23/29], p. 286, and I.5.10 [34/41], p. 306.

[125] *Hist.*, I.5.10 [33/41], p. 306: 'Igitur hae seditiones, quae propter ambitionem atque dignitatem summi sacerdotii inter praedictos turpiter gerebantur fratres, atque dissensiones quae inter Hyrcanum Iosephi filium, de quo supra meminimus, eiusque fratres crudeliter actae sunt, maxima pullularunt calamitatum semina in populo Iudaeorum, dum aduersum se alienigenarum arma prouocantes propria dilaniauerunt uiscera, dum aliqui Seleucum eiusque principes, alii uero Anthiochum illius successorem ad desolationem templi destitutionemque populi euocauerunt, ut praemissimus.'

[126] *Chron.*, pp. 138 ('Verum fratris eius seditione contra eum mota magnarum calamitatum Iudaeae genti causa extiterunt') and 139 ('Itaque ob sacerdotii dignitatem orta seditione inter principes ingentium miseriarum semina pullulauerunt').

[127] *Hist.*, I.5.1 [1.2], p. 273, I.5.4 [1.2], p. 285, I.5.6 [1.2], p. 289, I.5.8 [1/5], p. 300, I.5.10 [1.2], p. 304.

[128] For example, *Hist.*, I.5.8, pp. 300–2 was drawn from *Antiquities*, 12.131–46; *Hist.*, I.5.4, pp. 285–7 was drawn from *Antiquities*, 12.157–224. On Josephus's problematic sense of chronology, see Dov Gera, 'Unity and Chronology in the *Jewish Antiquities*', in *Flavius Josephus: Interpretation and History*, eds Jack Pastor, Pnina Stern and Menahem Mor, Supplements to the Journal for the Study of Judaism

both the chronological flow and the narrative focus of the *Histories*. In all these chapters, Frechulf drew heavily on Josephus, but the organisation of material, and the message conveyed, owed much more to the Christian historiographical tradition from which his *Histories* emerged. Frechulf claimed in the prologue to Part I that Helisachar had instructed him to set out the 'calamities that befell the Jewish people' up until Christ's birth. He did not fail to deliver.

In Book 6, this narrative continues, again using the words of Josephus, but following Eusebius-Jerome's lead. Although there were undoubted high points, such as the Maccabean revolt, a narrative of decline and fall continues to be charted, and Jewish affairs and Roman politics come into ever-increasing contact. Under Judas Maccabeus, the Temple was purified and worship restored, but at the same time a treaty with Rome was established.[129] Friendly relations between Rome and Judea continued with Jonathan, the high priest.[130] With the sons of John Hyrcanus, Alexander and Aristobulus, things again took a turn for the worse, which Hyrcanus himself was said to have predicted. The next crucial fallout, however, was between Hyrcanus II and Aristobulus II. Although it seems peace was in place, Antipater, father of Herod the Great, encouraged Hyrcanus to wrest power from Aristobulus. During this conflict, both brothers petitioned Pompey for aid, who at that time was campaigning in Asia Minor; eventually, joining forces with Hyrcanus and turning on Aristobulus, Pompey attacked Jerusalem, and entered the Temple. Although he did not seize anything, long after the event his transgression continued to be perceived as a shock to the Jewish system: 'Nothing, however, in that calamity seemed more serious to the Jewish people than that that sacred space, which previously had not been seen by anyone, was exposed to foreigners.'[131] Pompey, admittedly, did not touch the Temple's treasure, but Crassus, who was the governor of Syria, plundered its riches. Cassius later sold the Jews into slavery.

As the above-quoted conclusion to Book 6 of the *Histories* shows, civil and external wars, both for Romans and Jews, had become intermingled. Antipater, Herod's father, fought for Julius Caesar against Mithridates and earned his friendship; he then fought on the side of Octavian and Mark Antony against Cassius and Brutus. After Antipater's death, Herod's star continued to wax. He and his brother were appointed tetrarchs of Jerusalem, and later Antony crowned Herod king, both because he remembered Antipater's good service and appreciated Herod's evident talents.[132] By the end of I.7.12, Antigonus II, the last Hasmonean king of Judea, had been overthrown and executed.

---

146 (Leiden: Brill, 2011), 125–47. On Eusebius and Josephus, see Timothy D. Barnes, *Constantine and Eusebius* (Cambridge, MA: HUP, 1981), 118, and 342, n. 93.

[129] *Hist.*, I.6.1, pp. 317–19; cf. *Chron.*, p. 141–2.

[130] *Hist.*, I.6.2 [6.7], p. 320: 'suamque potentiam Romanorum amicitia conroborauit'.

[131] *Hist.*, I.7.1 [85/7], p. 367: 'Nihil autem grauius in illa clade Iudaeorum genti uisum est quam sanctum illud archanum, neque cuiquam prius uisum, alienis esse detectum.'

[132] *Hist.*, I.7.12 [42/44], p. 398.

Josephus wrote from a particular perspective and with a particular purpose in mind. Frechulf exploited Josephus's rich narrative but also integrated it with Orosius's focus on the rise of Rome and the turmoil which this generated; he was, moreover, able to recast Josephus's narrative in explicitly Christian terms. With Herod secure on the throne, Frechulf's Christian perspective and exegetical purpose reveal themselves.

Herod: History and Exegesis

Herod's turbulent reign forms a climax to Book 7. He murdered his family, his sons and his wife, and after 'immense slaughter' he turned his sights against Christ, which ultimately led to his gruesome death.[133] My focus here, however, is not on how Herod met his end, but the importance of his elevation to the kingship of Judaea.

After Herod is installed as king, Frechulf sets out an exegetically tinged chapter, the importance of which has not yet been fully appreciated.[134] Half of it was excerpted directly from Eusebius-Jerome's *Chronicle*. Although after the restoration of the Temple the *Chronicle* had assumed a single-page format, the accession of Herod saw the return of a double spread, in which time comes to a standstill: a visually striking pause for intensified effect.[135] Frechulf introduced this long passage from the *Chronicle* by recapping events which had already been covered (primarily through excerpts from Josephus and Hegesippus): with the capture of the High Priest Hyrcanus together with the death of his successor, Antigonus II, 'the kingdom and priesthood of the Jews came to an end'.[136] The deep resonances of this were then spelled out.

Herod's non-Jewish background is first made clear. He was a 'foreigner (*alienigena*)', who had 'absolutely nothing to do with Judaea'.[137] His father, Antipater, was from the Idumaean city of Ascalon, and his mother from Arabia.[138] His position was bestowed upon him by the Romans (*contradentibus Romanis*), and as a result, 'the kingship and priesthood of the Jews, which previously was held through the succession, that is, of judges, kings, priests, and kings and priests again (*iudicum, regum, sacerdotum, iterumque regum et sacerdotum*), was at this time destroyed'.[139] Frechulf's emendation of the *Chronicle*'s shorter note that

---

[133] *Hist.*, I.7.18, pp. 421–9.

[134] *Hist.*, I.7.13 [1/46], pp. 402–5. Staubach, '*Christiana tempora*', 179.

[135] *Chron.*, pp. 160–1. On the movement of time in the *Chronicle*, see Kelly, 'Shape of the Past', 22–6.

[136] *Hist.*, I.7.13 [1/4], p. 402: 'Hyrcanus uero, ut supra diximus, a Parthis captus, ac deinde Antigono eius successore, quem Parthi sacerdotem fecerant, a Romanis conprehenso atque interempto Iudaeorum defecit regnum et sacerdotium.'

[137] *Hist.*, I.7.13 [5], p. 403: 'Siquidem Herodes, alienigena et nihil omnino pertinens ad Iudaeam.'

[138] Frechulf earlier dwelled on Antipater's Idumaean background: *Hist.*, I.7.2 [28/36], p. 370.

[139] *Hist.*, I.7.13 [8/10], p. 403: 'regnum et sacerdotium Iudae, quod prius per successiones tenebatur, id est iudicum, regum, sacerdotum, iterum que regum et sacerdotum, quod eo tempore destructum est'.

the kingship and the priesthood had been 'held by a succession of lesser men' is remarkable.[140] In the prologue to Helisachar, Frechulf explained that he would chart the passing years in the pagan kingdoms, but also 'in the people of God, *per patriarchas, iudices, reges et sacerdotes, iterumque reges*'. Likewise, in the prologue before Book 2, Frechulf restated that he would set out the 'series of years', 'from the birth of Abraham, through the *patriarchas, iudices, reges, atque sacerdotes*, who were in charge of the people of God'. With Herod, this long thread of history came to a definite end.

Herod's assumption of the throne marked not only the destruction of the combined kingship and priesthood of the Jews, but also the fulfilment of Mosaic prophecy. Frechulf cited Genesis 49:10 (via the *Chronicle*), in which Jacob, speaking to his sons, predicted that 'there will not lack a prince from Judah, nor a leader from his loins, until he shall come in to whom it was promised, and he himself is the expectation of the gentiles'.[141] Frechulf had first quoted Jacob's prophecy (again via the *Chronicle*) much earlier in *Histories* in the context of Jacob's death, which occurred in the reign of the tenth king of the Assyrians, Altadas: Jacob, in the 147th year of his life, prophesied 'about Christ and the calling of the gentiles'.[142] Five books and over 1500 years later, this prophecy was complete, the fulfilment of which Frechulf revealed through his historical narrative. His excerpts from Josephus and Orosius worked towards realising the necessary historical conditions that Herod's rule was believed to have met: this infamous ruler was not from the Jewish line, but instead 'was confirmed in the kingdom of the Jews by a decree of the [Roman] senate and the support of Antony and Caesar'.[143] Josephus had his own reasons for linking Herod's accession to the Romans; Christian exegetes appropriated Josephus's narrative for their own ends.[144]

Until Herod, the 'judges, priests and kings had successively led the Jewish people'; from Herod onwards, 'no priests from the [ancient] sacerdotal class were established'.[145] The completion of Mosaic prophesy was then augmented with further stress on fulfilment. 'All these things', Frechulf continued, 'the prophet Daniel designated long ago'. These prophesies were contained in Daniel 9:26–7: firstly, that 'after seven and sixty-two weeks the anointing will perish, and there

---

[140] *Chron.*, p. 160 [5/8]: '... regnum et sacerdotum Iudaeae, quod prius per successiones minorum tenebatur, destructum est'. Compare Prosper, *Chronicle*, c. 335, p. 405.

[141] *Hist.*, I.7.13 [10/13], p. 403: 'Completa namque est prophetia quae ita per Moysen loquitur: Non deficiet ex Iuda princeps, neque dux de femoribus eius, donec veniet, cui repromissum est, et ipse est exspectatio gentium.'

[142] *Hist.*, I.2.11 [5/8], p. 106.

[143] *Hist.*, I.7.17 [1/3], p. 418: 'Igitur Herodes senatus consultu, Antonii que atque Caesaris fauore, in regno Iudaeorum confirmatus, ut superius enarrauimus.' This referred back to *Hist.*, I.7.11–12, pp. 394–402.

[144] In general, see Jan Willem van Henten, 'Herod the Great in Josephus', in *A Companion to Josephus*, eds Honora Howell Chapman and Zuleika Rodgers (Chichester: Wiley Blackwell, 2016), 235–46.

[145] *Hist.*, I.7.13 [14/17], p. 403.

will be no sound judgment there and the people will defile the Temple and the sanctuary with the leader who is coming: and they will be struck down in the flood of war'; and then that 'upon the Temple an abomination of desolation: and until the fulfilment of the time, a fulfilment will be given upon the desolation'.[146]

Book 1, as we saw in the previous chapter, is unusual because of the extensive use of exegetical sources. Deep into Book 7, Frechulf turned again to biblical commentary. To supplement excerpts from Eusebius-Jerome, he consulted another work of Jerome: his *Daniel Commentary*, written c. 407.[147] Jerome had set out an extensive overview of previous interpretations of Daniel 9:24–27, but Frechulf extracted only a single passage that expanded the *Chronicle*'s pared-down entry:

> Therefore seven and sixty-two weeks, which together become sixty-nine, and make up 484 years, in which the christs, that is priests consecrated by unction, ruled from the restoration of Temple under Darius up to Hyrcanus, in whom finally the unction and priesthood of the Jews came to an end. Therefore in the reign of Herod over the Jews and Augustus over the Romans, Christ, the son of God, was born, who built up the worship of the true God for many, [namely] the Apostles and other believers. For whatever took place in the Temple after the passion of the Lord was not a valid sacrifice to God but a mere worship of the devil, while they all cried out together, 'His blood be upon us and upon our children' [Matt. 27:25]; and, 'We have no king but Caesar' [John 19:15]. That, however, the number of years to be reckoned from the completion of the Temple to the tenth year of the Emperor Augustus, that is, when Hyrcanus was slain and Herod obtained Judaea, amounts to a total of seven plus sixty-two weeks, that is 484 years, we may check it in the following fashion: the building of the Temple was finished in the the first year of the sixty-sixth Olympiad, which was the sixth year of Darius; in the third year of the 186th Olympiad, that is, the tenth year of Augustus, Herod seized the rule over the Jews; this makes up in total 484 years, reckoning up by the individual Olympiads and computing them at four years each.[148]

The central importance of both Genesis 49:10 and Daniel 9:26–7 was that their respective fulfilments pointed towards Christ. Frechulf's chapter heading expressed this succinctly: 'after Herod the foreigner was made king of the Jews, the prophecies which predicted the coming of Christ and the destruction of the Jewish

---

[146] *Hist.*, I.7.13 [23/28], pp. 404. Adapted from online trans. of Eusebius-Jerome. Compare Frechulf's alteration of the *Chronicle*'s 'Quae omnia etiam Daniel Propheta vaticinatur, dicens' (p. 161) to 'Quae omnia ita se habentia longe prius prophetando designavit Danihel propheta ita dicens.'

[147] Jerome, *In Danielem*.

[148] *Hist.*, I.7.13 [29/46]; Jerome, *In Danielem*, III, ix. 24, pp. 875–6; I have made use of the translation by Gleason L. Archer which is based upon the *PL* edition: http://www.tertullian.org/fathers/jerome_daniel_02_text.htm [last accessed 18 May 2020]. (The passage in question was Jerome's summary of Eusebius's (now lost) commentary; Frechulf excised Jerome's note that 'Any reader who is interested may look up this passage in the *Chronicle* of this same Eusebius, for I translated it into Latin many years ago.')

kingdom were fulfilled'.[149] For exegetically minded historians and historically minded exegetes, the respective prophecies of Moses and Daniel were of the utmost importance. Read retrospectively, they signalled the specific time in which Christ was born. Eusebius's scholarship seems to have been foundational. Jerome transmitted parts of it to the Latin west through his translation of the *Chronicle* and his *Daniel Commentary*. Eusebius had also offered a more detailed rendering of the significance of Genesis 49:10, and also referred briefly to Daniel 9, in his *Ecclesiastical History*, which was translated and continued by Rufinus of Aquileia.[150]

Genesis 49:10 was a particular favourite of Christian historians, since its fulfilment not only lay at the very heart of the Christian understanding of the past but also was tied to historical events and persons who existed outside of the Old Testament. It was for both these reasons that this prophecy can be found in many of the sources utilised by Frechulf.[151] Pseudo-Hegisippus, in his epitome of Josephus's *Jewish Wars*, echoed Jacob's prophecy in his work's prologue.[152] Augustine offered a reading in his *City of God*, which marked the culmination of the chapter that looked at Jewish history between the Second Temple and Christ.[153] In Cassiodorus's *Historia Ecclesiastica Tripartita*, it was noted that Jacob's inspired words 'clearly referred to the reign of Herod, who was an Idumean, on his father's side, and on his mother's, an Arabian, and the Jewish nation was delivered to him by the Roman senate and Augustus Caesar'.[154] Frechulf would also have known about the pairing of these prophecies from exegetical sources. Claudius of Turin, in his *Genesis Commentary*, likewise stressed that Herod was a 'foreigner', picked not from the sacred priestly line but imposed upon the Jews by the Romans.[155] This

---

[149] *Hist.*, I.7.13 cap., p. 363: 'Herode alienigena rege facto Iudaeorum prophetiae completae sunt quae Christum tunc venturum praedixerunt et Iudaeorum regnum destruendum.'

[150] Eusebius-Rufinus, *Ecclesiastical History*, I.6.1–10, pp. 49–53.

[151] Compare *Chronicon Moisiacense*, ed. Hans Katz and David Claszen, 'Chronicon Moissiacense Maius: A Carolingian World Chronicle from Creation until the First Years of Louis the Pious', 2 vols (unpublished research master thesis, University of Leiden, 2012), vol. 2, pp. 1–150, at p. 48.

[152] Pseudo-Hegesippus, *De excidio*, Prol. 1, ed. Vincenzo Ussani, *Hegesippi qui dicitur Historia libri V*, CSEL 66/1 (Vienna: Hoelder-Pickler-Tempsky, 1932), p. 4. The key study on Hegesippus is Richard Matthew Pollard, 'The *De Excidio* of "Hegesippus" and the Reception of Josephus in the Early Middle Ages', *Viator*, 46(2) (2015): 65–100.

[153] Augustine, *DCD*, XVIII.45 [76/90], p. 643.

[154] Cassiodorus, *Historia ecclesiastica tripartita*, eds Walter Jacob and Rudolf Hanslik, *Cassiodori-Epiphanii historia ecclesiastica tripartita: historiae ecclesiasticae ex Socrate, Sozomeno et Theodorito*, CSEL 71 (Vienna: Hoelder-Pichler-Tempsky, 1952), p. 10: 'Iacob autem expectationem gentium in eo nunc existentem nec non et tempus, quo venit, praenuntiavit, ubi ait tunc deficere duces Hebraeorum ex genere Iudae principis tribus eius. Significabat autem principatum Herodis; qui cum Idumaeus esset genere paterno, Arabs autem a matre, commissa ei est gens Iudaeorum a senatu Romano et Caesare simul Augusto.'

[155] Claudius of Turin, *Commentarii in Genesim*, col. 1017A: 'Herodes … erat enim alienigena nec enim sacramento illo mysticae unctionis tamquam conjugali foedere cohaerebat, sed tamquam extraneus dominabatur, quam potestatem a Romanis et a Caesare acceperat.'

marked the end of the Judean kingdom and the sacred priestly line of the Jews, which, Claudius added, Daniel had also foretold, while also heralding the advent of Christ.[156] In 840, in the context of a debate between Eleazar, a recent Jewish convert and former deacon at Aachen, and Álvaro of Córdoba, the interpretation of Genesis 49:10 was a prominent matter of contention.[157] There was a very simple reason why this passage mattered so much: the central claim that the New Testament had superseded the Old was in part built on it.

Conclusion

Christ was the event towards which all others worked. Frechulf's *summa annorum* at the very end of Part I continues to confound, but the salience of the moment at which he stops is unmistakable within the context of Christian history:

> We have taken care to narrate this series of years, from the creation of the first man up to the advent of our Lord, as well as narrate from the more celebrated facts [what happened] in each kingdom. Now, however, having at last, after the great waves of the open sea, escaped the barking of Scylla, a safe haven has been reached, and after the long darkness of past ages, we reach the true light in the coming of the Lord Christ. Bathed with that light, we have made the end of our books.[158]

Frechulf's concern for charting chronology (*series annorum*) along with narrating famous known deeds in every kingdom, takes us back both to Frechulf's prologues and their underlying source: the *Chronicle* of Eusebius-Jerome. In this survey of Part I of the *Histories*, I have sought to show how fundamental this text was, both as a source of information but also as a guide to the divine flow of history. We should take seriously Frechulf's remark that he had been shown an account of world history, 'as if depicted on a concise chart'. The *Chronicle* conveyed to Frechulf a pattern of the past, in which all events—sacred and secular, biblical and classical—were brought together. In engaging with this massively important source, Frechulf was not unusual. The way he engaged with it, however, was unparalleled. Rather than continuing the *Chronicle*, Frechulf instead produced a 'vast narrative

---

[156] Claudius of Turin, *Commentarii in Genesim*, cols. 1017B–C: 'Illo ergo tempore quo jam de tribu Juda regnum defecerat, veniendum erat ad Christum verum Salvatorem Dominum nostrum, qui non obesset, multumque prodesset, sic enim fuerat prophetatum: Non deficiet princeps ex Juda, neque dux de femoribus ejus, donec veniat cui repromissum est, et ipse erit exspectatio gentium (Gen. XLIX). Jam isto tempore omne quoque magisterium Judaeorum, et mystifica unde Christi vocabantur unctio, ipsa defecerat, secundum prophetiam etiam Danielis, tunc venit cui repromissum erat, qui est exspectatio gentium, et unctus est Sanctus sanctorum oleo exsultationis prae participibus suis ...'
[157] Frank Riess, 'From Aachen to Al-Andalus: The Journey of Deacon Bodo (823–76)', *EME*, 13(2) (2005): 131–57, at 142–23.
[158] *Hist.*, I.7.19 [56/62], p. 432: 'Hanc igitur annorum seriem, a protoplausto scilicet usque ad Domini aduentum, in singulis prout potuimus regnis ex celebrioribus factis enarrare curauimus. Nunc autem post inmensos pelagi fluctus, Scilleos tandem euasisse latratus, optata statione potiti, post longeuas saeculorum tenebras ad lucem uenimus ueram, qua respersi in Domini Christi aduentu librorum finem fecimus.'

enlargement' of it, which involved fundamentally recasting its distinct form by incorporating excerpts from a range of other, no less authoritative, histories.[159] This new narrative echoed, emphasised and even altered Eusebius-Jerome's stresses, and the effort expended on achieving this should not be underestimated. This narrative, furthermore, was exegetical, since it served to demonstrate the 'truth of history'. The ultimate demonstration of the *veritas historiae* was Christ's Incarnation.

When commenting on the Book of Maccabees, Hrabanus Maurus explained that he included passages from Josephus's *Jewish Antiquities* since it would aid the reader 'if the narrations from different histories are compared, for in combination they seem to enhance each other, to explain the chronological order of the matter and to uncover the truth at a historical level'.[160] And in the prologue to this same commentary, Hrabanus stated that, by combining the narrative of the 'divine history' with other, extra-biblical historical accounts, 'the truth of [this] sacred history (*veritas sacrae historiae*) will appear through the combination of many books and the meaning of its narration (*sensus narrationis eius*) may become more clear to the reader'.[161]

Frechulf's goal—'to hunt through the volumes of the ancients and to collect all that pertains to the truth of history'—was not identical to Hrabanus's. His task was not to explicate or reveal the truth of one particular biblical book, but the 'overarching story' that emerged from all of scripture.[162] The truth of this meta-history was to be found in all the *volumina antiquorum*, and it was underscored ultimately with the birth of Christ, about whose advent Moses and Daniel had prophesised. An exegete like Angelomus of Luxeuil, with whom we started this chapter, practised biblical *explanatio* to demonstrate that Christ marked the fulfilment of the Old Testament; Frechulf performed a parallel task through historical *narratio*. All history, as Frechulf presented it in Part I, was purposively directed towards the Incarnation. The exegetical thrust of the *Histories* thus extended well beyond its distinctive first book: the arc of world history began with Adam and reached fulfilment in Christ. In the next chapter, I examine in more detail the Roman imperial context of Christ's birth and how Frechulf worked between two (supposedly) conflicting interpretations of the empire's world-historical significance.

---

[159] Quotation from Allen, 'Universal History', 39.

[160] Hrabanus Maurus, *Commentaria in libros Machabaeorum*, PL 109, cols. 1125–56D, I, 8, col. 1175D: 'Quid Josephus hinc referat non indignum videtur huic opero inserere; nec grave debet videri lectori si diversarum historiarum invicem conferuntur narrationes, quia alterutrum se juvare videntur ad explanandam rei rectitudinem historice retexere veritatem.' Trans. from De Jong, 'Empire as *Ecclesia*', 220.

[161] Hrab. *Epist.*, no. 19, pp. 424–5: trans. De Jong, 'Empire as *Ecclesia*', 217.

[162] I borrow this term from Young, *Biblical Exegesis*, 18 and 112. See further Elisabeth Mégier, '*Ecclesiae sacramenta*: The Spiritual Meaning of Old Testament History and the Foundation of the Church in Hugh of Fleury's *Historia ecclesiastica*', in *Christliche Weltgeschichte im 12. Jahrhundert: Themen, Variationen und Kontraste. Untersuchungen zu Hugo von Fleury, Ordericus Vitalis und Otto von Freising*, Beihefte zur Mediaevistik 13 (Frankfurt am Main: Peter Lang, 2010), 361–82 at 363.

4

Incarnation and Empire:
Orosius and the Exegesis of History

Between Parts I and II: Orosius at the Heart of the *Histories*

The birth of Christ marked the conclusion to Part I of Frechulf's *Histories* and the inception of Part II. That a Christian intellectual should centre their narrative of human history on the person of Jesus of Nazareth may not seem at all surprising. Yet, what at first glance appears as a prosaic facet reveals itself upon closer inspection to be extraordinary. Frechulf placed the birth of Christ at the heart of his *Histories* in such a way that cannot be paralleled in medieval historiography. Almost all of the material that comprised his *opus conpendiosum* was extracted from existing historical sources, yet none of these offered a model for organising a narrative in two separate halves, corresponding to history before Christ and after. Frechulf's decision to do so, beyond underscoring his own creative ingenuity, should be taken as a further, forceful, indication of the exegetical mindset that shaped his work. The bipartite structure of his *Histories* echoed the bipartite nature of the Christian scriptural canon, in which the books of the New Testament were understood as the fulfilment or completion of those of the Old. Jean Leclercq, in his classic overview of medieval monastic spirituality, wrote the Old and New Testaments 'were considered … not as two collections of "books", but as two periods, two "times" which echo each other. The time of the law (*tempus legis*) and the time of grace (*tempus gratiae*) are different stages of one and the same salvation, and each of them includes, over and above the scriptural texts, the sum of the realities told us in the texts.'[1] The *Histories* embody this conception of the past superbly.

The significance of Frechulf's structure would have been most conspicuous to readers of a pandect edition of the *Histories* in which both parts were joined together, although the work's Christocentric organisation would still have been

---

[1] Jean Leclercq, *The Love of Learning and the Desire for God: A Study of Monastic Culture*, trans. Catharine Misrahi (New York: Fordham University Press, 1974), 80–1.

clear to those who had at their disposal only one of the two volumes. For example, Frechulf began his Part II by recapping what preceded it:

> In [my] prior books, with God's support and with no small effort, I took care to excerpt from the many works of holy and pagan writers all that seemed to my smallness useful and beneficial for readers, beginning from the first parent, that is, the propagator of all mortal life; then, after the great darkness of past ages, we arrived finally at the birth of the new man, the Lord Jesus Christ, son of God and man. At this point, I decided to end my books, so that they would reach their conclusion just as the ceremonies of the Law and the shadows and ancient errors [of the pre-Christian past] came to an end.[2]

Three things stand out. Firstly, Frechulf here hinted at the typological association between Adam and Christ who bookended Part I, something implied by the overall structure of the volume but never explicitly stated or developed.[3] Second, the transition from Part I to Part II was presented as the passage from darkness to light. This was an established Christian motif,[4] which Frechulf deployed at the end of Part I and had already used earlier, in his sketch of the establishment of the Two Cities: throughout the world's first five thousand or so years, the presence of the *civitas Dei* paled in comparison to the city of iniquity, 'until the Lord Christ, son of God, God before the ages, man in our time, appeared from the womb of the most holy Virgin Mary', at which point 'the true God and true man, one person from two substances, radiated new light to the world'.[5] Even when human history was at its earliest stage, the advent of Christ was already anticipated. Third: the termination of the ceremonies of the Law. This referred back to a pair of influential Old Testament prophecies (Genesis 49:10 and Daniel 9:26–7), whose fulfilment marked one of the climaxes to Part I, as we saw in the previous chapter.

The fulfilment of these prophecies was deliberately restated near the start of Part II: 'as we revealed in [our] previous books', Frechulf explained, 'Herod, an outsider with no links at all to the Jewish people, was established as *princeps* by the Romans', after extended bouts of destabilising internecine strife left the Jewish

---

[2] *Hist.*, II.1.1, p. 440: 'In prioribus libris, Domino suffragante, ex multorum opusculis agiographorum seu gentilium, non modico labore desudans, decerpere curaui quaeque utilia paruitati meae sunt uisa et legentibus profutura, sumens exordium a primo parente mortalium propagatore; tandem post multas saeculorum tenebras ad noui natiuitatem hominis peruenimus, Domini scilicet Iesu Christi, Dei et hominis filii, ubi priorum finem decreui facere librorum, ut cum legalibus ceremoniis et umbris atque erroribus pristinis terminarentur.'
[3] See also *Hist.*, I.Prol. [16.17], p. 18: 'a conditione quidem primi hominis usque ad Christi nativitatem.' Staubach, 'Christiana tempora', 178, 203; Savigni, 'Storia universale', 167–70; Mégier, 'Ecclesia sacramenta', 372.
[4] For example, John 1:5–9, 8:12; Matthew 5:14; Acts 26:18; Ephesians 5:8; Isaiah 9:2.
[5] *Hist.*, I.1.9 [45/49], p. 36: '... tamen in paucis aedificata est ad conparationem iniquorum quoadusque Dominus Christus Deique filius, Deus ante saecula, homo in nostro tempore ex utero uirginis Mariae sacratissimae procederet: uerus Deus uerusque homo, ex duabus substantiis et una persona, nouum lumen mundo resplenduit.'

kingdom without an indigenous leader.[6] Already in the fourth century, Christian intellectuals had argued that Herod's reign marked the realisation of these scriptural passages, which signalled Christ's imminent arrival. By the ninth century, the completion of these predictions was firmly established in the Christian collective consciousness as a prime demonstration of divine providence; at the same time, the idea of completion underlined for Christian readers that the Nativity marked a radically transformative moment, bringing to an end the Jews' special relationship with God and inaugurating a new phase of history. By highlighting that the Nativity overturned established, Old Testament, traditions of divine worship and brought the light of the New Testament into a world hitherto obscured by darkness, Frechulf couched the central juncture of his work in the sort of Christian interpretive discourse that pervades biblical commentaries, sermons and the liturgy. If the two-part framing of the *Histories* was innovative, the message it conveyed would have been standard and orthodox for an educated Christian audience.

Frechulf's central focus on the Incarnation depended on a further, no less critical, foundation, namely that Christ's birth happened not only when Herod's rise to power broke the sequence of native Jewish leadership, but when the Roman Empire was established under Augustus, the first Roman emperor (ruled 27 BC–14 AD). The coincidence of Christ's birth and Augustus's reign was far from unique to Frechulf. Since at least the second century, Christian apologists had argued that the *pax Augusta*, the period of peace established by Augustus, was the work of God, who had used the Roman Empire to prepare the world for the coming of Christ and the church.[7] In the early medieval west, no source expressed this argument more decisively than Orosius's *Seven Books of History against the Pagans* (hereafter referred to as the *Historiae* to avoid confusion with Frechulf's *Histories*).[8] Orosius's *Historiae* were very widely read throughout the entire Middle Ages, and for very many reasons. Frechulf himself made considerable use of the text, and extensive excerpts from all seven of Orosius's books can be found throughout Parts I and II. Over a hundred years ago, Max Manitius could baldly state that 'Orosius [was] the most important source for the whole work'.[9] Insufficient attention, however, has been paid to unpacking the implications of this reception, especially insofar as it pertains to that central moment of his *Histories*: the birth of Christ and its coincidence with the establishment of the Roman Empire.

---

[6] *Hist.*, II.1.3 [1/6], p. 442: 'Igitur, ut in praecedentibus libris ostendimus, depulsos esse a regno Iudaeorum uel ducatu ex semine Iuda duces et principes dum de summa rerum acriter contenderent, Herodes a Romanis constitutus est princeps, alienigena et nihil omnino pertinens ad Iudaeos, qui Antipatri Aschalonitae et matris Cypridis Arabicae filius fuit.'
[7] For background, IIona Opelt, 'Augustustheologie und Augustustypologie', *Jahrbuch für Antike und Christentum*, 4 (1961): 44–57; Kershaw, *Peaceful Kings*, 49; James Corke-Webster, *Eusebius and Empire: Constructing Church and Rome in the* Ecclesiastical History (Cambridge: CUP, 2019), 82–4.
[8] Translation's of Frechulf's borrowings from Orosius all derive from Fear, *Orosius*.
[9] Max Manitius, *Geschichte*, 666, n. 1: 'Orosius ist die wichstige Quelle für das ganze Werk'. See further *Prolegomena*, 214*–216*.

A major reason for this neglect is that there has been more interest in unpacking what Frechulf learned from Augustine, Orosius's more illustrious 'teacher' and the dedicatee of his *Historiae*. The relationship between these men, as reconstructed by modern scholars, carries a lot of baggage. A view prevalent in much twentieth-century scholarship was not only that Augustine was *the* pre-eminent patristic authority of the Latin west, but also that Orosius was a mere historian, and a second-rate one at that, who tried and spectacularly failed to convert his teacher's intricate theology into a blunt, straightforward narrative. Recent work on Orosius by Peter van Nuffelen and Victoria Leonard has fundamentally overturned unhelpful assumptions about the *Historiae* as an unsuccessful attempt to construct a history along Augustinian lines; approaching things from a very different, but for my purposes complementary angle, Josh Timmermann has emphasised the degree to which Augustine was, of course, an exceptionally important figure within the Carolingian world, but as one authority among many.[10] This chapter uses Frechulf's reception of the *Historiae* to connect these perspectives. In so doing, I not only aim to shed new light on Frechulf's project but also to lock it even more tightly within the ninth-century intellectual culture that shaped it. More specifically, I argue that is necessary to remove Orosius from 'the shadow of Augustine' in order to appreciate the distinctive contribution his *Historiae* made to early medieval understandings of the historical conditions into which Christ was born. Second, I demonstrate that, in the context of elite Carolingian Christianity, predicated as it was upon the interpretation of the Bible and the collected writings of the 'holy fathers', Orosius was not simply a historian, but a fully fledged Christian authority, counted amongst the patristic canon.[11]

Frechulf's Orosius

Running through the first volume of the *Histories* was the successive transfer of pre-eminent power, the so-called *translatio imperii*, that started with the Assyrian ruler Ninus and reached its end with Augustus, or as Frechulf tended to call him, Octavian Caesar, who was 'the first to obtain the monarchy of the world'.[12] In making Augustus

---

[10] Van Nuffelen, *Orosius* and Victoria Leonard, *In Defiance of History: Orosius and the Unimproved Past* (Abingdon: Routledge, 2022); Josh Timmermann, 'An Authority among Authorities: Knowledge and Use of Augustine in the Wider Carolingian World', *EME*, 28(4) (2020): 532–59.

[11] This chapter develops ideas first tested out in Graeme Ward, 'All Roads Lead to Rome? Frechulf of Lisieux, Augustine and Orosius', *EME*, 22(4) (2014): 492–505 and Graeme Ward, 'Exegesis, Empire, and Eschatology: Reading Orosius's *Histories Against the Pagans* in the Carolingian World', in *Cultures of Eschatology II: Time, Death and Afterlife in Medieval Christian, Islamic and Buddhist Communities*, eds Veronika Wieser, Vincent Eltschinger and Johann Heiss (Berlin: De Gruyter, 2020), 674–97.

[12] *Hist.*, I.Prol. [25.26], p. 18: 'usque Octoviani Caesaris monarchiam'; I.2.Prol. [17.18], p. 85: 'usque ad Augusti Caesaris monarchiam'; I.4.25 [22], p. 258: 'usque ad Caesaris Octoviani monarchiam'; II.1.2 [19.20], pp. 441–2: 'Octovianus Caesar—qui primus monarchiam obtinuit mundi'. *Octovianus* was a common enough medieval spelling of Octavian: checked via Brepols cross database searchtool.

the culmination of this schema, Frechulf broke with the overview of history laid out in Eusebius-Jerome, which otherwise guided his framework of secular history. There, Julius Caesar was 'the first of the Romans to obtain sole power', and his reign was the point at which the Roman *fila regnorum* began to occupy the *Chronicle*'s left-most column. For Frechulf, however, Julius Caesar was only 'the architect of empire rather than the emperor'.[13] This observation, along much else about Augustus which we find in the *Histories*, depended directly upon Orosius.[14]

The Roman thread of the narrative in the final book of Part I (which more or less corresponded to Orosius's Book 6) followed the major events of the last century of the Republic, with an emphasis on expansion and conquest: Pompey's wars in the east (I.7.3) and Julius Caesar's in Gaul (I.7.4–6); civil war between Caesar and Pompey (I.7.7–9); then finally the ascent of Octavian (I.7.14–16). I.7.16 was the final chapter of Part I taken from Orosius (= VI.20–2), and it contains much of the material that will come up again below. After having defeated Antony in Egypt, Octavian returned to Rome and in 29 BC closed the gates of Janus for the first time and on 6 January took the name of Augustus, the same day that Christians 'observe Epiphany, that is the appearance or manifestation of the Lord's sacrament'.[15] The gates of Janus were opened, shut and opened again as further campaigns were undertaken as Rome's *imperium* continued to be extended all across the earth, quelling violence and hostility along with it. Then, 752 years *ab Urbe condita*, as the whole world enjoyed a period of singular serenity, Augustus closed the gates of Janus for a third and final time. Augustus not only encouraged this peace but also prohibited anyone from calling him 'master (*dominus*)'. The reason for all this was clear:

> in the year when Caesar, through God's decree, had established the most secure and stable peace on earth, Christ, for Whose coming that peace was a servant and upon Whose birth angels exultantly sang to listening men, 'Glory to God in the Highest, and on the Earth peace towards men of good will' [Luke 2:14], was born. At that same time he to whom all earthly power had been granted, did not suffer, or rather did not dare, to be called master of mankind, since the True Master of all the human race was then born among men.[16]

Not only was God shown to be the engineer of the empire and the so-called *pax Augusta*, but 'in His deep mysteries', God also 'predestined' that Augustus would order an imperial census to be carried out, in which Christ, as God born in the flesh, would be counted.[17]

---

[13] *Hist.*, II.1.2 [20.21], p. 442: 'quamvis avvunculus eius Iulius Caesar ante eum [that is, Augustus] existeret potius metator imperii quam imperator'. Trans, Fear, 322.

[14] Michael C. Sloan, 'Augustus, the Harbinger of Peace: Orosius' Reception of Augustus in *Historiae Adversus Paganos*', in *Afterlives of Augustus, AD 14–2014*, ed. Penelope J. Goodman (Cambridge: CUP, 2018), 103–21.

[15] *Hist.*, I.7.16 [1/10], pp. 413–14; Oros., VI.20.1-3, pp. 226–7; trans. Fear, 308–9.

[16] *Hist.*, I.7.16 [99/105], pp. 417–18 = Oros. VI.22.5, p. 235; trans. Fear, 316.

[17] *Hist.*, I.7.16 [106/16], p. 418 = Oros. VI.22.6, p. 236; trans. Fear, 316.

Drawing on Orosius Book 7 at the beginning of Part II, Frechulf then added that Christ was born at the very end of the forty-second year of Augustus's reign, bringing 'true light to a world lethargic from foul darkness of past ages (*veram mundo torpenti in tenebris a saeculis saeculorum tetris adferens lucem)*'. Moreover, he highlighted that:

> And so it came to pass that while the holy man Abraham, to whom divine promises were given and from whose seed Christ was promised to come forth, was born in the forty-third year of the rule of Ninus, the first king of the *gentes*, the birth of Christ came at the end of the forty-second year, so that instead of coming forth in part of this forty-third year, it should come forth from Him. I believe that it is well enough known how much that year abounded with both new and unaccustomed blessings without me listing them: an all-embracing peace came to all the lands of the globe, there was not a cessation but an abolition of all wars; the gates of Janus of the two faces were closed as the roots of war were not pruned, but torn out; this was when the first and greatest census was held, when all God's creation of great nations unanimously swore loyalty to Caesar alone, and at the same time, by partaking of the census were made into one community.
>
> So 752 years after the foundation of the City, Christ was born and brought to the world the faith that gives salvation. Truly, He is the Rock set at the heart of things, where there is ruination for whoever strikes against Him, but where whoever believes in Him is saved. Truly, He is the blazing Fire that lights the way for whoever follows Him, but consumes whoever makes trial of Him. Jesus Christ, son of God, consecrated the sixth age of the world with his advent. [18]

In short: through extensive quotation, Frechulf's *Histories* became infused with characteristically Orosian flavours. The Roman Empire was established and consolidated under Augustus according to God's designs, which he had arranged in advance for the sake of his Incarnation. When excerpting from an anonymous series of imperial biographies, the *Epitome de Caesaribus* (written c. 400), Frechulf revised that text's assessment of Augustus, which attributed his long reign to his own personal merits, so that it was clear that everything happened *pro causa nativitatis Domini*.[19] Orosius's version of events thus coloured Frechulf's interpretation of a text from which it was originally absent. In addition to the peace, a number of other episodes and events were understood as signs of God's governance of history: the coincidence of Epiphany and Augustus's acclamation; the story about Augustus taking umbrage at being called *dominus* (which Orosius got from Suetonius); the Roman census as a sort of foreshadowing of the Christian eucharistic community (compare Luke 2:1);[20] parallels between Abraham/Ninus/

---

[18] *Hist.*, II.1.2 [24/42], p. 442. Compare Oros., VII.2.16, p. 20 and VII.3.1-2, pp. 20-1; trans. Fear, 322 and 323.

[19] *Hist.*, II.1.4 [58/60], pp. 446-7: 'Imperauit annis LVI, XII cum Antonio, XLta uero et quattuor solus. Qui certe numquam aut rei publicae potentiam ad se traxisset aut tamdiu ea potiretur nisi pro causa natiuitatis Domini hoc fieret.'

[20] On this theme, see further Tiziana Faitini, 'Towards a Spiritual Empire: Christian Exegesis of

Belus on the one hand and Christ/Augustus/Caesar on the other. I will return to these signs later, but first I shall sketch the wider context of Orosius's status, as perceived by early medieval readers as well as modern scholars.

Orosius vs Augustine: Political Theology and Historiography in Late Antiquity and the Early Middle Ages

Orosius completed his *Historiae* around 417 at the behest of Augustine. His seven books were constructed as a defence of Christianity against the religion's critics, who held it responsible for the sack of Rome by the Goths in 410.[21] The book's central argument was that, by comparing the Christian and pre-Christian pasts, it could be shown that Christianity had significantly lessened the misery and brutal hardships which humans, stained by sin, had endemically suffered since Adam's fall from grace. While rooted firmly in a specific fifth-century milieu, the *Historiae* remained deeply meaningful to readers for at least the next millennium, as is attested by the text's staggering medieval reception.[22] Nearly 250 manuscripts are extant, including numerous abbreviated and glossed copies.[23] In addition to being continuously transcribed, read and studied, the *Historiae* served as a vital source of historical information for subsequent medieval historians and chroniclers from the fifth century onwards; and Orosius's description of the world in the first of his seven books (which also circulated independently) was an equally vital source of geographic knowledge.[24] By the tenth century, Orosius's work had been translated into Old English and, more remarkably still, Arabic.[25] Taken together, these are

the Universal Census at the Time of Jesus's Birth', in *The Church and Empire*, eds Stewart J. Brown, Charlotte Methuen and Andrew Spicer, *Studies in Church History*, 54 (2018): 16–30.

[21] Van Nuffelen, Peter, 'Not Much Happened: 410 and All That', Journal of Roman Studies, 105 (2015): 322–9.

[22] Heidi Eisenhut, *Die Glossen Ekkeharts IV. von St. Gallen im Codex Sangallensis 621* (St. Gallen: Verlag am Klosterhof, 2009), 56–61 provides a handy summary of the 'reasons for the success [of the text]'; see also J. N. Hillgarth, 'The *Historiae* of Orosius in the Early Middle Ages', in *De Tertullien aux Mozarabes: mélanges offerts à Jacques Fontaine, à l'occasion de son 70ᵉ anniversaire, par ses élèves, amis et collègues*, eds Louis Holtz and Jean-Claude Fredouille, 3 vols (Paris: Institut d'Études Augustiniennes, 1992), vol. 2, 157–70.

[23] Lars Boje Mortensen, 'The Diffusion of Roman Histories in the Middle Ages. A List of Orosius, Eutropius, Paulus Diaconus, and Landolfus Sagax', *Filologia Mediolatina*, VI–VII (1999–2000), 101–200, at 119–65. On glosses: Heidi Eisenhut, *Die Glossen*, together with digital edition http://91.250.103.102/heidieisenhut/cd/index.php [last accessed 9 June 2021]. See also Olivier Szerwiniack, 'Un commentaire hiberno-latin', in *Archivum Latinitatis Medii Aevi*, 51 (1992/3): 5–137 and 65 (2007): 165–208. Robert Evans and Rosamond McKitterick, 'A Carolingian Epitome of Orosius from Tours: Leiden VLQ 20', in *Historiography and Identity III: Carolingian Approaches*, eds Rutger Kramer, Helmut Reimitz and Graeme Ward (Turnhout: Brepols, 2021), 123–53; Coz, 'Quelques interprétations'.

[24] Oros., I.2.1–106, pp. 13–42. Merrils, *History and Geography*, 35–99; Natalia Lozovsky, '*The Earth is Our Book': Geographical Knowledge in the Latin West, ca. 400-1000* (Ann Arbor, MI: University of Michigan Press, 2000), 69–78. Lozovsky, 7, rightly notes that Orosius eschewed biblical references, but exegetes still managed to make connections between the *Historiae* and scripture: see below.

[25] *The Old English History of the World: An Anglo-Saxon Rewriting of Orosius*, ed. and trans. Malcolm R. Godden (Cambridge, MA: HUP, 2016); Christian Sahner, 'From Augustine to Islam: Translation and

all sure signs of the text's recognised importance. (Less well appreciated is the fact that Orosius was consulted as an exegetical aid, and here geographical and historical knowledge dovetailed: see below.)

Orosius's authority can also be sampled by briefly surveying how early medieval writers described him.[26] In the sixth-century *Decretum Gelasianum*, a highly influential list of approved and condemned authorities attributed to Pope Gelasius I (died 496), Orosius was labelled a *vir eruditissimus*, 'a most learned man'.[27] In seventh-century Iberia, Braulia of Zaragoza referred to Orosius as a 'holy man', *sanctus*; and in a stunning codex produced at the nunnery of Sainte-Marie-Saint-Jean at Laon in the mid-eighth century in a fine pre-Caroline minuscule (Laon, BM 137), there is a copy of the *Historiae* prefaced by Gennadius of Marseilles' bio-bibliography of Orosius, strikingly arranged in the shape of the cross with the text author introduced as *sanctus Orosius*.[28] A little later in the eighth century, Alcuin wrote a poem celebrating York's cathedral library that housed 'the legacy of the ancient fathers (*veterum vestigia partum*)', a phrase which was often used by early medieval exegetes to stress their humble dedication to received wisdom. Included amongst these *vestigia* were 'the writings of astute Orosius'.[29] The *Historiae* were even treasured amongst the secular elite: in the will of Eberhard of Friuli and Gisela drawn up c. 863–4, books as well as land and treasure were apportioned to their children, amongst which was a 'volume [containing] the seven books of the great Paul Orosius (*volumen VII librorum magni Orozii Pauli*)'.[30] Frechulf praised Orosius for having 'nobly and usefully composed seven books *Adversus paganos*' and, more generally, counted him amongst his *hagiographi*: his was but one in a long list of positive endorsements.

In stark contrast to these indicators of the *Historiae*'s vibrant medieval *Nachleben*, modern assessments of Orosius as a fifth-century writer have often

---

History in the Arabic Orosius', *Speculum*, 88(4) (2013): 905–31.

[26] Hillgarth, '*Historiae*' assembled the references and at 162 wrote of the '"canonisation" of Orosius'.

[27] *Decretum Gelasianum*, c. 4, ed Ernst von Dobschütz, *Das Decretum Gelasianum de Libris Recipiendis et non Recipiendis*, Texte und Untersuchungen zur Geschichte der altchristlichen Literatur 38:4 (Leipzig: J. C. Hinrichs, 1912), 46–7. See Mirela Ferrari, 'Mira Brevitate: Orosio e il Decretum Gelasianum', in *Roma, magistra mundi. Itineraria culturae medievalis. Mélanges offerts au Père L. E. Boyle à l'occasion de son 75e anniversaire*, ed. Jacqueline Hamesse, Textes et études du Moyen Âge, 3 vols (Louvain-la-Neuve: F.I.D.E.M., Collège Mercier, 1998), vol. 1, 225–31. Quodvultdeus of Carthage went for *historiographus eruditissimus*.

[28] 'Sanctus' was not originally included in Gennadius's text. Compare Felice Lifshitz, *Religious Women in Early Carolingian Francia: A Study of Manuscript Transmission and Monastic Culture* (New York: Fordham University Press, 2014), 154. There is at least one manuscript (from the 10th century) where Orosius is referred to as *beatus Orosius*: Vatican, Reg. Lat. 772, fol. 2r.

[29] Alcuin, *The Bishops, Kings, and Saints of York*, ed. and trans Peter Godman (Oxford: Clarendon Press, 1982), 122–3. Orosius's name is sandwiched between Jerome, Hilary, Ambrose, Augustine on the one side, and Gregory the Great, Leo I, Basil, Fulgentius, Cassiodorus, and John Chrysostom on the other. Alcuin borrowed part of this (including reference to *Orosius acutus*—from Venantius Fortunatus.

[30] *Cartulaire de l'abbaye de Cysoing et ses dépendances*, ed. M. Ignace de Coussemaker (Lille, 1885), n. 1, pp. 1–5 at p. 4.

been critical, even to the point of outright disparagement. Historians of the later Roman Empire, such as John Matthews, wrote him off for not having written the sort of detailed political narrative they found in Ammianus Marcellinus.[31] More pertinently for my purposes, specialists of late antique Christian culture were once equally dismissive, primarily because of Orosius's relationship to Augustine. Orosius had explained in his preface that his *Historiae* elaborated a line of argument Augustine himself had encouraged him to develop. Although this connection bolstered Orosius's authority in the Middle Ages, it later came to compromise it: in the twentieth century the two authors were compared, and Orosius's Augustinian credentials were seen to be hollow.[32] As a prominent expert on Augustine once said, 'Orosius must have been a very unsatisfactory pupil if he could so mistake his master's mind as to think that this sort of stuff was what Augustine wanted.'[33]

What did Orosius allegedly get so wrong? The Roman Empire and its role within Christian history lies at the heart of things. According to Robert Markus (the above-mentioned expert), Augustine had gradually but boldly moved away from the dominant fourth- and early fifth-century understanding of the Roman Empire, and especially the Christian Roman Empire, 'as God's chosen instrument for the salvation of men'. In contrast to Orosius as well as other renowned apologists such as Eusebius of Caesarea, Augustine reassessed the historical importance of the empire, rendering it 'no longer indispensable for the unfolding of [God's] providential plan in history'.[34] Orosius, on the other hand, 'once more reverted' to the Christian imperial optimism of Eusebius: 'the Empire founded by Augustus was the providentially established vehicle of Christianity, and the history of the period since the Incarnation (under Augustus!) could be read as the progressive realisation of divine purpose'.[35] Put differently, for Augustine, the city of God was always an eschatological concept, in that it could only be realised at the end of time. Its future citizens were to be recruited from earth, but the city itself could never occupy the place of the empire or the *ecclesia* or some fusion of the two. Orosius, however, came 'perilously close to the positions that gave Augustine concern'. For Orosius, '[i]f not heaven on earth … Christian Rome will certainly bring heaven closer to earth'.[36]

Amongst Anglophone students, Markus's work remains highly influential, not only in delineating Augustine's conception of history but also in setting it apart

---

[31] For example, John Matthews, *The Roman Empire of Ammianus* (Baltimore, MD: Johns Hopkins University Press, 1989), 6.
[32] Hillgarth, '*Historiae*'.
[33] Robert Markus, 'The Roman Empire in Early Christian Historiography', *Downside Review*, 81 (1963): 340–53, at 352.
[34] Markus, *Saeculum*, 54–5.
[35] Markus, *Saeculum*, 161–2. In a similar vein, see Peter Brown, *Augustine of Hippo, A Biography*, 2nd edn (Berkeley, CA: University of California Press, 2000), 294, 307–8, 321.
[36] Fear, *Orosius*, 23.

from Orosius's approach to the past, which took a serious bashing in the process. Markus was not alone. Henri-Irénée Marrou, another expert on Augustine, thought of Orosius as 'un disciple zélé, mais pechant par exces de zèle, pour notre malheur, point trop intelligent'.[37] In place of the nuance of the *City of God*, Marrou found in the *Historiae* only 'a sort of naïve providentialism', in which the good were invariably rewarded, the bad punished, and God's hand and judgment was all too readily identified throughout secular (that is, extra-scriptural) history.[38] Even when the point was not to critique Orosius for being a substandard student, there has been sustained interest in parsing the fundamental differences between Orosius's and Augustine's theologies of history, with especial emphasis on their conflicting views on the Christian significance of the Roman Empire.[39]

Recent work by late antique specialists has positively transformed our understanding of the *Historiae* as a sophisticated and independent work of early fifth-century scholarship, that overlapped as much as it was at odds with Augustine's oeuvre, above all his *De civitate Dei*.[40] Yet the old dichotomy that master and pupil produced works with diametrically opposed views still shapes the interpretation of the early medieval evidence. For example, Paul Kershaw, in his superb study of the ideology of peace in the early Middle Ages, uncovered a sense of imperial, Orosian, optimism during the reign of Louis the Pious. This mood is best captured in the writings of Ermoldus Nigellus, an exiled cleric and poet who, in an epic celebrating the life and deeds of Louis the Pious, described the frescoes adorning the walls of the palace at Ingelheim: these frescoes, if Ermoldus is to be trusted, were based directly on scenes and imagery extracted from the *Historiae*. Set in relation to these historical paintings were more recent images,

---

[37] Henri Irénée Marrou, 'Saint Augustin, Orose et l'augustinisme historique', in *La storiografia altemedievale*, Settimane 17 (Spoleto: Centro italiano di studi sull'alto Medioevo, 1970), 59–87 at 79.

[38] For both Markus and Marrou, Augustine's historical theology—or at least their interpretation of it—resonated deeply with their own personal Catholic outlooks on the world; Orosius, by contrast, either represented the political theology of Eusebius or set the scene for the (un-Augustinian) 'sacral Christianity' of the Middle Ages (Marrou, 'Saint Augustin', 86-7). If Augustine felt modern to these scholars, in that his ideas about secularity reflected their present-day theological concerns, Orosius implicitly encapsulated a more backward and simplistic way of thinking, where God routinely rewards the just and punishes the proud. There is some irony that early medievalists still look to a body of scholarship that took a dim view of the Middle Ages: see now Robin Whelan, 'After Augustine, after Markus: The Problem of the Secular at the End of Antiquity', *EME*, 29(1) (2021): 12–35.

[39] Theodor E. Mommsen, 'Orosius and Augustine', in *Medieval and Renaissance Studies*, ed. Eugene F. Rice Jr (Ithaca, NY: Cornell University Press, 1959), 325–48; Hans-Werner Goetz, *Die Geschichtstheologie des Orosius* (Darmstadt: Wissenschaftliche Buchgesellschaft, 1980), 136-47; Sabine Tanz, 'Orosius im Spannungsfeld zwischen Eusebius von Caesarea und Augustin', *Klio. Beiträge zur alten Geschichte*, 65 (1983): 337–46; W. H. C. Frend, 'Augustine and Orosius on the End of the Ancient World', *Augustinian Studies*, 20 (1989): 1–38; Antonio José Meseguer Gil, 'La obra histórica de Paulo Orosio y sus diferencias con Agustín de Hipona: transmisión de conceptos historiográficos en la Antigüedad Tardía', *Onoba*, 5 (2017): 89–101.

[40] Van Nuffelen, *Orosius*, esp. 3–9 and 197–206 and Leonard, *In Defiance of History*, with comprehensive bibliographies between them.

which depicted the Carolingian dynasty in triumph.[41] This mood, however, was not to last: the destructive Frankish civil wars of the 840s engendered in their wake much more pessimistic perceptions of the state of the world, as can be seen in the poetry of Florus of Lyon. 'Just as', Kershaw notes, 'the disruptions of the later fourth and early fifth centuries put paid to an optimistic celebration of earthly imperial authority and the peace of the Church, so the events of the middle years of the ninth century had in their turn driven Florus ... into an Augustinian distance from the fallen world, and towards a focus upon the peace of the Heavenly Jerusalem and its *vestigia* in the world'.[42] Seen as such, fifth-century debates about the relationship between empire and Christianity—or what Markus termed the 'eschatological dimension of Christian hope'—were played out again in Carolingian Francia. Advocates for Christian empire stand in contrast to those who viewed the contemporary saeculum with the sort of detached agnosticism of which Augustine would have been proud.

The study of Frechulf further exemplifies this point. Like Orosius, Frechulf was initially understood to have unsuccessfully rendered Augustine's theological understanding of history into a more straightforward narrative of events; 'in some ways', he is now even regarded as 'a better pupil of Augustine' than Orosius himself ever was.[43] Frechulf's perception of the Roman Empire is crucial here. When discussing the *Histories'* account of the coincidence of Christ's birth and Augustus, Staubach argued that Frechulf, following Eusebius and Orosius, accepted the 'salvific-historical and providential significance of Augustus's *monarchia mundi*' on the one hand, while denying the empire any further meaning on the other. It was ultimately no different than any of the *eminentiora regna* that had preceded it.[44] This, according to Staubach, was a conspicuously Augustinian sentiment, since in the *City of God* Augustine had 'perceived the imperial optimism, as propagated by Eusebius and still advocated by his own pupil Orosius, as a disastrous misinterpretation of the processes of salvation history'.[45] Building on Staubach's work, Michael Allen has refined our appreciation of what Frechulf learned from the *City of God*, and has drawn attention to further ways that Frechulf engaged with Orosius's *Historiae* through an Augustinian lens. For instance, Frechulf 'quietly dropped [Orosius's] Christian-Roman imperial typologies that had prompted

[41] Kershaw, *Peaceful Kings*, 186. For the text, see: Ermoldus Nigellus, *In honorem Hludowici Christianissimi Caesaris Augusti elegiacum carmen*, ed. Edmond Faral, *Ermold le Noir: poème sur Louis le Pieux et* épitres *au roi* Pépin, Les classique de l'histoire de France au moyen age 14 (Paris: Les Belles Lettres, 1964), 164; English trans. Thomas F. X. Noble, *Charlemagne and Louis the Pious: The Lives by Einhard, Notker, Ermoldus, Thegan, and the Astronomer* (University Park, PA: State University of Pennsylvania Press, 2009), 127–86, at 176.
[42] Kershaw, *Peaceful Kings*, 203. For a detailed study of another 'Augustinian' Carolingian, see Sumi Shimahara, *Haymon d'Auxerre, exégète carolingien* (Turnhout: Brepols, 2013).
[43] Goez, 'Zur Weltchronik' and Staubach, '*Christiana tempora*', 183–4.
[44] Staubach, '*Christiana tempora*', 188.
[45] Staubach, '*Christiana tempora*', 199.

specific, if anonymous, reproofs from Augustine: namely, the supposed *translatio imperii* culminating in Rome, and the far-fetched typological alignment of the Ten Plagues of Egypt and the 'ten imperial persecutions'.[46]

Frechulf's Augustinianism has thus in part been defined in relation to his (implied) disavowal of characteristically Orosian conceptions of history. There are a number of problems with this approach. At a general level, 'Augustinian' is a frustratingly nebulous term which, on account of Augustine's vast literary oeuvre, can encompass more ideas than a single adjective can helpfully contain.[47] To be sure, there were concrete 'Augustinian' issues with which Carolingian intellectuals grappled, such as double predestination and the nature of the eucharist.[48] It is, however, less clear that his work, and especially the *City of God*, was read in the ninth century as though it contained an identifiable and analysable theology of history, which could be demarcated from that of other writers. Second, and more specifically to the subject at hand, Frechulf incorporated many of the Orosian trappings that have been dismissed as un-Augustinian, such as the *Historiae*'s 'naïve providentialism'. Even Frechulf's real emphasis on Augustus could be seen in this light, since he is a figure who makes only a brief appearance in the *City of God*.[49] That, quantitatively speaking, such aspects outstrip those absorbed from the bishop of Hippo (directly, or indirectly via Claudius of Turin) seems clear enough;[50] that, qualitatively speaking, Augustine's theology of history has been privileged and understood as the lens through which all of Frechulf's work as compiler ought to be viewed therefore strains the evidence. The source of this tension lies ultimately in the modern understanding of Augustine and Orosius as advocates of competing *Geschichtstheologien*: for Frechulf to properly 'get' the ideas of the former requires that he questioned those of the latter.[51] Frechulf's achievement, however, was not to champion one authority over the other, but to synthesise them.

Frechulf's chapter about King Ninus offers a first example of synthesis.[52] There was disagreement between Orosius and Augustine as to whether Ninus or his

---

[46] Augustine, *DCD*, XVIII.52, pp. 650–2. *Prolegomena*, 214*. See also Allen, 'Frechulf of Lisieux', 1010; compare 1011: 'F[rechulf] recognized the ongoing ambiguous presence and intersection of both "cities" as ethical segments of humanity; he did not embrace the far more usual Orosian expedient of equating either with some conventional political fellowship.' In other words, he did not equate the city of God with the empire or *ecclesia*; Allen 'Frécult', 71.

[47] Pollman and Otten (eds.), *Oxford Guide to the Historical Reception of Augustine*.

[48] See for example Gillis, *Heresy and Dissent*, 90–146 and Pezé, *Le virus d'erreur*.

[49] Augustine, *DCD*, III.30, p. 96 and XVIII.46, p. 643.

[50] Book 1 notwithstanding, most of Frechulf's excerpts do not relate to Augustine's sweeping vision of history but rather to more mundane matters, such as events and persons from Greek mythology in Book 2 (extracted from the 18th book of *De civitate Dei*) or accounts of Socrates and Plato in Book 4 (from the 8th book of *De civitate Dei*).

[51] Compare Van Nuffelen, *Orosius*, 191–7, who discusses Orosius's 'Eusebianism'. His conclusion (206) that 'many of the confrontations between Orosius, Eusebianism, and Augustine start out from modern reconstructions of these theological systems' very much applies to Frechulf too.

[52] *Hist.*, I.2.2, pp. 92–3.

father Belus ought to be considered the first Assyrian ruler.[53] Frechulf took the middle path. Ninus was the 'Assyriorum primux rex', who 'took up arms out of lust to spread his power abroad' (= Orosius I.4.1; trans. Fear, 51). Frechulf also noted (echoing Orosius I.1.1) that 'pagan writers began their histories from Ninus, who is considered to have been the first king of the Assyrians'. It was not to be concluded from this, however, that 'there were no kings before [Ninus], as it pleases some [to say]'; rather, what distinguished him from the others was that 'lured by the desire to rule, [Ninus] was the first to lay waste kingdoms beyond his own borders'.[54] Frechulf then inserted an excerpt from Justin about Ninus (via Augustine, *DCD* IV.6—though without Augustine's critique of Justin's trustworthiness; this very same passage from Justin underlay Orosius I.4.1, from which Frechulf had already quoted), then added that 'hence it is clear what Augustine accurately explained, that Belus was the first to have ruled amongst the Assyrians', but like some other early kings, Belus was content to exert power [only] within his own kingdom.[55] Despite showing awareness of tensions and differences in his sources, Frechulf's aimed to iron them out. The differences he perceived, furthermore, related to *historia*, in the sense of (the record of) what happened in the past, not to how his authorities reflected on History, in the sense of an overall interpretation of the past.

A second example concerns the intertwined fates of Rome and Babylon. Following Augustine, Frechulf considered Babylon, the capital of the Assyrian kingdom, to be the 'city of the impious'. 1200 years later, Rome would be founded 'as if another Babylon in the west'.[56] Further parallels were drawn between these two famed cities. Rome's rise coincided precisely with destruction of the Assyrian kingdom, at which point a number of Old Testament prophets 'erupted together, as it were, like fountains of prophecy'. The prophet Abraham had uttered his promises to Gentiles 'in the first days of the Assyrian empire', and these promises were to be fulfilled with the birth of Christ. Following the foundation of Rome, the western Babylon under whose dominion Christ would later appear, there was another outburst of prophecy that primarily concerned the *gentes*. '[I]t was fitting', therefore, 'that this should occur at the same time as the foundation of that city which was to rule all the Gentiles'.[57] Christ's advent, however, was not only

---

[53] Oros., I.1.1, p. 10, I.4.1, p. 43 and VII.2.13, p. 19; Augustine, *DCD*, IV.6, p. 103, XVI.17, pp. 521–2, XVIII.2., pp. 593–4.

[54] *Hist.*, I.2.2 [16/20], p. 92: 'Quod ergo a Nino, ut in superiore libro diximus, gentium scriptores suas inchoasse historias, qui primus rex fuisse Assyriorum fertur, ob hoc nequaquam datur intellegi reges ante eum non fuisse, ut quibusdam placuit, sed quia ipse cupiditate regnandi allectus externa primus demoliuit regna.'

[55] *Hist.*, I.2.2 [34/37], p. 93: 'Hinc apparet, quod Augustinus accurate dilucidat, apud Assyrios Belum prius regnasse et apud Sycionios Aegialeum (unde et Egialea nuncupata est), sed propriis regnis contenti fuerunt.'

[56] *Hist.*, I.2.1 [20/26], p. 91. Trans. derived from Dyson, *City of God*, 725.

[57] *Hist.*, I.3.12, pp. 175–6; Augustine, *DCD*, XVIII.27, p. 618; trans. Dyson, *City of God*, 856. See also. Augustine, *DCD*, XVIII.22, pp. 612–13.

foretold by the Hebrew prophets. Frechulf added that at the same time a song of the Erythraean Sibyl, 'which the blessed Augustine translated from Greek into the Latin language (*quae beatus Agustinus* [sic] *ex Greco in Latinum vertit eloquium*)', was written down and spoke 'openly about Christ'.[58] A secular text thus pointed in the same direction as its sacred counterparts.

Augustine, however, was not alone in aligning Rome with Babylon: the intertwined fates of these two cities also ran through Orosius's *Historiae*. As already noted above, Frechulf took from Orosius (VII.2.13–15) the very similar coincidence that the prophecies of Abraham, uttered in the reign of Ninus, the first gentile king (*primo gentium rege*), were fulfilled in Christ in the reign of Augustus, the first world monarch.[59] Orosius had supplied material for an additional parallel, namely that the Persian conquest of Babylon was concurrent with the beginning of the Roman republic: drawing on this, Frechulf once again labelled Rome another Babylon. On this occasion, his source was not Augustine's *City of God*; moreover, Frechulf began this second synchronisation by stating that 'I recall now that the apostle Peter quite rightly called Rome 'Babylon in his writings' (I Peter 5:13).[60] Scripture, more so that Augustine or Orosius, framed Frechulf's thinking. Even if often only in the background of his text, the Bible was surely always at the forefront of Frechulf's mind.

This assimilation of Orosius and Augustine, as filtered through scripture, can be seen again at the start of Part II:

> Therefore now with the birth of the Saviour and with darkness removed and the world illuminated by his rays, another road must be trodden, nor will my pen be wearied, as before, writing about the kingdoms of various peoples, seeing that the ferocity and savagery of individual peoples and their great lust for empire, as we have touched upon in passing in our previous books, have passed together into all kingdoms being under a single power [viz. Rome], which had never previously existed anywhere. This came about not by the strength or wisdom of men, but by the omnipotence of God, something the prophet predicted long before, saying 'nation shall not lift sword against nation', and those things which follow [Isaiah 2:4]. And thus it was fitting that when he who is the one God in the substance of the Father and Holy Spirit, was born, the whole world was placed under the census of one man [that is, Augustus]. And so this birth was celebrated, having been predicted by the prophets and proclaimed by the angels: 'Glory to God in the Highest and on Earth peace towards men of good will' [Luke 2:14], when the whole world rested under one peace in a miraculous manner, unheard of in the preceding ages. Not only did the sacred writings predict this birth and peace long ago, but so too did the pagan oracles, as they are contained in the Sibylline books and in other songs.[61]

---

[58] *Hist.*, I.3.12 [30/66], pp. 176–8. See also I.3.12. cap., p. 156.

[59] *Hist.*, II.1.2 [19/35], pp. 441–2.

[60] *Hist.*, I.3.17 [94/110], p. 192. For a translation of this passage, see Ward, 'All Roads Lead to Rome', 500–1.

[61] *Hist.*, II.1.2 [1/18], pp. 440–41: 'Igitur iam saluatore nato, eius que radiis remotis tenebris, inlustrato

Frechulf here distilled the essence of Orosius's argument about the providential significance of the empire of Augustus, while also harking back to the passage from *City of God* about the eruption of sacred and secular prophecy. Into this mix, moreover, he stirred yet another biblical reference, Isaiah 2:4, the completion of which also was long associated with the worldwide peace established on earth under Augustus at the time of Christ's birth. The underlying authority here was neither Orosius nor Augustine, but Jerome, whose commentary on Isaiah conveyed this point to the Latin west.[62]

Orosian Omissions: Signs of the Time(s)?

To more fully grasp the significance of Frechulf's synthetic approach, as a means of understanding the composition of his work together with the wider intellectual culture that informed it, it is helpful to take into account what was excluded as well as what was included from the *Historiae*. One chapter of Orosius in particular underpins what follows: a catalogue of miraculous events from Augustan history which highlighted God's agency working through the emperor to prepare the world for Christ's arrival.[63] These included a rainbow-like apparition that illuminated the sky when Augustus returned to Rome after Julius Caesar's assassination in 44 BC, a fountain that flowed for a full day when Augustus was made tribune for life, and the coincidence of Octavian's acclamation as Augustus and the Christian feast of Epiphany. Frechulf incorporated Orosius's initial observation that Octavian was acclaimed as Augustus on 6 January, the very day on which the liturgical feast of Epiphany was later to be celebrated.[64] Yet he dropped the subsequent clause, where Orosius delivered his rhetorical punch: 'no believer, nor even anyone who opposes the faith is ignorant of this fact (*nemo credentium siue etiam fidei contradicentium nescit*)'. He also passed over Orosius's subsequent interpretation of each of these

---

mundo, alia terenda est uia, nec de diuersarum ut prius fatigabitur calamus gentium regnis scripturus, dum feritas atque rabies singularum gentium inmensa que libido dominandi, ut in prioribus libando perstrinximus libris, in unius ditionis pariter omnia conciderunt regna. Et hoc non hominum fortitudo uel prudentia, sed Dei omnipotentia, quod antea nusquam fuerat, praeparauit, quod longe ante propheta praeuidens ait: *Non leuabit gens contra gentem gladium*, et quae sequuntur. Dignum itaque erat ut illo nascente qui unus est Deus in substantia patris et spiritus sancti, sub unius censu totus subderetur mundus. Itaque haec natiuitas celebrata est prophetis praedicentibus et angelis proclamantibus *Gloria in excelsis Deo, et in terra pax hominibus bonae uoluntatis*, quando totus sub una pace mundus mirabili modo et praecedentibus saeculis inaudito quiescebat: quam uidelicet natiuitatem et pacem non solum diuini eloquii scripta, sed etiam gentilium oracula longe prius praedixerunt, ut in Sybillinis et ceterorum carminibus continetur.'

[62] Jerome, *Commentarii in Esaiam*, I (2:4), p. 30.

[63] Oros., VI.20.1–9, pp. 226–9; compare VI.22.1–8, pp. 234–6. For commentary, Sloan, 'Augustus', 113–17.

[64] Exactly what Orosius understood by Epiphany is ambiguous: see Theodor E. Mommsen, 'Aponius and Orosius on the Significance of the Epiphany', in *Medieval and Renaissance Studies*, ed. Eugene F. Rice Jr. (Ithaca, NY: Cornell University Press, 1959), 299–324. Incisive analysis in Leonard, *In Defiance of History*, ch. 3.

events, which were presented as a series of signs that demonstrated 'that Caesar's rule had been ordained in advance entirely to prepare for the future coming of Christ'.[65] Raffaele Savigni noted these omissions: in line with most scholarship on Frechulf, he understood them to be part of Frechulf's strategy to soften the political ideology of his late Roman source.[66] I propose a different approach.

It is now well established that silences and omissions are vital clues for the interpretation of early medieval texts. Yet by the very nature of their absence, teasing out the meaning of silences and omissions can amount to not much more than educated guesswork: this is meant less as critique of existing work than as a caveat for what follows. Scholarship on Frechulf has insisted that the bishop of Lisieux deliberately sought to excise the specific Christian imperial ideology or political theology of Orosius. To be sure, Frechulf's omissions suppressed many of the more obviously Roman flavourings of the *Historiae*. With one conspicuous exception, he excluded Orosius's central chronological spine, the counted years 'from the foundation of the City [of Rome] (*ab Urbe condita*)', which aligned all history in relation to a thoroughly Roman moment.[67] Even more significantly, Frechulf undercut the entire apologetic architecture of the source: when making his excerpts, he studiously avoided the book prologues where Orosius spelled out most clearly his main arguments about history and, for instance, extolled the values of Roman citizenship; he also omitted the frequent authorial interjections through which Orosius argued his main case, namely that because of Christianity the woes of the (fifth-century) present paled in comparison to those of the past. Although this can be interpreted as a strategy by Frechulf to distance himself politically from Orosius's often emphatic Romanness, there is also a vital cultural factor to be taken into account. Orosius—and also Augustine—wrote apologetically, to argue and persuade, in world in which there was a competing, non-Christian system of elite values and cultural memory to be challenged.[68] In the four hundred years separating the early fifth and early ninth centuries, much had changed. The late Roman understanding of the past that Orosius aimed to destabilise no longer existed; Frechulf's goal was not to bring non-Christian, or insufficiently Christian readers over to his side, but to summarise and digest received material for an audience already convinced of its truth and authority. There was thus no sense in including elements of an argument that already had been won. By ignoring those passages where Orosius's rhetoric was most pronounced, Frechulf was motivated by pragmatic, cultural concerns, not political ones.

---

[65] Oros., VI.20.3–4, p. 227; trans. Fear, 309.

[66] Savigni, 'Storia universale', esp. 176–9. Here Savigni specifically sought to tease out Frechulf's 'precise political-ideological purpose'.

[67] The exception is the nativity: 752 years *Ab Urbe condita*. Orosius also marked time by noting the sitting Roman consuls: Frechulf often removed these references, but less consistently.

[68] Van Nuffelen, *Orosius*.

Other eighth- and ninth-century historians and chroniclers had no qualms about including what Frechulf excluded, and this can be observed frequently enough that it seems insufficient to chalk it up to political ideology. Paul the Deacon's *Historia Romana* (written c. 770) was an extended and Christianised reworking of Eutropius's fourth-century *Breviarium ab Urbe condita*. When Paul came to Eutropius's account of Augustus, it was to Orosius (as well as Eusebius-Jerome's *Chronicle*) he turned to augment it:

> Having concluded wars throughout the entire world, Octavian Augustus returned to Rome in the twelfth year from when he was consul, and obtained sole [rule] of the state for 44 years, for he had held it previously for 12 years with Antony and Lepidus. When he returned victoriously from the east, he entered the city for a triple triumph. At this time, Augustus first was hailed because he enlarged the republic, and then obtained the highest power, which the Greeks call monarchy. In these days, a fountain of oil across the Tiber gushed forth from a lodging house and flowed for a full day with a most abundant stream, signifying the grace of Christ from the gentiles. And then appeared a circle of light, which looked like a rainbow around the sun. And so, in the 42nd year of his reign, when Caesar had composed a most secure and stable peace, the lord Christ was born in Bethlehem, whose advent that peace served. [69]

Around half a century before Paul, Bede drew on Orosius as a source of information for the chronicle embedded in his treatise on time, *De temporum ratione* (completed c. 725); an important example of this was the Nativity:

> In the forty-second year of Caesar Augustus, and the twenty-seventh [year] after the death of Cleopatra and Antony, when Egypt was turned into a [Roman] province, in the third year of the one hundred and ninety-third Olympiad, in the seven hundred and fifty-second from the foundation of the City [of Rome], that is to say the year in which the movements of all the peoples throughout the world were held in check, and by God's decree Caesar established genuine and unshakeable peace, Jesus Christ, the Son of God, hallowed the Sixth Age of the world by His coming. [70]

---

[69] Paul the Deacon, *Historia Romana*, ed. Amedeo Crivellucci (Rome, 1914), pp. 100–1: 'Ita bellis toto orbe confectis Octavianus Augustus Romam rediit duodecimo anno quam consul fuerat. ex eo rem publicam per quadraginta et quattuor annos solus obtinuit, ante enim duodecim annis cum Antonio et Lepido tenuerat. [Orosius, VI.20.1–2=] denique <cum de Oriente victor reversus esset Urbemque triplici triumpho ingressus esset, tunc primum Augustus eo, quod rem publicam auxerit, consalutatus est atque ex tunc summam rerum potestatem, quam Graeci monarchiam vocant, adeptus est. [VI, 18, 34=] his diebus trans Tiberim de taberna meritoria fons olei e terra exundavit ac per totum diem largissimo rivo fluxit significans ex gentibus Christi gratiam [=Eus-Jer, *Chronicle*]. [VI, 20, 5=] tunc etiam circulus ad speciem caelestis arcus circa solem apparuit. [Orosius, VI, 22, 5=] igitur cum quadragesimo secundo anno firmissimam verissimamque pacem Caesar composuisset, Christus dominus in Bethleem natus est, cuius adventui pax ista famulata est>.' [<> denotes text added to Eutropius.]

[70] Bede, *DTR*, c. 66, 268, p. 495: 'Anno Caesaris Augusti XLII, a morte vero Cleopatrae et Antoni, quando et Aegyptus in provinciam versa est, anno XXVII, olympiadis centesimae nonagesimae tertiae anno tertio, ab urbe autem condita anno DCCLII, id est eo anno, quo conpressis cunctarum per orbem terrae gentium motibus firmissimam verissimamque pacem ordinatione dei Caesar conposuit, Iesus

The ninth-century writers who substantially expanded and continued Bede's chronicle incorporated much more of Orosius's *Historiae*: these are the *Chronicon universale*, the *Chronicle of Moissac* and Ado of Vienne's *Chronicle*. The *Chronicle of Moissac*, perhaps written in southern Francia in the reign of Louis the Pious, included a slightly condensed version of the story of the fountain of oil that erupted and flowed for a day on the far side of the Tiber (at the site that would become Santa Maria in Trastevere) and Orosius's explanation of its significance. This text also emphasised the meaning of the peace that engulfed the world in the year of the Nativity, and that at this time Augustus forbade being addressed as master.[71] Ado of Vienne, writing around 870, also stressed the context of universal peace and that Augustus declined to be called master. Like Frechulf, Ado added that 'Christ, the true lord of all man was thus born amongst men, and immediately was inscribed on the Roman census, and this first and most clear declaration marked out Caesar as lord of all, and the Romans as masters of the world both individually and as a people.' Yet earlier, Ado had included all of Orosius's arguments that Christ's coming was foreshadowed in events from secular history, that is, those arguments which Frechulf overlooked.[72]

If pragmatic/cultural needs guided Frechulf's excerpts, they were nonetheless buttressed by specific theoretical considerations. I want to suggest, however, that these considerations were rooted in a discipline that, unlike political or historical theology, would certainly have been recognised by Carolingian intellectuals: biblical commentary. As already noted above, Frechulf omitted Orosius's 'far-fetched' typological comparison between the ten plagues and ten imperial persecutions, yet this does not have to reflect a conscious response to 'the quintessentially Orosian political exegesis that Aug[ustine] himself rejected'.[73] Scriptural exegesis offers an alternative angle. In his commentary on Exodus, Hrabanus Maurus included almost the entirety of the passage from the *Historiae* that Frechulf left out.[74] This should not be taken to mean that Hrabanus was less sensitive to Augustinian theology than Frechulf, but rather that his task, as he conceived it, was different.[75] Hrabanus's main aim was to collect patristic exegesis pertaining to the allegorical interpretation of Exodus, and he explained this clearly in the dedicatory preface to his commentary, which he sent to none other than

---

Christus filius dei sextam mundi aetatem suo consecravit adventu'. Trans. Wallis, 195.

[71] *Chronicle of Moissac*, ed. Katz and Claszen, p. 47. On this chronicle, see Kramer, 'A Crowning Achievement' and 'The Bede Goes On'.

[72] Ado, *Chronicon, PL* 123, cols. 73B–75D.

[73] Allen, 'Frechulf', 1010.

[74] Hrabanus Maurus, *Commentaria in Exodum, PL* 108, cols. 43C–47B, at 45C–47B. The passage of Orosius is Oros., VII.27.1–16, pp. 70–4.

[75] On Hrabanus and Augustine, see Silvia Cantelli Berarducci, 'Hrabanus Maurus', in *The Oxford Guide to the Historical Reception of Augustine*, eds Karla Pollmann and Willemien Otten, 3 vols (Oxford: OUP, 2013), vol. 2, 1158–60.

Frechulf himself sometime in the second half of the 820s.[76] The relevant excerpt from Orosius, which followed comments by Isidore and Origen on the 'mystical' and 'moral' interpretations of the plagues, respectively, was introduced as follows: 'these ten plagues by which Egypt was struck can also be compared to the times of the Roman kingdom, because these things were done as our examples'.[77] It was precisely the figurative quality of Orosius's analogy that made it valuable for Hrabanus but unsuitable for Frechulf. It clashed with Frechulf's understanding of historical narration and the 'truth of history' vis-à-vis the spiritual exegesis of scripture, not with his Augustinian sensibilities. This point can be further developed by moving away from Frechulf and examining in more detail how Carolingian biblical commentators engaged with the *Historiae*, specifically in the context of the Gospel of Matthew and its account of the birth of Christ.

The Carolingian Orosius: Exegesis and Historiography

Of the many contexts in which Orosius was read and used in the early Middle Ages, biblical commentary remains curiously neglected.[78] But the context is crucial, since, more so than historiography, exegesis more readily reveals the extent to which Orosius, over the course of the early Middle Ages, began to be read as part of the patristic canon and as such could be applied to the study of scripture. Bede, as is often the case, stands out as an innovator, though he drew on the *Historiae* only as an aid to understanding the names of cities or regions mentioned in three separate books of the Bible.[79] It fell to Carolingian exegetes of the ninth century to squeeze out further value from the *Historiae*. Hrabanus Maurus's commentaries furnish numerous examples of how Orosius's narrative could be viewed in direct relation to the places and persons mentioned in the holy books. In addition to

---

[76] Hrab. *Epist.*, no. 9, p. 395.

[77] Hrabanus Maurus, *Commentaria in Exodum*, col. 45C: 'Possunt praeterea et hae decem plagae quibus Aegyptus verberata est propter Israelitas, Romani regni comparari temporibus, quia haec in figuram nostri facta sunt [I Cor. 10.6].' The Pauline tag was already in Orosius: Oros., VII.27.2, p. 70; trans. Fear, 363. Compare Alcuin, *Epistolae*, Ep. 81, ed. Ernst Dümmler, MGH *Epp.* IV (Berlin: Weidmann, 1895), p. 123 on comparing OT and NT numbers: 'per decim plagas percussa est Aegyptus, ut populus Dei liberaretur. Per decim persecutions coronata est ecclesia Christi'. For a tenth-century example, see Roberts, *Flodoard*, 161

[78] Ward, 'Exegesis, Empire, and Eschatology'. Compare Opelt, 'Augustustheologie', who notes parallels between Orosius's three proofs and the Hiberno-Latin synoptic Gospel commentary attributed to Pseudo-Jerome (*PL* 30, cols. 531–90, at cols. 568D–569B). There is clear emphasis on the miracles in extant Hiberno-Latin exegesis: for an introduction plus texts and translations, see *Apocrypha Hiberniae, I. Evangelia Infantiae*, ed. Martin McNamara, Jean-Daniel Kaestli and Rita Beyers, CCSA 14 (Turnhout: Brepols, 2001), 521–37.

[79] Bede, *Nomina regionum atque locorum de Actibus apostolorum*, ed. M. L. W. Laistner, CCSL 121 (Turnhout: Brepols, 1983), 167–78; see, for example, 174: 'Parthi: inter flumen Indum, quod est ab oriente, et inter flumen Tigrim, quod est ab occasu, siti sunt, ut supra dictum est' (= Oros., 1.2.17..., p. 16). This is also how Orosius was used in Bede, *Libri Quatuor in Principium Genesis*, ed. Charles Jones, CCSL 118 (Turnhout: Brepols, 1967), III (10:10), pp. 146–7 and III (11: 8–9b), p. 157. Bede, *In Ezram et Neemiam*, ed. David Hurst, CCSL 119A (Turnhout: Brepols, 1969), II (8:17–18), p. 320.

Exodus, referred to above, passages from the *Historiae* were keyed to verses of Jeremiah, Judith and I Maccabees.[80] The exegetical use of Orosius, however, is most pronounced in Hrabanus's first commentary, his *expositio* of the Gospel of Matthew, which he undertook in 821/2, before becoming abbot of Fulda.[81]

We encountered Hrabanus's Matthew commentary in Chapter 1, since in it he indicated his working methods. Hrabanus's prologue was itself a patchwork of sorts, mixing his own words with excerpts from Jerome's preface to his commentary on Matthew (written c. 398) and Bede's preface to his commentary on Luke (c. 709–16). Bede stated that, in compiling his commentary, he began by investigating what Ambrose, Augustine, Gregory, Jerome and the 'other fathers' had written about Luke.[82] Hrabanus repurposed Bede's words to fit a different Gospel, and expanded the list of named authorities:

> Having gathered together from here and there the most excellent and worthy masters of scripture, I diligently set about inspecting what they had thought and what they had said in their works about the words of the blessed Matthew: I name Cyprian and Eusebius, Hilary [of Poitiers], Ambrose, Jerome, Augustine, Fulgentius [of Ruspe], Victorinus [of Pettau], Fortunatianus [of Aquileia], Orosius, Leo [the Great], Gregory of Nazianzus, Gregory the Roman Pope, John Chrysostom and the other fathers, whose names are written in the book of life.[83]

Remarkably, Orosius appears here not as a historian, but rather as one of the *artifices sacrae lectionis*, masters [of the art] of scripture, named alongside those who today are more typically thought of as patristic, exegetical, authorities. Such a perception may seem at odds with the contents of the *Historiae*, which overwhelmingly dealt with ancient and imperial Roman history. But discerning exegetes such as Hrabanus hunted through all the authoritative material they could get their hands on in their efforts to interpret whatever book of the Bible they were studying. Orosius clearly had significant insights to offer. (The overlaps uncovered, it is worth remembering, were not intended by Orosius, who explicitly

---

[80] Hrabanus Maurus, *Expositio super Hieremiam Prophetam*, PL 111, cols. 793–1272, at 1166A–167A; *Commentariorum in libros Machabaeorum*, PL 109, cols. 1125–1256, at 1129A–1130C, 1132A–C; *Commentariorum in Iudith*, PL 109, cols. 539–592, at 541D–543A, 544C–D. Importantly, these were commentaries for which Hrabanus had no patristic models: for example, the Orosius citation appears in the second half of his Jeremiah commentary, which covered the chapters of Jeremiah which Jerome had not commented upon. In one ninth-century manuscript of this commentary, one of the excerpts from Orosius was marked up with a marginal 'OROS': St. Gallen, Stiftsbibliothek, Cod. Sang. 282, p. 96.
[81] Silvia Beraducci Cantelli, *Hrabani Mauri Opera Omnia: Repertorium Fontium*, 3 vols (Turnhout: Brepols, 2006), vol. 1, 345–58; Phelan, 'Carolingian Renewal'.
[82] Bede, *In Lucae evangelium expositio*, Prol. [96/102], ed. Hurst, p. 7.
[83] Hrab. *Exp.*, Praef. [51/57], pp. 2–3: 'Adgregatis igitur hinc inde insignissimis sacrae lectionis atque dignissimis artificibus, quid in opusculis suis in beati Matthaei uerbis senserint, quid dixerint, diligentius inspicere curaui; Cyprianum dico atque Eusebium, Hilarium, Ambrosium, Hieronimum, Augustinum, Fulgentium, Victorinum, Fortunatianum, Orosium, Leonem, Gregorium Nazanzenum, Gregorium papam Romanum, Iohannemque Crisostomum et ceteros patres, quorum nomina sunt scripta in libro uitae.'

wanted to avoid retelling scripture, but compilers did not worry about respecting authorial intention when it came to culling excerpts.) If Bede first identified this potential, Hrabanus Maurus pushed it to its limits.

The bulk of Hrabanus's use of Orosius in this commentary was keyed to Matthew 2:1, which announced the birth of Jesus 'in Bethlehem of Juda, in the days of King Herod'.[84] Hrabanus began with an excerpt from Augustine's *De consensu evangelistarum* comparing Matthew's and Luke's accounts of the Nativity, before illustrating how Herod's reign marked the fulfilment of Genesis 49:10: Herod was an outsider, who received 'the power of the kingdom from the Romans and Augustus, after Hyrcanus, the priest of the Jews was captured and handed over by the Parthians'.[85] Extracts from Orosius then follow. There are overlaps with Frechulf: on account of the Nativity, Augustus created global peace on earth and refused to be called master. Otherwise, Hrabanus integrated those passages from the *Historiae* that Frechulf worked around; what is more, it quickly becomes apparent that Hrabanus edited and augmented said passages to such an extent that he became an out-and-out exegete of the text. For instance, he repeated (though simplified and purposefully altered) Orosius's argument that it was no coincidence that 'Abraham, to whom Christ was promised, was born in the forty-second year of the reign of Ninus, king the Assyrians' and later 'Christ was born at the very end of the forty-second year of the Augustus Caesar, who first held the monarchy [of the world]'.[86] The point that Hrabanus wished to convey, however, was very much his own, and was linked to the underlying object of his study: Matthew's Gospel. Matthew 1:1–17 enumerated Jesus's genealogy, linking him back through successive generations to David and then Abraham. Fourteen generations were counted between Abraham and David, fourteen from David to the Babylonian exile, then fourteen again from exile to Christ: a total of forty-two. Seizing on a previously unnoticed overlap, Hrabanus sprang into action and pointed out that 'the births of the patriarch [that is, Abraham] and of our saviour [that is, Christ] agree in number with the genealogical sequence [that runs] between them, as enumerated by Matthew the Evangelist'. Such intertextual harmony, it was concluded, 'was not free from mystery'.[87] Orosius's

---

[84] But see also Hrabanus's commentary on Matthew 4:24 ('his fame went throughout all Syria'), where it was noted that (drawing on Oros., I.2.23–5, pp. 17–18) 'Syria itaque generaliter dicitur omnis regio a flumine Eufrate usque ad mare magnum, a Capodocia et ab Armenia usque ad Aegyptum, habens maximas prouincias in se, hoc est Commagenam, Pheniciam et Palestinam, in qua gens Iudaeorum inhabitat': Hrab. *Exp.*, II (4.24) [87/91], p. 117. This is another example of Orosius's geographical knowledge being applied exegetically.

[85] Hrab. *Exp.*, I (2.1) [11/15], p. 52.

[86] Compare Oros., VII.2.13–15, pp. 19–20, where Abraham was born in the 43rd year of Ninus's reign, while Christ was born right at the end of the 42nd year of Augustus. Hrabanus modified the regnal year of Abraham's birth to make his point work. Bending facts and numbers to make them align is common in commentary, and was also a classic Orosian move: see Sloan, 'Augustus', 115.

[87] Hrab. *Exp.*, I (2:1) [16/22], p. 52: 'Notandum autem, quod, sicut Abraham, cui Christus promissus est, quadragesimo secundo anno Nini primi regis Assiriorum natus est, ita et Christus quadragesimo secundo anno Augusti Caesaris, qui primus monarchiam tenuit, emenso natus est. Nec hoc uacat a

parallelism between Abraham/Ninus and Christ/Augustus was recast with modified emphasis. Scriptural and extra-scriptural data were fused together to produce new sacred meaning.

Hrabanus next recounted the 'miraculous things which appeared in the time of Augustus as proof of the coming of [Christ]'.[88] What followed reproduced the very chapter of the *Historiae* that Frechulf omitted, when Orosius interpreted a series of events from Augustan history as prefigurations of the Nativity. Hrabanus's interventions demonstrate plainly that he was not interested in articulating an *Augustustheologie* but rather in underlining the exegetical value of Orosius, as an extra-scriptural but nevertheless authentically patristic transmitter of material that showed how Christ's advent was foreshadowed in the deeds of Augustus. Sometimes his interventions were minor: to Orosius's report of the rainbow that lit up the sky when Julius Caesar was assassinated, Hrabanus added that it signalled that in Augustus's day Christ would come 'to preach the faith of Holy Trinity'.[89] Others were more elaborate. Once Augustus had defeated Antony and Lepidus in Sicily, he took charge of all their troops, giving him forty-four legions in total. The troops rioted. Once this was taken care of, Augustus 'restored 30,000 slaves to their present masters and crucified another 6000 whose masters could be not be found' (VI.18.33; trans. Fear, 305). He then 'stationed the 44 legions over which he had sole command in positions to keep the world', before returning to Rome, whence 'he decreed that all previous debts of the Roman people be rescinded, and even ordered the records of them to be destroyed' (VI.20.6, trans. Fear, 310). According to Hrabanus, the 30,000 slaves restored to their masters signified that 'whoever, in the service of Christ, worthily fulfilled the ten commandments of the law in the faith of the holy trinity, shall live in eternity with the grace of God' (that is, 10*3=30[000]); the 6000, by contrast, signified 'those, who, spurning [God's] rule by involving themselves in various vices, have deviated throughout the [first] six ages [of the world] and will be punished with perpetual torture'.[90] Together, the legions and the abolishment of debts 'signified' that 'Christ, born in these

---

mysterio; concordant enim in numero natiuitas patriarchae ac Saluatoris nostri et ordo genealogiae inter ipsos per Matthaeum euangelistam enumeratae.'

[88] Hrab. *Exp.*, I (2:1) [23/25], p. 52: 'Nec onerosum debet esse lectori, si res mirandae, quae temporibus Augusti in testimonium aduentus Saluatoris nostri exstiterunt, breuiter commemorentur.'

[89] Hrab. *Exp.*, I (2:1) [25/31], pp. 52–3: 'Nam cum primo Gaio Caesare auunculo suo interfecto ex Apollonia rediens Vrbem ingrederetur, hora circiter diei tertia repente lucido ac puro sereno circulus ad speciem caelestis arcus orbem solis ambit, quasi eum unum ac potentissimum in hoc mundo solumque clarissimum in orbe monstraret, cuius tempore uenturus esset ad sanctae Trinitatis fidem praedicandum, qui ipsum solem solus mundum que totum et fecisset et regeret.'

[90] Hrab. *Exp.*, I (2:1) [32/39], p. 53: 'Quod autem Augustus XXX milia seruorum dominis reddidit et VI milia, quorum domini non exstabant, in crucem egit, significat eum ipsis temporibus uenturum, cuius seruituti quicumque se rite manciparent et digne in sanctae Trinitatis fide operantes decalogum legis implerent, in aeternum ipsi per Domini sui gratiam uiuerent, illos uero, qui eius dominatum spernentes per VI aetates istius saeculi uariis uitiis se implicantes aberrauerunt, perpetuo cruciatu omnes esse puniendos.'

times, sent out his preachers to defend the world against perfidy, and he ordered repentance and forgiveness of the sins in all peoples to be preached in his name'.[91] Lastly, the coincidence of Augustus's appellation and Epiphany. Orosius said:

> What could be more plausibly or credibly believed than that, given this co-incidence of the peace, his name, and the date, this man had been predestined by the secret ordering of events in order to prepare the way for His coming when he took up the banner of peace and assumed the title of power on the same day on which He would shortly make Himself known to the world?[92]

Hrabanus, by contrast, wrote:

> And what does this demonstrate, other than that this man had been predestined by the secret ordering of events in order to prepare the way for His coming when he took up the banner of peace and assumed the title of power, that on the day on which He, who restrained idolatry when He closed the pagan temples and bestowed true peace and unity of worship upon the whole earth, would shortly make himself known to the world.[93]

Once again, Hrabanus modified his source enough to ensure the stress was more on Christ than on Augustus. A final example is less obviously tied to a passage from the *Historiae*, but perhaps stems from a Hiberno-Latin source:[94]

> That therefore in these times there was an eclipse of the sun and a severe famine in the Roman Empire, these things witness the coming of the 'sun of justice' and the 'bread of life'. And rightly so the sun of the world then vanished and bodily need was vanquished, when 'true light' came, 'which illuminated every man coming into the world' and food and drink was given from the heavens, from which he who tastes it will neither be hungry nor thirsty till eternity.[95]

---

[91] Hrab. *Exp.*, I (2:1) [50/56], p. 53: 'Illud quoque, quod Augustus legiones suas ad tutamen orbis terrarum distribuisset ouansque omnia superiora populorum debita donanda, litterarum etiam monumentis abolitis, censuisset, significat, quod Christus ipsis temporibus natus praedicatoribus suis orbem terrarum contra perfidiam tuendum distribuit et iussit praedicari in nomine eius paenitentiam et remissionem peccatorum in omnes gentes.'
[92] Oros., VI.20.8, p. 229: 'quid fidelius ac uerius credi aut cognosci potest, concurrentibus ad tantam manifestationem pace nomine die, quam hunc occulto quidem gestorum ordine ad obsequium praeparationis eius praedestinatum fuisse, qui eo die, quo ille manifestandus mundo post paululum erat, et pacis signum praetulit et potestatis nomen adsumpsit?' Trans. Fear, 310.
[93] Hrab. *Exp.*, I (2:1) [66/71], p. 54: 'Et quid hoc aliud demonstrat, quam hunc occulto quidem gestorum ordine ad obsequium praeparationis eius praedestinatum fuisse, ut eo die, quo ille manifestandus mundo post paululum erat, qui idolatriam clausis idolorum templis conpescuit et pacem ueram cunctis terris atque unitatem religionis obtulit, in ipso iste et pacis signum praeferret et potestatis nomen adsumeret?'
[94] This is quite a distinctive passage and Verri's source synopsis suspects this is original to Hrabanus (Cantelli, *Hrabani Mauri Opera*, vol. 2, 952). There are, however, tantalising parallels in the Hiberno-Latin tradition: see above, note 78.
[95] Hrab. *Exp.*, I (2:1) [72/77], p. 54: 'Quod ergo his temporibus solis eclipsis facta est et fames ualida in Romano imperio, *solis iustitiae* (Mal 4.2) et *panis uitae* (John 6.35) testatur aduentum. Et merito tunc sol mundanus defectionem patitur et penuria corporei uictus erat, quando *lux uera* uenit, *quae inluminat omnem hominem uenientem in hunc mundum* (John 1. 9) et ille cibus ac potus de caelis datus est, de quo qui gustauerit non esuriet neque sitiet in aeternum.'

In each of these examples, Hrabanus added extra, more explicitly Christian, emphases to the text of Orosius. Two things jump out: firstly, Hrabanus's additions, like Frechulf's omissions, can be tied to the transformation in the context of learning between late antiquity and the Carolingian period. Hrabanus's audience would not have comprised educated 'pagans' or Christians schooled in Roman rhetoric. The initial reason for producing his commentary, as he explained in his preface, was that his Fuldan brethren lacked detailed patristic exegesis of Matthew. Excerpts from the *Historiae* were thus repackaged in such a way as to make them speak directly to monks and clerics seeking authoritative explication of the world into which Christ was born, as recorded in Matthew's Gospel. This leads to the second point: by further Christianising (or monasticising?) Orosius, Hrabanus subjected key passages to exegesis, even it seems allegorical exegesis, almost as though they were scriptural. Michael Sloan has convincingly argued that Orosius himself drew on the exegete's tool kit by 'allegorising of the person and events of Augustus': this corresponds to the signs and prodigies catalogued above.[96] Crucially, however, it is not Augustus *the person* but Orosius *the text* that is the object of Hrabanus's analysis. An analogue to this can be found in Bede, who extracted allegorical meaning from Josephus's description of the tabernacle.[97] The exegetical utility of Josephus's Latin corpus has long been recognised, and evidence of it can be found from the fourth century onwards. In the eighth and especially ninth centuries, Orosius also aided students of scripture, above all those interested in the birth of Christ, that most central of Christian moments. The bond between Orosius's account of Augustus and Matthew's Gospel became as intimate as that between Josephus and the books of the Old Testament.

This bond can be inferred from the fact that a number of other Carolingian exegetes turned to Orosius to elucidate Matthew 2:1. Hrabanus's commentary was itself digested into Otfrid of Wissembourg's glosses on Matthew. Paschasius Radbertus's commentary, which he began in the late 820s though only completed in the early 850s, and that of Christian of Stavelot (written in the 860s) offer better material for comparison. In both we find points of contact with Hrabanus as well as divergences. Christian of Stavelot, for example, made a brief note of the 'many prodigies [that] appeared, which revealed [Christ] as the creator of the world', though he implied that these happened on the day of the Nativity, rather than before it, as they were set out in Orosius.[98] Christian also repeated the anecdote that Augustus refused to be called *dominus*. Concerning the *pax Augusta*, the angels—as they always did—sang '*Glory to God in the highest and peace on earth*

---

[96] Sloan, 'Augustus', 114–17 (quotation at 115).

[97] Conor O'Brien, *Bede's Temple: An Image and its Interpretation* (Oxford: OUP, 2015), 32 and literature cited at n. 63.

[98] Christianus dictus Stabulensis, *Expositio*, p. 91: 'Et ipso die [of Christ's birth] multa prodigia exstiterunt quae eum creatorem orbis ostenderunt.'

for all good men' (Luke 2:14 and another example of Orosius's own exegesis), but Christian added his own flourishes: for example, working in further biblical passages, including Isaiah 2:4, which Frechulf also incorporated. He wrote it:

> So that that voice might be fulfilled, so great a peace was established in the Roman world for twelve years such as no king could have brought about in a single province, and thus, just as the prophet said, 'they shall turn their swords into ploughshares, and their spears into sickles' [Isaiah 2:4] and the psalmist said, 'in His days an abundance of peace shall arise' [Ps 71.7].[99]

Paschasius Radbertus (or Radbert) read closely the writings of *noster Paulus Orosius*, 'our Paulus Orosius', above all in the context of Matthew 2:1. Of all these exegetes, Radbert was alone in stating that the *pax Augusta* was enacted by God so that Christ's 'preachers would have an unimpeded path to follow across the whole earth'.[100] Remarkably, Radbert later repeated Orosius's stress on the *pax Augustua* in the context of a reworked excerpt from a letter of Augustine, in which the bishop of Hippo set out at length his ideas about eschatology, ideas which, it should be remembered, are generally considered antithetical to Orosius's understanding of the past. In the context of Matthew 24:6 ('You will hear of wars and rumours of wars, but see to it that you are not alarmed. Such things must happen, but the end is still to come'), Radbert began with Augustine's argument that wars are endemic to human history and therefore cannot be taken as signs of the end of days. There, was, however, one exception: 'under Augustus Caesar, through the dispensation of God's providence, there was a cessation from war at the time of Christ's Advent and then a little later so that the Gospel could be preached freely throughout the whole world. But not long after this, the barbarian nations frequently tore everywhere through the Roman provinces, just as the Romans themselves had done when they first subjugated the whole world through war.'[101] Orosius and Augustine were read in conjunction, ideas from each blended together to provide nuanced commentary of the Gospel.

Conclusions

Like Radbert, Frechulf was a keen reader of Augustine's *City of God* and Orosius's *Historiae*. Around midway through Part II, he included a potted biography of Orosius which centred on how Orosius, having been sent to the Holy Land to

---

[99] Christianus dictus Stabulensis, *Expositio*, ed. Huygens, p. 92: 'Eodem die angeli cantauerunt gloria in excelsis deo et in terra pax hominibus bonae uoluntatis, et ut ista uox conpleretur tanta pax in orbe Romano facta est per XII annos, quantam nullus rex potuit facere in una prouintia, ita ut, sicut propheta dixit, *conflarent gladios suos in uomeres et lanceas suas in falces*, et psalmista dixerat *orietur in diebus eius abundantia pacis*.'

[100] Paschasius Radbertus, *Expositio in Matheo libri XII*, II (2:1), ed. Bede Paulus, 3 vols, CCCM 56, 56A, 56B (Turnhout: Brepols, 1984), vol. 1, p. 143.

[101] Paschasius Radbertus, *Expositio*, XI (24:6), vol. 3, p. 1158.

study with Jerome, was given the relics of St Stephen and carried them back with him to North Africa, where they produced a number of miracles which Augustine included in Book 22 of the *City of God*. It was also at Augustine's behest that Orosius, his disciple (*discipulus*) wrote the *Historiae*.[102] Although Orosius's connection to Augustine was prominently broadcast through his prologue, Frechulf's mini-biography is in fact the earliest indirect attestation of the perception that Orosius and Augustine were master and student. Elisa Brilli has sketched the broad contours of the aspect of the reception history of Orosius.[103] Yet underpinning her survey was the commonly held notion that political ideology shaped Orosius's reception: 'Within the Carolingian cultural framework of the Holy Roman Empire, the Romanising providentialism of the *Historiae* provided an ideological instrument and a teleological narrative of secular history that one would have sought for in vain in the writings of the Father of the church', that is, Augustine; Brilli also noted of the other medieval authors she cites, that they were ideologically aligned, in that they were 'keen to see the role of the empire, ancient and contemporary, recognised in the historical accomplishment of Christendom'. Frechulf, as 'a partisan of the imperial politics of Louis the Pious and Judith of Bavaria', was one such figure.[104]

This chapter has argued against such a view. The extent to which political theology emerged from either the *Historiae* or the commentaries covered at the end of the chapter is open to question. Rather, I suggest that what unifies the different texts covered above is the central impulse of Carolingian intellectual culture: the study of scripture and the fathers. Otherwise, there is no single straightforward explanation for the different ways that the various authors discussed in the chapter interreacted with Orosius's *Historiae*: fuller analyses of each of these understudied texts would first be necessary and this is far beyond the scope of this monograph. But what deserves emphasis is that Orosius served as a foundational source for all, and this is especially evident with regard to the Nativity. Whether chronicling world history or commenting on Matthew's Gospel, Orosius became an indispensable tool for locating the birth of Christ, one of the most important events within all of Christianity, in space and time. Herod had long been important for understanding Christ's birth; through Matthew 2:1, his reign was inscribed within Christian sacred history as the historical setting of the Nativity. By the Carolingian period, so too had Augustus's empire, both within historical texts but also in a number of Matthew commentaries, a Gospel from which Augustus was in fact absent. What begins to emerge is a pronounced Carolingian moment in the reception history of Orosius, in which passages of the *Historiae*—not least those relating to the birth of the Christ—became evermore deeply entwined in the textual fabric of Christianity.

---

[102] *Hist.*, II.5.12, pp. 694–5.
[103] Elisa Brilli, 'L'entente entre Orose et saint Augustin: contribution à l'étude de la réception médiévale des *Histoires*', *Sacris Erudiri*, 51 (2012): 363–90.
[104] Brilli, 'L'ententre', 385.

5

Christiana tempora? The Conclusion of the *Histories* and the Creation of a Patristic Past

Introduction

The previous chapter examined Frechulf's reception of Orosius's *Historiae*, in part so as to underline the exegetical framework and focus of his compendium as a whole. At the end of the chapter, I concluded that Frechulf and the biblical commentors I surveyed alongside him were not reading Orosius as intellectuals steeped in late Roman culture, but rather as Frankish exegetes of the received writings of ancient Christianity. Armed with Orosius, as well as many other authorities, they adopted and adapted inherited knowledge to make sense of Christ's birth, as recorded in Matthew's Gospel; or, in the case of Frechulf, to articulate the overall shape of the past and the transformative effect the Incarnation was believed to have had on it. In short, Orosius was read as part of a wider engagement with the Latin patristic corpus. To be sure, Orosius stands out from this corpus on account of how emphatic he was in advertising his Christian Roman identity.[1] Yet to a certain degree this applied to the rest: when Carolingian intellectuals looked back to the voluminous writings of Christian antiquity—and they did so habitually—they looked to authors who lived, wrote and died in the Roman Empire, as well as to the saints and martyrs who suffered but ultimately triumphed within the Roman world. Even a towering figure such as Gregory the Great (died 604), who lived and wrote after the fall of the western empire, was still integrated into an imperial world. Indeed, one of the very last chapters of the *Histories* implied as much: before becoming pope, Gregory proved his theological credentials before the Emperor Tiberius II in Constantinople (died 582) and later died during the reign of Tiberius successor, Phocas (610).[2] Gregory's world,

---

[1] See especially Oros., V.2.1–8, pp. 86–7; this was one of the prefatory passages that Frechulf studiously avoided.

[2] *Hist.*, II.5.24, pp. 720–21. Context: Matthew Dal Santo, 'Gregory the Great, the Empire and the Emperor', in *A Companion to Gregory the Great*, eds Bronwen Neil and Matthew Dal Santo (Leiden

moreover, remained Roman, but a Rome at the centre of a universal church rather than a global empire.

It is against the backdrop of the sustained scrutiny of the textual heritage of Latin late antiquity and the era that generated it that I want to examine the most controversial aspect of the *Histories*: its seventh-century conclusion.[3] No other part of the text has generated quite so much interest, and it continues to puzzle students and specialists alike: if early medievalists are aware of Frechulf at all, it tends to be because he was a Carolingian historian who did not write about Carolingian history. The Incarnation, as we saw in the previous chapter, was undoubtedly a meaningful moment at which to divide a Christian history of the world, yet the reasons for and implications of Frechulf's end point require more explanation. Why did Frechulf break off his narrative over 200 years before his own day? In addressing this central question, this chapter has three principal goals: firstly, continuing my overview of the *Histories*, I provide a critical synopsis of the narrative of Part II; second, in so doing, I stress the bookishness of Frechulf's project and its inherent (inter)textuality; lastly, and most importantly, I argue that Frechulf's decision *not* to provide narrative coverage of the eighth and ninth centuries brings into sharp focus the extent to which his *Histories* were a Carolingian creation. In order to set the scene, it will be helpful first to think about when and why other historians ended their narratives.

To the Ends of Histories

Just how odd was Frechulf's decision to end his *Histories* so long before his own day? If Frechulf is compared exclusively against Carolingian chronicles and ruler biographies, then his work can feel idiosyncratic. In his exhaustive study of eighth- and ninth-century annals, that most characteristic of Carolingian historiographical genres, Helmut Reimitz emphasised that these texts were 'future-orientated': their form—reports on what happened in a given year—was readily updatable, and as such allowed 'for an endlessly expandable story'.[4] If one annalist wrote an account that culminated in the events of their own day, continuators could add to and revise existing blocks of narrative in order to reflect or even shape new political circumstances. The *Histories*, by contrast, appear to be wedded to the distant past and, from the vantage point of their early seventh-century terminus, look towards a future that was already known, not least from the very narratives and compendia of Frankish history that Reimitz has analysed.[5] Frechulf, furthermore, would not

and Boston, MA: Brill, 2013), 57–82.
[3] What follows substantially expands upon Graeme Ward, 'The Sense of an Ending in the *Histories* of Frechulf of Lisieux', in *Historiography and Identity III: Carolingian Approaches*, eds Rutger Kramer, Helmut Reimitz and Graeme Ward (Turnhout: Brepols, 2021), 291–315.
[4] Reimitz, *Frankish History*, 336.
[5] Compare Goetz, 'Vergangenheitswahrnehmung', 205, who suggested that Frechulf produced 'a

fit easily into a study such as Reimitz's, focused as it is upon the mutability of texts within the manuscript record. Frechulf's ending, for example, was fixed and stable: his *Histories* were often copied but never directly continued.[6] The manuscript evidence offers no indication that later readers were as concerned with Frechulf's conclusion as modern students have been.

Moving beyond the usual Carolingian suspects shows that Frechulf was not the only historiographer (broadly defined) who left a gap between the worlds they narrated and lived in. There are numerous possible reasons why such gaps might exist. Chroniclers could refrain from covering events from the very recent past. Jerome, for example, stopped his *Chronicle* in 378, leaving 'the remaining period under Gratian and Theodosius for a more wide-ranging historical treatment, not because I was afraid to write freely and truthfully about those who were still living (for the fear of God drives out the fear of men) but because, with barbarians still running riot in our land, everything is uncertain'.[7] In the early tenth century, Regino of Prüm also voiced caution about narrating the near past, though this, he stated, was 'so as not to offend certain people who are still alive', leaving it up to later generations 'to pursue these matters more fully'.[8]

Examples of authors leaving more than simply the recent past untouched are harder to come by, but nevertheless can be found scattered amongst the diffuse corpus of extent medieval historiography. The ninth-century Byzantine chronicler George Syncellus only recounted events up until the accession of the Roman Emperor Diocletian in 285, though this was far from intentional: according to Theophanes the Confessor, his continuator, Syncellus died (in 810) before completing his task.[9] Paul the Deacon's *Historia Romana*, written c. 770 and addressed to Adalperga of Benevento, was an abridgment of ancient and Christian Roman history, which extended from the first rulers of Italy through to the age of

---

universal pre-history of the Frankish realm and thus an addendum to the Frankish and contemporary histories already in circulation'.

[6] See, however, *Prolegomena*, 159*–62*.

[7] *Chron.*, Eus. Praef., p. 7 [3/9]: 'Quo fine contentus reliquum temporis Gratiani et Theodosii latioris historiae stilo reservavi, non quo de viventibus timuerim libere et vere scribere—timor enim Di hominum timorem expellit – sed quoniam dibacchantibus adhuc in terra nostra barbaris inverta sunt omnia.'; trans. Lake, *Prologues*, 68. J. H. W. G. Liebeschuetz, 'Ecclesiastical Historians on their Own Times', *Studia Patristica*, 24 (1993): 151–63, at 157: 'Political caution was surely what prevented writers from including highly controversial contemporary issues.' A similar idea was developed in Paul A. Holloway, 'Inconvenient Truths: Early Jewish and Christian History Writing and the Ending of Luke-Acts', in *Die Apostelgeschichte im Kontext antiker und frühchristlicher Historiographie*, eds Jörg Frey, Clare K. Rothschild, Jens Schröter and Bettina Rost (Berlin: De Gruyter, 2009), 418–33.

[8] Regino of Prüm, *Chronicle*, ed. Kurz, p. 1; trans. MacLean, *Regino*, 61–2. For analysis: MacLean, 'Insinuation'.

[9] *The Chronography of George Synkellos: A Byzantine Chronicle of Universal History from the Creation*, ed. and trans. by William Adler and Paul Tuffin (Oxford: OUP, 2002), 473 and 501 together with their 'Introduction', xxix–lxxxviii at xlvii; *The Chronicle of Theophanes Confessor: Byzantine and Near Eastern History, A.D. 284–813*, trans. Cyril A. Mango, Roger Scott and Geoffrey Greatrex (Oxford: Clarendon Press, 1997), 1–2.

Justinian (ruled 527–65).[10] Paul hoped to carry the story through to his own time, although this was never realised.[11] Towards the end of the tenth century, Aimoin, a monk at Fleury, compiled a Frankish history that served to digest a selection of Merovingian texts and render them in a more polished Latin style. The work, as it was originally conceived, was to run from the Trojan origins of the Franks through to Pippin III's royal coronation in 751, although the text breaks off suddenly at 654.[12] Karl Ferdinand Werner argued that this non-Carolingian history of the Franks was commissioned by Abbot Abbo of Fleury (died 1004) to catch the eye of the recently crowned king of west Francia, Robert II (died 1031), whose father—Hugh Capet— had recently replaced the last Carolingian monarch, Louis V. But the personal and political circumstances which motivated the text's production unexpectedly changed and the project was abandoned.[13] Over a century later, Hugh, another Fleury monk, wrote his *Historia ecclesiastica* (completed c. 1110), which, despite its name, was a universal history built upon extensive excerpts from many of the sources Frechulf himself used, and perhaps also from the *Histories* themselves. This text stopped with the succession of the sons of Louis the Pious.[14] Hugh wrote a later work, 'The Deeds of the Modern Kings of the Franks (*Liber modernum regum Francorum actus*)', which began at the Battle of Fontenoy in 844, from which point onwards 'the regnum Francorum remained separated and divided from the Roman Empire'.[15] Hugh thus saw the reign of Louis the Pious as a break between the ancient history of the Church, defined as it was by the framework of empire, and the 'modern' history of the Franks.[16]

[10] Paul the Deacon, *Historia Romana*, Pref., p. 4: 'usque ad Iustiniani Augusti tempora perveni'. On Adelperga and her family, see Janet L. Nelson, 'Making a Difference in Eighth-century Politics: The Daughters of Desiderius', in *After Rome's Fall: Narrators and Sources of Early Medieval History. Essays Presented to Walter Goffart*, ed. Alexander Callander Murray (Toronto: University of Toronto Press, 1998), 171–90; repr. in her *Courts, Elites, and Gendered Power in the Early Middle Ages: Charlemagne and Others* (Aldershot: Asghate, 2007). On the *Historia Romana*, see most recently Christopher Heath, *The Narrative Worlds of Paul the Deacon: Between Empires and Identities in Lombard Italy* (Amsterdam: Amsterdam University Press, 2018), 39–66.

[11] Paul the Deacon, *Historia Romana*, Pref., p. 4: 'si tamen aut vestrae [that is, Adalperga's] sederit voluntati aut mihi vita comite ad huius modi laborem maiorum dicta suffragium tulerint, ad nostram usque aetatem eandem historiam protelare'. See also *Historia Romana*, XVI.23, p. 238: 'Quia vero restant adhuc quae de Iustiniani Augusti felicitate dicantur, insequenti Deo praesule libello promenda sunt.'

[12] Aimoin of Fleury, *Historia Francorum*, PL 139, cols. 627B–797A.

[13] Karl-Ferdinand Werner, 'Die literarischen Vorbilder des Aimoin von Fleury und die Entstehung seiner *Gesta Francorum*', in *Medium Aevum Vivum: Festschrift für Walther Bulst*, eds H. R. Jauss and D. Schaller (Heidelberg: C. Winter, 1960), 69–103, esp. 93–5. Werner's thesis was broadly accepted by Justin Lake, 'Rewriting Merovingian History in the Tenth Century: Aimoin of Fleury's *Gesta Francorum*', *EME*, 25(4) (2017): 489–525, at 492–3 and 522.

[14] Hugh of Fleury, *Historia ecclesiastica*, ed. Georg Waitz, MGH SS 9 (Hanover: Hahn, 1851), 337–54; a complete critical edition is available in Leendert Martin de Ruiter, '*Hugo van Fleury: Historia ecclesiastica, editio altera: Kritische teksteditie*' (unpublished thesis, University of Groningen, 2016).

[15] Hugh of Fleury, *Liber modernum regum Francorum actus*, ed. Georg Waitz, MGH SS 9 (Hanover: Hahn, 1851), pp. 376–95, at 376.

[16] In contrast to Frechulf, Hugh's *Historia* was more obviously indebted to typological interpretation: see various articles by Mégier collected in her *Christliche Weltgeschichte* and Julian Führer, 'Hugues de

Premature death, anxiety about live political issues, plans to compose a continuation which never materialised, and shifting historical circumstances: while they offer fascinating factors to think with, none can readily be applied to Frechulf. He wanted his *Histories* to stop at the point at which they did. There is no evidence to suggest that he planned to extend the story to his own day, and it would be fruitless to posit a lost or unfinished portion of the text that covered the Merovingian and Carolingian periods: such speculation only makes sense in the light of the expectation that a historical narrative ought to extend to within sight of an author's time of writing. Frechulf defined the limits of his narrative on four separate occasions: 1) in the dedicatory prologue which accompanied Part II; 2) at the end of Part II's final chapter; 3) in the *explicit* that appears as a colophon in the earliest manuscripts; 4) and finally in the letter-preface to his edition of Vegetius, which was composed nearly ten years after the *Histories* were finished. Over the course of a decade, therefore, Frechulf remained clear and consistent as to the scope of Part II. What exactly did he say?

On all four occasions, the end point was given as the establishment of the kingdoms of the Franks and the Lombards in Gaul and Italy.[17] In the prologue to Judith, Frechulf stated:

> I set about writing a second volume, beginning with Octavian Augustus and the birth of our Lord and Saviour, and carrying it down to the kingdoms of the Franks and the Lombards, when the emperors and governors of the Romans disappeared from Italy and Gaul, and the kings of the Goths, who had succeeded them, were likewise driven out by these peoples. I have divided this work into five books.[18]

At the very end of Part II, Frechulf restated his end point, though this time providing a little more information:

> On account of the love for my *domina*, Judith Augusta, I have undertaken a second volume, which I have carried through from the birth of the Lord Jesus Christ to the death of the extraordinary doctor, Gregory [the Great]. Next I selected certain of the deeds of Pope Boniface. I then decided to set the end of my books when the Franks and the Lombards took charge of the kingdoms of Gaul and Italy, after the governors of the Romans and the Goths had been driven out.[19]

Fleury: l'histoire et la typologie', in *La typologie biblique comme forme de pensée dans l'historiographie médiévale*, ed. Marek Thue Kretschmer (Turnhout: Brepols, 2015), 97–118.

[17] The partial exception is Frechulf's preface to his edition of Vegetius, where the Lombards were dropped: *Prol. Veg.*, p. 729: 'ab inicio mundi usque ad regna Francorum'. On the implications of this, see *Prolegomena*, 26*–28*.

[18] *Hist.*, II.Prol, p. 436: 'Igitur ab Octouiano Augusto et Domini natiuitate saluatoris nostri secundum adgressus sum scribendo opus, quod peregi usque ad regna Francorum et Longobardorum, deficientibus Romanorum imperatoribus seu iudicibus ab Italia et Galliis, Gothorum quoque regibus qui successerant ab eis etiam depulsis; quod uidelicet opus quinque distinxi in libris'. Trans. adapted from Lake, *Prologues*, 113.

[19] *Hist.*, II.5.27, pp. 723–4: 'Igitur a natiuitate Domini Iesu Christi ob amorem dominae meae Augustae Iudith secundum adgressus sum scribendo opus, quod usque ad Gregorii eximii doctoris obitum perduxi.

The additional reference points given in this epilogue correspond to three of the final four chapters of Part II: II.5.24 sketched the life and writings of Gregory the Great (died 604); II.5.25 noted the Lombard invasion of Italy under Alboin, before mentioning the martyrdom of the Visigothic prince Hermenegild (in 585) and the conversion of his brother King Reccared to orthodox Christianity (*ad catholicam fidem*) (in 587); II.5.26 listed two 'deeds of Boniface', the first of which was that, at the pope's request, the eastern emperor Phocas (ruled 602–10) recognised the primacy of the Roman see and the second was the conversion of the Pantheon to the Church of Mary and all the Martyrs (in 609), again decreed by Phocas at Boniface's request. Both deeds were attributed to one pope, but Frechulf—or rather Frechulf's source, Bede's *Chronica maiora*—conflated Boniface III (died 607) and Boniface IV (died 615). II.5.27, the very last chapter, comprised a summary of the six ecumenical councils, also drawn from Bede's *Chronica*. Not only was this chapter not signalled in the epilogue, but it also considerably post-dated the three chapters which preceded it, since the sixth council, III Constantinople, took place in 680–1.

Frechulf was clear enough in letting his readers know where he decided to halt his narrative: rulership of the areas of the former western Roman Empire was now in the hands of the Franks and the Lombards, which roughly aligned with the territorial extent of Charlemagne's and Louis the Pious's realms.[20] Moreover, under Gregory and then especially his successor(s), the western world was still 'Roman, however, but Roman ecclesiastical'.[21] Yet at no point did he attempt to articulate *why* he chose to end when he did. In order to make sense of what was left unexplained, a range of solutions have been put forward. Broadly speaking, they have been organised around two main focal points: interpretations which have prioritised the establishment of the kingdoms of the Franks and the Lombards in Gaul and Italy, or those which homed in on ecclesiastical developments, signalled by the deeds of Gregory the Great and his papal successor(s). Both of these strands of argument have reached comparable conclusions, albeit from radically different angles: Frechulf's ending was distinctive, significant, even singular, because it reflected his awareness of the end of one era and the inception of a new phase of world history.[22]

De gestis etiam Bonefacii papae quaedam deinceps praelibando perstrinxi. Romanorum iudicibus et Gothis ab Italia et Galliis depulsis, his Francis et Langobardis succedentibus in regnis, hic terminum censui meorum inponere librorum. In St Gall, 622, p. 517 there is no *secundum* to qualify *opus*, but there is a still a clear echo of the prologue, which does mention *secundum*: see *Prolegomena*, 57*–58*.

[20] Allen, 'Universal History', 40.

[21] Noble, *Images*, 353.

[22] In general, see Reinhart Herzog and Reinhart Koselleck (eds), *Epochenschwelle und Epochenbewußtsein* (Munich: Fink, 1987). Related concepts, such as Zeitbewußtsein and Geschichtsbewußtsein, have been much studied in German-language scholarship: see, for instance, extensive work by Hans-Werner Goetz, helpfully collected in his *Vorstellungsgeschichte: gesammelte Schriften zu Wahrnehmungen, Deutungen und Vorstellungen im Mittelalter* (Bochum: Dieter Winkler, 2007).

A version of the political reading had already been advanced as early as 1858, when Wilhelm Wattenbach put forth the idea that the bishop of Lisieux sought to dispel the myth that the Roman Empire, as the fourth and final monarchy of Daniel's eschatological vision, would persist until the end of time; rather, Frechulf 'ventured to consider the new realms (of the Franks and Lombards), which were established on Roman soil, as effectively new entities, and to regard their foundation as the beginning of a new age'.[23] Over the next century and a half, the idea that Frechulf gave expression to an 'awareness of an epochal break between the world of the Roman Empire and Carolingian Christianity (Epochenbewußtsein eines Bruches zwischen der Welt des Imperium Romanum und der karolingischen Christenheit)' was repeated and refined.[24] Anna-Dorothee von den Brincken's survey of medieval universal chronicles, which remains an important reference work, credited Frechulf with identifying c. 600 as a 'new epoch of world history', which represented nothing less than 'the break, which today we label the transition from Antiquity to the Middle Ages'.[25] Matthew Innes grouped Frechulf with a number of ninth-century writers who 'began to sense a more radical discontinuity between their world and that of Rome',[26] and likewise Tom Noble stated that Frechuf 'was the first (or perhaps the first after Isidore) medieval writer to see the post-Roman west as something new'.[27] Hans Hubert Anton has suggested that the new era Frechulf identified was a specifically western one dominated by new post-Roman *regna*.[28]

Nikolaus Staubach offered a critical modification to this 'political/secular' reading of the *Histories'* controversial finale. Staubach maintained that the turn of the seventh century was, as an 'Epochenzäsur', a moment of immense significance

---

[23] Willhelm Wattenbach, *Deutschlands Geschichtsquellen im Mittelalter bis zur Mitte des dreizehnten Jahrhunderts*, 2 vols (Berlin: W. Hertz, 1893–4) 6th edn, vol. 1, 178. Compare Josef Adamek, *Vom römischen Endreich*, 70.

[24] For example, Heinz Löwe's update of Wattenbach and Levison, *Deutschlands Geschichtsquellen*, 352 (where the quote is from); Fritz Landberg, *Das Bild der alten Geschichte in mittelalterlichen Weltchroniken* (Berlin: E. Streisand, 1934), 54; Natunewicz, 'Freculphus', 122–3: 'it must be concluded that he regarded the "Holy Roman Empire" as a new and separate entity, not bound by any connections with ancient Rome. There can be no other explanation for the fact that the chronicle concludes so abruptly with the establishment of Frankish and Lombard kingdoms and does not continue to [Frechulf's] own time. It is also interesting that Freculphus ends his narrative by emphasizing the growing power of the Church: in the last two chapters he respectively notes the recognition by Phocas of Boniface III as the spiritual head of all Christendom and describes the six universal synods. The reader is thus prepared for the Middle Ages, in which both the new political order based on feudalism and the authority of the Church, particularly of the Papacy, played important roles. The fact that Freculphus was the first writer to be aware of both these aspects of medieval history, even though he modestly left to others a detailed account of that period, entitles him to a unique position in the realm of historiography ...'

[25] Von den Brincken, *Studien*, 125.

[26] Innes, 'Carolingians and the Germanic Past', 234–6 (quotation at 235).

[27] Noble, *Images*, 352.

[28] Hans Hubert Anton, 'Anfänge säkularer Begründung von Herrschaft und Staat im Mittelalter. Historiographie, Herkunftssagen, politische Metaphorik (*Institutio Traiani*)', *Archiv für Kulturgeschichte*, 86 (2004): 75–122, at 86.

for Frechulf, but this was not because the post-imperial kingdoms of the Franks and Lombards inaugurated a new world historical epoch; rather, the ecclesiastical events with which Frechulf ended (the empire's recognition of papal primacy and the consecration of the Pantheon) brought to a close an Augustinian metanarrative that had started with Cain's murder of Abel. The end of ancient history was not to be found at the fall of the western empire, but the point at which Christian worship had replaced pagan cults. Here Frechulf situated the 'conclusive breakthrough of Christian times', the final stage of a long and gradual process that had begun with Christ's Incarnation.[29] Staubach's rich essay convincingly refuted an earlier interpretation by Werner Goez, who had suggested that Frechulf's failure properly to grasp Augustine's *Geschichtstheologie* led him to believe that the Carolingian Empire was part of the *civitas terrena* and so he cut short his narrative in order to fudge any awkward identifications.[30] Against Goez's characterisation of Frechulf's conclusion as premature ('Der vorzeitige Abbruch des Werkes'), Staubach showed that it was carefully and consciously chosen. This, to be sure, is a sentiment with which I fully agree, yet it is one I hope to demonstrate by decentring Augustine.

In this chapter, my point of departure is that neither the secular nor ecclesiastical events highlighted by Frechulf ought to take priority over the other, and that any attempt to distinguish them distances us from one of the central aspects of the *Histories*: namely, that the text was a compilation. The objects of Frechulf's analysis were not, strictly speaking, the events that lay beneath his assembled sources, but the very sources themselves. The political transformations and ecclesiastical developments that ran throughout Part II and which reached their denouement at the end of the volume emerged from and responded to Frechulf's own critical (or even exegetical) reading of the canon of Christian historiography. My own contribution to the problem of the *Histories*' end point, therefore, is framed in relation to the bishop's engagement with this canon as a canon, as a collection of distinct but interlinked texts which contained complementary perspectives on the same essential story. It was the job of the exegete to extract this story from the myriad voices of the 'volumes of the ancients'. I have already touched upon this issue throughout this study. Here, I want to develop it further, and to this end the notion and perception of a wider Christian canon plays a parallel role within this chapter. The *Histories* were built upon a recognised corpus of chronicles and histories, but canonical

---

[29] Staubach, '*Christiana tempora*', 189–90. Compare 186: 'Mit der Vollendung dieser Metamorphose und der Erfüllung von Noes Verheißung war für Frechulf die bedeutendste Zäsur der Weltgeschichte erreicht, eine Epochenwende, die das Ereignis der Inkarnation erst zu voller historischer Geltung gebracht hatte. Kein anderer Einschnitt erschien ihm ähnlich geeignet, als Grenzdatum seiner Chronik die Einheit der alten Zeit einer an Stadt und Staat, Volk und Stamm gebundenen Gottesverehrung gegenüber der Neuheit der *chrstiana tempora* zu bezeichnen'. The importance of Noah's promise to the gentiles (Gn. 9:27) was also underlined by Mégier, 'Frechulf und Ado', 42.

[30] Goez, 'Zur Weltchronik', esp. 103.

texts appear regularly throughout Part II, from the various items that make up the New Testament all the way through to the oeuvre of Gregory the Great. It has already been noted that 'the development of Christian literature greatly occupied Frechulf', but the implications of this have not yet been explored.[31] Towards the end of this chapter, I argue that Frechulf not only worked with texts that, on account of being written by *sancti patres*, were themselves authoritative, but at the same time also outlined the history of patristic Christianity. As we shall see, if the boundary hinted at by *Histories*'s end point can be said to have marked the end of an era, it was the age of the church fathers.[32] There is much ground to cover first: some overall orientation will help set the scene.

Emperors, Ecclesiastics and the Growth of the Church

In Part I, Frechulf showed that all history, from its origins at the world's creation, worked towards the preordained historical conditions within which Christ was to be born. Part II traced how history radiated out from the Nativity. It dealt with the Christian emperors who persecuted then later supported Christianity, and traced how the *ecclesia*, the community of the faithful established in one corner of Augustus's worldwide empire, gradually spread throughout, and even beyond, the limits of the Roman world (*orbis Romanus* was a favoured term of Frechulf's) and in the process fulfilled Old and New Testament prophecy.[33] In all the many sources that fed into Part II, divine providence was the guiding thread that unified the whole edifice of excerpts: God meted out punishments, bestowed rewards, and steered the course of the past, despite the best efforts of the Ancient Enemy (*hostis antiquus*) to frustrate things, either by spreading heretical doctrine or inciting imperial persecution. Providence, as the driving force of history, was present in most of the core resources marshalled for Part II, but the bishop of Lisieux also added his own particular emphases at crucial moments.

On the one hand, Frechulf's was not a new narrative: the triumphal history of the early church in the face of the enmity of the Devil was integral to Christian collective memory and identity and remained so throughout the Middle Ages; what is more, this history was, to a considerable degree, the product of the fourth- and especially fifth-century sources with which Frechulf worked.[34] On

---

[31] Von den Brincken, *Studien*, 126.

[32] This was indicated but not developed by Savigni, 'Storia universale', 191: 'Con la conversione dei popoli germanici e la morte di Gregorio Magno si era chiusa un'epoca storica, quella dell'ecumene mediterranea e dei Padri.'

[33] On prophecy, see, for example, *Hist.*, I.1.31, p. 62; I.7.13, pp. 402–5; II.1.3, pp. 443–4; II.1.8 [23/27], pp. 452–3; II.1.24 [12/30], pp. 489–90.

[34] See, for example, Peter Brown, *Authority and the Sacred: Aspects of the Christianisation of the Roman World* (Cambridge: CUP, 1995), 1–26; Robert A. Markus '*Tempora christiana* Revisited', in *Augustine and his Critics. Essays in Honour of Gerald Bonner*, eds Robert Dodaro and George Lawless (London: Psychology Press, 2000), 201–13.

the other hand, it needs to be stressed that this foundational narrative had never previously been told in such a way: the overall structure of books and chapters, the wide range and particular combinations of source extracts that were inserted into this structure, and the extension of the core story, first told in the fourth and especially fifth centuries, through to the era of Gregory the Great at the turn of the seventh were all unprecedented. I deal with each of these three things in turn.

Libri: *Structure and Organisation*

In Part II as in Part I, books (*libri*) were the largest organisational units. Although not explicitly stated, the overall theme of the volume was Christianisation and one way this was emphasised was through book conclusions. The dissolution of the structures and symbols of non-Christian worship marked the end points of all but one of Part II's five books. Book 1, which began with Christ/Augustus, ended with the destruction of the Second Temple in AD 70. The rupture of traditional and—in the minds of hostile Christian exegetes—legitimate Jewish worship took place at the Nativity, even if the full effects of this were not felt until the Roman siege of Jerusalem. Accordingly, it was at this moment that Frechulf 'decided to make the end of the first book of my undertaken work, when the legal sacrifices together with the Temple and the most heinous people of the Jews were irrecoverably brought to ruin'.[35] Vespasian and Titus, the emperors who had waged the Jewish War, marked the point of departure of Book 2, which concluded with a catalogue of authors who had written during the reigns of Severus (ruled 193–211) and Caracalla (ruled 198–217). Staubach labelled this a 'makeshift conclusion', which served to portion up material but did not develop the overall theme: I shall return to this point below.[36]

The thematic focus of the conclusions to the next three books was much clearer. Book 3 ran from the reigns of Severus and Caracalla through to Constantine (died 337): amongst his many celebrated deeds that comprised the later chapters of this book, Constantine was said to have issued an edict by which pagan temples were to be closed without bloodshed. According to Frechulf:

> In this, the omnipotence of our Lord Jesus Christ must be praised and marvelled at, that when He willed it, soon, by the edict of one devout ruler, the shrines and temples of the idols, which wondrously had been built by the hard work of mighty and wise men and by the most powerful of all the kings and emperors of the past, were closed. With almost no resistance from the worshippers throughout the whole world, [these shrines and temples] were reduced to nothing.[37]

---

[35] *Hist.*, II.1.24 [39/41], p. 490: 'Hic autem coepti operis decreui primi finem facere libri, ubi legales hostiae pariter cum templo ac populo Iudaeorum sceleratissimo inrecuperabiliter conciderunt.'

[36] Staubach, '*Christiana tempora*', 181. See also p. 102, n. 116, above.

[37] *Hist.*, II.3.21 [92/6], p. 612: 'Et in hoc Domini nostri Iesu Christi laudanda atque miranda est

Book 4, which ran from the beginning of the reigns of Constantine's sons (in 338), Constantius, Constantine II and Constans, through to the death of Theodosius I (395). In this book, Christianisation continued apace, and Egypt served as a token. During Valens' reign, the teachings of the desert fathers 'fulfilled the Apostle [Paul's] words that "where sin abounded, grace did more abound" (Romans 5:20)'. 'For Egypt', Frechulf added, 'more so than all other nations formerly served the various monsters of idolatry with deeply misplaced devotion'.[38] Even in Alexandria, 'where pagan superstition had become especially ingrown', the shrines to the old gods, most notably the Serapeum, were soon destroyed following another imperial decree, this time of Theodosius I.[39] This event was Book 4's end point and was presented as the completion of a process already underway: 'In the preceding book, we set out the limit [of our narrative] when, under the pious prince Constantine, the temples of the pagans were closed; let this [book's] terminus be in the destruction of false gods and the subversion of the temples'.[40] A final point in the long-term and pre-ordained downward trajectory of pagan worship was added at the very end of Book 5. Following a request from Pope Boniface, the emperor Phocas decreed that the Pantheon in Rome be converted from a pagan shrine to a Christian church, 'so that where once the worship, not of all the gods but rather of all the demons had taken place, there should thenceforth be a memorial to all the saints'.[41]

The neatness of this narrative strongly suggests deliberate emplotment. This is by no means a novel observation: Nikolaus Staubach and Michael Allen have already traced the broad contours of Part II's narrative and have shown the extent to which it developed a focus on cult and worship first articulated in Part I.[42] There is, however, more to appreciate if we look in closer detail at the contents of the chapters that comprised the five books of Part II.

---

omnipotentia, ut quando uoluit, mox unius religiosi principis edicto, omnium regum et imperatorum potentissimorum et retro saeculis fortium ac sapientium industria fana ac mirabiliter idolorum fabricata templa clausa, nullo resistente cultore poene per omnem orbem, et ad nihilum sunt redacta.' Compare Oros., VII.28.28, p. 79.

[38] *Hist.*, II.4.18 [10/12], p. 647: 'Aegyptus enim prae omnibus nationibus superstitiosissime diversis idolorum monstris quondam servierat.'

[39] *Hist.*, II.4.30, p. 668. For background: Johannes Hahn, 'The Conversion of the Cult Statues: The Destruction of the Serapeum 392 A.D. and the Transformation of Alexandria into the "Christ-loving" City', in *From Temple to Church: Destruction and Renewal of Local Cultic Topography in Late Antiquity*, ed. Johannes Hahn (Leiden: Brill, 2008), 335–66.

[40] *Hist.*, II.4.30 [23/6], p. 669: 'Igitur praecedenti libro ubi sub pio principe Constantino paganorum clausa sunt templa finem inposuimus. Huic autem terminus sit in destructione deorum falsorum et in subuersione templorum.'

[41] *Hist.*, II.5.26 [4/8], p. 722; trans. adapted from Wallis, 226. For background, see Susan Rankin, '*Terribilis est locus iste*: The Pantheon in 609', in *Rhetoric Beyond Words: Delight and Persuasion in the Arts of the Middle Ages*, ed. Mary J. Carruthers (New York: CUP, 2010), 281–310.

[42] Staubach, '*Christiana tempora*', esp. 175–81 and Allen, 'Universal History', 40–1.

Themes and Sources I: Orosius and Eusebius, Empire and Ecclesia

Frechulf began Part II's second book with a preamble which summarised the ground his first book had just covered:

> In succinct prose, I took care to compile together from the various books of authors the deeds of emperors and the acts of ecclesiastics, from the birth of the Lord Christ until his passion, and from there through to the destruction of the Temple of Jerusalem, the dispersion of the Jewish people via the just retribution of God, and the massacre they suffered, on account of [divine] vengeance, not only for the passion of Christ, son of God and man, but also the persecution and slaughter of his servants.[43]

Beyond summarising the contents of II.1, the reference to the 'deeds of emperors and the acts of churchmen' captures the basic shape of the narrative and reflects the main sources Frechulf used. Emperors appear throughout Part II: their successive reigns, from Augustus to Phocas, supplied the main chronological reference points around which excerpts were grouped together, just as the rulers from the left-most column of Eusebius-Jerome's *Chronicle* had done in Part I. Imperial deeds themselves also were given considerable attention. One of Frechulf's chief sources was Orosius, whose seventh and final book *contra paganos* 'deal[t] with the times when the Christian faith germinated, the times when it grew all the more amid the hands of those who would have stopped it'.[44] On the whole, the various chapters of this book took the form of a series of biographies of Roman emperors, from Augustus through to Honorius I (died 423). In addition, Frechulf also made notable use of another collection of imperial biographies, the late fourth-century *Epitome de Caesaribus* of Pseudo-Aurelius Victor, which—as per its title in the earliest, ninth-century, manuscript—dealt with the 'lives and habits of the emperors, from Caesar Augustus to Theodsoius I'.[45] This text was possibly written by a non-Christian author, and at the very least contained none of the distinctly Christian trappings of Orosius's narrative. Nevertheless, Frechulf read it as he did all his sources, as a ninth-century intellectual studying a world created and governed by God: even if the text originally presented a non-Christian overview of the lives of the caesars, it was embedded within an explicitly Christian framework. We have already encountered one example of this: the *Epitome* had attributed Augustus's remarkably long reign due to his natural disposition, but for Frechulf the reason was at root Orosian: to prepare the world for Christ's Incarnation.[46]

---

[43] *Hist.*, II.2.1, p. 496: 'Igitur in priore libro a Domini natiuitate Christi usque ad eius passionem, ac deinde usque ad templi Hierosolimitani destructionem populique Iudaici iusta Dei ultione dispersionem ac diuersis mortibus internitionem propter passionis Christi, Dei hominisque filii, uindictam, eiusque seruorum persecutiones ac neces, tam de gestis imperatorum quamque et de ecclesiasticorum actibus succincto sermone ex diuersis auctorum libris colligere curaui.'

[44] Oros., VI.22.10–11, p. 237; compare VII.3.2–3, pp. 20–1.

[45] *Pseudo-Aurélius Victor: Abrégé des Césars*, ed. and trans. Michel Festy, Collection des universités de France (Paris: Les Belles Lettres, 1999).

[46] For a comparable example, see *Hist.*, II.3.14 [41/61], pp. 590–1 where a spree of imperial deaths in

For the *acta ecclesiasticorum,* Frechulf worked closely with the tradition that developed out of Eusebius's *Ecclesiastical History.*[47] Eusebius defined his subject at the outset of the work: in addition to detailing 'the disasters which devastated the Jewish people on account of the plots which they prepared against the saviour'—this was reflected clearly in the quotation from Frechulf above—another important theme was the 'famous men ... who lead the most celebrated churches' and 'who, in each generation, nobly strengthened the word of God through their writings and teaching'.[48] While Orosius's seventh book was a collection of imperial biographies, Eusebius's *History* was also essentially a collective biography of apostles, saints and martyrs, through whose written and physical *acta* the church came into being.[49] When it came to these luminaries, however, Frechulf normally had recourse to Jerome's *On Illustrious Men,* a late fourth-century catalogue of authorities, from the apostle Peter through to Jerome himself, which essentially served as a ready-made distillation of the lives and writings of the many holy men who populated the *Ecclesiastical History.* Despite having a less obvious narrative form, Jerome's work performed a comparable function: to chart 'the number and the quality of men who founded, built, and adorned the church'.[50] Of Jerome's 135 bio-bibliographies—that is, biographies defined by what people had written— Frechulf included 120, and most of them verbatim. The people and texts by which the church came into being were central to the narrative of Part II.

In combining *gesta imperatorum* and *acta ecclesiasticorum,* Frechulf effectively amalgamated two complementary historiographical approaches which can,

---

the early fourth century is attributed to Christian persecution, a theme alien to the *Epitome.*
[47] On Eusebius, see most recently, Corke-Webster, *Eusebius and Empire.* On the genre of ecclesiastical history: Robert A. Markus, 'Church History and the Early Church Historians', in *The Materials, Sources and Methods of Ecclesiastical History,* ed. Derek Baker, *Studies in Church History* 11 (Oxford: Blackwell, 1975), 1–17; repr. in his *From Augustine to Gregory the Great: History and Christianity in Late Antiquity* (London: Varorium Reprints, 1983), item III; Glen F. Chesnut, *The First Christian Histories: Eusebius, Socrates, Sozomen, Theodoret and Evagrius,* 2nd edn (Macon, GA: Mercer University Press, 1986); Peter Van Nuffelen, 'Ecclesiastical History', in *A Companion to Late Antique Literature,* eds Scott McGill and Edward J. Watts (Hoboken, NJ: John Wiley, 2018), 161–75. On Rufinus: Françoise Thelamon, *Païens et chrétiens au IVᵉ siècle: l'apport de l'Histoire ecclésiastique de Rufin d'Aquilée* (Paris: Études augustiennes, 1981); Françoise Thelamon, 'Écrire l'histoire de l'Église: d'Eusèbe de Césarée à Rufin d'Aquilée', in *L'historiographie de L'église des premiers siècles,* eds Bernard Pouderon and Yves-Marie Duval (Paris: Éditions Beauchesne, 2001), 207–35; Mark Humphries, 'Rufinus's Eusebius: Translation, Continuation and Edition in the Latin *Ecclesiastical History', Journal of Early Christian Studies,* 16(2) (2008): 143–64. On Cassiodorus's *Historia Tripartita:* Désirée Scholten, 'Cassiodorus' *Historia tripartita* before the Earliest Extant Manuscripts', *The Resources of the Past in Early Medieval Europe,* eds Clemens Gantner, Rosamond McKitterick and Sven Meeder (Cambridge: CUP, 2015), 34–50 and Emerance Delacenserie, 'Beyond the Compilation: The Two *Historiae tripartitae* of Theodore Lector and Cassiodorus', *Sacris Erudiri,* 56 (2017): 415–44; on the text of the *Historia* used by Frechulf, see Jürgen, Dummer, 'Frechulf von Lisieux und die *Historia ecclesiastica tripartita', Philologus,* 115 (1971): 58–70.
[48] Eusebius-Rufinus, *Historia ecclesiastica,* I.1.1, p. 7: 'qui etiam insignes viri in locis maxime celeberrimis ecclesiis praefuerunt vel qui singulis quibusque temporibus seu scribendo seu docendo verbum dei nobiliter adstruxere...'.
[49] For example, Schott, 'General Introduction', 17 and Corke-Webster, *Eusebius and Empire,* 74, 80.
[50] Jerome, *DVI,* Prol., ed. Richardson, p. 2; trans. Halton, 2; McKitterick, *History and Memory,* 223–6.

albeit cautiously, be termed 'Orosian' and 'Eusebian'.[51] Following a seminal article by Karl-Ferdinand Werner, Orosius's *Historiae* have been seen as the Christian transformation of the moral mode of history characteristic of the Old Testament: God rewarded his followers and made grim examples of his enemies.[52] Eusebius's *History*, by contrast, has been understood almost as an extension of the New Testament: it traced the expansion of Christian communities throughout the Roman Empire, picking up where the Gospels and the Acts of the Apostles left off.[53] There were moments of overlap between these two sources, which contributed to Frechulf's own representation of the past. Divine vengeance was one such theme: Eusebius, for instance, had influentially argued that Josephus's account of the *Jewish War* was evidence that the Roman siege was punishment for the crucifixion; Orosius, on the other hand, claimed that Titus had pondered whether to destroy the Temple after the conclusion of the siege, 'but as the Church of God was now springing up in abundance throughout the whole world, God decided this building, now it was exhausted from giving birth, empty, and fit for no good purpose, ought to be removed'.[54] More often than not, however, Orosius and Eusebius told parallel narratives. Christian persecution, for example, was a common theme, but while Orosius concentrated on the Roman emperors who initiated persecutions and the often swift punishments that typically befell them, Eusebius was more interested in those who were persecuted, especially those who became saints and martyrs.[55] Frechulf stood between these traditions, blending together their respective focal points for the benefit of readers for whom both approachs represented the historical foundations of their collective identity.

[51] On Eusebius and Orosius, see Kempshall, *Rhetoric*, 59-78, with quotation at 78: 'It is difficult to overestimate the importance and influence of Eusebius and Orosius as models of Christian historiography in the Middle Ages.'
[52] Karl Ferdinand Werner, 'Gott, Herrscher und Historiograph: der Geschichtsschreiber als Interpret des Wirkens Gottes in der Welt und Ratgeber der Könige (4. Bis 12. Jahrhundert)', in *Deus qui mutat tempora: Menschen und Institutionen im Wandel des Mittelalters: Festschrift für Alfons Becker zu seinem fünfundsechzigsten Geburtstag*, eds Ernst-Dieter Hehl, Hubertus Seibert and Franz Staab (Sigmaringen: Thorbecke, 1987), 1-31 and Werner, 'L'*Historia* et les rois', in *Religion et culture autour de l'an mil: royaume capétien et Lotharingie: actes du colloque Hugues Capet 987-1987, la France de l'an mil, Auxerre, 26 et 27 juin 1987, Metz, 11 et 12 septembre 1987*, eds Dominique Iogna-Prat and Jean-Charles Picard (Paris: Picard, 1990), 135-43. See also G. W. Trompf, *Early Christian Historiography: Narratives of Redistributive Justice* (London: Continuum, 2000), 292-322 and Kempshall, *Rhetoric*, 64-81.
[53] For example, Inglebert, *Les Romains chrétiens*, 213. Compare Roland Kany, 'Warum fand die Apostelgeschichte keine Fortsetzung in der Antike? Elf Thesen zu einem ungelösten Problem', in *Die Apostelgeschichte im Kontext antiker und frühchristlicher Historiographie*, eds Jörg Frey, Clare K. Rothschild and Jens Schröter (Berlin: De Gruyter, 2009), 327-48, at 330, who questions any direct continuity.
[54] Oros., VII.9.5, p. 39; trans. Fear, 338. This passage was reproduced by Frechulf: *Hist.*, II.2.3 [34/42], p. 500. In general, Trompf, *Early Christian Historiography*.
[55] On persecution in Eusebius, see William Tabbernee, 'Eusebius' "Theology of Persecution": As Seen in the Various Editions of his Church History', *Journal of Early Christian Studies*, 5 (1997): 319-34 and Thomas O'Loughlin, 'Eusebius of Caesarea's Conceptions of the Persecutions as the Key to Reading his *Historia ecclesiastica*', in *The Great Persecution: Proceedings of the Fifth Patristic Conference, Maynooth, 2003*, eds D. Vincent Twomey and Mark Humphries (Dublin: Four Courts Press, 2009), 91-105.

Before going further, some qualification is needed. 'Orosian' and 'Eusebian' are purposely loose terms, and I use them to not evoke any particular political theologies.[56] As already seen in the last chapter, Frechulf borrowed much from Orosius but excised many of the rhetorical/apologetic features that are usually considered characteristic of the *Historiae*. Furthermore, in tracing 'imperial deeds' and 'ecclesiastical acts', Frechulf made no rigid distinction between the pool of texts from which he drew. Ecclesiastical sources were also replete with imperial history: this becomes especially so from Constantine onwards, when the history of the church and the empire became increasingly intertwined. Both Rufinus's Latin continuation of the *Ecclesiastical History* and Cassiodorus's *Tripartite History*, which was a compilation of three of Eusebius's fifth-century Greek continuators, were mined for ecclesiastical acts as much as for imperial deeds. Frechulf reproduced Orosius's account of how Theodosius I overcame the usurpers Arbogastes and Eugenius (in 394) through the power of prayer; this was paralleled by the account of Theodosius II's similarly secured victory against the usurper Johannes (c. 424), taken from Cassiodorus.[57] Lastly, these two categories fail to capture the range and variety of sources on which Frechulf drew and the intricate editorial work he performed in order to weave his chosen extracts together. They remain useful, nevertheless, since they capture in broad brushstrokes the narrative of Part II; they also help explain Frechulf's ending.

Themes and Sources II: Emperors and Authors

Frechulf's second book began with chapters on the 'good acts of Vespasian' (II.2.2) and 'the magnificent works of Titus' (II.2.3), both of which comprised passages from Orosius augmented by the *Epitome de Caesaribus*. The next chapter was introduced with a short framing note:

> I shall attempt to set out briefly who the illustrious doctors of the churches were after the Ascension of the Lord Jesus Christ in the times of the above-mentioned princes [that is, Titus and Vespasian]: [these doctors], as the practice of reading [*usus legendi*] has transmitted to us, were also authors of books. [I shall also relate] what parts of the world the apostles accepted as their lot to spread the Gospel, and in which places they triumphed in their battle and attained the eternal palm [of martyrdom].[58]

---

[56] On this, see Van Nuffelen, *Orosius*, 191–7.

[57] *Hist.*, II.4.28 [12/45], pp. 661–2 and II.5.8 [7/29], p. 689.

[58] *Hist.*, II.2.4 [1/7], p. 500: 'Per horum tempora praefatorum principum post Domini ascensionem Christi, quique inlustres fuerunt ecclesiarum doctores, librorum etiam quos usus legendi tradidit auctores, quas quidem mundi partes apostoli ad praedicandum per sortes proprias acceperunt, quibus etiam locis agonizando triumphatores aeternam consecuti sunt palmam, succincta breuitate expedire conabor.' Compare *Hist.*, II.2.4 cap., p. 491: 'sub praefatis principibus apostolici uiri et reliqui doctores sacri qui tunc floruerunt, quas mundi partes ad praedicandum susceperunt, et quibus in locis consecuti sunt palmam martyrii, per ordinem continetur.'

What follows is a survey of the lives, writings and deaths of the evangelists and apostles, based primarily on three sources: Eusebius-Rufinus's *Ecclesiastical History*, Jerome's *De viris illustribus* and Isidore of Seville's *De ortu et obitu patrum*, another collection of holy lives completed sometime between 600 and 636 in Visigothic Iberia.[59] This chapter provides yet another example of Frechulf synthesising received traditions: while Jerome focused on Christ's closest followers and what they had written, Isidore's *De ortu et obitu patrum* was more concerned with the post-scriptural (that is, 'apocryphal') history of apostles, a subject of long fascination and deep meaning within medieval Christianity.[60] Entries from both sources could even be melded together: to the end of Jerome's entry for the evangelist Matthew, Frechulf tacked Isidore's note that the author of the first Gospel 'initially evangelised in Judaea, before preaching in Macedonia. He is at rest in the Parthian mountains.'[61] An earlier critic of Frechulf claimed that this chapter was 'keine Geschichte', but merely a 'series of brief biographies of the apostles and the evangelists'.[62] Yet this biographical series has a clear narrative function: following the destruction of the Second Temple, Christianity began to spread all throughout the world by means of 'the disciples of the Lord, the preachers of faith and the teachers of the gentiles'.[63] Frechulf's brief introduction to this potted history of Christianity's beginnings not only explained the chapter's meaning, but also acknowledged the importance of written, textual, authority: through the 'practice of reading'—presumably both the reading of scripture in the context of the liturgy and the frequent reading of authoritative histories such as Jerome's *De viris illustribus*—it was known that these *doctores ecclesiasiarum* were also *auctores librorum*.

---

[59] Isidore of Seville, *De ortu et obitu patrum*, ed. César Chaparro Gómez (Paris: Les Belles Lettres, 1985). See also César Chaparro Gómez, 'El *De ortu et obitu patrum* de Isidoro de Sevilla. El problema de su composición y transmisión', in *L'édition critique des oeuvres d'Isidore de Séville: les recensions multiples: actes du collque organisé à la Casa de Velázquez et à l'Université Rey Juan Carlos de Madrid (14–15 janvier 2002)*, eds Ma A. Andrés Sanz, J. Elfassi and J. C. Martín (Paris, 2008), 49–62 and Hervé Inglebert, 'Renommée et sainteté: historiographie et hagiographie dans les chroniques tardo-antiques latines et dans le *De ortu et obitu patrum* d'Isidore de Séville', *Salesianum*, 67 (2005): 977–88.
[60] Els Rose, *Ritual Memory: The Apocryphal Acts and Liturgical Commemoration in the Early Medieval West (c. 500–1215)* (Leiden: Brill, 2009); see further the articles by François Dolbeau collected in his *Prophètes, apôtres et disciples dans les traditions chrétiennes d'Occident. Vies brèves et listes en latin* (Brussels: Sociétés des Bollandistes, 2012).
[61] *Hist.*, II.2.4 [9/20], pp. 500–1.
[62] Schelle, 'Frechulf', 125.
[63] *Hist.*, II.2.4 [120/122], p. 505: 'Igitur Domini discipuli, praedicatores fidei et doctores gentium, qui dum omnes unum sint, singuli tamen certis locis in mundo ad praedicandum partes proprias acceperunt, quod ut breuiter repetam: Petrus namque Romam accepit, Andreas Achaiam, Iacobus Hispaniam, Thomas Indiam, Iohannes Asiam, Matheus Macedoniam, Philippus Gallias, Bartholomeus Liconiam, Symon Zelotis Aegyptum, Mathias Iudaeam, Iacobus frater Domini Hierusalem, Iudas frater Iacobi Mesopotamiam. Paulo autem cum ceteris apostolis nulla sors propria traditur, quia in omnibus gentibus magister et praedicator eligitur. Nam sicut Petro et reliquis circumcisionis apostolatus est datus, ita Paulo praeputii in gentibus. Hic tamen septem ecclesiis et tribus euangelizat discipulis.'

For much of Part II, the history of the church was inseparable from that of the empire. Although already present in Frechulf's core sources, one way this was made more explicit was by situating the production of Christian literature in the context of Christian persecution. Take, for example, Trajan: II.2.9 dealt with the 'marvellous deeds of Trajan'; II.2.10 offered a biography of John the Evangelist, who Frechulf knew had died 'under Trajan, sixty-seven years after Christ's passion'.[64] II.2.11 then covered some famous victims of Trajan's persecution, introduced by a short preamble:

> At this time, the Old Enemy, the foe of all good things, was eying humanity's salvation with envy and was grieving that the belief of truth and the universal cult of religion had illuminated the world: for this reason, he incited Trajan to pursue the preachers of true light and root out [Christ's] worshippers. Throughout the whole Roman world many were crowned [martyrs] due to their open confession of Christ: it is pleasing to insert the memory of some of these men in this work.[65]

Frechulf's first example was Clement of Rome, whose biography was constructed through three separate sources: Jerome's *De viris illustribus*, the *Passio sancti Clementi*, and Rufinus's Latin translation of the Pseudo-Clementine *Recognitiones*. II.2.12 summarised the lives of two other holy men who were killed at this time: Simon son of Clopas (from the *Historia ecclesiastica*) and Ignatius of Antioch (from *De viris illustribus*).

Trajan's was the third of ten cardinal imperial persecutions, which Orosius had enumerated but Eusebius had not. By the time we get to the fourth, that of Marcus Aurelius, a pattern emerges. Following a description of Marcus Aurelius's virtues, Frechulf wrote:

> Nevertheless, having been deceived by error, he spoiled his many good deeds: the fourth after Nero, he moved to persecute Christians by his edict. Here it is pleasing to gather together brief notices (*sub brevitate perstringere*) of those men who flowered in our doctrine or from amongst the well-known individuals who were crowned with martyrdom.[66]

Our compiler's examples were primarily taken from Jerome's *De viris illustribus*. By framing these excerpts in direct relation to Marcus Aurelius's persecution, however,

---

[64] *Hist.*, II.2.10 [60/61], p. 516. This chapter spliced Eusebius-Rufinus with Isidore, with the latter adding the performance of miracles (for example, turning pebbles into precious stones, bringing the dead back to life) to the former's account of John's pastoral achievements.

[65] *Hist.*, II.2.11 [1/8], p. 517: 'Qua tempestate dum hostis antiquus, omnium bonorum inimicus, inuidens saluti hominum, dolens fidem ueritatis ac religionis cultum uniuersum inlustrasse orbem: qua de re Traianum iam praefatum principem ad insequendos ueri luminis praedicatores ac cultores extirpandos incitauit, sub quo per uniuersum orbem Romanum multi clara confessione Christi coronati sunt. Ex quibus aliquorum memoriam huic operi inserere libuit.'

[66] *Hist.*, II.2.16 [65/69], p. 533: 'Qui tamen errore deceptus multa suae honestatis bona foedauit, dum quartam post Neronem in Christianos persecutionem suo mouit edicto. Vnde libet sub breuitate perstringere qui eo imperante in nostro maxime floruerunt dogmate uel ex notioribus martyrio coronati sunt.'

Jerome's concise bio-bibliographies were embedded in a much clearer and simpler narrative structure. This did not generate something completely new or profound, but rather conveyed in a novel way a foundational understanding of early Christian history: in the face of the malign efforts of the Ancient Enemy, bishops and intellectuals wrote treatises to defend and advance their religion, often suffering torment and death for it. The same approach, in which a flourishing *ecclesia* was set against the efforts of its persecutors, can be observed in Frechulf's chapters on Severus and Antoninus,[67] Decius,[68] Valerian,[69] and Diocletian and his colleagues.[70]

The final chapter of Book 2 surveyed 'the illustrious men who flourished in Christian teaching and the martyrs who achieved salvation' during the persecution of Severus and Antoninus (comprising no fewer than nineteen consecutive entries of Jerome's *On Illustrious Men* (chapters 36–54)). Book 3 begins:

> And so I have taken care to note down how many and what kind of doctors of the church and robust defenders of our faith existed at this time of persecution, so that, discerning the wonderful dispensation of God, his omnipotence, and his clemency towards mankind, we may busy ourselves to praise and to thank [him] more willingly just as He himself granted, since he miraculously deigned to extend the *ecclesia* that his blood had redeemed, even while the whole world stood up against it. Grieving over human salvation, the arrogant Ancient Enemy did not cease to inflict upon us diverse schismatic doctrines, while also determining to inflict terrors and murders on the church from outside [that is, via imperial persecution]. But even though the church of Christ was pressed hard from all sides more greatly than before by perfidious and schismatic men deceived by diabolic trickery, nobly it grew in size and, by thriving in more places, was further strengthened.[71]

The conclusion to Book 2, as noted above, has been judged 'makeshift', since it sits a little uneasily in relation to the others of Part II, seeing it does not treat the

---

[67] *Hist.*, II.2.23 [1/149], pp. 545–52; introduced at II.2.22 [5/9], p. 545: 'Imperantibus Severo et filio eius Antonino, quintam post Neronem in Christianos persecutionem fieri decernentibus, quique inlustres in nostros floruerint dogmate vel martyrii palmam adsecuti quorum memoriam repperi, breviter adnotare curabo.'

[68] *Hist.*, II.3.7 [56/147], pp. 568–72, esp. [57/60], p. 568: 'Qui sub praefatis principibus floruerint doctores et scribendo agonizandoque enituerint, quamvis quorundam iam fecerimus mentionem, breviter eorum actus memoria dignos repetendo adnotare curabimus.'

[69] *Hist.*, II.3.8 [68/140], pp. 575–9.

[70] *Hist.*, II.3.14 [62/120], pp. 591–3, esp. [62/4], p. 591: 'Igitur tempore praedictorum principum memoriam replicare curabo.'

[71] *Hist.*, II.3.1, p. 558: 'Igitur hac tempestate persecutionum quanti qualesue ecclesiarum extiterint doctores ac robusti pro fide nostra propugnatores ex parte adnotare curaui, ut miram Dei dispensationem cernentes, illius omnipotentiam et circa genus humanum eiusdem clementiam propensius laudare ac gratias agere prout ipse donauerit satagamus, quoniam mirabiliter ecclesiam suo redemptam sanguine dilatare dignatus est, dum totus aduersus eam adsurgeret mundus. Ab externis terrores et mortes, a nostris diuersa scismatum dogmata superbus hostis antiquus non cessabat inferre, dolens humanam salutem seque expoliari dum cerneret. Sed ut magis undique premebatur a perfidis et ab scismaticis uiris diabolica fraude deceptis, eo amplius nobiliter propagabatur et crescendo confortabatur in plurimis Christi ecclesia.'

theme of 'temple-based worship'.[72] The proem to Book 3, however, shows that the dissolution of non-Christian cult was not Frechulf's only theme. Rather, it vividly illustrates the Orosian/Eusebian focal points of his narrative and, apart from the dedicatory prologue to Part II, it is about as close as Frechulf gets to spelling out what effect he hoped his *Histories* would have on contemporary readers: confronted with the production of Christian literature, the suffering of martyrs and the overall control of divine providence on human affairs, readers were to be brought into contact with God. History was to be read as an act of worship. This flash of exposition is all the more revealing because it was announced in relation to one of the many chapters scattered throughout Part II, which gathered together entries from Jerome's *De viris illustribus*. Although in terms of form and content this short-form source can appear prosaic and lacklustre today, especially when contrasted with a work as theologically rich and dense as Augustine's *City of God*, this view was not held by Frechulf. Jerome's catalogue of authors offered a useful digest of one of the central nubs of ecclesiastical history. Moreover, it helped define a two-fold sense of canon. It was littered with a dizzying array of early Christian writings, most of which were lost and known only through this single text (or its source, the *Ecclesiastical History*). Jerome thus set out a history of written authority, and in turn—or, rather, as a result—his own catalogue was invested with authoritative status.

In Book 3, a decisive transformation took place: Constantine became the first Christian emperor (or at least the first since Philip the Arab). From this point and until well into Book 5, Frechulf's core resources continued to shape his project and contributed to the overall narrative of ecclesiastical growth. In Constantine's reign, Christianity spread to new corners of the world where it had previously not existed, such as 'Outer India' (that is, the kingdom Aksum in modern-day Ethiopia), a region that 'was so distant that the plow of the apostolic preaching had made no furrow in it' but where soon 'many apostolic virtues were accomplished and a countless multitudes of barbarians were converted to Christianity'.[73] 'The seeds of faith sprouted in Outer India' and the gospel also reached the Georgians and the Armenians. The king of the Armenians, Tiridates, was said to have encouraged all his subjects to convert, and so 'the Christian dogma spread across the other borders [of the Roman world], and the multitude [of believers] was enlarged'.[74] Frechulf's source for this latter passage was the *Tripartite History*, from which he also knew that later, in the reign of Theodosius II, the holy man Maruthas brought Christianity

---

[72] See above, note 42. The phrase is from Allen, 'Universal History', 40.
[73] *Hist.*, II.3.18 [18/20], p. 604: '... uirtutes apostolicae patratae sunt plurimae et infinitae barbarorum multitudines ad Christianismum conuersae'; first quote from Eusebius-Rufinus, *Historia ecclesiastica*, trans. Philip R. Amidon, *The Church History of Rufinus of Aquileia, Books 10 and 11* (New York and Oxford: OUP, 1997), 19.
[74] *Hist.*, II.3.19 [15/22], p. 605.

to the Persians and roughly at this same time the Jews of Crete 'converted to the Christian faith'.[75] Alongside this was the struggle between orthodox and heterodox Christianity, another central aspect of fifth-century ecclesiastical history and a recurrent theme throughout Books 4 and 5 of the *Histories*.

All of this is worth spelling out because it encompasses the lion's share of the narrative of Frechulf's second volume. His core resources, most of which were products of fifth-century imperial Christianity, supplied material well into Book 5. The narrative of Orosius ran until II.5.7; the last excerpt from the *Tripartite History* is found at II.5.11, roughly a third of the way through the book. As a Carolingian compiler, however, Frechulf also had at his disposal numerous other texts that post-dated his main late antique narratives, which allowed him both to augment and, moreover, continue, the story he had already been unfolding across some two hundred manuscript pages. These included Jordanes' *Getica* and *Romana* (sixth-century productions), the *Chronicle of Fredegar* (first created in the seventh century), and Bede's *Greater Chronicle* (finished c. 725).[76] While the succession of (eastern Roman) emperors still supplied the chronological spine until the reign of Phocas (ruled 602–10), attention was increasingly paid to the *partes Hesperiarum*, and especially their post-imperial transformations.

Partes Hesperiarum: Post-imperial Transformations

I: End of the Western Empire

Orosius concluded his *Histories against the Pagans* on an optimistic note, something which modern critics once held against him since they knew that events would soon begin to subvert his rosy hopes for the empire. Throughout the second half of Book 5, Frechulf traced these events. Attila the Hun and his allies attacked the empire (II.5.15); they were repelled partly by the patrician Aetius, 'the great salvation of the western empire'; however, 'returning from Italy after having liberated Gaul … [he] was killed, and with him the western realm (*Hesperiarum regnum*) also died'.[77] Two chapters later, this point was restated but in a different context. II.5.17 dealt with 'the frequent changes of rulers' between the death of Majorian and the last western emperor, Romulus Augustulus, and its disastrous consequences. (The chapter heading is: *De crebris mutationibus principum, et sic perdiderunt Occidentis imperium Romani* (Concerning the frequent changes of rulers, and [how] thus they ruined the western Roman Empire). With Romulus Augustulus's death, 'the

---

[75] *Hist.*, II.5.10, pp. 691–2.

[76] Of these, Jordanes was the only authority mentioned by name: *Iordanis historicus* (*Hist.*, II.5.18 [70/1], p. 710).

[77] *Hist.*, II.5.15 [1/4], pp. 700–1: 'Aetius autem patricius, magna Occidentalis rei publicae salus, ab hostibus liberata Gallia reuertitur Italiam. Denique factione Eraclii spadonis a Valentiniano principe occiditur, cum quo Hesperiarum cecidit regnum.' Trans. Wallis, 222.

res publica of the Romans, which hitherto had held sway over the *gentes*, now, with a groan, lay under the rule of their kings'.[78] The phrasing here was distinctive to the bishop of Lisieux, but the basic perception was well established: the fall of the western empire, dated to the death of Romulus Augustulus, was manufactured by Latinate historians active in sixth-century Constantinople. This sixth-century view was transmitted to Frechulf directly through Jordanes's writings, and indirectly by Bede, whose source was Marcellinus Comes.[79]

Most of the remaining 'political/secular' chapters followed the rise and fall of Ostrogothic power in Italy (II.5.18, 21, 23). This was finally accomplished by Justinian's general Narses, who 'liberated Italy from the yoke [of the Goths]' and 'restored [it] to the body of the republic'.[80] Yet, having done so, Narses also sent word to Alboin, king of the Lombards, who (two chapters later) invaded Italy.[81] Frechulf's treatment of the Franks is even less detailed, and arguably more idiosyncratic. Readers looking for accounts of Clovis's baptism, or really any of the exciting stories found within Gregory of Tours or Fredegar will be disappointed, as only the barest outlines of post-imperial Gaul are traced. Clothar I (died 561), for example, suppressed a rebellion by his son Chram and subjected the Bretons and Saxons to Frankish rule.[82] Clovis appears only fleetingly, and there is no mention of his Christian identity: firstly, Theoderic the Great wanted to make an alliance with the *gens Francorum*, and so arranged to marry Clovis's sister, Audofleda; a little later, Clovis's army lined up against that of Alaric II's Goths and defeated them at the battle of Vouillé (in 507), which resulted in the destruction of the Gothic kingdom of Narbonne.[83] The stress on this event, nevertheless, makes it clear that political change was not the focus per se; rather, Frechulf discovered in the record of Frankish history (here Fredegar's *Chronicle*) further evidence of God's ordering of the past. Earlier in Book 5, Frechulf had incorporated Orosius's account of Alaric I's sack of Rome in 410. In his own words, he added: 'Alaric, by the wonderful

---

[78] *Hist.*, II.5.17, p. 707: 'Hinc iam res publica Romanorum partibus Hesperiarum quae actenus gentibus imperaverat, regibus gentium gemens subcubuit.' See further Fritz Lošek, '*Non ignota canens*? Bemerkungen zur Chronik (*Historia*) des Frechulf von Lisieux', in *Ethnogenese und Überlieferung: angewandte Methoden der Fruhmittelalterforschung*, eds Karl Brunner and Brigetta Merta, Veröffentlichungen des Instituts für Österreichische Geschichtsforschung 31 (Vienna: Oldenbourg, 1994), 223–31.

[79] See Brian Croke, 'A.D. 476: The Manufacture of a Turning Point', *Chiron*, 13 (1983): 81–119.

[80] *Hist.*, II.5.23, pp. 719–20.

[81] *Hist.*, II.5.23 [25/6], p. 720: 'Scripsit genti Langobardorum ut venirent et possiderent Italiam'; II.5.25 [1/4], p. 722: 'Qua tempestate Albuinus rex Langobardorum, a Narsite ut praemisimus inuitatus, relinquens atque incendens Pannoniam in qua habitabat, cum omni populo suo ueniens comitante fame et mortalitate inuadit Italiam.'

[82] *Hist.*, II.5.22 [27/37], p. 718. Compare II.5.20 [17/21], p. 713 (King Sigismund, having been captured by the Franks, was dressed up as a monk and thrown in a well; then the Merovingian king Chlodomer died (c. 524) fighting against the Burgundians). See also *Hist.*, I.4.5 [7/12], p. 622.

[83] *Hist.*, II.5.18 [68/75], p. 710; II.5.22 [1/19], pp. 717–18. In the first case, Frechulf called Clovis *Ludouuic* and in the second, *Chlodoues*—it is not clear whether he thought these were the same person.

dispensation of God, stormed and ransacked the City [of Rome], and rebuked the Roman people, more through terror than slaughter, since in many ways they had offended God.'[84] The defeat of Alaric II was viewed through the same providential lens, which also took into account the fall of the western empire:

> It was determined by the wonderful dispensation of God that Alaric I—whom the Goths made king when military service was taken away from them as a result of the greed of the Roman consuls, and who plotted to take up arms against the Romans due to hunger and need, ravaging Illyricum, invading Italy and plundering Rome, the mistress of the *gentes*—rejoiced in his various prosperous successes and raised up his people and his kingdom; [divine providence also determined that] in Alaric II's reign, the people and kingdom of the Goths ultimately came to an end. This was just like how, in the west under Octavian Augustus, the Roman Empire became mistress of other nations, and then in the end, perishing under Augustulus, the empire became subjected to the rule of those other nations.[85]

Orosius had ended his work with the peace established between the Gothic ruler Vallia, one of Alaric's successors, and Honorius; using the same providential logic that undergirded the *Historiae*, Frechulf took this story forward to the point at which the Gothic kingdom, established under Alaric, was no more, and the western empire over which Honorius had ruled, was now in the hands of the Franks (and the Lombards). The reshaping of western rulership and the beginnings of the Frankish (and, by implication, Carolingian) realm was integrated into the same divinely guided story that gave shape and meaning to Alaric's sack of Rome as well as to the foundations of Augustus's empire.

II: Ecclesia: *Authors and Orthodoxy*

As Michael Allen has observed, 'the topos of the Temple punctuates [Frechulf's] books'.[86] Within these books, further aspects of the *ecclesia*'s history were

---

[84] *Hist.*, II.5.5 [82/4], p. 685: 'Alaricus autem mira Dei dispensatione, Vrbem inrupit atque vastavit, populumque qui in multis Deum offenderat Romanum magis terrore quam caede corripuit; post triduum ab Urbe discessit.'

[85] *Hist.*, II.5.22, pp. 717–18: 'Mira Dei dispensatione actum est: ut Alaricus—quem Gothi regem creauerant quando auaritia consulum Romanorum stipendiae sunt subtractae ab eis, qui fame et penuria coacti conspirauerunt contra Romanos in arma, Illyricum depopulantes, Italiam inuadentes, Romam gentium dominam depraedantes—Alaricus ouans diuersis successibus prosperitatum sublimauit gentem suam et regnum, demum in Alarico gens et regnum Gothorum defecit, sicuti et Romanorum in Hesperia sub Octouiano Augusto aliarum gentium domina, et nouissime in Augustulo deficiens, ut supra retulimus, gentibus est aliis subiecta.' See also Staubach, '*Christiana tempora*', 188–9. This is considerably more elaborate than Jordanes, *De origine actibusque Getarum* [=*Getica*], 245, ed. Theodor Mommsen, MGH *Auct. Ant.* 5,1 (Berlin: Weidmann, 1882), 53–138, at 21: 'Nam pari tenore ut de Augustis superius diximus, et in Alaricis evenisse cognoscitur: et in eis saepe regna deficiunt, a quorum nominibus incoharunt.' Trans. Peter Van Nuffelen and Lieve Van Hoof, *Jordanes: Romana and Getica* (Liverpool: LUP, 2020), 334: 'For in the same way as we have said above for the Augusti, it is known to have happened with the Alarici: a kingdom often ends under one who bears the name of the one with whom it started.'

[86] Allen, 'Universal History', 40.

developed. God's providence had allowed the *ecclesia* to grow, in times of both imperial persecution and support. Frechulf's post-imperial sources allowed him to extend this line of thought in directions that were alien to his core fifth-century sources. Using Bede, it was possible to show how Christianity, soon after having reached Persia, was transmitted to early medieval Britain.[87] The struggles between 'Arian' and 'catholic' Christianity, which had begun in the reign of Constantine, found partial resolution in Book 4: Hilary of Poitiers and Ambrose of Milan were said to have freed Gaul and then Italy 'from the Arian plague'.[88] In Book 5, Frechulf could introduce a further front in this conflict, which although it fell outside the scope of the traditional ecclesiastical histories nevertheless appears in the *Histories* in direct continuation of them: Vandal North Africa.[89] Bede again was Frechulf's chief source. The Vandals crossed over to Africa under the leadership of Geiseric and defiled 'everything with sword, rapine and the Arian heresy'.[90] (Gaiseric later sacked Rome, but without human costs thanks to the divine supplications of Pope Leo I.[91]) Five chapters later, Huneric followed in the footsteps of previous Arian rulers such as Valens who had persecuted their 'catholic' subjects; despite his best efforts he was unable to 'eliminate the expression of the catholic confession'.[92] But then under Hilderic, the persecutions of his Vandal predecessors were reversed and 'heretical profanations' were expelled from North Africa.[93] The final act in this long-running drama occurred in Visigothic Spain, where King Reccared (586–601), at Bishop Leander of Seville's insistence, 'converted to the catholic faith the whole Gothic people over whom he ruled'.[94]

The history of orthodox Christianity here conveyed was deliberately simple. It was told in largely symbolic terms, leaving aside all the complexities and nuances of Christological doctrine. Arianism regularly appears but was never defined: alongside Simon Magus, 'the head of all depravity and the beginning of all heresy', Arius/Arianism stands as a totem for all beliefs that self-professed orthodox authorities condemned as heterodox.[95] This comes into focus in Frechulf's very last chapter, which listed in order (again via direct quotation from Bede) the

---

[87] *Hist.*, II.5.13, pp. 696–7; II.5.16, p. 703; II.5.24, p. 721.

[88] *Hist.*, II.4.14 [40/42], p. 641: 'Qui [Hilary] ab exilio reversus velut splendidum lumen Gallias inradiavit ceterasque provincias suo sacro dogmate a peste Arriana liberavit'; II.4.26 [13/16], pp. 658–9: 'Quorum uirtutibus uenerabilis antistes suffultus, sapientia ac uitae honestate insignibus que exemplis ornatus, Mediolanensium ecclesiam muniuit et a peste Arriana Italiam liberauit.'

[89] Robin Whelan, *Being Christian in Vandal Africa: The Politics of Orthodoxy in the Post-imperial West* (Oakland, CA: University of California Press, 2018).

[90] *Hist.*, II.5.13 [1/9], p. 605. Frechulf spliced together passages from Jordanes, Fredegar and Bede, from whom the quotation derives (trans. Wallis, 220).

[91] *Hist.*, II.5.15 [6/23], p. 701. Frechulf's source was Prosper of Aquitaine.

[92] *Hist.*, II.5.20 [1/4], p. 712; trans. Wallis, 223.

[93] *Hist.*, II.5.20, p. 712; trans. Wallis, 224.

[94] *Hist.*, II.5.25, p. 722 [10/11]: 'omnem Gothorum cui praeerat gentem, insistente Leandro Hispalitano episcopo [...] catholicam convertit ad fidem'; trans. adapted from Wallis, 226.

[95] Simon Magus: see *Hist.*, II.1.20, pp. 475–9.

six ecumenical councils, which cumulatively created and defined mainstream understandings of correct Christianity. Chronologically, it took Frechulf back in time to the Council of Nicaea (325), 'convened … against Arius, with three hundred and eighteen bishops, in the time of Pope Julius and under the Emperor Constantine', and stretched forward to III Constantinople (680-1), 'written up in Greek in the time of Pope Agatho, enforced and presided over by the most pious Prince Constantine [IV] in his palace, together with the legates of the Apostolic See and with one hundred and fifty bishops taking part'.[96] Frechulf recognised that this chapter broke the flow of his narrative when he wrote: 'So as briefly to go over what was omitted above, let us set out those six universal synods, which the whole east—or rather, those there who soundly uphold the catholic faith— receives and celebrates in common'.[97] Of all the Christological disputes contained within this list, only Nicaea was mentioned in the context of doctrine, and even then no details were actually given as to what beliefs Arius was alleged to have held.[98] This is yet another example of what the process of abridging the corpus of Christian historiographical writing entailed: streamlining and simplifying a larger, more complex body of texts. There is also a bigger point. By providing a concise overview of the recognised and accepted definitions of orthodoxy, Frechulf ended on a clear high note. The councils fittingly capped off his intertwined story of ecclesiastical acts and imperial deeds: even if they were never highlighted by him when delineating the overall scope of his work, they offered a logical end point for a narrative which traced the triumphal growth of the *ecclesia*, often in the face of heretical schism and persecuting emperors.

The universal councils were potent symbols of Christian orthodoxy. Other Carolingian authors drew attention not to all six, but only to the first four: Nicaea, I Constantinople, I Ephesus and Chalcedon.[99] One source that did stress all six was the *Opus Caroli*, attributed to Theodulf of Orléans and written primarily to refute the eastern empire's claims that the Second Council of Nicaea, convoked in 787, was the seventh ecumenical council. Remarkably, there is a direct connection to Frechulf here, since the main issue of contention—the worship of images—was debated again at the 825 Council of Paris, where he gave evidence following a

---

[96] *Hist.*, II.5.27 [3/17], p. 723; trans. Wallis, 231–2.

[97] *Hist.*, II.5.27, p. 23 [1/3]: 'Ut omissa superius paulisper repetamus, quae sunt uniuersales sex sinodi quas totus Oriens recipit et concelebrat, qui catholicam fidem sana mente retinent, ostendamus.'

[98] *Hist.*, II.3.16 [48/52], p. 509: 'Igitur uenerabili huic concilio ex paucorum memoria conici potest quam magni interfuerunt Deo amabiles uiri, qui leges ecclesiasticas, quos canones uocamus, sanxerunt, et peruersum dogma Arii cum ipso auctore anathematizantes dampnauerunt.'

[99] Following Isidore's *Etymologiae*, VI.16.1–10, see Hrabanus Maurus, *De rerum naturis*, V.7, cols 124C–125D; *Capitula Parisiensia*, c. 1, ed. Rudolf Pokorny, MGH *Capit. Episc.* III (Hanover: Hahn, 1995), pp. 25–35, at p. 26; Odilbert of Milan's treatise on baptism, quoted in Owen M. Phelan, *The Formation of Christian Europe: The Carolingians, Baptism, and the Imperium Christianum* (Oxford: OUP, 2014), 174. Bede's Carolingian continuators cited the six councils. See also Hincmar, *Opusculum LV capitulorum*, c. 20, ed. Rudolf Schieffer, MGH *Conc.* 4, Suppl. 2 (Hanover: Hahn, 2003), p. 219.

diplomatic mission to Rome. In the letter sent by the eastern emperors, Michael II and his son and co-ruler, Theophilos, which kickstarted the second round of debate on image worship in the west, they appealed to Louis the Pious for help in dealing with iconodule opponents who had fled to Rome.[100] To demonstrate their religious affinity with Louis, they stressed that they 'proclaim ... the creed/symbol of the six holy and universal synods, which is held by all orthodox Christians' and that they accepted 'whatever was passed on from the blessed apostles and established in these same councils by the most holy fathers'.[101] Frechulf's formulation at the end of the *Histories*—that all those in the east who—in the present tense— 'soundly uphold the catholic faith'—may very well be an allusion to contemporary discussions about image worship and the disputed canonicity of II Nicaea.[102]

There is also, however, an indirect connection that I want to tease out. Like the eastern emperors cosying up to Louis the Pious in 825, Theodoulf defined in the *Opus Caroli* the tenets of Frankish orthodoxy in similar terms: 'accepting the six holy and universal synods, which were guided by the holy and venerable fathers in order to deal with the various assaults of heretical belief, we [that is, western Christians] [are] sustained by the writings of the prophets, evangelists and apostles, instructed by the commands of the holy, orthodox fathers, who in no way in their teachings deviate from [Christ], who is the way, the truth and the life (John 14:6) ...'.[103] This tripartite division of scriptural, patristic and canonical authority is ubiquitous within medieval Christianity. Collectively, this is what is often referred to as 'tradition'.[104] We have now seen that Frechulf capped off his narrative of imperial and ecclesiastical history with the six ecumenical councils. A second core aspect of tradition—'the instructions of the holy and orthodox fathers'—also formed a thread running throughout Part II. Frechulf's ending ought to be seen in this light too.

---

[100] Council of Paris (825), *Epistola*, pp. 475–80.

[101] Council of Paris (825), *Epistola*, p. 479. For context, Noble, *Images*, 260-6; see further Claudia Sode, 'Der Briefe der Kaiser Michael II. und Theophilos an Kaiser Ludwig den Frommen', in *Zwischen Polis, Provinz und Peripherie: Beiträge zur byzantinischen Geschichte und Kultur*, eds Anuscha Monchizadeh and Lars Martin Hoffmann (Wiesbaden: Harrassowitz, 2005), 141–58.

[102] Savigni, 'Storia universale', 160, 190–1; Allen, 'Fréculf', 70 and 76.

[103] Theodulf of Orléans, *Opus Caroli regis contra synodum*, Pref., ed. Ann Freeman, MGH *Conc.* 2, Suppl. 1 (Hanover: Hahn, 1998), p. 101: 'Nos denique propheticis, evangelicis et apostolicis scripturis contenti et sanctorum orthodoxorum patrum, qui nullatenus in suis dogmatibus ab eo, qui est via, veritas et vita, deviarunt, institutis inbuti et sanctas et universales sex synodos, quae pro variis hereseorum infestationibus a sanctis et venerabilibus patribus gestae sunt, suscipientes, omnes novitates vocum et stultiloquas adinventiones abicimus et non solum non suscipimus, verum etiam tamquam purgamenta dispicimus, sicut et eam, quae propter adorandarum imaginum inprudentissimam traditionem in Bithiniae partibus gesta est, synodum.'

[104] Karl F. Morrison, *Tradition and Authority in the Western Church, 300-1140* (Princeton, NJ: Princeton University Press, 1969); David M. Gwynn, 'The Council of Chalcedon and the Definition of Christian Tradition', in *Chalcedon in Context: Church Councils 400-700*, eds Richard Price and Mary Whitby (Liverpool: LUP, 2009), 7–26.

Running through Part II are regular summaries of Christian literature, from the texts of the New Testament onwards. A crucial source of this was Jerome's *De viris illustribus*, excerpts from which were scattered throughout all five books of Part II, often in coherent groupings. The last dump of bio-bibliographies is to be found at II.5.3, which surveyed 'the illustrious men who shone like twinkling stars during the reigns of Arcadius and his brother Honorius'.[105] Already in this chapter, Frechulf's Carolingian retrospect is detectable. Jerome's somewhat ambiguous entry on Ambrose ('Ambrose, bishop of Milan, continues writing down to the present day. Concerning him I postpone judgment in that he is still alive lest I get blamed for flattery, on the one hand, or, on the other, for telling the truth.') was recast in a considerably more positive light: 'Ambrose, bishop of the church of Milan ... died at this time. Marvellously, he published many little works: I believe it is unnecessary to summarise them, since they are known through constant reading'.[106] One of the striking features of *De viris illustribus* was that Jerome included himself amongst the great ecclesiastical writers: in his work's final chapter, he 'raised his own monument long before he was ready to be inhumed'.[107] His own bibliography was completed in 392/3, but was presented as a work in progress: 'many other [commentaries] on the work of the Prophets which I have on hand, and are not yet finished'.[108] Frechulf, writing well over four hundred years later, supplied a more rounded entry by including the names of some of the works completed in the three decades between the *De viris illustribus* and its author's death: 'usefully [Jerome] published an explanation of Isaiah in [several] large volumes, and he also explained [the book of] Jeremiah as well as Daniel. Furthermore, he produced a commentary on Matthew along with many more little works'.[109]

Frechulf embedded into his overview of history a number of authors who were regarded as authoritative but were not part of Jerome's canon.[110] The last, and arguably most significant added author was Pope Gregory I, who was the subject of an entire chapter, titled 'De beato Gregorio et eius gestis'. It amounts

[105] *Hist.*, II.5.3 [3/6], p. 676.
[106] *Hist.*, II.5.3 [37/40], p. 678: 'Ambrosius Mediolanensis ecclesiae episcopus, de quo supra mentionem fecimus, qui multa nobiliter edidit opuscula quae quidem propter notitiam assidue legentium reor non esse recapitulare necessarium, eo tempore defunctus est.' Jerome, *DVI*, ed. Richardson, 124, p. 53; trans. Halton, p. 158. On the Carolingian cult of Ambrose, see Giorgia Vocino, 'Framing Ambrose in the Resources of the Past: The late Antique and Early Medieval Sources for a Carolingian Portrait of Ambrose', in *The Resources of the Past in Early Medieval Europe*, eds Clemens Gantner, Rosamond McKitterick and Sven Meeder (Cambridge: CUP, 2015), 133–54.
[107] Vessey, 'Reinventing History', 279.
[108] Jerome, *DVI*, 135, p. 56: 'multaque alia de opere prophetali, quae nunc habeo in manibus, et necdum expleta sunt.' Trans. Halton, 168.
[109] *Hist.*, II.5.4, pp.679–80: 'Esaiam utiliter explanando grandia volumina edidit, Hieremiam etiam exposuit, Danielem quoque explanavit; commentarium etiam In Matheum et alia quam plura opuscula fecit.' See also *Prolegomena*, 67*.
[110] *Hist.* II.5.20 [22/6], p. 713 (Boethius); cf. II.5.3 [71/8], p. 680 is ostensibly about Martin of Tours, but with the note that 'Sulpicius Severus made Martin's life and his miraculous acts famous.'

to an extended bio-bibliography, consisting of some renowned episodes from Gregory's life alongside a catalogue of his writings. As such, it appears as the last in a long line of chapters centred on the *acta ecclesiasticorum*, principally drawn from Jerome's *De viris illustribus*, but also from other ecclesiastical histories and hagiographies. Frechulf, however, had no obvious model for constructing this chapter. By the early ninth century, several biographies of Gregory the Great— both long and short—had been composed, most of which included references to his writings.[111] (One of the consequences of Jerome's catalogue, and its Eusebian origins, was that patristic biography increasingly became incomplete without an accompanying bibliography.) Seemingly he did not know of any of them: if he had to hand Isidore's entry on Gregory from his contribution to the *De viris illustribus* tradition, he presumably would have quoted from it. Instead, Frechulf gathered together some unconnected snippets from Bede's *Greater Chronicle* to provide an account of Gregory's memorable deeds, to which he added his own résumé of Gregory's transmitted texts:

> Guided by divine inspiration, [Gregory] wrote his *Moralia in Job*, and set out most clearly his *Pastoral Rule*; moreover, he transmitted to future readers his *Dialogues*, which were addressed to the venerable men of his own time for them to imitate. He created the very splendid work on Ezekiel, and his *Homilies* offer up for [our] enjoyment the healthiest of spiritual foods. His many extant letters are useful to readers, on account of the tasks for which they were written.[112]

Frechulf's descriptive language suggests direct knowledge of the Gregorian sources, something which, considering Gregory's illustrious patristic status, may come as no great surprise. The fact that he included them is nevertheless significant, not only because it was in the Carolingian period that Gregory's status was firmly established but also because it takes us back to the ending: the 'obitus

---

[111] Isidore, *De viris illustribus*, 27, ed. Carmen Codoñer Merino, *El 'De viris illustribus' de Isidoro de Sevilla* (Salamanca, 1964), pp. 148–9; *Liber pontificalis*, c. 66, ed. Louis Duchesne, *Le Liber pontificalis: texte, introduction et commentaire*, 2 vols (Paris: E. Thorin, 1886–92, repr. 1955), vol. 1, p. 312; Bede, *Ecclesiastical History*, II.1, pp. 122–35 (esp. pp. 126–9); *Vita Gregorii*, ed. and trans. Bertram Colgrave, *The Earliest Life of Gregory the Great, by an Anonymous Monk of Whitby* (Cambridge: CUP, 1985), cc. 24–7, 31, pp. 116–25, 135–7; Paul the Deacon, *Vita Gregorii*, ed. Sabine Tuzzo, *Vita Sancti Gregorii Magni* (Pisa: Scuola normale superior, 2002), cc. 8 and 12, pp. 11–12 and 21–2; *De Convivio Monachorum (Ordo Romanus XIX)*, ed. Josef Semmler, CCM 1 (Siegburg: F. Schmitt, 1963) pp. 53–63, at 59–60. In general, see Conrad Leyser, 'The Memory of Gregory the Great and the Making of Latin Europe, 600–1000', in *Making Early Medieval Societies: Conflict and Belonging in the Latin West, 300–1200*, eds Kate Copper and Conrad Leyser (Cambridge: CUP, 2016), 181–201 and, more specifically, Conrad Leyser, 'The Memory of Pope Gregory the Great in the Ninth Century: A Redating of the Interpolator's Vita Gregorii (BHL 3640)', in *Gregorio Magno e le origini dell'Europa: atti del Convegno internazionale, Firenze, 13–17 maggio 2006*, ed. Claudio Leonardi (Florence: Sismel, 2014), 449–62.

[112] *Hist.*, II.5.24, p. 721: 'Qui Moralia in Iob gratia diuina inspirante conscripsit, librum etiam Pastoralem luculentissime edidit, Dialogorum uero ad imitandos uenerabiles uiros qui per haec tempora claruerunt libros dictans ad nostram porrexit legendos posteritatem. In Ezechihel opus praeclarum condidit, Omeliarum eius liber saluberrimas et spiritales gustantibus ministrat dapes, epistolae uero exstant eius plures pro negotiis quibus sunt conpositae legentibus utiles.'

Gregorii eximii doctoris', along with the deeds of Boniface and the ascendancy of the Franks and Lombards, was one of the stated moments that marked the *Histories*' terminus.

The Age of the Fathers?

The closure of non-Christian sites of worship, the victory over heresy and the definition of orthodoxy, and the enumeration of a patristic canon, running from the early church to Gregory the Great: these various strands coalesce at Frechulf's conclusion. Although the ending was marked by the displacement of Roman rulership in the West, what the overall narrative points towards is the end of the patristic era, that is, of the golden age of Christianity during which divine providence was readily discernible in human affairs, the *ecclesia* spread throughout the world, orthodox doctrine was gradually shaped and defined, and a canon of texts came into being that taught correct Christian belief and practice. With the death of the Roman emperor Trajan, Frechulf added that, according to the second-century author Hegesippus, the apostolic age of the church came to a close.[113] The *Histories* intimated a comparable sense of closure, but of the age of the church fathers, located, roughly speaking, around the death of Gregory the Great.

Over sixty years ago, Von den Brincken thought that c. 600 signified for Frechulf 'the break, which today *we* [my italics] label the transition from Antiquity to the Middle Ages'.[114] If nothing else, reframing this observation in terms of a boundary between patristic and later Christianity has the clear advantage of working with categories of periodisation that would have been more recognisable to Carolingian readers. The study of authoritative, patristic, knowledge is inscribed throughout all sorts of Carolingian sources. Carolingian intellectual culture was predicated upon the writings of the *sancti patres*, and it fed directly into practice: at church councils, the patristic heritage was mined for authoritative and applicable insights that shaped the norms and organisation of the contemporary church. The religious and intellectual cultures of the eighth and ninth centuries were fundamentally oriented on the Latin fathers and the ecumenical councils, along with the wider tradition of ecclesiastical law associated with them. The Big Four of the patristic canon were Ambrose, Jerome, Augustine and Gregory, though for the Carolingians many other names existed between them and some even post-dated them, such as Isidore of Seville, Bede, and occasionally also Alcuin.[115] Extant library catalogues are one of the clearest representations of the patristic orientation of Carolingian Christianity, since the major institutions

---

[113] *Hist.*, II.2.12 [43/53], p. 524. Source: Eusebius-Rufinus, *Historia ecclesiastica*, III.32.7–33.1, pp. 271–2.
[114] Von den Brincken, *Studien*, 125.
[115] Kaczynski, 'Authority of the Fathers'.

whose inventories have survived classified their collections by authorities. The Reichenau list of 822, for example, began with the books of the Bible, followed by the books of Augustine, Jerome, Gregory the Great and so forth; at nearby St Gall in the later ninth century, the abbey's book list (*breviarium librorum*) began with scripture, then the first handful of subsections were devoted to Gregory the Great, Jerome, Augustine and Ambrose, respectively; at Lorsch (c. 860), the most extensive survey of its holdings began with liturgical books followed by scripture, then history, then the assembled works of Augustine, Jerome, Gregory, Bede and Ambrose; at St Riquier, where Helisachar, the dedicatee of Part I was abbot, the books of monastery, the organisation of scripture, then Jerome, Augustine, Gregory and Isidore.[116] What I want to suggest is that Frechulf's *Histories* emerged out of the same overall concern for authoritative, patristic knowledge, but here it found expression as a historical narrative.

Frechulf's *Histories* worked to produce a patristic history at two different levels. On the one hand, Frechulf's was an account of Christianity stitched together from texts whose authors were themselves regarded as authoritative. Most of Frechulf's texts are also found enumerated amongst monastic library holdings. This holds true for his core resources, those which he excerpted most frequently and often namechecked, as well as those he drew on silently: examples of the latter group include two authors/texts encountered above, Isidore's *De obitu et ortu patrum* and Bede's *Greater Chronicle*, both of which certainly were counted amongst the Carolingian patristic canon.[117] On the other hand, he tracked the development of Christian writing across time, from the apostle Peter, the first of Jerome's illustrious men, through to Gregory the Great, who wrote over a century and half after Jerome had died. As a result of integrating Jerome's catalogue (almost in its entirety) amongst excerpts from narrative histories, and moreover by extending it to reflect ninth-century perspectives, Frechulf generated a synopsis of Christian history that did not previously exist. Jerome's catalogue itself lacked a defined narrative; by contrast, early medieval chroniclers, many of whom followed Jerome (as translator and continuator of Eusebius's *Chronicle*) in commemorating Christian writers, tended not to list what these writers had written.[118] Rosamond McKitterick previously highlighted that 'one of the most crucial aspects of the reception and dissemination of Christian writings in the Carolingian world was

---

[116] Reichenau: Lehmann, *Mittelalterliche Bibliothekskataloge*, pp. 240–252; St Gall: Lehmann, *Mittelalterliche Bibliothekskataloge*, pp. 71-82; Lorsch: Häse, *Mittelalterliche Bücherverzeichnisse*, pp. 136–67 and Reimitz, *Frankish History*, 363-68; St Riquier: Hariulf, *Chronicon Centulense*, 3, 3, pp. 86–94.
[117] Melissa Markauskas, 'Rylands MS Latin 12: A Carolingian Example of Isidore's Reception into the Patristic Canon', in *Isidore of Seville and his Reception in the Early Middle Ages: Transmitting and Transforming Knowledge*, eds Andrew T. Fear and Jamie Wood (Amsterdam: Amsterdam University Press, 2016), 177–208; on Bede see Hill, 'Carolingian Perceptions' and Westgard, 'Bede and the Continent'.
[118] On Jerome, see Vessey, 'Reinventing History'.

the perception of their original contexts'.[119] No other single source reflects this general perspective quite so vividly as Frechulf.

In Part I, for example, there are sporadic recommendations for further reading, which I briefly discussed in Chapter 1. Readers who wanted to know more about certain episodes from Jewish history were pointed in the direction of the relevant book of Josephus's *Antiquities*; a reader keen to learn more about the tree of life and the tree of good and bad knowledge was advised to consult 'the books of Augustine *On the City of God*'; on four occasions the diligent student was directed to Orosius's *Historiae*. Cross-referencing the core resources from which the compilation was made was one way by which a notion of canon was reified, yet the full effect of this only comes to light in Part II, since the lives and writings of these previously referenced authorities appear themselves as historical actors. In some cases, Frechulf was able to insert relevant bio-bibliographies directly from Jerome's *On Illustrious Men* or the *Ecclesiastical History*. Thus, after the chapter on the doctors, apostles and martyrs who spread out over the world after the destruction of the Temple in AD 70, a separate chapter was added on Josephus the *historiographus*, who was taken from Judaea to Rome as a prisoner by Vespasian. Remaining at Rome once he was released from captivity, he wrote 'his seven books about the *Jewish War*' as well as 'twenty books of *Antiquities*, from the beginning of the world up until the fourteenth year of Domitian (that is, AD 93/4).[120] Jerome's biography of Josephus served as the basic introduction to his life throughout the Middle Ages.

More revealing are the cases in which Frechulf added or emended existing bio-bibliographies, using what was known about a given author, as extracted from the sources they had written. We encountered one of these examples at the end of Chapter 4. The main subject of II.5.12 was Orosius, who, during the reign of Honorius, had transported the relics of St Stephen from Jerusalem to North Africa. This topic also offered an opportunity to provide brief portraits of two of the main actors involved: Orosius, who carried the relics back from the Holy Land, but also Augustine, who in the first place had sent him there to study with Jerome. This much was already known, since Frechulf lifted it verbatim from Bede's *Greater Chronicle*, and Bede had previously taken it from Gennadius's bio-bibliography of Orosius. The bishop of Lisieux then improvised: once the relics reached North Africa, they set off a wave of miracles, and after Augustine had learned of them, he made a record them in the *City of God*: this was likely known through direct knowledge of Book 22 of Augustine's magnum opus. Augustine, moreover, was known to have written much more besides his famed tome. Indeed, he wrote 'so many lofty volumes' that, according to a certain teacher (*quidam doctorum*, that is, Isidore), anyone who claimed to have read the lot of them was surely lying. Lastly,

---

[119] McKitterick, *History and Memory*, 245. See also, McKitterick, *Perceptions*, 61.
[120] *Hist.*, II.2.5, pp. 506–7; trans adapted from Halton, 28.

to round off this series of connections, Frechulf returned to Orosius: it was at Augustine's insistence that Orosius, his *discipulus*, 'nobly and usefully composed seven books *Adverus gentes*'.[121] The connection between Orosius and Augustine was clearly broadcast in the preface to the *Historiae*, yet prior to Frechulf no indirect source had stressed it. Readers, therefore, were not only presented with masses of excerpts taken from all seven books of the *Historiae*, but were also provided with a useful sketch of the context on its creation.

Eusebius of Caesarea provides a second example. Frechulf inserted Jerome's bio-bibliography of Eusebius at the end of the Book 3, in amongst the 'diverse doctors who flourished under Constantine'. Included there were Eusebius's 'ten books of *Ecclesiastical History*'. In the early medieval west, however, no such ten-book version was known; instead, readers had at their disposal only the translation of Rufinus, in which Eusebius's tenth book was done away with and two new books were added, which covered church history from the sitting of Nicaea through to the death of Theodosius I. Frechulf clearly differentiated between Eusebius and Rufinus.[122] Interested readers wanting to know more about Nicaea were encouraged to consult 'the *Ecclesiastical History* of Eusebius of Caesarea, which was translated into the Latin tongue (*in nostrum eloquium*) by Rufinus'; on the difficulties that Athanasius faced in the reign of Constantius II, detailed accounts were to be found in the *Tripartite History*, Athanasius's own writings, and 'Rufinus, the author of the history of the church during this time'.[123]

Significantly, Eusebius also appeared as a historical actor. Firstly, Frechulf augmented a note (from Book 10 of Rufinus) that many big names were at Nicaea: Rufinus had named only a young Athanasius, but alongside him were added 'the great Eustathius of Antioch' as well as 'Eusebius Pamphilius, *pontifex* of the church of Caesarea, who nobly endured in faith in the time of persecution and who was a most sage writer of many illustrious works'.[124] Jumping back two chapters, this was spelled out even more clearly: Eusebius was referenced as the key source for the imperial persecution begun under Diocletian, which 'as if from a small spark set aflame almost the whole of the Roman world'.[125] Two choice examples of this persecution were selected, before Frechulf added that:

> It is not possible to set out how many torments were devised at that time for the holy martyrs of God, or how many thousands of saints were killed by new and unusual instruments of torture. Bishop Eusebius of Caesarea, the author of the *Ecclesiastical History*, strove in part to reveal these things in the eighth and ninth

---

[121] *Hist.*, II.5.12, pp. 694–5.
[122] *Prolegomena*, 218*.
[123] *Hist.*, II.3.16 [99/101], p. 601; II.4.2 [49/52], p. 619.
[124] *Hist.*, II.3.16 [87/94], pp. 600–1.
[125] *Hist.*, II.3.14 [91/5], p. 593: 'Igitur Eusebio referente haec persecutio sub Diocletiano … exordium cepti, et velut ex parva scintilla paene totum Romanum inflammavit orbem …'

books of his histories, which, since he was present, he discovered in truth and observed first-hand.[126]

A careful reading of Books 8 and 9 of the *Ecclesiastical History* would have revealed that they reflected Eusebius's experiences of the so-called Great Persecution, which began c. 303 and ceased c. 313.[127] Yet by highlighting this, and in the context of an excerpt from the work in question, the bishop of Lisieux reinforced the distinctly intertextual quality of his *Histories*. Readers were not only offered a summation of Eusebius's foundational narrative, but were also informed of when and in what circumstances it was written, and were even offered a helpful assessment of the quality of its evidence.

The implications of this are considerable. Firstly, it once again points towards the ecclesiastical centres of learning as the site for the composition and consumption of the *Histories*. The text offers a digest and exegesis of received historiography, catering for an audience for whom these texts were canonical and thus deemed essential to know. The *Histories* are best approached as a sort of study aid or handbook that set out a panorama of the past in which a vast amount of knowledge was rendered into a practical, carefully ordered, compendium (of either one or two volumes). Frechulf's compendium addressed an audience for which the basic twofold division of scripture (and by extension, the basic understanding of the world that stemmed from it) was central: the Old Testament was fulfilled in the New; and the gospel was then spread throughout the world as the Christian *ecclesia* grew, triumphing over paganism. Likewise, the *Histories* spoke to an audience for whom scriptural interpretation (and much else besides) was derived from the church fathers, a collection of highly esteemed authorities whose thoughts and opinions on all matters of doctrine and practice were sought out and applied. The last of the major fathers was Gregory the Great. The *Histories* thus offered a synopsis of Christian history that reinforced the broad currents of Carolingian intellectual culture, fixated as it was on the *sancti patres*.[128] Walter Berschin once noted that 'If you read the first great Carolingian

---

[126] *Hist.*, II.3.14 [114/20], p. 593: 'Itaque explicari non ualet quanta Dei sanctis martyribus excogitabantur tormenta ea tempestate, seu quanta sanctorum milia nouis et inauditis cruciatuum tormentis interempta sunt. Quibus Eusebius Caesariensis episcopus, Ecclesiasticae scriptor historiae, dum interesset, quae in ueritate conperit et cernendo conspexit octauo historiarum et nono libris partim manifestare studuit.'

[127] See, for example, Eusebius-Rufinus, *Historia ecclesiastica*, I.1.2, p. 7 ('martyria nostris suscepta temporibus ...'; VII.32.32, p. 731; VIII.1 (cap.), p. 733 ('De nostri temporis, id est Diocletiani, Maximiani et Maximini persecutione'); VIII.1.proem., p. 737 ('Apostolorum successionibus intra septem libros a nobis conclusis, in hoc octavo volumine dignum credidi etiam ea, quae nostris temporibus gesta sunt, posterorum memoriae derelinquere, et hinc iam nobis sermo sumat exordium.') On persecution, see Corke-Webster, *Eusebius and Empire*, 266–71.

[128] Mayke de Jong, 'From the Order of the Franks to the World of Ambrose: The *Vita Adalhardi* and the *Epitaphium Arsenii* Compared', in *Historiography and Identity III: Carolingian Approaches*, eds Rutger Kramer, Helmut Reimitz and Graeme Ward (Turnhout: Brepols, 2021), 39–63 and Conrad Leyser, 'From Maternal Kin to Jesus as Mother: Royal Genealogy and Marian Devotion in the Ninth-century

catalogue which was compiled by Reginbert of Reichenau [died 846] around 822 and quotes more than 400 books, you are looking not only into a monastic library of the early ninth century, but also into the mind of those who wrote those books and studied them.'[129] Examining the *Histories* produces a similar effect.

Appreciating the *Histories* in this light also takes us out of Frechulf's *scriptorium*. Carolingian reform—whether understood in the more traditional sense of Carolingian rulers, bishops and abbots imposing ecclesiastical legislation and policy from above, or more current, bottom-up approaches to eighth- and ninth-century religious and social change—was predicated upon a canon of orthodox texts.[130] As a consequence, Carolingian reformers established a boundary between the past and present phases of the universal church. This boundary could be a hard one, captured by the Old Testament injunction against 'transgressing the limits of the Fathers' (Proverbs 22:28), which became a catchphrase of sorts for weeding out disapproved practices or establishing new norms with specific reference to the writings of the church fathers as transmitters and upholders of orthodoxy.[131] It was also, however, a porous and dynamic boundary, since the main intention of looking back to the past ages of correct Christianity was to recreate it in the present; this was not a lost age, but one which, through correct texts and morally sound leadership, could be recreated.

One particular significant attempt to remould society in line with this golden age is preserved in the acta of the Council of Paris in 829, which are usually attributed to Jonas of Orléans. Frechulf himself was in attendance, and we shall learn more about this in the next chapter.[132] The bishops at Paris concluded the prologue to their acta by assuring their imperial audience that, in producing such bulky provisions (which run to 74 pages in the MGH edition) for correcting and improving the church, they had 'not dared to transgress the boundaries of the holy fathers'. The *capitula*, the bishops continued, were not to be judged excessive, but were of such length because each provision had to be reinforced by 'the utterances of divine eloquence and the words of the holy fathers', so that no-one could accuse

---

West', in *Motherhood, Religion, and Society in Medieval Europe, 400–1400: Essays Presented to Henrietta Leyser*, eds Conrad Leyser and Lesley Smith (Farnham: Ashgate, 2011), 21–39 (at 39) both show how Paschasius Radbertus inhabited the world of (late) antiquity.

[129] Walter Berschin, 'An Unpublished Library Catalogue from Eighth-century Lombard Italy', *Journal of Medieval Latin*, 11 (2001): 201–9, at 201.

[130] Recent approaches: Kramer, *Rethinking Authority in the Carolingian Empire: Ideal and Expectations during the Reign of Louis the Pious* (Amsterdam: Amsterdam University Press, 2019); Carine van Rhijn, 'Royal Politics in Small Worlds: Local Priests and the Implementation of Carolingian *Correctio*', in *Kleine Welten: Ländliche Gesellschaften im Karolingerreich*, eds Thomas Kohl, Steffen Patzold and Berhard Zeller (Ostfildern: Thorbecke, 2019), 237–53.

[131] Edward M. Peters, 'Transgressing the Limits Set by the Fathers: Authority and Impious Exegesis in Medieval Thought', in *Christendom and its Discontents: Exclusion, Persecution, and Rebellion, 1000–1500*, eds Scott L. Waugh and Peter D. Diehl (Cambridge: CUP, 1996), 338–62, esp. 341–5.

[132] Council of Paris (829), pp. 605–80.

them of fabrication.[133] Jerome, Ambrose, Augustine and Gregory are cited and namechecked throughout. In the Paris acta, we even find the sorts of cross-references that I briefly discussed above. Frechulf's improvised bio-bibliography of Gregory the Great had listed his 'many extant letters [that] are useful to readers on account of the tasks for which they were written'. Amongst the Paris dossier, in a chapter on simony (that is, purchasing clerical ordination), the bishops drew attention to one such practical use of the Gregorian register:

> If anyone wishes to learn more about what has been written regarding the heresy of simony, which must be shunned and despised, they should read the book of letters of the blessed Gregory, in which it is manifestly clear that, back then, when the same doctor was sending his letters to Gallic provinces, the seat of the blessed Peter, of which he was in charge, was free from this plague.[134]

To read the letters of Gregory was to see how things once were, and by implication could again become.

Conclusion

If Frechulf's sense of time can be recovered from his seventh-century ending, neither the emergence of Augustine's *Christiana tempora* nor the break between antiquity and the Middle Ages seems fully convincing. Rather, his conclusion hints at the boundary between the Carolingian *ecclesia* and the era of patristic Christianity, an era understood not simply as a period of time but as corpus of orthodox authors, to whom learned Carolingian men and women routinely turned to define their own sense of correct belief and practice. The unexpected irony of Frechulf's ending is that, in saying nothing about the events of the eighth and ninth centuries, it offers a profound insight into the thought world of Carolingian Christianity. We may learn little of the complex manoeuvrings and processes by which successive Carolingian rulers convinced the ecclesiastical and secular elite of their authority and legitimacy to rule, but a close reading of Part II and its conclusion lets us appreciate core aspects of intellectual life, as practised within the ecclesiastical centres of learning which bolstered and sustained Carolingian power.

---

[133] Council of Paris (829), p. 609.

[134] Council of Paris (829), c. 11, p. 618: 'Si quis igitur copiosius pleniusque de vitanda ac detestanda symoniaca herese scriptum nosse cupit, librum epistolarum beati Gregorii legat, in quibus manifeste apparet, quod eo tempore, quando easdem epistolas idem doctor ad Gallias mittebat, sedes beati Petri, cui prelatus erat, ab eadem luc immunis erat.' See Robert A. Markus, *Gregory the Great and his World* (Cambridge: CUP, 1997), 170–4, and more broadly Timothy Reuter, 'Gifts and Simony', in *Medieval Transformations: Texts, Power and Gifts in Context*, eds Esther Cohen and Mayke de Jong (Leiden: Brill, 2001), 157–68.

6

Past and Present in the *Histories*

Introduction

The extensive acta from the Council of Paris communicated to the imperial court the outcomes of the deliberations carried out by the bishops who had assembled on 6 June 829: Frechulf, as bishop of Lisieux, was present. It has long been known that the acta are a highly important window into Carolingian ideals of religious leadership.[1] As noted in the last chapter, the council's outcomes, attributed to Bishop Jonas of Orléans, are also richly illustrative of the role that ancient, authoritative, Christianity played in Carolingian discussions about the present. Scriptural and especially patristic examples, as transmitted in key texts, supplied the rationale and justification for the prescriptions enumerated throughout the bulky *capitula*, which concerned the church as a whole, then the priestly office, before turning to kings and the laity. These wide-reaching prescriptions aimed, no less, at defining the fundamentals of Christian belief, society and governance, as interpreted by the Carolingian episcopate. Jerome, Ambrose, Augustine and Gregory and other *sancti patres* were all regularly cited; particularly pertinent to my purposes, late antique historiography, in the form of Eusebius-Rufinus's *Ecclesiastical History* also made an appearance. It is thus not only Frechulf's presence amidst the west Frankish ecclesiastical elite in 829 that places him within the orbit of contemporary debates about *ecclesia* and empire.

The Paris council was one of four separate meetings called throughout the empire, though the records of the others—held at Lyon, Toulouse and Mainz—have not survived. The councils were conceived of as a collective attempt to allay deeply held anxieties about the state of the realm: a number of political and military setbacks in 827-8 were interpreted as evidence of systemic crisis and thus

---

[1] There are a number of excellent recent overviews: Patzold, *Episcopus*, 149–68; De Jong, *Penitential State*, 170–84; Michael Edward Moore, *A Sacred Kingdom: Bishops and the Rise of Frankish Kingship, 300–850* (Washington, DC: CUA Press, 2011), 314–27. Hans Hubert Anton, 'Zum politischen Konzept karolingischer Synoden und zur karolingischen Brüdergemeinschaft', *Historisches Jahrbuch*, 99 (1979): 55–132, at 55–74 remains valuable.

divine displeasure at a sinful and morally lax *ecclesia*. Intense introspection and collective correction were needed to placate what was perceived as God's manifest wrath. Addressing Louis the Pious and Lothar, his eldest son and co-emperor, the bishops, in whose joint name the acta were written, sketched the background to the council: 'For when the divine sword was, on account of our iniquity, deservedly grinding down the empire entrusted to you by God with many-fold disasters, both internally and externally', the emperors swiftly responded, sending out letters to 'all the pastors of the churches' requesting help; to the emperors' credit, they 'wisely' had recognised the empire's ills had come about 'sheerly as a result of the just judgment of God'.[2] To placate God, religious professionals, the bishops, were needed.

Two aspects of this council in particular have been stressed in recent decades. Although the initial impulse came from emperors, the bishops set themselves up in the vanguard of this attempt at empire-wide moral improvement. In the light of this, Steffen Patzold made this council the cornerstone of his study of the development of the Carolingian episcopate over the course of the ninth and tenth centuries: the 820s, Patzold argued, witnessed a new understanding of episcopal authority, defined as a God-granted ministry (*ministerium*) which was responsible for the well-being of the realm and the salvation, both of its subjects and its rulers.[3] This radically new conception of the episcopal office crystallised in 829. The second, related, aspect is that the conception of empire set out was thoroughly ecclesial. It is now well known that, at least during the reign of Louis the Pious, the boundaries between empire and *ecclesia* were blurred to such a degree that the terms became almost synonymous with one another.[4] The Paris acta included one episcopal letter

---

[2] Council of Paris (829), *Epistola episcoporum*, p. 667: 'Nam cum mucro divinus imperium vobis divinitus commissum interius exteriusque merito nostrae iniquitatis multifariis adtereret cladibus, prudenter animadvertentes, quod haec nonnisi iusto iudicio Dei evenirent, ilico scriptis serenitatis vestrae anno praeterito cunctos ecclesiarum pastores admonuistis ...'

[3] Patzold, *Episcopus*. There is a helpful overview and assessment by Theo Riches: https://reviews. history.ac.uk/review/961.

[4] Nikolaus Staubach, '*Cultus Divinus* and karolingische Reform', *Frühmittelalterliche Studien*, 18 (1984): 546–81 and Staubach, '*Chistiana tempora*', esp. 200–2; De Jong has written much on this: see, for example, 'Empire as *Ecclesia*'; '*Sacrum palatium et ecclesia*: L'autorité religieuse royale sous les Carolingiens (790–840), *Annales*, 58 (2003), 1243–69; and 'The Sacred Palace, Public Penance and the Carolingian Polity, in *Great Christian Jurists and Legal Collections in the First Millennium*, ed. Philip L. Reynolds (Cambridge: CUP, 2019), 155–81; '*Ecclesia* and the Early Medieval Polity', in *Staat im Frühen Mittelalter*, eds Stuart Airlie, Walter Pohl and Helmut Reimitz (Vienna: Austrian Academy of Sciences Press, 2006), 113–32; *The Penitential State: Authority and Atonement in the Age of Louis the Pious, 814–840* (Cambridge: CUP, 2009); 'The Empire That was Always Decaying: The Carolingians (800–888)', *Medieval Worlds*, 1(2) (2015): 6–25 and 'The Two Republics: Ecclesia and the Public Domain in the Carolingian World', in *Italy and Early Medieval Europe: Papers for Chris Wickham*, eds Ross Balzaretti, Julia Barrow and Patricia Skinner (Oxford: OUP, 2018), 486–500. See also Steffen Patzold,'"Einheit" versus "Fraktionierung"': zur symbolischen und institutionellen Integration des Frankenreichs im 8./9. Jahrhundert', in *Visions of Community in the Post-Roman World: The West, Byzantium and the Islamic world, 300–1100*, eds Walter Pohl, Clemens Gantner and Richard Payne (Farnham: Ashgate, 2012), 375–90. For a different take, see Raffaele Savigni, 'L'Eglise et l'épiscopat en tant que corps social', in *La productivité d'une crise: le règne*

(quoted from above) addressed to the 'most excellent Lords, Louis and Lothar, the most orthodox and invincible *Augusti*, by the grace of piety', and stated that their 'empire (*imperium*)' had been entrusted to them by God. Yet earlier, in the preface to the council, the bishops stressed this differently: it was not the *imperium* that was suffering, but 'the *ecclesia*, which Christ [had] redeemed with his precious blood' and it was the church that, 'through his hidden providence', Christ had 'entrust[ed] to his orthodox servants, the glorious emperors Louis and Lothar, to rule and protect'.[5] A little later, the bishops then explained that 'the holy universal church of God' consisted of a single body, whose head was Christ; within that single, ecclesial body, there were two 'eminent persons', the 'sacerdotal' and the 'royal'. In stating this, the bishops modified their patristic source texts—a famous letter of Pope Gelasius I and Fulgentius of Ruspe's treatise on predestination—to associate the competences of episcopal and royal leadership specifically with the 'church'; Gelasius, for instance, had spoken of leadership within the 'world (*mundus*)'.[6]

According to Geoffrey Koziol, 'Much of what is most important about Carolingian political discourse can be seen as both illustration and application of the principle that "empire" and "church" were different aspects of a single indivisible Body of Christ'.[7] To what extent did Frechulf's work reflect or contribute to this discourse? So far, emphatically positive answers have been given to this question. Raffaele Savigni noted that Frechulf's account of bishops and Christian emperors clearly echoed the Gelasian flavour of Carolingian ecclesiology of the late 820s; Nikolaus Staubach more explicitly placed the *Histories* 'in the wider context of the contemporary efforts (i.e. in 829) to redefine the Frankish *imperium Christianum* and its organs and functions' and considered the work to be 'a thoroughly useful information tool and aid for current discussion about reform'.[8] Lastly, Steffen Patzold detected in the *Histories* a clear reflection of what he termed the 'Paris Model' of episcopal authority.[9] Central to all these approaches is Frechulf's dedicatory prologues, especially that to Part II: its framing as a *speculum principum*, a 'mirror for princes', demonstrated that the ideals of imperial Christianity that Frechulf's second volume contained were intended to be disseminated directly to the court and absorbed by a young ruler, who, it was hoped, would one day put them into practice.

---

de Louis le Pieux (814-840) et la transformation de l'Empire carolingien = Produktivität einer Krise: die Regierungszeit Ludwigs des Frommen (814-840) und die Transformation des karolingischen Imperiums, eds Philippe Depreux and Stefan Esders (Ostfildern: Thorbecke, 2018), 289–312.

[5] Council of Paris (829), p. 607: 'Cum igitur haec ita fideliter se habeant et liquido pateat ecclesiam, quam Christus, qui eam suo pretioso sanguine redemit suisque orthodoxis famulis Hludowico et Chlothario, gloriosis Augustis, regendam tuendamque committere occulta sua dispensatione voluit ...'

[6] Council of Paris (829), cc.2–3, pp. 610–11. For recent discussion of these authorities in context, see Whelan, 'After Augustine', 19–26.

[7] Geoffrey Koziol, 'Christianizing Political Discourses', in *The Oxford Handbook of Medieval Christianity*, ed. John H. Arnold (Oxford: OUP, 2014), 473–89, at 483.

[8] Savigni, 'Storia universale', 155, 182–3; Staubach, '*Christiana tempora*', 200 and 202.

[9] Patzold, *Episcopus*, 173–5.

By contrast, I have until now explicitly decentred political questions from my analysis and instead have implicitly focused on the perspectives of monastic and clerical readers: that is, readers for whom the *Histories* would have been a handy historiographical primer to be consulted in the context of biblical and patristic study. Can these perspectives be reconciled? In what follows, I argue that they can. It is precisely in relation to the basic context of Carolingian biblical culture that I want to frame my own assessment of the political resonances of the *Histories*. I suggest that, above all, what draws Frechulf's work into contemporary debates about church, state and society was the study and use of authoritative texts. To this end, the use of canonical early Christian historiography in Carolingian political discourse is the focus of the second part of this chapter. In order to get there, however, I first discuss the concomitant question of audience: before considering what functions the text might have served, it is necessary to think more about who might have read it. The high-profile dedicatees and stated expectations of use that Frechulf communicated though his prefaces have served to situate most previous discussions of audience and purpose, and for good reason. Yet I take a different approach, in part because insufficient attention has been paid to unpacking these thorny documents. I aim to set out a more nuanced reading of the prologues in order to generate a wider, more inclusive, view of audience, which in turn offers new ways to consider how the study of authoritative texts informed contemporary ideals of church and society. My contention is not that we have to envisage an immediate reception between text and court in order to appreciate impact; rather the educative settings the *Histories* evoke—that is, the study of authoritative texts by court-connected intellectuals and budding students—was the crucial link that made the centres of learning also centres of power in the Carolingian world.

Problematising Prologues

As I noted briefly in my Introduction, prologues, prefaces and other dedicatory letters are notoriously hard to handle. They are generally highly stylised texts, loaded with biblical allusions and rhetorical commonplaces. They are self-fashioning and at times also self-serving: they were opportunities for authors to demonstrate their Latinity, often combining prose and verse (as did Frechulf); Amalarius of Metz, for example, dedicated his extended commentary on the liturgy, the *Liber officialis*, to Louis the Pious to win back lost imperial favour.[10] Studies of Carolingian prologues and dedications have highlighted how such learned gifts could be sent at moments of heightened political tension to reaffirm

---

[10] Amalarius of Metz, *Liber officialis*, Praef., ed. Jean-Michel Hanssens, *Amalarii episcopi opera liturgica omnia II: Liber officialis*, Studi e Tesi 139 (Vatican City: Biblioteca apostolica vaticana, 1950), pp. 19–20; Christopher A. Jones, *A Lost Work by Amalarius of Metz: Interpolations in Salisbury Cathedral Library MS 154* (Woodbridge: Boydell & Brewer, 2001), esp. 164–74.

relational bonds between sender and recipient. Aspiring scholars might send their work to superiors to ward off accusations of impudence and to acknowledge ecclesiastical hierarchies, and friends and colleagues addressed each other to maintain horizontal bonds and social networks over space and time.[11] Yet the local production and the later circulation of texts amongst elite circles meant that authors likely did not expect their work to be read only by the person to whom it was dedicated, and the decision to dedicate may only have come later, rather than at the beginning of the process of creating a text.[12] A work such as Frechulf's implies multiple audiences, from students at the local cathedral school getting to grips with the outline and events of sacred history to other members of the ecclesiastical, courtly elite. The decision to undertake such a compilation may have responded initially to the immediate needs of a local community, while prefatory material, added subsequently, invested the end product with court-facing qualities. Although authors are often more explicit in prologues about their reasons for writing than elsewhere in their works, these reasons should not be taken as clear-cut statements of fact. Consequently, the political impact of texts, if judged primarily on the basis of prologues, must be queried.

Take, for example, the prologue to Part I. Here Frechulf centred his relationship with Helisachar, his 'most beloved teacher'. It was Helisachar, we are told, who, after 'insistently spurring on others' into action, had urged Frechulf to put his mind to good use. Besides placing himself at the bottom of Helisachar's pecking order, thereby emphasising his lowly status, Frechulf warded off negative assumptions about his own ambition by presenting his work as the fulfilment of a command. It was 'not out of presumptuousness but for the sake of obedience', Frechulf explained, that 'I, an uneducated novice, have seized upon this great undertaking, which ought to have been entrusted to wiser men'. Helisachar prompted the bishop of Lisieux to begin work on the *Histories*, and the prologue implied that he had signed off on the finished product: 'I am sending it for you to examine, and if you judge that it will be useful, it will be attributed to the corrector (*censor*) no less than the author.'[13] Readers were thus told up front that the text they had before them had been assessed and approved.

The status and reputation of this *censor* were important. Helisachar had been close to Louis the Pious when he was still king of Aquitaine, serving as his chancellor between 808 and 813; with Louis' accession in 814, Helisachar became

---

[11] De Jong, 'Empire as Ecclesia' and 'Exegesis for an Empress'; Sita Steckel, 'Between Censorship and Patronage: Interaction between Bishops and Scholars in Carolingian Book Dedications', in *Envisioning the Bishop: Images and the Episcopacy in the Middle Ages*, eds Sigrid Danielson and Evans A. Gatti (Turnhout: Brepols, 2014), 103–26, as well as more extensive treatment in *Kulturen des Lehrens*, 515–688.

[12] *Prolegomena*, 29*: Frechulf's dedicatory letter to his edition of Vegetius 'seems to have arisen at a middle point in the accretion of [the] bishop's edition, perhaps itself as an ad hoc accretion'.

[13] *Hist.*, I.Prol, pp. 18–20; trans. Lake, 111–12.

arch-chancellor, a position he held until 819. Thereafter, he was an abbot of at least two west Frankish monasteries, St Aubin in Angers and St Riquier, and throughout the 820s remained an important figure at the imperial court.[14] Along with other pre-eminent abbots of the empire, Helisachar's name is featured prominently in the St Gall and Reichenau confraternity books, dating from 810/15 and 824, respectively.[15] When Agobard of Lyon wished to air his complaints about Jewish slave owners to the emperor in 822, he had to speak to Helisachar, Adalhard and Wala, who then—much to Agobard's chagrin—spoke to Louis on his behalf, leaving him out of the loop: Helisachar was one of the key men who physically controlled access to the ruler.[16] His close proximity to the emperor can also be seen in Ermoldus Nigellus's panegyric poem *In Honour of Louis*, and especially the poem's depiction of the baptism of the Danish king Harold Klak in 826: after the baptismal ceremony, all gathered to celebrate Mass, which began with a procession to the altar, with the emperor flanked by Hilduin of St Denis and Helisachar.[17] If Frechulf presented his text as having stemmed from such a high-profile figure, he was also tacitly locating it near the emperor's inner circle.

Helisachar's status, furthermore, can be linked with the production and evaluation of texts, exegetical, homiletic, liturgical and hagiographical.[18] As discussed briefly in Chapter 2, Helisachar was singled out by Bernhard Bischoff

[14] Overviews in Theo Kölzer, *Die Urkunden der Karolinger. Zweiter Band, Die Urkunden Ludwigs des Frommen* (Wiesbaden: Harrassowitz, 2016), xxix and Depruex, *Prosoprographie de l'entourage de Louis le Pieux (781-840)*, Instrumenta I (Sigmaringen: Thorbecke, 1997), no. 143, 236–40; Sarah Patt, *Studien zu den 'Formulae imperiale': Urkundenkonzeption und Formulargebrauch in der Kanzlei Keiser Ludwigs des Frommen (814-840)* (Wiesbaden: Harrassowitz, 2016), 58.
[15] Dieter Geuenich, 'Gebetsgedenken und anianische Reform: Beobachtungen zu den Verbrüdersbeziehungen der Äbte im Reich Ludwigs des Frommen', *Monastische Reformen im 9. und 10. Jahrhundert*, eds Raymund Kottje and Helmut Maurer (Sigmaringen: Thorbecke, 1989), 79–106, esp. 87–9. In the St Gall *Liber vitae*, Helisachar was bracketed by Benedict of Aniane and Einhard: Dieter Geuenich, 'Benedikt von Aniane, Helisachar und Einhard im St Galler Verbrüderungsbuch', in *Schatzkammer Stiftsarchiv St. Gallen. Miscellanea Lorenz Hollenstein*, eds Peter Erhart and Klaus Amann (Dietikon: Graf, 2009), 27–9; Dieter Geuenich and Uwe Ludwig (eds), *Die St. Galler Verbrüderungsbücher*, MGH, Libri memorialies, nova series 9 (Wiesbaden: Harrassowitz, 2019), p. 235.
[16] Agobard of Lyon, *De baptismo manciporum Iudaeorum*, ed. Lieven van Acker, *Agobard Lugdunensis opera omnia*, CCCM 52 (Turnhout: Brepols, 1981), pp. 115–17, at 115. Agobard encountered a similar problem a year or two later in the context of ecclesiastical property: Agobard, *De dispensatione ecclesiasticarum rerum*, c. 4, ed. Lieven Van Acker, *Agobardi Lugdunensis Opera Omnia*, CCCM 52 (Turnhout: Brepols, 1981), pp. 119–42, at p. 123: 'Cum haec igitur a me dicerentur, responderunt pie reuerentissimi uiri Adalardus et Helisacar abbates. Vtrum uero audita retulerint domno imperatori, nescio ...' For context, see Irene van Renswoude, *The Rhetoric of Free Speech in Late Antiquity and the Early Middle Ages* (Cambridge: CUP, 2019), 212–19.
[17] Ermoldus, *In Honorem Hludowici*, IV, ll. 2294–6, p. 176: 'Hilduinus habet dextram, Helisacharque sinistram/Sustentat'. Cf. I, ll. 1039–40, p. 82: 'mox vero famulum revocat Helisachar amatum'; III, ll. 1548–9, p. 119: 'carus Helisachar'; IV, ll. 2006, p. 153. The *Annales regni Francorum*, s.a. 826, ed. Georg Petz and Friederich Kurze, MGH SRG 6 (Hanover: Hahn, 1895), 169– 70 and Astronomer, *Vita Hludovici*, c. 40, p. 432 states this took place at St Alban's, Mainz (*Mogontiaci apud sanctum Albanum*), whereas Thegan suggests Ingelheim at c. 33, p. 220 (*in palatio regio Ingilenheim*).
[18] Huglo, 'D'Helisachar'.

as the likely instigator of a series of (unedited and largely unstudied) biblical commentaries.[19] He likewise has been considered the likely author of a homily on All Saints.[20] When Amalarius of Metz created a new antiphonary c. 831, a book central to the performance of the Divine Office, he recalled Helisachar's own efforts to revise this particular liturgical book, undertaken around a decade earlier in collaboration with Archbishop Nibridius of Narbonne. Amalarius considered Helisachar 'a most learned man, exceptionally devoted to reading and the divine cult, who was foremost amongst the leading men of the palace of the most excellent emperor Louis'.[21] There is even another extant source which was offered to him for appraisal. Ardo, Benedict of Aniane's biographer, addressed his *Vita* to the monastic community of Inde, but specified that, once the brethren there had examined it, they should pass it on to Helisachar, since he was so beloved by Benedict: 'should he decide for it to be supressed', Ardo wrote, 'I beg forgiveness for my error. But should he deem it useful, let those who freely obeyed Benedict when he was alive, now devote themselves to imitating his life although he is absent.'[22]

Frechulf characterised Helisachar as being 'revered for [his] insatiable love of wisdom': in the light of the other extant mini-portraits of him, this rings true.[23] More to the point, he was not the only author who styled his text as having been examined by this well-regarded man. That both Part I of the *Histories* and the *Vita Benedicti* are extant, implies that these texts secured Helisachar's approval: that, at least, is the effect that such prologues create. But Frechulf went a step further. Helisachar not only approved of the text, but it appears as though he had been given partial ownership of it: he was presented not only as a peer reviewer but also as a co-author or collaborator. It is precisely this impression that cautions

---

[19] Bischoff, 'Libraries and Schools', 111–13. Paul-Irénée Fransen, 'Le dossier patristique d'Hélisachar.' See above, pp. 56–7.

[20] Edited and analysed in J. E. Cross, '"Legimus in ecclesiasticis historiis": A Sermon for All Saints, and its Use in Old English Prose', *Traditio*, 33 (1977): 101–35, with Helisachar's authorship considered at 128; authorship more confidently stated by Christina Rauer, 'Female Hagiography in the Old English Martyrology', in *Writing Women Saints in Anglo-Saxon England*, ed. Paul Szarmach (Toronto: University of Toronto Press, 2014), 13–29, at 24–5. Bullough, however, was 'unconvinced': Donald A. Bullough and Alice L. Harting-Corrêa, 'Texts, Chant, and the Chapel of Louis the Pious', in *Carolingian Renewal: Sources and Heritage* (Manchester: MUP, 1991), 241–71, at 259, n. 6. Michael Allen made a tantalising connection between this sermon, which touches on the consecration of Pantheon, and Frechulf's conclusion: *Prolegomena*, 207* and 'Fréculf', 75.

[21] Amalarius of Metz, *Prologus antiphonarii*, 10, ed. Jean-Michel Hanssens, *Amalarii episcopi opera liturgica omnia I: Introductio—opera minora*, Studi e Testi 138 (Vatican City: Biblioteca apostolica vaticana, 1948), p. 362: 'adprime eruditus, et studiosissimus in lectione et divino cultu, necnon et inter priores primus palatii excellentissimi Hludovici imperatoris'. On Helisachar's antiphonary, see Kenneth Levy, 'Abbot Helisachar's Antiphoner', *Journal of the American Musicological Society*, 48 (1995): 171–86.

[22] Ardo, *Vita Benedicti Abbatis Anianensis et Indensis*, c. 33, ed. Georg Waitz, MGH SS 15/1 (Hanover: Hahn, 1887), pp. 198–220, at 220; Trans. Thomas F. X. Noble and Thomas Head, eds, *Soldiers of Christ: Saints and Saints Lives from Late Antiquity and the Early Middle Ages* (University Park, PA: Pennsylvania State University Press, 2000), pp. 213–54 at 216.

[23] *Hist.*, I.Prol [9], p. 17; trans. Lake, p. 111.

against accepting the prologue at face value. Even if Frechulf's phrasing reflects a pre-existing relationship, it still served rhetorical ends. Presenting a work as being the fulfilment of a commission was itself a topos, examples of which even can be found in some of Frechulf's core resources.[24] Rufinus explained in his prologue that Chromatius of Aquiliea had urged him to undertake his translation and continuation of the *Ecclesiastical History*, and then he had asked him to 'approve and bless' the finished product.[25] Orosius offers a more redolent example. The very first words of the *Histories against the Pagans* were: '*Praeceptis tuis parui, beatissime pater Augustine*'—'I have obeyed your instructions, most blessed father Augustine.' 'If you publish [these books]', Orosius then asked Augustine at the work's conclusion, 'they must be approved of by you, but if you destroy them, you will have disapproved of them.'[26] Peter Van Nuffelen has argued that Orosius used his own preface 'to cash in on the status of Augustine.'[27] Frechulf's dedication may well have performed a comparable function: by subordinating his own authority to that of prominent figure at court, Frechulf emphasised his humility while also using Helisachar's reputation for erudition, his high standing at court and his close proximity to Louis the Pious to bolster his project's credentials. (This likely was also a two-way street: prominent courtiers such as Helisachar would have welcomed dedications, since they would enhance their own status, as patrons and supporters of learning.[28])

Whether or not Helisachar did in fact commission the *Histories* is beside the point; there are compelling reasons to suppose that he did at least offer material support, in the form of a copy of Eusebius-Jerome's *Chronicle* and perhaps other texts from St Riquier's hoard of history books. In the prologue to Part II, Frechulf set his sights on a figure even closer to the emperor: the Empress Judith. At first glance, the dedicatory prologue to Part II has a different register and conveys a different writing process. Rather than being the fulfilment of a commission, Frechulf presents Part II as the product of his own initiative. Awed by Judith's learning, as he explains, he 'resolved to offer to the ardour of [her] beneficence a small gift assembled by my own efforts' and thus 'set about writing a second volume ... divided ... into five books'. In place of the topoi of humility and subservience that run through the dedication to Helisachar, this document can be best described as a panegyric: its main purpose was to praise, and it did so through a heightened, hyperbolic,

[24] Simon, 'Untersuchungen', Part II, 132. See also Van Nuffelen, *Orosius*, 32.
[25] Eusebius-Rufinus, *Historia ecclesiastica*, Praef., pp. 951–2; trans Amidon, *Church History*, 3–4.
[26] Oros., I.Prol.1, p. 6 , trans. Fear, 31 and VII.43.20, p. 132, trans. Fear, 414.
[27] Van Nuffelen, *Orosius*, 31–41, at 36.
[28] See further Rosamond McKitterick, 'Royal Patronage of Culture in the Frankish Kingdoms under the Carolingians: Motives and Consequences', in *Committenti e produzione aristico-letteraria nell'alto medioevo occidentale*, Settimane 39 (Spoleto: Centro italiano di studi sull'alto Medioevo, 1992), vol. 2, 93–129.

register.[29] Judith, Frechulf wrote, had it all: a superlative husband, unrivalled beauty and a young son who was 'the glory' of the world and the delight of men'. Since 'there was nothing to be found in the affairs of this world' that she lacked, Judith turned herself to learning, 'so that', as far as 'the pursuit of wisdom' was concerned, '[she] might be deemed to surpass the empresses of past ages'. Judith's god-granted *sapientia* and natural *scientia* was, continued Frechulf, the catalyst for the second instalment of his *Histories*: 'For I was amazed when I became aware of the fluency of your erudition in divine and liberal studies, and so I resolved to offer to the ardour of your beneficence a small gift assembled by my own efforts.'[30]

Judith's status as imperial wife was noted, but the real emphasis was on her status as mother: family and especially dynasty play a notable role in Frechulf's praise. Charles was still young in years, but his eminently royal name evoked the memory of Charlemagne:

> [Charles] conquers and surpasses his own immature years through the elegance of his person, his superior habits, and his active pursuit of wisdom, so that his grandfather appears not to have perished but to have wiped away the haziness of sleep and illuminated the world anew. For his grandson there shines brightly his same immortal mind, his name, his elegance, and his virtue.[31]

Judith, as Charles's mother, was expected to contribute to his upbringing, and it was to this this end that Frechulf hoped his work would be put.[32] Through Judith's 'urging and command (*admonitionem atque iussionem*)', Charles was 'to see in these [histories] as in a mirror (*velut in speculo*) what should be done and what should be avoided'.[33] Frechulf thought it would be 'fitting' for Judith to 'instruct [her] only and venerable son, the king of our joy and of a new age'. In this appeal to education, he asked Judith to look back to the world of the Old Testament and recall the example of Queen Bathsheba, 'who taught Jedidiah [Solomon], the wisest king of antiquity'. Frechulf then cited Proverbs 4:3–6 (introducing this with 'as [Solomon] sa[id] of himself'):

> 'For I was my father's son, tender, and as an only son in the sight of my mother. And [s]he taught me, and said, "Let your heart receive my words, keep my commandments, and you will live. Get wisdom, get prudence. Do not forget, nor turn away from the words of my mouth. Forsake her [i.e. Bathsheba] not, and she will keep you; love her, and she will preserve you"'.[34]

---

[29] For a study of the function of panegyric in a later context, see Erik Niblaeus, 'Beautiful Power: Panegyric at the Court of Henry II (1039–56)', *Journal of Medieval History*, 47(1) (2021): 1–21.

[30] *Hist.*, II.Prol., pp. 435–6; trans. Lake, 113.

[31] *Hist.*, II.Prol. [9/14], p. 435; trans. Lake, 113. On other contemporary perceptions of Charles's illustrious name, see William Diebold, '*Nos quoque morem illius imitari cupientes*: Charles the Bald's Evocation and Imitation of Charlemagne', *Archiv für Kulturgeschichte*, 75 (1993): 271–300, at 289–94.

[32] Airlie, *Making and Unmaking*, 110.

[33] *Hist.*, II.Prol. [28/32], p. 436; trans. Lake, 113.

[34] *Hist.*, II.Prol. [32/5], pp. 436–7; trans. Lake, 113–14.

Fulfilling the role of educator, Judith's loving, maternal admonitions (*maternae dilectionis admonitiones*) would encourage Charles 'to entrust these books (*codicellos*) to his memory'. To round things off, Frechulf made a final plea: 'It is my desire for your affection, therefore, my ever august lady, that has compelled me to write these volumes, which now await the judgement of your beneficence and immortal wisdom.' By way of conclusion, he added a further biblical allusion, this time the empress's Old Testament namesake: 'If they obtain praise in your eyes, it will be ascribed eternally to your memory, since your most holy name Judith means "judging" or "praising".'[35]

Each of Frechulf's volumes was offered up for appraisal by high-ranking individuals of the realm. Although the prologues to Parts I and II presented different scenarios in which the corresponding volumes were written, they shared a common backdrop: the court. The court is to be understood as a physical location but also as a mental construct, 'a frame of mind' (Nelson) or 'a palace of memory' (Airlie), that authors evoked, even if in far-off locations such as Lisieux, to signal the learned world to which they belonged.[36] Frechulf's prologues capture the courtliness of ninth-century intellectual culture, in part because they advertised his closeness to the imperial centre: Louis the Pious, his family and his closest advisors. Indeed, when Frechulf expressed his astonishment at Judith's wisdom, he made it clear he was not alone: the other men who heard her speak (*inter ceteros auditores*) were likewise amazed. These 'other listeners' presumably were other men at court, and Frechulf is again stressing his close proximity to the heart of imperial power. It is important to note that other contemporary courtiers, such as the exiled poet Ermoldus Nigellus and Walahfrid Strabo, praised Judith for her beauty, her learning and her status as mother.[37]

Frechulf's Prologue to Part II in particular highlights the immediate reception and intended use of the *Histories*. With Judith's encouragement, Charles ought to see in the *Histories*, 'as in a mirror', good and examples to imitate or reject: 'enlightened by the deeds of emperors, the triumphs of the saints, and the instruction of eminent teachers, he will discover ... what is to be done and what is to be avoided'.[38] Frechulf's prologue was very much framed as what is now known as a *Fürstenspiegel*, a 'mirror for princes'.[39] For this reason, it is common to read

[35] *Hist.*, II.Prol. [47/52], p. 437; trans. Lake, 114.
[36] Nelson, 'History-Writing', 439; Stuart Airlie, 'The Palace of Memory: The Carolingian Court as Political Centre', in *Courts and Regions in Medieval Europe*, eds Sarah Rees Jones, Richard Marks and A. J. Minnis (Woodbridge: York Medieval Press, 2000), 1–20; repr. in his *Power and its Problems in Carolingian Europe* (Farnham: Ashgate Variorum, 2012), item VII.
[37] Ward, 'Caesar's Wife', 216–225.
[38] *Hist.*, II.Prol. [43/6] p. 437; trans. Lake, 114.
[39] On this genre, see Hans Hubert Anton, *Fürstenspiegel und Herrscherethos in der Karolingerzeit*, Bonner Historische Forschungen 32 (Bonn: Bonn Röhrscheid, 1968); Alain Dubreucq, 'La littérature des 'Specula': Délimitation du genre, contenu, destinataires et réception', in *Guerriers et moines. Conversion et sainteté aristocratiques dans l'Occident médiéval (IXᵉ-XIIᵉ siècle)*, ed. Michel Lauwers

that Frechulf compiled his text with the education of Charles in mind, and his *Histories* are often counted amongst the numerous examples of advice-giving literature written in the eighth and ninth centuries.

It is safe to assume that Frechulf hoped that Charles, by reading his work or having it read to him, might learn a thing or two about how to be a morally upright person and a successful ruler. History, after all, was a didactic genre.[40] The notion that history was the teacher of life (*historia vitae magistra est*) went back to Cicero and the basic principle further back still; in Isidore's phrasing, the key 'utility of history' was 'the instruction of the living'. In dedicating his *Ecclesiastical History* to King Ceolwulf of Northumbria, Bede stated that 'Should history tell of good men and their good estate, the thoughtful listener is spurred on to imitate the good; should it record the evil ends of wicked men, no less effectually the devout and earnest listener or reader is kindled to eschew what is harmful and perverse.'[41] The Astronomer, in his *Vita Hludowici*, asserted that 'when the good or bad deeds of the ancients, especially of princes, are drawn back into memory, a twofold advantage is conferred upon those who read about them: the one serves to benefit and edify them, and the other to warn them.'[42] Hrabanus Maurus presented his commentaries on Old Testament *historia* to ninth-century rulers for their moral improvement. Nevertheless, Carolingian sources labelled *specula* generally did not take the form of historical narrative. Alcuin's 'lay mirror' for Count Wido/Guy (written 799–800) and the various mirrors of Jonas of Orléans, including the acta of the Council of Paris 829, are usually taken as prime examples of this mode of writing.[43] Frechulf thus can be situated within a wider web of Carolingian texts addressed to secular elites that were framed as guidebooks for sound ethical living.

Should Frechulf's prologue be taken at face value? Can it be read as a straightforward statement of how he intended the book to be used? The courtliness

---

(Turnhout: Brepols, 2002), 17–39; Rachel Stone, 'Kings are Different: Carolingian Mirrors for Princes and Lay Morality', in *Le prince au miroir de la literature politique de l'Antiquité aux Lumières*, eds Frédérique Lachaud and Lydwine Scordia (Mont-Saint-Aignan: Publications des Universités de Rouen et du Havre, 2007), 69–86; Monika Suchan, 'Gerechtigkeit in christlicher Verantwortung: Neue Blicke in die Fürstenspiegel des Frühmittelalters', *Francia*, 41 (2014): 1–23.

[40] Although not considered here, there is an exegetical angle, since moral instruction was also the point of tropological commentary. This would repay further study: see, for example, Sigbjørn Sønnesyn, 'Eternity in Time, Unity in Particularity: The Theological Basis of Typological Interpretations in Twelfth-Century Historiography', in *La typologie biblique comme forme de pensée dans l'historiographie médiévale*, ed. Marek Thue Kretschmer (Turnhout: Brepols, 2014), 79–95, at 89–91.

[41] Bede, *Historia ecclesiastica*, Praef., pp. 2–3.

[42] Compare Astronomer, *Vita Hludowici imperatoris*, Prol., p. 280: 'Cum gesta priscorum bona malave, maxime principum, ad memoriam reducuntur, gemina in eis utilitas legentibus confertur: alia enim eorum utilitati et aedificationi prosunt, alia cautelae.' English trans. Noble, *Charlemagne and Louis the Pious*, 226–8. See also Savigni, 'Storia universale', 180 and n. 98. On this topos, see further Simon, 'Untersuchungen', Part I, 71, 77, 112 and Part II, 105–6.

[43] Rachel Stone, 'Translation of Alcuin's *De virtutibus et vitiis liber* (Book about the Virtues and Vices)', *The Heroic Age*, 16 (2015).

of Frechulf's prologues encourages some caution: the panegyric form suggests that praising Judith (for whatever purposes), rather than shaping the mind of her young son, was at the forefront of Frechulf's mind; praise was an immediate goal, whereas princely formation was a longer term hope. If so, then royal advice giving was just one function that Frechulf expected his *Histories* to perform. Further hints support this. The dedicatory prologues to Parts I and II present strikingly different scenarios of composition: Frechulf's first volume was allegedly commissioned by Helisachar and tailored to his specifications; Part II rather was presented as Frechulf's own initiative. Yet, if we peel away these outer layers, the inner workings and organisation of material were consistent and coherent across each volume; these correspond to what must have been Frechulf's own designs, which likely were developed independently of Helisachar's commission and for reasons distinct from praising Judith/educating Charles. Each volume even begins with its own prefatory material that frames what follows and does not depend on the material presented in dedicatory prologues.

Frechulf's prologue to Helisachar may have served to acknowledge thanks for providing sources. The dedication to Judith, if dated to 829, perhaps used Charles's sixth birthday—an important milestone in the aristocratic lifecycle—to make his support for the imperial family known, or at least to remind them of his support; Frechulf was not alone in praising Judith's beauty and status as mother of a significantly named prince, which seems to have been a common strategy for courtiers. If dated later, say to 831, the dedication would have arrived after Judith had been freed from monastic confinement following the rebellion of 830, when the empress and her family were especially in need of displays of loyalty. Other scenarios are also possible. Hrabanus Maurus, for example, first dedicated his commentary on Kings to Hilduin, the abbot of St Denis and imperial arch-chaplain in 829, before re-dedicating it to Louis the German in 832: in Mayke de Jong's reading, Hrabanus 'tested the water' with his first dedication before setting his sights higher.[44] Frechulf may have been playing a similar game, by addressing Helisachar before turning his attention to the empress. What is more, Hrabanus also stated that, even before Hilduin requested a sample of his scholarship, he had produced the commentary on Kings for an internal audience: the monks at Fulda.[45] Biblical commentary provided 'a practical guide to Christian kings', especially because it aided 'the royal understanding of the deeper and truly Christian meaning' of the histories of the kings of the Old Testament.[46] Yet it was

---

[44] For example, Mayke de Jong, 'Carolingian Political Discourse and the Biblical Past: Hraban, Dhuoda, Radbert', in *The Resources of the Past in Early Medieval Europe*, eds Clemens Gantner, Rosamond McKitterick and Sven Meeder (Cambridge: CUP, 2015), 87–102, at 92.

[45] Hrab. *Epist.*, nos. 14, pp. 401–3 and 18, pp. 422–4.

[46] De Jong, 'Empire as *Ecclesia*', 205.

also an essential resource for studious and liturgically active monks.[47] The fact that more than one of Hrabanus's commentaries had multiple dedications, and that they initially may have been produced to satisfy the local needs of his own monastic community, serves as a further reminder that audiences were mutable and that dedications tell only part of the story.[48]

Put simply, the relation between text/prologue and audience/use is complicated. This is not to say that we ought to reject the veracity of dedications out of hand, but rather they need to be handled cautiously. For my purposes, this does not limit the contemporary impact of the *Histories* but helps to outline a wider context of reception. To develop this, I want to look more closely at the didactic and moral uses of imperial Roman historiography in the ninth century; instead of thinking narrowly about who might have read the *Histories* and why, I situate Frechulf's creative engagement with Roman texts in relation to the activities of his contemporaries.

Reading Roman History

In the Christian empire of the Carolingians, Roman history supplied a vocabulary of power and a 'symbolic language of authority', especially after Charlemagne's imperial coronation in 800.[49] The writings of ancient Rome also became a source of real interest. Frechulf distinguished himself as a diligent editor of Vegetius's fourth-century military handbook, a text he thought was especially fit for a king;[50] that Hrabanus Maurus sent excerpts of Vegetius to Lothar II, and Hartgar of Liège dedicated a copy to Eberhard of Friuli, confirms both ecclesiastical and secular interest. Frechulf also made notable use of the *Epitome de Caesaribus*, a collection of imperial biographies, most likely written by a non-Christian author sometime towards the end of the fourth century or beginning of the fifth.[51] The

---

[47] Caroline Chevalier-Royet, 'Le commentaire de Raban Maur sur les *Livres des Rois*: manuel scolaire à l'usage des moines et guide pratique à l'usage des rois', in *Raban Maur et son temps*, eds Philippe Depreux, Stéphane Lebecq, Michel J.-L. Perrin and Olivier Szerwiniak (Turnhout: Brepols, 2010), 293–303. A similar point is also made in Allen, 'Brede and Frechulf', 69.

[48] Hrabanus dedicated his Maccabees commentary to Louis the Pious's arch-chaplain, Gerholt, before later gifting it to Louis the German: Hrab. *Epist.*, nos. 19 and 35, pp. 424–5 and 469–70. Two dedications to his *De rerum naturis* likewise are extant: Hrab. *Epist.*, nos. 36–7, pp. 470–4. This list could be expanded.

[49] Ildar H. Garipzanov, *The Symbolic Language of Authority in the Carolingian World (c. 751–877)*, Brill Series on the Early Middle Ages 16 (Leiden: Brill, 2008) as well as his 'The Communication of Authority in Carolingian Titles', *Viator*, 36 (2005): 41–82 with a useful table at 69–82. In this they followed other post-imperial western rulers who turned to Roman titles to project their authority.

[50] Charles was addressed as *inclitus rex* ('glorious king'), a term favoured by Charles's court in the late 830s, which combined royal and late Roman imperial political vocabulary: Garipzanov, *Symbolic Language*, 118.

[51] See the introduction by Michel Festy, in *Pseudo-Aurélius Victor*; Timothy D. Barnes, 'The *Epitome de Caesaribus* and its Sources', *Classical Philology*, 71 (1976): 258–68; Giorgio Bonamente, 'Minor Latin Historians of the Fourth Century A.D.', in *Greek and Roman Historiography in Late Antiquity: Fourth to*

Epitome's contents are neatly encapsulated in the *inscriptio* with which the text was accompanied: 'the short work about the life and character of emperors, abbreviated from the six books of Aurelius Victor, from Augustus Caesar up until Theodosius [I]'.[52] There are two extant ninth-century manuscripts of the *Epitome*, one of which, it has been suggested, was copied at Fulda and may even have been annotated by Lupus of Ferrières.[53] In 844, around fifteen years after Frechulf addressed his *Histories* to Judith, Lupus sent a letter to Charles the Bald, exhorting him to rule wisely and justly. Lupus concluded his letter, saying:

> I have had a very brief summary of the deeds of the emperors presented to Your Majesty so that you may readily observe from their actions what you should imitate or what you should avoid. I especially commend to your consideration, however, Trajan and Theodosius because you can most profitably find many things among their deeds to imitate.[54]

Although a firm identification is impossible, it seems likely that 'the very brief summary' Lupus was speaking of was the *Epitome*. In another letter of 844, this time to Marcward of Prüm, Lupus requested that the now-lost Fulda manuscript of Suetonius's *Lives of the Caesars* be taken to Prüm to be copied, before being sent on to Ferrières.[55] Lupus had seemingly become acquainted with Suetonius as a student at Fulda, and his pupil Heiric of Auxerre epitomised it, or at least another copy of it, in his *Collectanea*.[56] It is in the pages of Einhard, another intellectual educated at Fulda, that the most well-known ninth-century uses of Suetonius are to be found.[57] The *Historia Augusta*, another collection of imperial biographies, was also to be found at Fulda and Murbach, and like Suetonius, was epitomised in a ninth-century florilegia, though this time by Sedulius Scottus.[58] Even in this brief

---

Sixth Century A.D., ed. Gabrielle Marasco (Leiden: Brill, 2003), 85–125, at 100–3.

[52] *Epitome de Caesaribus*, p. 2: 'LIBELLUS DE VITA ET MORIBUS IMPERATORUM BREVIATUS EX LIBRIS SEXTI AURELII VICTORIS A CAESARE AUGUSTO USQUE AD THEODOSIUM.'

[53] *Prolegomena*, 201*. See also Veronika von Büren, 'Une edition critique de Solin au IXᵉ siècle', *Scriptorium*, 50 (1996): 22–87 at 42–3 and 86.

[54] Lupus of Ferrières, *Letters*, ed. Léon Levillain, *Loup de Ferrières: Correspondance*, 2 vols., Les classiques de l'histoire de France au Moyen Age 10 (Paris: Les Belles Lettres, 1964), no. 37, vol. 1, p. 164; English trans. Graydon W. Regenos, *The Letters of Lupus of Ferrières* (The Hague: Springer, 1966), 55.

[55] Lupus, *Letters*, no. 35, vol. 1, pp. 154–8.

[56] Heiric of Auxerre, *Collectanea*, ed. Riccardo Quadri, *I Collectanea di Eirico di Auxerre*, Spicilegium Friburgense 11 (Freiburg: Edizioni universitarie, 1966), 104–13. Heiric included excerpts from Orosius on Trajan and Jovian amongst the quotations from Suetonius' *Lives of the Caesars* (see p. 113).

[57] On Suetonius, see L. D. Reynolds (ed.), *Texts and Transmission: A Survey of the Latin Classics* (Oxford: Clarendon Press, 1983), 400 and Matthew Innes, 'The Classical Tradition in the Carolingian Renaissance: Ninth-Century Encounters with Suetonius', *International Journal of the Classical Tradition*, 3 (1997): 265–82. On Einhard, see David Ganz, 'Einhard's Charlemagne: The Characterisation of Greatness', in *Charlemagne: Empire and Society*, ed. Joanna Story (Manchester: MUP, 2005), 38–51.

[58] Sedulius Scottus, *Collectaneum Miscellaneum*, ed. Dean Simpson, CCCM 67 (Turnhout: Brepols, 1988), c. lxxxviii (*ex vita Caesarum*), pp. 305–13. Sedulius Scottus also used the *Historia Augusta* in his *De rectoribus christianis*, ed. and trans. by R. W. Dyson, *De rectoribus christianis: On Christian Rulers* (Woodbridge: Boydell Press, 2010), c. 9, p. 130. David Ganz has suggested that Einhard borrowed an

sketch, it is possible to see at least the outlines of a cluster of scholarship centred around Fulda with an interest both in the histories of Roman emperors and in their perceived edifying value.[59] Frechulf—if we can accepted that he was a monk at Fulda—can also be placed in this context.

Unsurprisingly, Rome's Christian emperors occupied a more conspicuous place in the minds of secular and ecclesiastical elites in the first decades of the ninth century. When the bishops at Paris in 829 addressed Louis and Lothar as 'the most orthodox and invincible *Augusti*', or when Frechulf addressed Judith as the most 'blessed of the empresses' and asked 'who among emperors is nobler or wiser in both sacred and secular learning than the unconquered Caesar Louis', it was the memories of the celebrated rulers from the fourth and fifth centuries that were called to mind. It has been suggested that Louis the Pious's official monogram, found on his charters, was modelled on that used by Theodosius II (died 450) on his coins; Garipzanov suggested, moreover, that Helisachar—whom we encountered in some detail above—was responsible for this change, since it already appears on charters in 808, when Helisachar is first attested as Louis' chancellor in Aquitaine.[60] The figure of Theodosius II also exerted influence through narrative texts: the *Tripartite History* described this emperor as a paragon of Christian virtue, who had a pious wife, who stood out on account of his extraordinary clemency, who ran his court like a monastery, knew scripture by heart, conversed with bishops as if he was once a priest and collected 'sacred books' and the commentaries written on them. Frechulf digested this material into a chapter on 'the most noble life of Theodosius and his wife'.[61] It is hard not read it without thinking of ninth-century representations of Louis the Pious. On the one hand, Thegan's depiction of Louis' devotion, his austere, quasi-monastic discipline and self-restraint as well as the fact that he was au fait with allegorical exegesis; and on the other hand, the Astronomer's tag, that Louis' only fault was that he was all too merciful.[62] According to the *Tripartite History*, Theodosius II's clemency meant that those condemned to death always had their sentences repealed, even if only at the last minute; the Astronomer's Louis, going against the mood of his advisers, refused the death penalty for his nephew Bernard.[63]

---

unusual word (*diaculus*, 'talkative') from the *Historia Augusta*: 'Einhard's Charlemagne', 49.

[59] See further Innes, 'Classical Tradition'.

[60] Ildar H. Garipzanov, *Graphic Signs of Authority in Late Antiquity and the Early Middle Ages* (Oxford: OUP, 2018), 259–60.

[61] *Hist.*, II.5.11, pp. 693–4.

[62] Thegan, *Gesta*, c. 19, pp. 200–4: on this passage, see Innes, 'Politics of Humour' and Staubach, '*Christiana tempora*', 203–4; Astronomer, *Vita*, Prol., p. 284, on which, see Andrew J. Romig, 'In Praise of the Too-clement Emperor: The Problem of Forgiveness in the Astronomer's *Vita Hludowici Imperatoris*', *Speculum*, 89(2) (2014): 382–409.

[63] Astronomer, *Vita*, c. 30, p. 384.

Constantine and Theodosius[64]

It is, however, Constantine and Theodosius I who appear as the Christian emperors 'par excellence'.[65] In Ermoldus Nigellus's poetic description of the frescoes at the palace of Ingelheim (also written in late 820s), representations of Constantine and Theodosius I were followed immediately by the Carolingian rulers.[66] Theodosius I in particular was to be held up as emblematic of Louis the Pious's reign. In part, this was because the Astronomer, one of the emperor's biographers, made a direct comparison between the penance that Louis undertook at Attigny in 822 and Theodosius's. Louis' penance was to atone for the botched blinding of his nephew in 818 that resulted in Bernard's unintended death; Theodosius's came about in 390 after the emperor clamped down on a civil uprising in Thessaloniki with excessive force, reportedly leading to the death of some 7000 of the city's inhabitants.[67] According to the Astronomer: 'imitating the example of Theodosius, Louis accepted a penance on his volition for … the things that he had done to his own nephew'.[68] Mayke de Jong called the Astronomer's account 'the imperial view of the matter'.[69] Conspicuously absent from the *Vita Hludowici*, however, is Bishop Ambrose of Milan, who castigated Theodosius for his immoral actions and urged him to make amends through penance. More often than not, when Carolingian writers remembered Theodosius's penance, they did so not only with explicit reference to Ambrose, but also with reference to one particular source: the *Tripartite History*. Frechulf exemplifies this tendency.

Frechulf devoted a brisk chapter to the penance.[70] It presented a pared-down rendition of the more extensive account found within the *Historia tripartita*, chopping unnecessary side characters and trimming much of the dialogue, leaving only the bare essentials in place. Ambrose was greatly vexed by the emperor's display of unrighteous anger in sanctioning the massacre and so confronted him when he returned to Milan: the emperor's hands were stained with blood and would need ritual cleansing before he would be allowed back into the cathedral

---

[64] Some of this section builds upon Graeme Ward, 'Lessons in Leadership: Constantine and Theodosius in Frechulf of Lisieux's *Histories*', in *The Resources of the Past in Early Medieval Europe*, eds Clemens Gantner, Rosamond McKitterick and Sven Meeder (Cambridge: CUP, 2015), 98–111.

[65] Karl Ferdinand Werner, '*Hludowicus Augustus*: gouverner l'empire chrétien: idées at réalités', in *Charlemagne's Heir: New Perspectives on the Reign of Louis the Pious*, eds Peter Godman and Roger Collins (Oxford: Clarendon Press, 1990), 3–123, at 56–61; Anton, *Fürstenspiegel*, 436–46. On the legal legacy of the Christian emperors, Janet Nelson, 'Translating Images of Authority: The Christian Roman Emperors in the Carolingian World', in *The Frankish World, 750–900* (London: Hambledon Press, 1996), 89–98.

[66] Ermoldus, *In Honorem Hludowici*, IV, ll.2148–63, p. 164

[67] For context, see Neil B. McLynn, *Ambrose of Milan: Church and Court in a Christian Capital* (Berkeley, CA: University of California Press, 1994), esp. 315–330.

[68] Astronomer, *Vita Hludowici Imperatoris*, c. 35, p. 406; trans. Noble, *Charlemagne and Louis the Pious*, 262. On Attigny and the various responses to it, see De Jong, *Penitential State*, 122–31.

[69] De Jong, *Penitential State*, 128.

[70] *Hist.*, II.4.27 [1/28], pp. 659–60.

church. Ambrose offered forthright rebukes. Theodosius, as a ruler 'nurtured in divine learning' who 'plainly knew what was proper to bishops and rulers', responded appropriately: he shed tears of contrition, and returned to the palace where he remained holed up for eight months weeping ceaselessly. Eventually he approached Ambrose, humbly asking how he might regain access to the cathedral church and receive again communion. In response, Ambrose ordered the emperor to issue a corrective law regarding Thessaloniki and to suspend any punishments for thirty days. Theodosius agreed to this, and the problem was resolved. Frechulf concluded with a punchy summary: 'enlightened by the rebukes of the venerable bishop, the most holy emperor made it known that he recognised Bishop Ambrose before all others in truth itself'.[71]

Theodosius was a 'most holy emperor' because he recognised the limits of his own authority: he received Ambrose's rebukes with all due humility and put his admonitions into practice. The emperor was 'enlightened (*inlustratus*)' by Ambrose: Frechulf, it should be remembered, hoped young Charles would be 'enlightened by the deeds of the emperors ... and the teaching of magnificent doctors'. This was a prime example of the sort of lesson from which present-day emperors could learn, with advice-giving bishops like Frechulf implicitly occupying the role of Ambrose. Yet to see princely education as Frechulf's primary aim misses the broader appeal that this influential story had within ninth-century society. That emperors ought to heed episcopal admonition, and indeed should even encourage bishops to extend it, is a theme deeply imprinted within the sources of the 820s.[72]

Other ninth-century bishops, such as Agobard of Lyon and Hincmar of Rheims, also drew on the example of Ambrose and Theodosius when proffering counsel.[73] In his moral handbook for the secular aristocracy, Jonas of Orléans argued that the lay elite, like Theodosius, ought to honour priests, since it was only through priests that sinners could be reconciled with God. Jonas wrote that:

> in adoring and obeying priests and with most abundant honour, [laymen] should imitate the orthodox emperor Theodosius who, having been elevated to power, humbly and reverently obeyed the memorable admonitions, rebukes, and excommunications of the blessed Ambrose. Certainly, Theodosius understood that the power of the emperor, with which he was distinguished, depended upon the power of God, whose servant and minister was Ambrose.[74]

[71] *Hist.*, II.4.27 [29/31], p. 660: 'His et aliis imperator sacratissimus a uenerabili episcopo correptionibus inlustratus eum prae omnibus fatebatur in ueritate se agnouisse episcopum.'
[72] De Jong, *Penitential State*, 112–47 is essential, but see also Van Renswoude, *Rhetoric of Free Speech*.
[73] See further Van Renswoude, *Rhetoric of Free Speech*, 195, n. 82.
[74] Jonas of Orléans, *De Institutione Laicali*, II.20, ed. Odile Dubreucq, *Instruction des Laïcs*, 2 vols (Paris: CERF, 2013), vol. 2, pp. 70–2 '... Imitentur igitur in uenerandis et obtemperandis sacerdotibus potentia, et copiosissimis honoribus sublimatum Theodosium orthodoxum imperatorem, quam humiliter reuerenterque beati Ambrosii memorabilis uiri monitis et increpationibus atque excommunicationibus paruerit. Sciebat nempe potestatem imperialem qua insignitus erat ab illius pendere potestate cuius famulus et minister Ambrosius erat. Hoc qui plenius nosse uoluerit, librum Historiae tripartitae

Kings and elites must respect a bishop's privileged place in Christian society. Jonas, moreover, made clear his source, citing it by book and chapter (thus employing the sort of cross-referencing I noted in Chapters 1 and 5): 'whoever wishes to learn more fully about this [episode] should read book nine, chapter thirty of the *Tripartite History*'. Writing a couple of decades later, and perhaps for Charles the Bald, Sedulius Scottus also excerpted from Cassiodorus's ecclesiastical compendium, although quoting much more of the relevant chapter. Following the account of the affair, he asserted that 'it is proper for good and godly princes to listen humbly and gladly to the wholesome corrections of bishops'.[75] A Christian emperor cannot rule without the men of God: their admonitions must be obeyed. Major decisions concerning the *ecclesia*/empire, moreover, must not be made without episcopal consent.

A model for such decision-making existed in the First Council of Nicaea, convened in 325 by Constantine.[76] Frechulf paid close attention to the Council of Nicaea, or more accurately, to the sources which preserved accounts of it, which he clearly listed: Rufinus's translation of Eusebius's *Ecclesiastical History* as well the *Historia ecclesiastica tripartita*, compiled from 'the histories of three illustrious men, Sozomen, Socrates and Theodoret'.[77] He began with an excerpt from Orosius, which provided a concise outline of the context: 318 bishops gathered together to combat the heretical doctrine of Arius, which had emerged around him at Alexandria.[78] Frechulf then turned to Cassiodorus's *Tripartite History* to set the scene. First, he used this source to describe the 'universality' of the council, and to highlight that it was the 'crown' that Constantine had 'dedicated to his saviour Christ'.[79] Constantine prepared the room for the bishops with chairs and benches as befitting their dignity. He then entered the room after them with a small following, placing a little stool in the middle of the bishops and taking his seat only when they had instructed him to do so. Then that most sacred group/chorus of bishops (*sacratissimus ille chorus*) sat down with him.[80]

---

nonum, sub titulo tricesimo legat.' Jonas's text further exemplifies complex links between dedications and audiences: see Veronese, 'Jonas', 419.

[75] Sedulius Scottus, *De rectoribus christianis*, c. 12, pp. 124 (Latin) and 125 (English). On Sedulius, see comments in Kershaw, *Peaceful Kings*, 223–34, and Nikolaus Staubach, *Rex christianus: Hofkultur und Herrschaftspropaganda im Reich Karls des Kahlen, II: Die Grundlegung der 'religion royale'*, Pictura et poesis 2 (Cologne: Böhlau, 1993), 105–97.

[76] For background, Mark Edwards, 'The First Council of Nicaea', in *The Cambridge History of Christianity, Vol. 1: Origins to Constantine*, eds Margaret M. Mitchell and Frances M. Young (Cambridge: CUP, 2006), 552–67.

[77] *Hist.*, II.3.16 [98/105], p. 601.

[78] *Hist.*, II.3 16 [1/9], p. 597.

[79] *Hist.*, II.3.16 [17/19], p. 598: 'Talem itaque solus a saeculo unus imperator Constantinus Christo coronam uinculo pacis exornans suo saluatori de uictoria inimicorum et hostium Deo decibilem dedicauit.' Compare Sedulius Scottus, *De Rectoribus Christianis*, c. 11, pp. 112 (Latin) and 113 (English), who also utilised the *Historia tripartita* when describing Nicaea.

[80] *Hist.*, II.3.16 [20/27], p. 598.

Rather than continue excerpting from Cassiodorus, Frechulf turned to the tenth book of Rufinus's *Historia ecclesiastica*. The shift from one source to another was seamless, and Rufinus's account perfectly complemented and continued what had come before it. Once everyone had taken their seats, bickering between the various bishops broke out, and Constantine was harassed incessantly by requests to resolve personal and local disputes, all of which came at the expense of dealing with the crucial issue which they had convened to discuss. Constantine's solution was to have the bishops write down their complaints on *libelli*, presumably small bits of parchment. When all the complaints had been gathered, the emperor addressed the quarrelsome bunch:

> God has appointed you as priests, and He has given you power to judge even
> ourselves, so that we are rightly judged by you. But you yourselves cannot be judged
> by men: You are to look forward to a judgment between you from the throne of
> God; for your disputes, whatever they may be, are reserved to that divine tribunal.
> You are gods, given to us by God; and it is not proper for a man to judge gods, but
> only Him of Whom it is written: 'God has stood in the assembly of the gods, and in
> the midst of them He judges the gods' [Psalm 81:1].[81]

The bishops were thus commanded 'to put aside these matters and without contention examine those things which belong to the faith of God'. To end this discord, the emperor ordered that all the gathered *libelli* were to be burned, 'lest the dissension between priests become known to anyone'.[82] To this, Frechulf grafted his own conclusion which stressed the vital point that was implied but not stated outright in the *Ecclesiastical History*: it was not the dissension that would be remembered, but rather that 'all had come together in harmony to attend adroitly to ecclesiastical business'.[83] In the end, the bishops, under the prudent oversight of the emperor, deliberated and acted in unison to defeat a common enemy, whose heretical beliefs had disrupted the peace and stability of the realm.

The image of consensus and harmony coupled with the proper relationship between emperor and bishops are the key features of this scene, to the extent that the religious controversies that sparked Nicaea appear only to play a background role. There is no mention of the Melitian schism or disagreements over the correct date for celebrating Easter, both of which, along with Arius's teachings, had disrupted the *ecclesia*.[84] More to the point, readers would find little in the way of explanation as to what beliefs Arius actually held, or more accurately, what beliefs he was alleged to have held.[85] The prehistory of the council was reduced down to

---

[81] *Hist.*, II.3.16 [36/44], pp. 598–9; trans. Amidon, *Church History*, 10.

[82] *Hist.*, II.3.16 [44/5], p. 599; trans. Amidon, *Church History*, 10.

[83] *Hist.*, II.3.16 [46/7], p. 599: 'sed ecclesiasticum omnes unianimes ad quod uenerant negotium agere solerter inuigilarent'.

[84] See Cassiodorus, *Historia ecclesiastica tripartita*, I.18, pp. 73–6 and I.20, p. 80.

[85] *Hist.*, II.3.15 [6/9], p. 597; cf. II.4.3 [24/9], p. 620.

its bare essentials, as were its outcomes: at this 'venerable council', Frechulf said, the 'great, God-beloved men who were present enacted ecclesiastic laws—which we call canons—and condemned as anathema the perverse doctrine of Arius along with its originator himself'.[86] Not only did the bishop of Lisieux omit any detailed reference to Arianism,[87] he also was silent about what the canons actually prescribed as well as about the Nicene creed, the other vital product of the church's first ecumenical council.

The Contemporaneity of Frechulf's Constantine

Constantine is in many ways a more interesting model than Theodosius, because his early medieval legacy was more complex.[88] Reading through the *Histories*, one would see that Constantine was a pious prince, an *optimus imperator*, who legislated on behalf of the church and adhered to the wisdom of God's earthly representatives. His concern for the *vera religio*, moreover, was such that he supported and defended Christians living beyond the frontiers of his empire, something which, as imperial rulers, both Charlemagne and Louis the Pious had sought to do.[89] Yet Frechulf also preserved one aspect of Constantine's problematic image when he wondered why 'such a man (*tantus vir*)' reportedly had his son Crispus and his nephew Licinius murdered.[90] A further reason, which Frechulf glossed over, pertained to Constantine's Christianity: competing traditions held that Constantine was either baptised at the very end of his life by Eusebius of Nicomedia, a known Arian, or in Rome by Pope Silvester. Both what Frechulf included about Constantine's role at Nicaea, and what he omitted concerning his baptism, illustrate aspects of the *Histories*' contemporaneity.

If Ambrose's rebuking of Theodosius evokes the central role of episcopal admonition in Carolingian society in the 820s, the example of Nicaea brings to mind the importance of councils, as the vital organs of collective decision-making and consensus building in the Carolingian empire, not least in the reign of Louis the Pious. Frechulf's account, despite being ostensibly 'unoriginal', captures

---

[86] *Hist.*, II.3.16 [48/52], p. 599: 'Igitur uenerabili huic concilio ex paucorum memoria conici potest quam magni interfuerunt Deo amabiles uiri, qui leges ecclesiasticas, quos canones uocamus, sanxerunt, et peruersum dogma Arrii cum ipso auctore anathematizantes dampnauerunt.' On knowledge of the outcomes of Nicaea, see Eusebius-Rufinus, *Historia ecclesiastica*, X.6, pp. 965–9; trans. Amidon, *Church History*, 13–16.

[87] See, for example, Eusebius-Rufinus, *Historia ecclesiastica*, X.1 and 5, pp. 960 and 964.

[88] Eugen Ewig, 'Das Bild Constantins des Großen in den ersten Jahrhunderten des abendländischen Mittelalters', *Historisches Jahrbuch*, 75 (1955): 1–46.

[89] *Hist.*, II.3.20 [1/40], pp. 605–7. On Charlemagne: Einhard, *Vita Karoli*, c. 27, pp. 31–2. Louis: Jonathan P. Conant, 'Louis the Pious and the Contours of Empire', *EME*, 22(3) (2014): 336–60.

[90] *Hist.*, II.3.20 [55/57], p. 607: 'Igitur inter haec latent causae cur tantus vir vindicem gladium et destinatam in impios punitionem etiam in proprios egit affectus. Nam Crispum filium suum et Licinium sororis filium interfecit, ut aiunt.' Compare Oros., VII.28.26, p. 78. *Tantus vir* was Frechulf's own addition. The murder of Fausta, Constantine's wife, was not mentioned.

something particular about the period; it is in fact precisely the derivative nature of the *Histories* that connects Frechulf to contemporary bishops, not least Jonas of Orléans.

Constantine's address to the bishops, as recorded in Eusebius-Rufinus, clearly struck a chord with Jonas and his circle. It can be found six times within writings that are attributed to him: it was used twice within the Paris acta, once in the rescript of the 829 acta that was sent to Louis the Pious, once each in his *De institutione laicali* (completed c. 828) and *De institutione regia* (831 or 834), and also as part of the assemblage of materials produced at a later council held in Aachen in 836.[91] In each instance, the moral message was the same: bishops/priests were godlike in that they could not be judged by mere mortals, and as such they must be honoured with fitting reverence. The secular elite must take priestly advice and admonitions to heart, because without the aid of the divine ministry of the priesthood, their souls will be jeopardised. Across his various tracts, Jonas argued this from two angles. Firstly, in his lay mirror, Constantine's address was one of several scriptural and patristic examples (alongside Theodosius's rebuke of Ambrose) that he used to demonstrate why 'honour ought to be displayed to priests': it is only through priests that 'men are reconciled with God'.[92] When pontificating on kingship, he argued that a basic job of a ruler was to ensure that his subjects 'recognise the name, power, force, authority and dignity of priests'.[93] In each of the conciliar examples, Eusebius-Rufinus was then followed by an excerpt from 'Prosper' (but in fact was Julianus Pomerius), in which the roles of priests as the builders and pastors of the church and as heaven's gatekeepers were stressed.[94] Following this excerpt, Jonas then offered the same conclusion:

> For although in life we are inferior to the holy priests of the past, nevertheless the same sacred ministry, which unworthily we have undertaken, exists [in us] with no less authority and dignity; and although we are unworthy of such a ministry, nevertheless on account of God, whose ministry we carry out, it ought not to be despised in us.[95]

---

[91] Jonas of Orléans, *De institutione laicali*, II.20, pp. 58–73; *De institutione regia*, II, ed. Alain Dubreucq, *Jonas d'Orléans: Le metier de Roi* (De institutione regia) (Paris: CERF, 1995), 180-2; Council of Paris (829), pp. 625 and 673; *Episcoporum ad Hludowicum imperatorem relatio*, eds Alfred Boretius and Victor Krause, MGH *Capit.* (Hanover: Hahn, 1897), no. 196, pp. 27–51, at 35-6; Council of Aachen (836), at p. 716.

[92] Jonas, *De institutione laicali*, II.20, p. 58 (*quod sacerdotibus, per quos homines Deo reconciliantur, honor debitus sit exhibendus*).

[93] *De institutione regia*, II, p. 180; cf. *Episcoporum ad Hludowicum imperatorem relatio*, p. 35; Council of Paris (829), p. 673; Council of Aachen (836), p. 716.

[94] Julianus Pomerius, *De vita contemplativa*, II.2, PL 59, cols. 411–520, at 444D-445B; Josh Timmermann, 'Sharers in the Contemplative Virtue: Julianus Pomerius's Carolingian Audience', *Comitatus*, 45 (2014): 1–45.

[95] For example, Council of Paris (829), p. 673: 'Licet enim sanctorum praecedentium sacerdotum vita et meritis longe inferiores simus, idem tamen sacrum ministerium, quod indigni suscepimus, non minoris auctoritatis et dignitatis existit et, quamquam tanto ministerio indigni simus, propter illum

What can we make of this? What does the overlapping use of texts tell us? Does this imply Frechulf and Jonas were both working in the service of moral reform? Jonas's focus was unmistakably upon the bishops at Nicaea, to the extent that the emperor plays only a supporting part. His exaltation of the men of God alone was repeated, but never in context. Frechulf, in contrast, devoted considerable space to what happened before and after the emperor's intervention. In so doing, he made a different point: under a strong and judicious emperor committed to orthodoxy, ecclesiastical unity could be achieved. A negative example of this was given at the beginning of Book 4. When looking at the more turbulent reign of Constantine's son, Constantius II, Frechulf included a densely compressed account of 'the various synods at which the Arians strove to subvert the catholic decrees of the council of Nicaea', which compressed many chapters' worth of events from Cassiodorus, Rufinus and Orosius into a couple of hundred words. The attempt, however, to replace the 'orthodox' church with a 'heterodox' one failed. Constantius, lacking the leadership of his father, was unable to bring the eastern and western bishops to unanimous agreement (*unanimitatem*), which led to even 'greater discord emerging in the churches'.[96]

Recently it has been noted that, in Charlemagne's reign, there was stress on 'unanimity' in the records of church councils, but that this emphasis lost traction over the course of the 820s. Moreover, when Charlemagne convoked a series of five reform councils in 813, he was depicted as having set the agendas as well as having reviewed and signed off on their outcomes.[97] Louis and Lothar, as we saw at the beginning of this chapter, got the ball rolling in 829, yet the bishops' word was final. There is no sense that the emperors were themselves present at the council's deliberations or consulted in the writing up of the acta.[98]

Frechulf's focus on Constantine's active involvement at Nicaea and the unanimity that it engendered might challenge this picture, though I think it would be unwise to see Frechulf's narrative as a direct allegory for contemporary politics, or to envisage that he and Jonas advanced competing, or even alternative, ideas about the roles of emperors and bishops within Christian governance. There are tantalising parallels between the *Histories* and the Paris acta, but to envisage too tight a connection may be counterproductive. It presupposes a shared intention

---

tamen, cuius ministerium gerimus, in nobis non contemnendum est.' Compare Rescript (829), p. 36 and Aachen (836), p. 717.

[96] *Hist.*, II.4.3, pp. 619–20.

[97] On these councils, see Kramer, *Rethinking Authority*, 61–91.

[98] See Florian Hartmann, 'Auf dem Weg zur bischöflichen Dominanz? Entscheidungsfindung und leitende Akteure auf den Konzilien von Frankfurt 794 bis Paris 829', in *Konzilien und kanonisches Recht in Spätantike und frühem Mittelalter: Aspekte konziliarer Entscheidungsfindung*, eds Wolfram Brandes, Alexandra Hasse-Ungeheur and Hartmut Leppin (Berlin: De Gruyter, 2020), 169–90 and Cristina La Rocca and Francesco Veronese, 'Cultures of Unanimity in Carolingian Councils', in *Cultures of Voting in Pre-Modern Europe*, eds Serena Ferente, Lovro Kuncevic and Miles Pattenden (London: Routledge, 2018), 39–57.

which, at least in the case of Frechulf, is overly reductive. Frechulf framed Part II as 'a mirror for princes', but ultimately he produced a very different sort of text than any of Jonas's *specula*: whatever similarities we might note will be overwhelmed by differences in content and form. On the one hand, Theodosius appears once in Jonas's writings, and Constantine, to a limited extent, six times; otherwise, the Roman imperial past is largely absent.[99] Put differently, Jonas drew on Christian Roman historiography, but very selectively. On the other hand, the lessons in imperial and episcopal leadership to which Frechulf drew attention were buried within an expansive narrative built upon the detailed study of the sort of historiographical texts Jonas generally did not use. Frechulf's concern with a progressive narrative, furthermore, stands in contrast to Jonas's more focused, targeted, approach, in which thematically organised chapters conveyed a central moral point (for example, honouring the clergy) and were exemplified through thick helpings of scriptural and patristic citation. Discerning readers of the *Histories* could of course locate particular events using Frechulf's handy *capitula*: for example, II.4.27: 'how Theodosius, having being reproached by Ambrose, earned satisfaction through penance'. Frechulf presumably could have written a more obvious *specula*-style text should he have wished to, but instead he fashioned an expansive *narratio rei gestae*, a narrative of events.

Steffen Patzold was surely correct to identity echoes of the Paris model in the *Histories*, but these are echoes of a broadly shared intellectual milieu rather than a clear reflection of common purpose. The basic unifying factor is that both Jonas and Frechulf were part of the same generation of ecclesiastics who grew up in the cultural boom of the early ninth century and who benefited from the increasing availability of intellectual resources; they were able to dedicate time and energy to digesting scripture and the writings of the fathers, and then put this received, authoritative, knowledge to various new uses. Despite the overlaps, therefore, I am inclined to read these texts as parallel responses to wider elite engagement with the patristic canon.

Frechulf's Constantine resonates with his time of writing in a second way. As Tom Noble once remarked, 'It was not until the ninth century that the Carolingians became comfortable with the ideal of the first Christian emperor.'[100]

[99] Compare Council of Aachen (836), *Epistola ad Pippinum*, III.23, pp. 765–6: 'Qualiter denique ecclesia Christi per successores apostolorum, pastores videlicet eiusdem ecclesiae, sub orthodoxis imperatoribus et, ut de multis unum ponamus, Constantino necnon regibus aliis ac principibus ceterisque fidelibus sua vota Deo offerentibus eamque ecclesiam diversis donariis incrementantibus atque ad alta sublimantibus excreverit, hic enumerare et prolixum est et laboriosum et huic opusculo incapabile.'
[100] Thomas F. X. Noble, 'Tradition and Learning in Search of Ideology: The *Libri Carolini*', in *'The Gentle Voices of Teachers': Aspects of Learning in the Carolingian Age*, ed. Richard E. Sullivan (Columbus, OH: Ohio State University Press, 1995), 227–60, at 247. See also Yitzhak Hen, 'Specula principum carolingi e l'immagine di Costantino', in *Constantino I. Enciclopedia Costantiniana sulla figura e l'immagine dell'imperatore del cosiddetto editto di Milano*, eds Peter Brown *et al.* (Rome: Istituto della

The largely positive image of Constantine in the *Histories* and in Jonas's oeuvre both testify to this. In a letter of 778, Pope Hadrian I called Charlemagne a 'new Constantine' as part of a strategy to get the Frankish king to honour a promise to transfer land conquered in southern Italy to the papacy, evoking the memory of Constantine's lavish gifts to Pope Silvester, as contained in the legendary *Donation of Constantine*.[101] Later in the eighth century, when Constantine's name was invoked in the context of the Christological dispute known as Adoptionism, it was as a warning: Constantine, although he embraced orthodox Christianity at the hands of Pope Silvester, shunned it for Arianism and so ended his life in disgrace.[102] Frechulf's sources offered him options from which to pick and choose what image he wanted to depict. On the one hand, the chronicles of Jerome and Isidore both emphasised the ignominy of Constantine's deathbed baptism at the hands of a known Arian, Eusebius of Nicomedia. Frechulf opted for the account of the *Tripartite History*, which did not draw attention to the Christian identity of Constantine's baptiser nor its implications for the emperor's dubious orthodox status, as perceived by the likes of Jerome. On the other hand, Bede's *Greater Chronicle* stated that Constantine was baptised at Rome.[103] Bede's source, the *Liber pontificalis*, further specified that Constantine was baptised by Pope Silvester, a story which ultimately went back to the fifth-century *Actus Silvestri*, a source which would circulate widely in western Europe and which was the basis of the *Donation of Constantine*, a classic statement of papal primacy that was to have enormous influence on the Latin church.[104] Either in its full or

---

enciclopedia italiana, 2013), online: https://www.treccani.it/enciclopedia/elenco-opere/Enciclopedia_ Costantiniana [last accessed 25 March 2021], who argues that Constantine failed to become an imitable emperor for the Carolingians.

[101] *Codex epistolaris carolinus*, no. 60, ed. Wilhelm Gundlach, MGH *Epp*. III (Berlin: Weidmann, 1892), pp. 469-658, at p. 587. Judson Emerick, 'Charlemagne: A New Constantine?', in *The Life and Legacy of Constantine: Traditions through the Ages*, ed. M. Shane Bjornlie (London: Routledge, 2017), 133–61; see further Thomas Grünewald, '*Constantinus novus*: zum Constantin-Bild des Mittelalters' in *Costantino il Grande: dall'antichità all'umanesimo: Colloquio sul cristianesimo nel mondo antico, Macerata, 18-20 dicembre 1990*, eds Giorgio Bonamente and Franca Fusco, 2 vols (Macerata: Universitá degli studi, 1992), vol. 1, 461–85, at 476-85.

[102] Relevant texts: *Epistola episcoporum Hispaniae ad Karolum Magnum*, ed. Albert Werminghoff, MGH *Conc*. II/1 (Hanover: Hahn, 1906), pp. 120–1, at p. 121, 3/10, and *Epistola Karoli Magni ad Elipandum et Episcopos Hispaniae*, ed. Albert Werminghoff, MGH *Conc*. II/1 (Hanover: Hahn, 1906), pp. 157–64, at p. 161, 32/33. See also Alcuin, *Epistolae*, no. 182, pp. 300–7, at p. 303, 1/4 and p. 307, 16. For comment, see Rutger Kramer, 'Adopt, Adapt and Improve: Dealing with the Adoptionist Controversy at the Court of Charlemagne', in *Religious Franks: Religion and Power in the Frankish Kingdoms: Studies in Honour of Mayke de Jong*, eds Dorine van Espelo, Bram van den Hoven van Genderen, Rob Meens, Janneke Raaijmakers, Irene van Renswoude and Carine van Rhijn (Manchester: MUP, 2016), 32–50, esp. 39–43 and in the same volume, Janneke Raaijmakers and Irene van Renswoude, 'The Ruler as Referee in Theological Debates: Reccared and Charlemagne', in *Religious Franks: Religion and Power in the Frankish Kingdoms: Studies in Honour of Mayke de Jong*, eds Dorine van Espelo, Bram van den Hoven van Genderen, Rob Meens, Janneke Raaijmakers, Irene van Renswoude and Carine van Rhijn (Manchester: MUP, 2016), 51–71, esp. 64–8.

[103] Bede, *DTR*, c. 66, 416, p. 509.

[104] On the *Actus*: see Kristina Sessa, 'Constantine and Silvester in the Actus Silvestri', in *The Life and*

its scaled-down Bedan form, this aspect of Constantine's legacy was ignored by Frechulf.[105] Why?

According to Johannes Fried, Frechulf expressed an anti-papal sentiment held by a prominent faction at Louis the Pious's court, whose leading figures included Part I's exulted dedicatee, Helisachar.[106] Frechulf's anti-, or at the very least non-papal vision of Constantine also fed into Fried's controversial argument, published twenty years later, that the above-mentioned *Donation* was not a product of late eighth-century Rome, as was traditionally believed, but was forged at St Denis or Corbie in the 830s.[107] To be sure, Fried's observation that, in the second volume of Frechulf's *Histories*, the bishops of Rome play an insignificant part is correct. Neither the popes, as historical actors, nor the papacy as an institution, are given much space at all. Also sound is Fried's observation that the penultimate chapter of the *Histories*, in which an imperial decree of Phocas recognised the 'Roman and apostolic see as the head of all churches', had little to do with the juridical primacy of the contemporary papacy. To see Frechulf's compendium as being deliberately anti-papal, however, is going too far. Carolingian ecclesiology, especially as conceptualised at the Council of Paris, was not explicitly papal; rather, it was more broadly episcopal. Bishops, by virtue of their *ministerium*, considered themselves to be the rightful successors of the Apostles. Bishops were the conduits of authentic Christianity and they, collectively, controlled access to heaven, since they were imbued with the special power of binding and loosing (Matthew 16:19), powers that by the eleventh century, the reform papacy would start to claim exclusively as prerogative.[108] Even if Frechulf did not shape his *Histories* explicitly with the 'Paris model' in mind, he was still part of an episcopate for whom the popes of Rome had not assumed the position of juridical primacy they later would. This picture already began to change around the middle of the ninth century with the creation of the Pseudo-Isidorean decretals, an audacious forgery project which

---

Legacy of Constantine: Traditions through the Ages, ed. M. Shane Bjornlie (London: Routledge, 2017), 77–91. On the *Liber pontificalis*, see Rosamond McKitterick, *Rome and the Invention of the Papacy: The Liber Pontificalis* (Cambridge: CUP, 2020).

[105] All Bede's Carolingian continuators preserved the Rome story. For example, Ado, *Chronicon*, col. 91D: 'Constantinus in fide eruditus a B. Silvestro papa, fecit miro opere baptisterium Romae, ubi baptisatus est iuxta basilicam B. Joannis Baptistae, quae appellatur Constantiniana.'

[106] Johannes Fried, 'Ludwig der Fromme, das Papsttum und die fränkische Kirche', in *Charlemagne's Heir: New Perspectives on the Reign of Louis the Pious (814–840)*, eds Peter Godman and Roger Collins (Oxford: Clarendon Press, 1990), 231–73, at 238–9. Kathleen G. Cushin, 'Papal Authority and Its Limitations,' in *The Oxford Handbook of Medieval Christianity*, ed. John H. Arnold (Oxford: OUP, 2014), 515–530 offers a clear overview.

[107] Johannes Fried, *Donation of Constantine and Constitutum Constantini: The Misinterpretation of a Fiction and its Original Meaning. With a contribution by Wolfram Brandes: 'The Satraps of Constantine'* (Berlin: De Gruyter, 2007), with discussion of Frechulf at 65–7. Caroline J. Goodson and Janet L. Nelson, 'The Roman Contexts of the "Donation of the Constantine"', *EME*, 18(4) (2010): 446–67, respond to Fried's argument and reaffirm the traditional dating.

[108] For example, Council of Paris (829), c. 4, pp. 611–12.

established some of the crucial foundations upon which papal reformers would draw in subsequent centuries.[109] The False Decretals are one of the earliest, and certainly most significant witnesses to the reception history of the *Donation of Constantine*; a version of Constantine's speech to the bishops at Nicaea was also incorporated into this canonical collection. Although separated by only around two decades, Frechulf's vision of the church and his understanding of the past were a far cry from those of Pseudo-Isidoreans.

Conclusion: *Historia, Ecclesia* and Empire

Detaching Frechulf from a focused context of political engagement reveals larger points about Christian history and the interlinked relationship between church and empire in the ninth century: by way of conclusion, I want to sketch out some of these larger points. To study the *Histories* would not just have been to learn about imperial-ecclesiastical relations, but rather to learn the basic shape and dynamics of Christianity, of a world created and governed by God, a world whose origins were detailed in the Old Testament and more fully revealed in the New. The Council of Paris, which was convoked by Louis the Pious and Lothar, had come to the conclusion that the sorry state of the world at the end of the 820s was the consequence of 'the just judgment of God'. *Historia*, in the form of the Old Testament and Christian historiography alike, was the record of God's vengeful interventions in human affairs.[110] The second volume of Frechulf's *Histories* was replete with such examples: the destruction of Jerusalem in AD 70 was believed to have been the result of divine punishment (*iusta Dei ultioni*) against the Jews for Christ's crucifixion; centuries later, the emperor Julian (died 363) 'deservedly suffered punishment [of death] because willingly he deserted God, the author of all'; Frechulf explicitly attributed an unusually potent storm that tore through Constantinople in 367 to 'God's indignation … on account of the exile and persecution of God's servants exacted by the emperor and the Arians'.[111] The death of the emperor in question—Valens—is especially pertinent. Frechulf's source was Orosius, who had written that Valens's death came about 'by the righteous judgment of God (*iusto iudicio Dei*)' and functioned as an *exemplum* of 'divine wrath for future generations'.[112] *Iusto iudicio Dei* was the very same phrase used by the bishops at Paris when taking stock of contemporary woes. Within this shared vocabulary can be found an essential link: God punished sinners in

---

[109] Much has been written: Erik Knibbs's website, https://pseudo-isidore.com/, is a good place to begin.
[110] Robert A. H. Evans, 'God's Judgment in Carolingian Law and History Writing', in *The Church and the Law*, eds Rosamond McKitterick, Charlotte Methuen and Andrew Spicer, *Studies in Church History*, 56 (2020): 60–77.
[111] *Hist.*, II.2.1 [1/6], p. 496; II.4.9 [87/9], p. 634; II.4.21 [19/21], p. 651. Similar examples: II.4.4 [29.30], p. 622; II.4.24 [40.41], p. 657; II.5.19 [23], p. 712.
[112] *Hist.*, II.4.20 [24/6], p. 650; trans. Fear, 383.

the past, and continued to do so in the present. Although this may be stating the obvious, it is worth bearing in mind that the *ecclesia* over which Louis the Pious and Lothar ruled, and which was seen to be in dire need of correction, was the very same *ecclesia* whose growth Frechulf had charted throughout Part II.[113] Church history—in the broadest sense of the term—and the contemporary ecclesia/empire were different eras of the same universal story, which began with the world's creation and was transformed by Christ's Incarnation. This implies a dynamic relationship between past and present: the study of authoritative texts informed current practices because these texts represented earlier phases of the same divinely created world that Carolingian ecclesiastics still inhabited.

   Christian *historiae* were a versatile and multipurpose group of texts, and for this reason their audiences and uses of are best thought of in the plural. Frechulf was in many ways unusual amongst other Carolingian compilers because of the extent to which he made Christian historiography the principal focus of his compendium. Yet his core resources, individually and collectively, were foundational and canonical, and they served a range of purposes within Carolingian intellectual life. Jonas of Orléans's repeated use of Constantine's address to the bishops, as preserved in Eusebius-Rufinus, offers one example of historiography's relevance.

   In addition to reinforcing moral norms amongst secular and ecclesiastical elites, history could also be put to exegetical uses. To understand the text of the Bible as well as the overall context in which its various books unfolded, eighth- and ninth-century churchmen turned to many of the very same histories and chronicles utilised by Frechulf. As we saw in Chapter 4, Orosius's *Histories against the Pagans* functioned as an aid for biblical commentators such as Hrabanus Maurus. The abbot of Fulda could also deploy the text in other, exegetically adjacent, texts. Towards the end of 834, he dedicated a treatise to Louis the Pious, known as *De honore parentum*, or 'Concerning the honour owed to parents and the submission required by sons'.[114] The work consists principally of biblical citations that exemplify a range of different issues that were offered to console Louis after he was deposed and forced to perform public penance in 833. Non-scriptural history makes an occasional appearance, for instance in a chapter about the importance of honouring the royal office and what happens to those who dishonour it. Hrabanus first selected some biblical passages that highlighted the importance of obedience, before offering some cases from the Old Testament about how 'arrogance' and 'rebellion' directed against legitimate rulers displeased God. Hrabanus then shifted to *Christiana tempora*:

---

[113] Cf. *Hist.*, II.3.1 [3/8], p. 558: '... quoniam mirabiliter ecclesiam suo redemptam sanguine dilitare ...' and Council of Paris (829), p. 607: 'ecclesiam, quam Christus, qui eam suo pretioso sanguine redemit'.
[114] Hrabanus Maurus, *De honore parentum*, ed. Ernst Dümmler, MGH *Epp.* V (Berlin: Weidmann, 189), pp. 403–15. On this treatise, see Mayke de Jong, 'Hraban as Mediator: *De Honore Parentum* (Autumn 834)', in *Splendor Reginae. Passions, genre et famille: Mélanges en l'honneur de Régine Le Jan*, eds Laurent Jégou, Sylvie Joye, Thomas Lienhard, and Jens Schneider (Turnhout: Brepols, 2015), 49–58.

> Although history records these ancient deeds from long ago, similar examples are not lacking from Christian times. For tyrants, who, with rash insolence rose up against their legitimate lords, did not escape unpunished; rather, condemned by the just judgment of God, suffered the punishment they deserved.[115]

Theodosius I, who was described as the 'most glorious and faithful emperor', provided a choice example of how unjust insurrection could be overcome when, through the power of prayer, he faced and defeated the usurping pagan Eugenius at the River Frigidus in 394 (Oros., VII.35). Old Testament *historia* was thus set against events from Christian times, as recorded by Orosius, with the latter flowing on from the former in a continuous stream. The *Historiae*, therefore, could be employed to make sense of scripture, or be read as an extension of its sacred narrative.

Or, take the example of the *Historia ecclesiastica tripartita*. Two liturgical exegetes, Amalarius and Walahfrid Strabo, mined this text for facts and arguments about the origins and development of Christian worship.[116] For Frechulf, it was an important source for Christian imperial history between Constantine and Theodosius II: in this chapter, we encountered it specifically in relation to the penance of Theodosius I. Irene van Renswoude has recently made the tantalising suggestion that the ninth-century copy of the *Tripartite History* made at Corbie (and now in St Petersburg, National Library of Russia, F.v.I. no. 11) played a role in Louis' decision to atone for his sins in 822. Adalhard of Corbie pored over this manuscript during his period in exile on the island abbey of Noirmoutier between 814 and 821/2, and its account of Ambrose's fearless admonition may have sparked his imagination. Upon his return to court, Adalhard urged the emperor to go on the penitential offensive at Attigny in 822.[117] What is more, in one of the most thrilling early medieval discoveries of recent decades, Klaus Zechiel-Eckes conclusively demonstrated that this very same codex was instrumental in the genesis of the False Decretals of Pseudo-Isidore, which we encountered very

---

[115] Hrabanus Maurus, *De honore parentum*, c. 3, p. 408: 'Sed et haec licet antiquitus facta veterum prodat historia, tamen huiuscemodi christianis temporibus non desunt exempla.Nam tyranni, qui contra dominos legitimos subita insolentia se aerexerant, non inpuniti evaserant, sed iusto iudicio Dei dampnati poenas condignas luebant.'

[116] Amalarius, *Liber officials*, IV.7.9, pp. 432–3 (singing of antiphons started by Ignatius of Antioch); I.14.9, p. 102 (on the roots of the adoration of the Holy Cross); Amalarius of Metz, *Epistula Amalarii ad Hilduinum abbatem*, 11, 75, 77, ed. Jean-Michel Hanssens, *Amalarii episcopi opera liturgica omnia I: Introductio—opera minora*, Studi e Testi 138 (Vatican City: Biblioteca apostolica vaticana, 1948), pp. 341–58, at 343, 354–5 (on liturgical diversity between different eastern and western churches). Walahfrid Strabo, *Libellus de exordiis et incrementis quarundam in observationibus ecclesiasticis rerum*, cc. 20 and 25, trans. Alice Harting-Correa, *Walahfrid Strabo's Libellus de exordiis et incrementis quarundam in observationibus ecclesiasticis rerum. A Translation and Liturgical Commentary* (Leiden: Brill, 1996), pp. 110–11 and 158–89. Both Amalarius and Walahfrid cited the *Historia tripartita* by chapter and book.

[117] The connection to Adalhard stems from an eleventh-century colophon: Van Renswoude, *Rhetoric*, 198.

briefly above. Short passages marked up with distinctive marginalia correspond exactly with the forged decretals of a number of early popes.[118] Engagement with the *Historia tripartita* thus shaped the interpretation of Christian worship as well as the creation of ecclesiastical procedural law.[119]

Even such a cursory sketch of the reception of particular sources reveals that Carolingian churchmen drew on historiography in various different contexts. This is not surprising. These were canonical texts, of which monks and clerics trained in monastic and cathedral schools would have had intimate knowledge. In making his *Histories*, Frechulf was not rescuing rare knowledge that was in danger of being forgotten, but was compressing what was essential to know in one practical compendium. The *Histories* themselves, just like the central components from which they were fashioned, would have served no one single purpose; rather, they helped to equip an ecclesiastical elite with a foundational knowledge of their Church's past, which they could activate and utilise elsewhere.

---

[118] Klaus Zechiel-Eckes, 'Ein Blick in Pseudoisidors Werkstatt. Studien zum Entstehungsprozess der falschen Dekretalen: Mit einem exemplarischen editorischen Anhang (Pseudo-Julius an die orientalischen Bischöfe, JK †196)', *Francia*, 28(1) (2001): 37–90.

[119] Erik Knibbs, 'Ebo of Rheims, Pseudo-Isidore, and the Date of the False Decretals', *Speculum*, 92(1) (2017): 144–83, at 158–64, 173.

Conclusion

History was written and read in the early Middle Ages for many different reasons and put to a wide variety of uses. The political functions and applications of historiography, and above all the writing of new contemporary narratives, have been intensively analysed by modern scholars over the past half-century. The contexts in which the authoritative histories of the earlier Christian past were copied and routinely studied by Carolingian ecclesiastics have received far less attention. This study has sought to address this imbalance. Using the *Histories* of Frechulf of Lisieux as my primary case study, this book has sought out the basic educative and exegetical functions that historiography served for monks and clerics in Carolingian Europe. Seen from this perspective, history was read in order to understand the world created and governed by God. History, as Cassiodorus had clearly already expressed in the mid-sixth century, served to 'instruct the minds of the readers in heavenly matters'. Cassiodorus in part helped to define a canon of Christian history, and it is precisely on this canon that my study has focused. The various components of the historiographical canon served myriad functions within ecclesiastical life, teaching students not only what happened in the past but also instructing them in chronology, geography and grammar. Moreover, authoritative texts, such as Josephus's *Antiquities* (which, although authored by a Jewish priest became absorbed into the Christian canon), Eusebius-Jerome's *Chronicle* and Orosius's *Histories against the Pagans*, also taught scripture. They helped set the events of the Bible in context as well as to frame the over-narrative in which scripture took place, beginning with the world's creation, as told in Genesis, before being transformed by the birth of Christ and the New Testament.

Biblical commentary has remained in the background throughout this book because it conditioned how history was encountered and guided its application: Cassiodorus's survey of Christian historians, after all, came in the context of a handbook on the study of scripture. Exegesis was ubiquitous to all medieval Christian intellectual culture. According to Chelia Chazelle and Burton van Name Edwards, 'most Carolingian scholarly work was essentially exegetical in orientation; it participated in or was influenced by the drive to understand the

Bible and patristic exegesis of its contents.'[1] A central objective of this study was to locate the study of the past in the Carolingian world within these broad contours. To this end, Frechulf is an especially valuable case study, not only because the substantial size of his text allows for in-depth analysis, but also because the means by which he compiled it reveal how he engaged with his resources. For the educated elite, these sources would have been well known. The evidence of library catalogues, manuscript transmission and indirect usage show clearly that historians such as Orosius, Josephus and Eusebius were copied, read and utilised throughout the early Middle Ages and especially during the Carolingian centuries. Nonetheless, the two-volume structure of the *Histories* and Frechulf's innovative use of exegetical language—'the truth of history'—supply unusually detailed insight into the hermeneutical approach to historical knowledge.

Despite the wide diffusion of the principal texts Frechulf used and the ubiquity of the form of compilation that he practised, his *Histories* have no direct antecedents in the early Middle Ages. The unusualness of the project, in terms of its shape, size and focus, should not, however, preclude us from appreciating the fact that it reveals a process—the study of Christian historiography—that often was ongoing in ecclesiastical centres of learning in the Carolingian age and well beyond. History books regularly would have been read, even if this cannot always be appreciated in the sort of detail that Frechulf's work allows. The *Liber tramitis*, an eleventh-century monastic customary produced under Abbot Odilo of Cluny (died 1049), listed which of the abbey's books were given out and to whom, in order to be read during Lent, as per the Rule of Benedict's prescription that monks, during this liturgical season, were to read one book the whole way through.[2] Amongst the many exegetical and patristic books distributed, we find also that a brother Wirardus was given the 'Historiam of Josephus', a brother Umbertus was given the 'Storia aecclesiastica of Eusebius of Caesarea', a brother Bernard given 'Orosium', another Umbertus given Augustine's *City of God* and a certain Girbertus was given Bede's 'Hystoriam Anglorum'. At Cluny, the reading of history was a liturgical act, an exercise in monastic discipline and devotion. Frechulf's exegetical compendium traces a broad intellectual context that later sources reveal more sharply.

The authoritative resources that Frechulf made the objects of his compendium continued to be read throughout the Latin Middle Ages, and the essential connection between history and exegesis continued to inform how intellectuals

---

[1] Chazelle and van Name Edwards, 'Introduction', 6.

[2] *Regula Benedicti*, c. 48, 15–16, ed. Rudolf Hanslik, CSEL 75 (Vienna, 1960), p. 117; *Liber tramitis aevi Odilonis abbatis*, ed. Peter Dinter, CCM 10 (Siegburg, F. Schmitt, 1980), 261–64. See also André Wilmart, 'Le couvent et la bibliothèque de Cluny vers le milieu du XIᵉ siècle', *Revue Mabillon*, 11 (1921), 89–124.

approached and conceptualised the past.[3] Did Frechulf's *Histories* contribute to this? The reception history of the bishop of Lisieux's work remains to be written, yet the raw materials for such an endeavour have already been prepared in the form of Michael Allen's detailed assessment of the text's manuscript transmission.[4] The pattern it suggests is to some extent a familiar one: after a burst of activity in the ninth century, there is an ostensible dip in the tenth before a resurgence of interest in the second half of the eleventh century. By the twelfth century, Frechulf himself was catalogued amongst the great authorities of the church when new versions of Jerome's bio-bibliographic dictionary, *On Illustrious Men*, were produced; around this time, his name also first appears in historiographical prologues when authors namechecked him amongst the past authorities they had consulted when compiling their own narratives.[5]

It has long been held that a similar story of a post-Carolingian dip reflects the fate of other authoritative compilations of the Carolingian age, such as liturgical commentary and above all biblical commentary.[6] According to an older historiographical tradition, this was taken as evidence that the tenth century was a period of rupture, characterised not only by the political fragmentation and the collapse in public authority that came about after the death of the last Carolingian emperor, Charles the Fat, but also a marked decline in intellectual culture that was only to be revived around the middle of the eleventh century. This was an age of iron and darkness that interrupted the Carolingian and twelfth-century 'renaissances'. Such a view is no longer tenable, and the period between c. 900 and c. 1050 is in the process of being thoroughly reassessed.[7] For example, although

---

[3] Mégier, *Christliche Weltgeschichte*.

[4] *Prolegomena*, pp. 55*–179*. Schelle, 'Frechulf von Lisieux', 150–71, although largely superseded, remains useful.

[5] See for example, Sigebert of Gembloux, *De viris illustribus*, c. 91, ed. Robert Witte, *Catalogus Sigeberti Gemblacensis monachi de viris illustribus. Kritische Ausgabe* (Bern and Frankfurt, Peter Lang, 1974), p. 79 and Wolfger of Prüfening, *De scriptoribus ecclesiasticis*, c. 61, ed. Francis R. Swietek, 'Wolfger of Prüfening's *De scriptoribus ecclesiasticis*: A Critical Edition and Historical Evaluation' (Unpublished PhD Dissertation, University of Illinois, 1978), p. 142; see also Allen, Prologomena, 80* and 126*. For examples of later chroniclers: Richard of Poitiers, *Chronicon*, ed. Georg Waitz, MGH SS 26 (Hanover: Hahn, 1882), 74–86, at 77: 'Hoc opusculum excerpsi de libris Augustini, Ieronimi, Ysidori, Theodulfi; Iosephi, Egesippi, Eutropii, Titi Livii, Suetonii, Aimoini, Iustini adbreviatoris seu excerptoris Pompeii Trogi, Friculphi, Orosii, Anastasii bibliothecarii Romane sedis, Annei Flori, Gregorii Turonensis, Bede, Adonis, Gilde Britonum hystoriographi, Pauli monachi Langobardorum hystoriographi et quorumdam aliorum ...'; the *Annales Parchenses*, s.a. 1, ed. Georg Heinrich Pertz, MGH SS 16 (Hanover: Hahn, 1859), 598–608, at 598: 'Iohannes baptista nascitur. Hucusque Freculphus historiographus. Hic incipit cronica Marianus Scotus et Regino abbas Prumiensis. 909 Regino abbas Prumiensis cronicam suam ab incarnatione Domini inchoatam usque ad hunc annum perduxit.'

[6] See for example, Roger Reynolds, 'Liturgical Scholarship at the Time of the Investiture Controversy: Past Research and Future Opportunities', *The Harvard Theological Review*, 71 (1978): 109–24.

[7] See especially recent collected volumes: Sarah Greer, Alice Hicklin and Stefan Esders (eds), *Using and not Using the Past after the Carolingian Empire, c. 900–c.1050* (London: Routledge, 2020) and Warren Pezé (ed.), *Wissen und Bildung in einer Zeit bedrohter Ordnung: der Zerfall des Karolingerreiches um 900 = Knowledge and Culture in Times of Threat: The Fall of the Carolingian Empire (ca. 900)* (Stuttgart:

no new biblical commentaries such as those compiled by Hrabanus Maurus were produced, Carolingian compendia themselves continued to be copied and read.[8] The efforts of Carolingian compilers to write 'useful' texts evidently paid off: the basic need to have patristic commentary on each book of the Bible had largely been met, and so later readers and teachers were content to adapt Carolingian compilations as they saw fit.

The transmission and reception of historical texts parallels this scenario. Regino of Prüm (died 915) is usually taken as the last of the Carolingian historians.[9] Rosamond McKitterick noted, however, that 'it is by no accident that the most important world chronicles of the eleventh and twelfth centuries by Hermann of Reichenau, Sigebert of Gembloux, and Marianus Scotus are all closely connected with centres associated with surviving manuscripts of Regino'.[10] Frechulf was a demonstrably valuable source for another prominent representative of the central medieval tradition of universal history-writing: the *Chronicle* of Frutolf. Frutolf was a monk at the abbey of Michelsberg in Bamberg who wrote on a wide range of topics; an extensive universal chronicle, which he completed c. 1099, is one of his best known texts.[11] As a chronicler, Frutolf has been studied for his trenchant views on Gregory VII and the Investiture Controversy.[12] A large part of the text, however, was a compilation of pre-existing historiographical sources, very much in the Frechulfian mode.[13] The resources he drew on will now be familiar, as they were part of the canon Frechulf helped consolidate: the historical writings of Josephus, Eusebius-Jerome's *Chronicle*, Orosius's *Historiae* and Augustine's *City of God*. More excitingly, Frechulf's *Histories* themselves were a crucial source for Frutolf: with some careful reading, they can very easily be discerned in the text published in the MGH. In Georg Waitz's now very out-of-date edition of 1844, passages excerpted directly from known sources were printed in a smaller font, to distinguish them visually from passages in a larger font, which were presumed

---

Hiersemann, 2020). On the question of political change, see Charles West, *Reframing the Feudal Revolution: Political and Social Transformation between Marne and Moselle, c. 800–c. 1100* (Cambridge: CUP, 2013).

[8] Sumi Shimahara, 'L'exégèse biblique de la fin du IXe siècle au milieu du XIe siècle. État des lieux', in *Wissen und Bildung in einer Zeit bedrohter Ordnung: der Zerfall des Karolingerreiches um 900 = Knowledge and Culture in Times of Threat: The Fall of the Carolingian Empire (ca. 900)*, ed. Warren Pezé (Stuttgart: Hiersemann, 2020), 103–46.

[9] See Koziol, 'Future of History'.

[10] McKitterick, *Perceptions of the Past*, 31.

[11] In the MGH edition, the text is misattributed to Frutolf's continuator, Ekkehard of Aura: *Ekkehardi Uraugiensis Chronica*, ed. Georg Waitz, MGH SS 6 (Hanover: Hahn, 1844), 33–211. A new edition is in preparation, partially now available online: https://mgh.de/die-mgh/editionsprojekte/bamberger-weltchronistik. There is an English translation of the entries between 1001 and 1101 by T. J. H. McCarthy, *Chronicles of the Investiture Contest: Frutolf of Michelsberg and his Continuators* (Manchester: MUP, 2014), 85–137.

[12] T .J .H. McCarthy, 'Frutolf of Michelsberg's Chronicle, the Schools of Bamberg, and the Transmission of Imperial Polemic', *Haskins Society Journal*, 23 (2001): 51–70.

[13] Horst Lößlein, 'Beobachtungen zur Arbeitsweise Frutolfs von Michelsberg', *DA*, 74 (2018): 585–638.

to have been Frutolf's own additions: this was, and often still is, common editorial practice. Remarkably, a considerable number of Frutolf's ostensibly 'original' contributions, which stand out clearly in Waitz's edition, were in fact direct borrowings from Frechulf. These borrowings matched Frechulf's own formulations, rather than those he had extracted from his sources: Frutolf was not citing one of the sources the *Histories* were based on.[14] Although it has not survived, there was a copy of the *Histories* at Bamberg cathedral, from which Frutolf likely worked.[15] In late eleventh-century Bamberg, therefore, the *Histories* thus served not only as a prior example of how the canon of Christian historiography could be effectively synthesised, but also illustrated Frechulf's own role in shaping and building upon this synthesis. Frutolf's work would go on to serve as one of the foundations of Otto of Freising's even more renowned universal chronicle.[16] Directly and indirectly, Frechulf thus contributed to the longer development of narrative- and exegetically-driven medieval histories of the world. As a work of Carolingian history-writing, the *Histories* can still seem odd to modern students due to the text's seemingly derivative content and lack of obviously Carolingian coverage. The creation and reception of Frechulf's work makes it clear, however, that in the ninth century and beyond his work instructed the minds of many ecclesiastical readers in how to interpret and make sense of the past.

[14] Examples of Frutolf's borrowings from Frechulf are given in the appendix.
[15] *Prolefomena*, p. 169*.
[16] Otto of Freising, *Chronica sive Historia de Duabus Civitatis*, ed. Adolf Hofmeister, MGH *SRG* 45 (Hanover: Hahn, 1912).

Appendix: Frutolf of Michelsberg's Borrowings from Frechulf

Passages from Frutolf's *Chronica* are from *Ekkehardi Uraugiensis Chronica*, ed. Georg Waitz, MGH *SS* 6 (Hanover: Hahn, 1844), pp. 33-211.

Example 1

Frutolf: Ex supra dictis autem liquido claret, exordium litterarum ab ipso primo homine coepisse, qui adhuc supererat, quando filii eius in sapientiae studio fervebant. (*Chronica*, p. 35, 22/24.)

Frechulf: Liquido namque claret ab ipso exordium litterarum primo homine coepisse, qui adhuc supererat quando filii ac nepotes sui in studio sapientiae feruebant. (*Hist.*, I.1.12 [6/8], pp. 40-1.)

Example 2

Frutolf: Divisiones autem linguarum 72 fuisse, hystoriae declarant, non quod solummodo tot homines tunc fuissent et non plures; sed tot iam principes familiarum ex filiis Noe procreatos ostendit, qui populos et gentes condiderunt. (*Chronica*, p. 35, 56/58.)

Frechulf: Diuisiones autem linguarum LXXII fuisse historia declarat, non ut solummodo tot homines tunc fuissent et non plures, sed tot iam principes familiarum ex filiis Noe procreatos ostendit qui populos et gentes condiderunt. (*Hist.*, I.1.28 [39/42], pp. 59-60.)

Example 3

Frutolf: Hic oritur dissonantia hystoriarum in annis videlicet Salomonis, qui in libro Regum dicitur annis quadraginta regnasse, Iosephus vero dicit, eum annis octoginta regnum tenuisse, et omne vitae illius spacium annorum 94 fuisse. (*Chronica*, p. 46, 12/14.)

Frechulf: Hic namque dissonantia oritur historiarum in annis uidelicet regni Salomonis, dum XL eum regnasse annis in libris legitur Regum, Iosepphus autem LXXX et omne uitae illius spatium ann. XCIIII fuisse adserit. (*Hist.*, I.3.5 [2/5], p. 165.)

Example 4

Frutolf: Hic tantae fuit fortitudinis, ut etiam Maiestenes in quarto Indicorum libro nitatur approbare, hunc regem fortitudine et actuum magnitudine Herculem transcendisse. (*Chronica*, p. 53, 61/63.)

Frechulf: Ergo Nabugodonosor tantae fuit fortitudinis ut etiam Maiestenis in quarto Indicorum libro nitatur adprobare hunc regem fortitudine et actuum magnitudine Herculem transcendisse. (*Hist.*, I.3.17 [52/54], p. 190.)

Example 5[1]

Frutolf: Hunc ergo finem regni Babylonici, quem diximus, fuisse cognovimus. Sed cum tam potentes atque famosi Babyloniorum existerent reges, queritur, quaenam causa sit, cur non in numero et ordine illustrium habeantur regum. Scimus enim, quoniam regnum Assyriorum, quod a Semiramide, Nini uxore, in Babylonia est fundatum, diuturno tempore in ea et usque ad Sardanapallum permansit. Quo interfecto, a Medorum prefecto Arbace regnum Assyriorum in Medos est translatum, Medorumque reges exinde in ordine et numero ab hystoriographis traduntur, donec ad Persas translatum est regnum. Ergo si regnum Assyriorum translatum est ad Medos, nunc regnum Babyloniorum quod sit si quis scire voluerit, recolat Asiam a Nino occupatam totumque orientem usque ad Indos, ab uxore vero eius insuper Aethyopas aliasque nationes regno Assyriorum esse subiectas. Ex quo apparet, discedentem ad Medos Arbacem maximam regni partem dignitatemque invasisse ac penes se in Media retinuisse. Chaldei vero Babyloniam sibi adversus Medos vendicaverunt, et ita potestas Babyloniae apud Medos, proprietas vero regni apud Chaldeos fuit. Chaldei autem propter antiquam regiae urbis dignitatem, non suam dignitatem, sed illius vocare maluerunt. Unde factum est, ut Nabuchodonosor ceterique post eum reges usque ad Darium et Cyrum, qui Chaldeorum regnum civitatemque Babyloniam destruxerunt, quamvis Chaldeorum viribus potentes, nomine tamen Babyloniae clari legantur. (*Chronica*, p. 54, 7/23.)

Frechulf: Igitur dum tam potentes atque famosi Babylloniorum existerent reges, quaeritur quaenam causa sit cur non in numero et cardine inlustrium habentur

---

[1] Already identified by Goez, *Translatio imperii*, 108–9.

regum. Scimus enim quoniam regnum Assyriorum, quod a Semiramide Nini uxore est in Babyllonia fundatum, diuturno tempore in ea et usque ad Sardanapallum permansit. Quo interfecto a praefecto Medorum Arbace regnum Assyriorum in Medos esse translatum, Medorumque reges in cardine et numero ab historiographis traduntur donec ad Persas translatum est. Ergo si translatum est Assyriorum regnum ad Medos et cum eis retentum, sicut historiae declarant, nunc Babylloniorum regnum quod sit si quis scire uoluerit, recolat Asiam a Nino occupatam totumque Orientem usque ad terminos Indiae, ab uxore uero eius insuper Ethiopas aliasque nationes regno Assyriorum esse subiectas. Ex quo apparet discedente Arbace ad Medos, partem regni maximam dignitatemque inuasisse ac paenes se in Media retinuisse; Chaldei uero Babylloniam sibi aduersus Medos uindicauerunt. Ita quippe potestas Babylloniae apud Medos, proprietas uero regni apud Chaldeos fuit. Chaldei autem propter antiquam dignitatem regiae urbis, non suam dignitatem, sed illius uocare maluerunt. Vnde factum est ut Nabugodonosor ceterique post eum reges usque ad Cyrum et Darium, qui Chaldeorum regnum ciuitatemque Babylloniam destruxerunt, quamuis Chaldeorum uiribus potentes, nomine tamen Babylloniae clari legantur. (*Hist.*, I.3.17 [70/93], pp. 191-2.)

Example 6

Frutolf: Phytagoras Samius, a quo ferunt phylosophiae nomen exortum, qui et arithmeticae artis et musicarum consonantiarum repertor **fuisse dicitur, eisdem temporibus fuisse fertur**. (*Chronica*, p. 54, 27/28.)

Frechulf: Phitagoras autem Samius, a quo etiam ferunt philosophiae nomen exortum, qui et arithmeticae artis inuentor **fuisse dicitur, eodem tempore claruisse fertur**. (*Hist.*, I.3.17 [172/74] p. 195. Bold text is not in Augustine, *DCD*, VIII.2, Frechulf's source, but is Frechulf's own addition.)

Example 7

Frutolf: Ergo venia reaedificandi templi sub Cyro exordium habuit, sed impedientibus inimicis mansit imperfectum usque ad Darium, cuius regni anno secundo a Zorobabel et Hiesu construitur, et quarto aedificationis anno, qui est Darii sextus, perficitur opus, iuxta Iosephum vero anno septimo, qui est Darii nonus, consummatur, prophetantibus ultimis Aggeo et Zachario et Malachia, qui Angelus dicitur apud Iudaeos. A prima autem aedificatione templi sub Salamone usque ad reaedificationem sub Dario secundum quosdam sunt anni quingenti duodecim, iuxta Iosephi vero assertionem 450. (*Chronica*, p. 57, 23/28.)

Frechulf: Ergo uenia aedificandi templi sub Cyro exordium habuit, causis uero existentibus impedimenti, ut praediximus, manet inperfectum usque ad Darii regis imperium. Cuius regni anno secundo a Zorobabele et Hiesu construitur et quarto opus aedificationis ab eis consummatur anno. Iosepphus enim septem annis perfectum dicit templum a praedictis uiris, qui est nonus regni regis Darii, prophetantibus ultimis Aggeo atque Zacharia et uno ex duodecim qui dicitur Angelus apud Iudaeos. Hic namque finis tertii nostri operis erit libri, qui continet in se a prima aedificatione templi sub Salomone usque ad secundam reaedificationem sub Dario, secundum quosdam quingentos XII annos, iuxta uero Iosepphi adsertionem quadringentos quadraginta. (*Hist.*, I.3.19 [29/41], pp. 205-06.)

Example 8

Frutolf: Socrates, magister Platonis, Athenis tunc claruit, qui primus universam phylosophiam ad corrigendos mores flexisse memoratur, cum ante illum omnes magis physicis, id est naturalibus, rebus perscrutandis operam darent, **finemque bonum fieri non posse nisi bene uiuendo docuit**. (*Chronica*, p. 60, 49/51.)

Frechulf: Socrates ergo primus uniuersam philosophiam ad corrigendos conponendosque mores flexisse memoratur, cum ante illum omnes magis phisicis, id est naturalibus, rebus perscrutandis operam maximam inpenderint, **finemque bonum fieri non posse nisi bene uiuendo docuit**. Nolebat itaque inmundos terrenis cupiditatibus animos extendere in diuina et coronari. (*Hist.*, I.4.14 [5/10], p. 230. Bold text is not in Augustine, *DCD*, VIII.3, Frechulf's source, but is Frechulf's own addition.)

Example 9

Frutolf: Nam usque ad Hyrcanum, Alexandri Iamnei filium, iudices, sacerdotes, reges per successiones populo Iudaeorum prefuerunt. (*Chronica*, p. 93, 67/68.)

Frechulf: Nam usque ad Herodemiudices, sacerdotes, reges per successiones populo praefuerunt Iudaeorum. (*Hist.*, I.7.13 [13/14], p. 403.)

Bibliography

Manuscripts cited

Berlin, Deutsche Staatsbibliothek Preussische Kulturbesitz
    Phillips 1879
Bern, Burgerbibliothek
    Cod. 219
Leiden Universiteitsbibliotheek
    MS Scaliger 14
    MS VLQ 110
London, British Library (BL)
    Add. Ms. 16974
Lucca, Biblioteca Capitolare Feliniana (Lucca Bibl. Capit.)
    Cod. 490
Paris, Bibliotheque Nationale de France (BNF)
    lat. 4871
    lat. 6042
St. Gallen, Stiftsbibliothek
    Cod. Sang. 282
    Cod. Sang. 622
Vatican, Biblioteca apostolica Vaticana
    Reg. lat. 2077
    Reg. lat. 772

Printed Primary Sources

Admonitio generalis, ed. Hubert Mordek, Klaus Zechiel-Eckes and Michael Glatthaar, *Die Admonitio generalis Karls des Grossen*, MGH *Fontes iuris* XVI (Hanover: Hahn, 2012).

Ado of Vienne, *Chronicon*, PL 123, cols. 23–138; ed. Georg Pertz, MGH *SS* 2 (Hanover: Hahn, 1829), pp. 315–23.

Agobard of Lyon, *De baptismo manciporum Iudaeorum*, ed. Lieven van Acker, in *Agobard Lugdunensis opera omnia*, CCCM 52 (Turnhout: Brepols, 1981), pp. 115–17.

Agobard, *De dispensatione ecclesiasticarum rerum*, ed. Lieven Van Acker, *Agobardi Lugdunensis Opera Omnia*, CCCM 52 (Turnhout: Brepols, 1981), pp. 119–42.

Alcuin, *De grammatica*, PL 101, cols. 849–902.

Alcuin, *De virtutibus et vitiis*, PL 101, cols. 613–38.

Alcuin, *Disputatio de rhetorica et de virtutibus*, ed. and trans. Wilbur Samuel Howell, *The Rhetoric of Alcuin and Charlemagne: A Translation* (Princeton, NJ: Princeton University Press, 1941).

Alcuin, *Epistolae*, ed. Ernst Dümmler, MGH *Epp.* IV (Berlin: Weidmann,1895), pp. 18–481.

Alcuin, *Interrogationes et responsiones in Genesin*, PL 100, cols. 515–66.

Alcuin, *Versus de patribus regibus et sanctis Euboricensis ecclesiae*, ed. and trans. Peter Godman, *The Bishops, Kings, and Saints of York* (Oxford: Clarendon Press, 1982).

Amalarius of Metz, *Epistula Amalarii ad Hilduinum abbatem*, ed. Jean-Michel Hanssens, *Amalarii episcopi opera liturgica omnia I: Introductio—opera minora*, Studi e Testi 138 (Vatican City: Biblioteca apostolica vaticana, 1948), pp. 341–58.

Amalarius of Metz, *Liber officialis*, ed. Jean-Michel Hanssens, *Amalarii episcopi opera liturgica omnia II: Liber officialis*, Studi e Tesi 139 (Vatican City: Biblioteca apostolica vaticana, 1950), pp. 13–543.

Amalarius of Metz, *Prologus antiphonarii*, ed. Jean-Michel Hanssens, *Amalarii episcopi opera liturgica omnia I: Introductio — opera minora*, Studi e Testi 138 (Vatican City: Biblioteca apostolica vaticana, 1948), pp. 361–3.

Angelomus of Luxeuil, *Commentarius in Genesin*, PL 115, cols. 551-628; *Epistolae variorum*, ed. Ernst Dümmler, MGH Epp. V (Berlin: Weidmann, 1895), no. 5, pp. 619-22.

Annales Parchenses, ed. Georg Waitz, MGH *SS* 16 (Hanover: Hahn, 1859), pp. 598–608.

Annales regni Francorum, ed. Friederich Kurze, MGH *SRG* 6 (Hanover: Hahn 1895).

Apocrypha Hiberniae, I. Evangelia infantiae, ed. Martin McNamara, Jean-Daniel Kaestli and Rita Beyers, CCSA 14 (Turnhout: Brepols, 2001).

Ardo, *Vita Benedictia abbatis Anianensis et Indensis*, ed. Georg Waitz, MGH *SS* 15/1 (Hanover: Hahn, 1887), pp. 198–220; trans. in Thomas F. X. Noble and Thomas Head (eds), *Soldiers of Christ: Saints and Saints' Lives from Late Antiquity and the Early Middle Ages* (University Park, PA: Pennsylvania State University Press, 2000), 213–54.

Astronomer, *Vita Hludowici imperatoris*, ed. and trans. Ernst Tremp, MGH *SRG* 64 (Hanover: Hahn, 1995), pp. 280–554; English trans. Thomas F. X. Noble, *Charlemagne and Louis the Pious: The Lives by Einhard, Notker, Ermoldus, Thegan, and the Astronomer* (University Park, PA: Pennsylvania State University Press, 2009), 226–302.

Augustine, *De doctrina christiana*, ed. and trans. R. P. H. Green (Oxford: OUP, 1995).

Augustine, *De civitate Dei*, eds Bernard Dombart and Alphonse Kalb, *Sancti Aurelii Augustini De civitate Dei*, CCSL 47 (Libri I–X) and 48 (Libri XI–XXII) (Turnhout: Brepols, 1955); English trans., R. W. Dyson, *The City of God against the Pagans* (Cambridge: CUP, 1998).

Bede *De temporibus*, ed. Charles W. Jones, CCSL 123C (Turnhout: Brepols, 1980), pp. 585–611. English translation: Calvin B. Kendall and Faith Wallis, *Bede: On the Nature of Things and* On Times (Liverpool: LUP, 2010), 107–31.

Bede, *De temporum ratione*, ed. Charles W. Jones, CCSL 123B (Turnhout: Brepols, 1977); English trans., F. Wallis, *Bede: The Reckoning of Time* (Liverpool: LUP, 1999).

Bede, *Historia ecclesiastica gentis Anglorum*, ed. and trans. Bertram Colgrave and R. A. B. Mynors, *Bede's Ecclesiastical History of the English People* (Oxford: OUP, 1969).

Bede, *In Ezram et Neemiam*, ed. David Hurst, CCSL 119A (Turnhout: Brepols, 1969).

Bede, *In Lucae evangelium expositio*, ed. David Hurst, CCCM 120 (Turnhout: Brepols, 1960), pp. 5–425.

Bede, *Libri quatuor in principium Genesis*, ed. Charles W. Jones, CCSL 118 (Turnhout: Brepols, 1967).

Bede, *Nomina regionum atque locorum de Actibus apostolorum*, ed. M. L. W. Laistner, CCSL 121 (Turnhout: Brepols, 1983), pp. 165–78.

Benedict of Aniane, *Concordia regularum*, ed. Pierre Bonnerue, CCCM 168A (Turnhout: Brepols, 1999).

Boniface, *Epistolae*, ed. Michael Tangl, *Die Briefe des heilgen Bonifatius und Lullus*, MGH *Epp. Sel.* 1 (Berlin: Weidmann, 1916).

Capitula Parisiensia, ed. Rudolf Pokorny, MGH *Capit. Episc.* III (Hanover: Hahn, 1995), pp. 25–35.

Capitularia missorum specialia, ed. Alfred Boretius, MGH *Capit.* 1 (Hanover: Hahn, 1883), no. 34, pp. 99–102.

Cartulaire de l'abbaye de Cysoing et ses dépendances, ed. M. Ignace de Coussemaker (Lille, 1885).

Cassiodorus, *Historia ecclesiastica tripartita*, ed. Walter Jacob and Rudolf Hanslik, *Cassiodori-Epiphanii historia ecclesiastica tripartita: historiae ecclesiasticae ex Socrate, Sozomeno et Theodorito*, CSEL 71 (Vienna: Hoelder–Pichler–Tempsky, 1952).

Cassiodorus, *Institutiones*, ed. R. A. B. Mynors (Oxford: Clarendon Press, 1937); trans. James W. Halporn with introduction by Mark Vessey, *Cassiodorus:* Institutions of Divine and Secular Learning *and* On the Soul (Liverpool: LUP, 2004).

Catalogi, ed. Paul Lehmann, *Mittelalterliche Bibliothekskataloge Deutschlands und der Schweiz*, vol. 1: *Die Bistümer Konstanz und Chur* (Munich: C.H. Beck, 1918).

Christianus dictus Stabulensis, *Expositio super librum generationis*, ed. R. B. C. Huygens, CCCM 224 (Turnhout: Brepols, 2008).

Chronicle of 452, ed. Richard Burgess, 'The Gallic Chronicle of 452: A New Critical Edition with a Brief Introduction', in *Society and Culture in Late Antique Gaul: Revisiting the Sources*, eds Ralph W. Mathisen and Danuta Shanzer (Aldershot: Ashgate, 2001), pp. 52–84.

Chronicon Moisiacense, ed. Georg Heinrich Pertz, MGH *SS* 1 (Hanover: Hahn, 1826), pp. 282–313; ed. Hans Katz and David Claszen, 'Chronicon Moissiacense Maius: A Carolingian World Chronicle from Creation until the First Years of Louis the Pious', 2 vols (unpublished research master thesis, University of Leiden, 2012), vol. 2, pp. 1–150, https://hdl.handle.net/1887/20005

Cicero, *De inventione*, ed. J. Henderson, trans. H. M. Hubbell, LCL 386 (Cambridge, MA: HUP, 1949).

Cicero, *De oratore*, books 1–2, ed. H. Rackham, trans. H. M. Hubbell, LCL 386 (Cambridge, MA: HUP, 1949).

Claudius of Turin, *Commentarii in Genesim*, PL 50, cols. 893–1048; *Epistolae*, ed. Ernst Dümmler, MGH, *Epp.* IV (Berlin: Weidmann, 1895), pp. 590–3.

Codex epistolaris carolinus, no. 60, ed. Wilhelm Gundlach, MGH *Epp.* III (Berlin: Weidmann, 1892), pp. 469–658.

Concilia aevi Karolini [742–842], ed. Albert Werminghoff, MGH *Conc.* II, 2 vols (Hanover: Hahn, 1904–1908).

Concilia aevi Karolini 843–859, ed. Wilfried Hartmann, MGH *Conc.* III (Hanover: Hahn, 1984).

Concilia Galliae a. 511–695, ed. Charles de Clercq, CCSL 148A (Turnhout: Brepols, 1963).

De convivio monachorum (Ordo Romanus XIX), ed. Josef Semmler, CCM 1 (Siegburg: F. Schmitt, 1963), pp. 51–63.

Decretum Gelasianum, ed. Ernst von Dobschütz, *Das decretum gelasianum de libris recipiendis et non recipiendis*, Texte und Untersuchungen zur Geschichte der altchristlichen Literatur 38:4 (Leipzig: J. C. Hinrichs, 1912).

Die St. Galler Verbrüderungsbücher, eds Dieter Geuenich and Uwe Ludwig, MGH, Libri memorialies, nova series 9 (Wiesbaden: Harrassowitz, 2019).

Einhard, *Vita Karoli*, ed. Oswald Holder-Egger, MGH *SRG* 25 (Hanover: Hahn, 1911), pp. 1–41; English trans. by David Ganz, *Two Lives of Charlemagne* (Harmondsworth: Penguin, 2008), 17–44.

Ekkehardi Uraugiensis Chronica [= Frutolf of Michelsberg], ed. Georg Waitz, MGH *SS* 6 (Hanover: Hahn, 1844), pp. 33–211; partial online edition, https://mgh.de/die-mgh/ editionsprojekte/bamberger-weltchronistik; partially translated in T. J. H. McCarthy, *Chronicles of the Investiture Contest: Frutolf of Michelsberg and his Continuators* (Manchester: MUP, 2014), pp. 85–137.

Episcoporum ad Hludowicum imperatorem relatio, ed. Alfred Boretius and Victor Krause, MGH *Capit.* 2 (Hanover: Hahn, 1897), no. 196, pp. 27–51.

Epitome de Caesaribus, ed. and trans. Michel Festy, *Pseudo-Aurélius Victor: Abrégé des Césars*, Collection des universités de France (Paris: Les Belles Lettres, 1999).

Ermoldus Nigellus, *In honorem Hludowici Christianissimi Caesaris Augusti elegiacum carmen*, ed. Edmond Faral, *Ermold le Noir: poème sur Louis le Pieux et épitres au roi Pépin*, Les classique de l'histoire de France au moyen age 14 (Paris: Les Belles Lettres, 1964); English trans. Thomas F. X. Noble, *Charlemagne and Louis the Pious: The Lives by Einhard, Notker, Ermoldus, Thegan, and the Astronomer* (University Park, PA: Pennsylvania State University Press, 2009), 127–86.

Eusebius-Jerome, *Chronicon*, ed. Rudolf Helm, *Eusebius Werke*, vol. 7: *Die Chronik des Hieronymus/Hieronymi Chronicon*, Die griechischen christlichen Schriftsteller der ersten Jahrhunderte 47, 2nd edn (Berlin: Akademie-Verlag, 1956); online English translation at https://www.tertullian.org/fathers/jerome_chronicle_00_eintro.htm [last accessed 23/09/21].

Eusebius, *Die Chronik aus dem Armenischen Übersetzung, mit textkritischem Commentar*, ed. Josef Karst, *Eusebius Werke*, vol. 5 (Leipzig: J. C. Hinrichs, 1911).

Eusebius-Rufinus, *Historia ecclesiastica*, eds Eduard Schwartz and Theodor Mommsen, *Eusebius Werke*, vol. 2: *Die Kirchengeschichte*, Die griechischen christlichen Schriftsteller der ersten drei Jahrhunderte 6, 3 vols (Leipzig: J.C. Hinrichs, 1903-9), 2nd end (Berlin: Akademie Verlag, 1999); English translation of Rufinus in Philip R. Amidon, *The Church History of Rufinus of Aquileia, Books 10 and 11* (New York and Oxford: OUP, 1997); Greek text translated in Jeremy M. Schott, *The History of the Church: A New Translation* (Oakland, CA: University of California Press, 2019).

Excerpta Rhetorica, ed. C. F. Halm, *Rhetores Latini minores* (Leipzig: Teubner, 1863), 585–9.

Exordium, ed. Alfred Schöne, *Eusebi Chronicorum Libri Duo*, 3rd edn, 2 vols (Berlin: Weidmann, 1999), vol. 1, appendix 2, pp. 41–9; *PL* 27, cols. 61–76.

Frechulf of Lisieux, *Epistola ad Hrabanum Maurum abbatem de pentateucho commentando*, ed. Michael I. Allen, *Frechulfi Lexoviensis episcopi opera omnia*, CCCM 169 A (Turnhout: Brepols, 2002), pp. 3–7.

Frechulf of Lisieux, *Historiarum libri XII*, ed. Michael I. Allen, *Frechulfi Lexoviensis episcopi opera omnia*, CCCM 169 A (Turnhout: Brepols, 2002), pp. 9–724; partial trans. Justin Lake, *Prologues to Ancient and Medieval History: A Reader* (Toronto: University of Toronto Press, 2013), 111–14.

Frechulf of Lisieux, *Prologus ad Karolum Calvum regem in libellos Flavii Vegeti Renati de re militari nuper emendatos*, ed. Michael I. Allen, *Frechulfi Lexoviensis episcopi opera omnia*, CCCM 169 A (Turnhout: Brepols, 2002), pp. 725–9.

Gesta fontanellensis coenobii, ed Pascal Pradié, *Chronique des abbés de Fontenelle (Saint-Wandrille)* (Paris: Les Belles Lettres, 1999).

Gregory the Great, *Homiliae in Hiezechielem prophetam*, ed. Marcus Adriaen, CCSL 142 (Turnhout: Brepols, 1971).

Gregory of Tours, *Libri historiarum X*, ed. Bruno Krusch and Wilhelm Levison, MGH *SRM* I:1, 2nd edn (Hanover: Hahn, 1951).

Hariulf, *Chronicon Centulense*, ed. Ferdinand Lot, *Chronique de l'abbaye de Saint-Riquier (Ve siècle–1104)* (Paris: Alphonse Picard et fils, 1894).

Heiric of Auxerre, *Collectanea*, ed. Riccardo Quadri, *I Collectanea de Eirico di Auxerre*, Spicilegium Friburgense 11 (Freiburg: Edizioni universitarie, 1966).

Historia translationis corporum ss. Ragnoberti et Zenonis, ed. Olivier Larue, 'La Translation de corps de saint Regnobert et de saint Zénon', *Bulletin de la Société des Antiquaires de Normande*, 51 (1952): pp. 215–64.

Hrabanus Maurus, *Commentaria in libros Machabaeorum*, PL 109, cols. 1125–56.

Hrabanus Maurus, *Commentariorum in Ezechielem libri viginti*, PL 110, cols. 493–1084.

Hrabanus Maurus, *De institutione clericorum libri tres*, ed. Detlev Zimpel, Freiburger Beiträge zur mittelalterlichen Geschichte 7 (Frankfurt am Main: Peter Lang, 1996).

Hrabanus Maurus, *De rerum naturis*, PL 111, cols. 9A–614B; trans. Priscilla Throop, *Hrabanus Maurus: De universo. The Peculiar Properties of Words and Their Mystical Significance*, 2 vols (Charlotte, VT: MedievalsMS, 2009).

Hrabanus Maurus, *Epistolae*, ed. Ernst Dümmler, MGH *Epp.* V (Berlin: Weidmann, 1899), pp. 381–516.

Hrabanus Maurus, *Expositio in librum Judith*, PL 109, cols. 539–92.

Hrabanus Maurus, *Expositio in Matthaeum*, ed. Bengt Löfstedt, CCCM 174, 2 vols (Turnhout: Brepols, 2000).

Hrabanus Maurus, *Expositionis super Hieremiam prophetam libri viginti*, PL 111, cols. 793–1272.

Hugh of Fleury, *Historia ecclesiastica*, ed. Georg Waitz, MGH SS 9 (Hanover: Hahn, 1851), 337–54; Leendert Martin de Ruiter, '*Hugo van Fleury*: Historia ecclesiastica, editio altera: *Kritische teksteditie*' (unpublished thesis, University of Groningen, 2016).

Hugh of Fleury, *Liber modernum regum Francorum actus*, ed. Georg Waitz, MGH SS 9 (Hanover: Hahn, 1851), pp. 376–95.

Hydatius, *Chronicon*, ed. R. W. Burgess, *The Chronicle of Hydatius and the Consularia Constantinopolitana: Two Contemporary Accounts of the Final Years of the Roman Empire* (Oxford: OUP, 1993).

Isidore of Seville, *Chronica*, ed. Jose Carlos Martin in *Isidori Hispalensis chronica*, CCSL 112 (Turnhout: Brepols, 2003); trans. by Sam Koon and Jamie Wood, 'The *Chronica maiora* of Isidore of Seville: An Introduction and Translation', *e-Spania* 6 (2008), available online at http://e-spania.revues.org/15552 [last accessed 2 June 2019].

Isidore of Seville, *De ortu et obitu patrum*, ed. César Chaparro Gómez (Paris: Les Belles Lettres, 1985).

Isidore of Seville, *De viris illustribus*, ed. Carmen Codoñer Merino, *El 'De viris illustribus' de Isidoro de Sevilla* (Salamanca, 1964).

Isidore of Seville, *Etymologiae*, ed. W. M. Lindsay (Oxford: Clarendon Press, 1911); English translation in Stephen A. Barney, W. J. Lewis, J. A. Beach and Oliver Berghof, *The Etymologies of Isidore of Seville* (Cambridge: CUP, 2006).

Jerome, *Commentarii in Abdiam prophetam*, ed. Marcus Adriaen, CCSL 76 (Turnhout: Brepols, 1969), pp. 349–75.

Jerome, *Commentarii in Amos prophetam*, ed. Marcus Adriaen, CCSL 76 (Turnhout: Brepols, 1969), pp. 211–348.

Jerome, *Commentarii in Danielem*, ed. Franciscus Glorie, CCSL 75A (Turnhout: Brepols, 1964); online trans. by Gleason L. Archer, http://www.tertullian.org/fathers/jerome_daniel_02_text.htm [last accessed 18 May 2020].

Jerome, *Commentarii in Esaiam*, ed. Marcus Adriaen, CCSL 73 and 73A (Turnhout: Brepols, 1963).

Jerome, *Commentarii in Hieremiam prophetam*, ed. Sigofried Reiter, CCSL 74 (Turnhout: Brepols, 1960).

Jerome, *Commentarii in Hiezechielem*, ed. Franciscus Glorie, CCSL 75 (Turnhout: Brepols, 1964); trans. Thomas P. Scheck, *St Jerome: Commentary on Ezekiel* (New York: Newman Press, 2017).

Jerome, *Commentarii in Malachiam prophetam*, ed. Marcus Adriaen, CCSL 76A (Turnhout: Brepols, 1970), pp. 901–42.

Jerome, *Commentarii in Matheum*, eds David Hurst and Marcus Adriaen, CCSL 77 (Turnhout: Brepols, 1969).

Jerome, *Commentarii in Michaeam prophetam*, ed. Marcus Adriaen, CCSL 76 (Turnhout: Brepols, 1969), pp. 421–524.

Jerome, *Commentarii in Zachariam prophetam*, ed. Marcus Adriaen, CCSL 76A (Turnhout: Brepols, 1970), pp. 747–900.

Jerome, *Commentarioli in Psalmos*, ed. Germanus Morin, CCSL 72 (Turnhout: Brepols, 1959), pp. 177–245.

Jerome, *Commentarius in Ecclesiasten*, ed. Marcus Adriaen, CCSL 72 (Turnhout: Brepols, 1959), pp. 247–361.

Jerome, *De viris illustribus*, ed. E. C. Richardson, *Hieronymus, Liber de viris illustribus. Gennadius, De virus illustribus* (Leipzig: J.C. Hinrichs, 1896); English trans. Thomas P. Halton, *Saint Jerome: On Illustrious Men*, The Fathers of the Church 100 (Washington, DC: CUA Press, 1999).

Jerome, *Epistulae*, ed. Isidorus Hilberg, 3 vols, CSEL 54–56 (Vienna: Verlag der österreichischen Akademie der Wissenschaften, 1996).

Jerome, *Hebraicae Quaestiones in Libro Geneseos*, ed. Paul de Legarde, CCSL 72 (Turnhout: Brepols, 1952), pp. 1-56.

Jerome, *Prologus in libro Regum*, ed. Robert Weber, *Biblia Sacra: iuxta Vulgatam* (Stuttgart: Deutsche Bibelgesellschaft, 1969), pp. 364–6.

Jonas of Orléans, *De institutione regia*, ed. Alain Dubreucq, *Jonas d'Orléans: Le metier de Roi (De institutione regia)* (Paris: CERF, 1995).

Jonas of Orléans, *De institutione laicali*, ed. Odile Dubreucq, *Instruction des Laïcs*, Sources chrétiennes 549–550 (Paris: CERF, 2012).

Jordanes, *De origine actibusque Getarum [= Getica]*, ed. Theodor Mommsen in MGH *Auct. Ant.* 5:1 (Berlin: Weidmann, 1882), pp. 53–138; trans. Peter Van Nuffelen and Lieve Van Hoof, *Jordanes: Romana and Getica* (Liverpool: LUP, 2020), 221–369.

Jordanes, *De summa temporum vel origine actibusque gentis Romanorum [= Romana]*, ed. Theodor Mommsen in MGH *Auct. Ant.* 5:1 (Berlin: Weidmann, 1882), pp. 1–52; trans. Peter Van Nuffelen and Lieve Van Hoof, *Jordanes: Romana and Getica* (Liverpool: LUP, 2020), 107–219.

Josephus, *Jewish Antiquities*, ed. Franz Blatt, *The Latin Josephus I: Introduction and Text. The Antiquities; Books I–V*, Acta Jutlandica 30 (Aarhus, 1958); *Flavii Iosephi … opera quaedam* (Basel, 1524).

Julianus Pomerius, *De vita contemplativa*, PL 59, cols. 411–520.

Liber pontificalis, ed. Louis Duchesne, *Le* Liber pontificalis: *texte, introduction et commentaire*, 2 vols (Paris: E. Thorin, 1886–92, repr. 1955).

Liber tramitis aevi Odilonis abbatis, ed. Peter Dinter, CCM 10 (Siegburg: F. Schmitt, 1980).

Lupus of Ferrières, ed. Léon Levillain, *Loup de Ferrières: Correspondance*, 2 vols., Les classiques de l'histoire de France au Moyen Age 10 (Paris: Les Belles Lettres, 1964); English trans. Graydon W. Regenos, *The Letters of Lupus of Ferrières* (The Hague: Springer, 1966).

Martianus Capella, *De nuptiis Philologiae et Mercurii*, ed. James Willis (Leipzig: B.G. Teubner Verlagsgesellschaft, 1983).

Orosius, *Historiae adversum paganos*, ed. Marie-Pierre Arnaud-Lindet, *Orose: Histoires (contre les païens)*, 3 vols. (Paris: Les Belles Lettres, 1990–1); trans. A. T. Fear, *Orosius: Seven Books of History against the Pagans* (Liverpool: LUP, 2010).

Otto of Freising, *Chronicle*, ed. Adolf Hofmeister, *Ottonis episcopi Frisingensis Chronica sive Historia de duabus civitatibus*, MGH *SRG* 45 (Hanover: Hahn, 1912).

Paschasius Radbertus, *Expositio in Matheo libri XII*, ed. Bede Paulus, 3 vols, CCCM 56, 56A and 56B (Turnhout: Brepols, 1984).

Paul the Deacon, *Historia Romana*, ed. Amedeo Crivellucci (Rome, 1914).

Paul the Deacon, *Vita Gregorii*, ed. Sabine Tuzzo, *Vita Sancti Gregorii Magni* (Pisa: Scuola normale superior, 2002).

Prosper of Aquitaine, *Chronicon*, ed. Theodor Mommsen, MGH *Auct. Ant.* 9 (Berlin: Weidmann, 1892), pp. 341–485.

Pseudo-Hegesippus, *De excidio*, ed. Vincenzo Ussani, *Hegesippi qui dicitur Historia libri V*, CSEL 66/1 (Vienna: Hoelder-Pickler-Tempsky, 1932).

Quintilian, *Institutio Oratorio*, books 3–5, ed. and trans. Donald A. Russell, LCL 125 (Cambridge, MA, and London: HUP, 2001).

Regino of Prüm, *Chronicle*, ed. Friederich Kurze, *Reginonis abbatis prumiensis Chronicon cum continuatione treverensi*, MGH *SRG* 50 (Hanover: Hahn, 1890); trans. Simon MacLean, *History and Politics in Late Carolingian and Ottonian Europe: The Chronicle of Regino of Prüm and Adalbert of Magdeburg* (Manchester: MUP, 2009).

Regula Benedicti, ed. Rudolf Hanslik, CSEL 75 (Vienna, Hoelder-Pichler-Tempsky, 1960).

Rhetorica ad Herennium, trans. Harry Caplan, LCL 403 (Cambridge, MA: HUP, 1954).

Richard of Poitiers, *Chronicon*, ed. Georg Waitz, MGH *SS* 26 (Hanover: Hahn, 1882), 74–86.

Rudolf of Fulda, *Miracula sanctorum in fuldenses ecclesias translatorum*, ed. Georg Waitz, MGH, *SS* 15/1 (Hanover: Hahn, 1887), pp. 328–41.

Sedulius Scottus, *Collectaneum miscellaneum*, ed. Dean Simpson, CCCM 67 (Turnhout: Brepols, 1988)

Sedulius Scottus, *De rectoribus christianis*, ed. and trans. by R. W. Dyson, *De rectoribus christianis: On Christian Rulers* (Woodbridge: Boydell Press, 2010).

Sigebert of Gembloux, *De viris illustribus*, ed. by Robert Witte, *Catalogus Sigeberti Gemblacensis monachi de viris illustribus. Kritische Ausgabe* (Bern and Frankfurt: Peter Lang, 1974).

Smaragdus, *Expositio libri comitis*, PL 102, cols. 13C–552D.

The Chronography of George Synkellos: A Byzantine Chronicle of Universal History from the Creation, ed. and trans. William Adler and Paul Tuffin (Oxford: OUP, 2002).

The Old English History of the World: An Anglo-Saxon Rewriting of Orosius, ed. and trans. Malcolm R. Godden (Cambridge, MA: HUP, 2016).

Thegan, *Gesta Hludowici imperatoris*, ed. Ernst Tremp, MGH *SRG* 64 (Hanover: Hahn, 1995), pp. 168–258; English trans. Thomas F. X. Noble, *Charlemagne and Louis the Pious: The Lives by Einhard, Notker, Ermoldus, Thegan, and the Astronomer* (University Park, PA: Pennsylvania State University Press, 2009), 194–218.

Theodulf of Orléans, *Opus Caroli Regis Contra Synodum*, ed. Ann Freeman, MGH *Conc.* 2, Suppl. 1 (Hanover: Hahn, 1998).

Theophanes the Confessor, *The Chronicle of Theophanes Confessor: Byzantine and Near Eastern History, A.D. 284–813*, trans. Cyril A. Mango, Roger Scott and Geoffrey Greatrex (Oxford: Clarendon Press, 1997).

Vita Gregorii, ed. and trans. Bertram Colgrave, *The Earliest Life of Gregory the Great, by an Anonymous Monk of Whitby* (Cambridge: CUP, 1985).

Walahfrid Strabo, *Libellus de exordiis et incrementis quarundam in observationibus ecclesiasticis rerum*, trans. Alice Harting-Correa, *Walahfrid Strabo's Libellus de exordiis et incrementis quarundam in observationibus ecclesiasticis rerum. A Translation and Liturgical Commentary* (Leiden: Brill, 1996).

Wolfger of Prüfening, *De scriptoribus ecclesiasticis*, ed. Francis R. Swietek, 'Wolfger of Prüfening's *De scriptoribus ecclesiasticis*: A Critical Edition and Historical Evaluation' (Unpublished PhD Dissertation, University of Illinois, 1978).

Secondary Literature

Adamek, Josef, *Vom römischen Endreich der mittelalterlichen Bibelerklärung* (Würzburg: Triltsch, 1938).

Adler, William, 'Eusebius' *Chronicle* and its Legacy', in *Eusebius, Christianity and Judaism*, eds Harold W. Attridge and Gohei Hata (Detroit, MI: Wayne State University Press 1992), 467–91.

Adler, William and Tuffin, Paul (eds and trans), *The Chronography of George Synkellos: A Byzantine Chronicle of Universal History from the Creation* (Oxford: OUP, 2002).

Airlie, Stuart, 'The Palace of Memory: The Carolingian Court as Political Centre', in *Courts and Regions in Medieval Europe*, eds Sarah Rees Jones, Richard Marks and A.J. Minnis (Woodbridge: York Medieval Press, 2000), 1–20; repr. in *Power and its Problems in Carolingian Europe* (Farnham: Ashgate Variorum, 2012), item VII.

Airlie, Stuart, '"Sad Stories of the Death of Kings": Narrative Patterns and Structures of Authority in Regino of Prüm's *Chronicle*', in *Narrative and History in the Early Medieval West*, eds Elisabeth M. Taylor and Ross Balzaretti (Turnhout: Brepols, 2006), 105–31. repr. in his *Power and its Problems in Carolingian Europe* (Farnham: Ashgate Variorum, 2012), item XII.

Airlie, Stuart, 'The World, the Text and the Carolingian: Royal, Aristocratic and Masculine Identities in Nithard's *Histories*', in *Lay Intellectuals in the Carolingian World*, eds Patrick Wormald and Janet L. Nelson (Cambridge: CUP, 2007), 51–76; repr. in *Power and its Problems in Carolingian Europe* (Farnham: Ashgate Variorum, 2012), item IX.

Airlie, Stuart, *Making and Unmaking the Carolingians, 751–888* (London: Bloomsbury, 2020).

Allen, Michael I., 'History in the Carolingian Renewal: Frechulf of Lisieux (fl. 830), his Work and Influence' (unpublished PhD thesis, University of Toronto, 1994).

Allen, Michael I., 'Bede and Frechulf at Medieval St Gallen', in *Beda Venerabilis: Historian, Monk and Northumbrian*, eds L. A. J. R. Houwen and A. A. MacDonald (Groningen: E. Forsten, 1996), 61–80.

Allen, Michael I., *Prolegomena*, in *Frechulfi Lexoviensis episcopi opera omnia*, CCCM 169 (Turnhout: Brepols, 2002).

Allen, Michael I., 'The *Chronicle* of Claudius of Turin', in *After Rome's Fall: Narrators and Sources of Early Medieval History. Essays Presented to Walter Goffart*, ed. Alexander Callander Murray (Toronto: University of Toronto Press, 1998), 288–319.

Allen, Michael I., 'Universal History 300–1000: Origins and Western Developments', in *Historiography of the Middle Ages*, ed. Deborah Mauskopf Deliyannis (Leiden: Brill, 2003), 17–42.

Allen, Michael I., 'Fréculf de Lisieux: l'histoire de l'antiquité comme témoignage de l'actualité', *Tabularia*, 8 (2008): 59–79.

Allen, Michael I., 'Frechulf of Lisieux', in *The Oxford Guide to the Historical Reception of Augustine*, eds Karla Pollmann and Willemien Otten, 3 vols (Oxford: OUP, 2013), vol. 2: 1010–11.

Allen, Michael I., 'Writing to Bishops in the Letter-Book of Lupus of Ferrières', in *Écriture et genre épistolaires: IVe-XIe siècle*, eds Thomas Deswarte, Klaus Herbers and Hélène Sirantoine (Madrid: Casa de Velàzquez, 2018), 59–68.

Allmand, Christopher T., *The De re militari of Vegetius: The Reception, Transmission and Legacy of a Roman Text in the Middle Ages* (Cambridge: CUP, 2011).

Anton, Hans Hubert, *Fürstenspiegel und Herrscherethos in der Karolingerzeit*, BonnerHistorische Forschungen 32 (Bonn: Bonn Röhrscheid, 1968).

Anton, Hans Hubert, 'Zum politischen Konzept karolingischer Synoden und zur karolingischen Brüdergemeinschaft', *Historisches Jahrbuch*, 99 (1979): 55–132.

Anton, Hans Hubert, 'Anfänge säkularer Begründung von Herrschaft und Staat im Mittelalter. Historiographie, Herkunftssagen, politische Metaphorik (*Institutio Traiani*)', *Archiv für Kulturgeschichte*, 86 (2004): 75–122.

Aris, Marc-Aeilko, '*Nostrum est citare testes*: Anmerkungen zum Wissenschaftsverständniss des Hrabanus Maurus', in *Kloster Fulda in der Welt der Karolinger und Ottonen*, ed. Gangolf Schrimpf, Fuldaer Studien 7 (Frankfurt: J. Knecht, 1996), 437–64.

Atsma (ed.), Hartmut, *La Neustrie. Les pays au nord de la Loire 650 à 850. Colloque historique international*, 2 vols (Sigmaringen: Thorbecke, 1989).

Banniard, Michel, 'Language and Communication in Carolingian Europe', in *The New Cambridge Medieval History, vol. 2, c.700–c.900*, ed. Rosamond McKitterick (Cambridge: CUP, 1995), 695–708.

Bardy, Gustave, 'La littérature patristique des *quaestiones et responsiones* sur l'Ecriture sainte', *Revue biblique*, 41 (1932): 210–36, 341–69, 515–37 and 42 (1933): 14–30, 211–29 and 328–52.

Barnes, Timothy D., 'The *Epitome de Caesaribus* and its Sources', *Classical Philology*, 71 (1976): 258–68.

Barnes, Timothy D., *Constantine and Eusebius* (Cambridge, MA: HUP, 1981).

Bassett, Paul M., 'The Use of History in the *Chronicon* of Isidore of Seville', *History and Theory*, 15 (1976): 278–92.

Berggötz, Oliver, 'Hrabanus Maurus und seine Bedeutung für das Bibliothekswesen der Karolingerzeit: zugleich ein Beitrag zur Geschichte der Klosterbibliothek Fulda', *Bibliothek und Wissenschaft*, 27 (1994): 1–48.

Bériou, Nicole, Berndt, Rainer and Fédou, Michel (eds), *Les réceptions des Pères de l'Église au Moyen Âge: le devenir de la tradition ecclésiale*, Archa verbi. Subsidia 10, 2 vols (Münster: Aschendorff, 2013).

Berschin, Walter, 'An Unpublished Library Catalogue from Eighth-century Lombard Italy', *Journal of Medieval Latin*, 11 (2001): 201–9.

Berschin, Walter, *Eremus und Insula: St. Gallen und die Reichenau im Mittelalter. Modell einer lateinischen Literaturlandschaft* (Wiesbaden: Ludwig Reichert, 1987).

Bischoff, Bernard, *Mittelalterliche Studien: ausgewählte Aufsätze zur Schriftkunde und Literaturgeschichte*, vol. III (Stuttgart: Hiersemann, 1981).

Bischoff, Bernard, *Die Abtei Lorsch im Spiegel ihrer Handschriften* (Lorsch: Heimat- und Kulturverein Lorsch mit Unterstützung der Stadt Lorsch, 1989).

Bischoff, Bernard, 'Libraries and Schools in the Carolingian Revival of Learning', in his, *Manuscripts and Libraries in the Age of Charlemagne*, trans. by Michael Gorman (Cambridge: CUP, 1994), 93–114.

Blair, Ann, *Too Much to Know: Managing Scholarly Information before the Modern Age* (New Haven, CT, and London: Yale University Press, 2010).

Blaise, Albert, *Dictionnaire Latin-Français des auteurs du Moyen-Age*, CCCM Lexicon Latinitatis medii aevi (Turnhout: Brepols, 1975).

Bonamente, Giorgio, 'Minor Latin Historians of the Fourth Century A.D.', in *Greek and Roman Historiography in Late Antiquity: Fourth to Sixth Century A.D.*, ed. Gabrielle Marasco (Leiden: Brill, 2003), 85–125.

Boodts, Shari, 'Les sermons d'Augustin', in *Les douze compilations pauliennes de Florus de Lyon*, eds Pierre Chambert-Protat, Franz Dolveck and Camille Gerzaguet (Rome: École française de Rome, 2017), 197–211.

Booker, Courtney M., *Past Convictions: The Penance of Louis the Pious and the Decline of the Carolingians* (Philadelphia, PA: University of Pennsylvania Press, 2009).

Brilli, Elisa, 'L'entente entre Orose et saint Augustin: contribution à l'étude de la réception médiévale des *Histoires*', *Sacris Erudiri*, 51 (2012): 363–90.

Brincken, Anna-Dorothee von den, *Studien zur lateinischen Weltchronistik bis in das Zeitalter Ottos von Freising* (Dusseldorf: Michael Triltsch, 1957).

Brincken, Anna-Dorothee von den, 'Hieronymus als Exeget "secundum historiam": Von der Chronik zum Ezechiel-Kommentar', *DA*, 49 (1993): 453–78.

Brown, Dennis, *Vir trilinguis: A Study in the Biblical Exegesis of Saint Jerome* (Kampen: Kok Pharos Publishing House, 1992).

Brown, Giles, 'Introduction: The Carolingian Renaissance', in *Carolingian Culture: Emulation and Innovation*, ed. Rosamond McKitterick (Cambridge: CUP, 1994), 1–51.

Brown, Peter, *Authority and the Sacred: Aspects of the Christianisation of the Roman World* (Cambridge: CUP, 1995).

Brown, Peter, *Augustine of Hippo: A Biography*, 2nd edn (Berkeley, CA: University of California Press, 2000).

Brunhölzl, Franz, *Geschichte der lateinischen Literatur des Mittelalters, I: Von Cassiodor bis zum Ausklang der karolingischen Erneuerung* (Munich: Fink, 1975).

Bührer-Thierry, Geneviève, 'Raban Maur et l'épiscopat de son temps', in *Raban Maur et son temps*, eds Philippe Depreux, Stéphane Lebecq, Michel J.-L. Perrin and Olivier Szerwiniak (Turnhout: Brepols, 2010), 63–76.

Bullough, Donald A. and Harting-Corrêa, Alice L., 'Texts, Chant, and the Chapel of Louis the Pious', in *Carolingian Renewal: Sources and Heritage* (Manchester: MUP, 1991), 241–71.

Büren, Veronika von, 'Une edition critique de Solin au IXe siècle', *Scriptorium*, 50 (1996): 22–87.

Burgess, Richard W., 'Jerome Explained: An Introduction to his Chronicle and a Guide to its Use', *Ancient History Bulletin*, 16 (2002), 1–32; repr. in his *Chronicles, Consuls, and Coins: Historiography and History in the Later Roman Empire* (Farnham: Ashgate Variorum, 2011).

Burgess, Richard W. and Kulikowski, Michael, *Mosaics of Time: The Latin Chronicle Traditions from the First Century BC to the Sixth Century AD, vol. 1: A Historical Introduction to the Chronicle Genre from its Origins to the High Middle Ages* (Turnhout: Brepols, 2013).

Burrows, Toby, 'Holy Information: A New Look at Raban Maur's *De naturis rerum*', *Paregon*, 5 (1987): 28–37.

Butzmann, Hans, 'Der Ezechiel-Kommentar des Hrabanus Maurus und seine älteste Handschrift', *Bibliothek und Wissenschaft*, 1 (1964): 1–22.

Campopiano, Michael and Bainton, Henry (eds), *Universal Chronicles in the High Middle Ages* (Woodbridge: York Medieval Press, 2017).

Canellis, Aline, 'Jerome's Hermeneutics: How to Exegete the Bible?', in *Patristic Theories of Biblical Interpretation: The Latin Fathers*, ed. Tarmo Toom (Cambridge: CUP, 2016), 49–76.

Cantelli, Silvia, *Angelomo e la scuola esegetica di Luxeuil*, Biblioteca di Medioevo Latino 1 (Spoleto: Centro italiano di studi sull'alto Medioevo, 1990).

Cantelli, Silvia Beraducci, *Hrabani Mauri Opera Omnia: Repertorium Fontium*, 3 vols (Turnhout: Brepols, 2006).

Cantelli, Silvia Beraducci, 'Hrabanus Maurus', in *The Oxford Guide to the Historical Reception of Augustine*, eds Karla Pollmann and Willemien Otten, 3 vols (Oxford: OUP, 2013), vol. 2, 1158–60.

Cavadini, John, 'Claudius of Turin and the Augustinian Tradition', in *Proceedings of the PMR Conference*, vol. 11, (Villanova: Villanova University, 1986), 43–50.

Cavadini, John, 'A Carolingian Hilary', in *The Study of the Bible in the Carolingian Era*, eds Celia Chazelle and Burton van Name Edwards (Turnhout: Brepols, 2003), 133–40.

Ceillier, Remy, *Histoire générale des auteurs sacrés et ecclésiastiques*, nouvelle edition, 14 vols (Paris: Louis Vivès, 1858–63).

Chambert-Protat, Pierre, Delmulle, Jérémy, Pezé, Warren and Thompson, Jeremy C. (eds), *La controverse carolingienne sur la prédestination: histoire, textes, manuscrits: actes du colloque international de Paris des 11 et 12 octobre 2013* (Turnhout: Brepols, 2018).

Chandler, Cullen J., *Carolingian Catalonia: Politics, Culture, and Identity in an Imperial Province, 778–987* (Cambridge: CUP, 2019).

Chazan, Mireille, 'La méthode critique des historiens dans les chroniques universelles médiévales', in *La méthode critique au Moyen Âge*, eds Mareille Chazan and Gilbert Dahan (Turnhout: Brepols, 2006), 223–56.

Chazan, Mireille, 'La *Chronique* de Jérôme: source, modèle ou autorité?', in *Apprendre, produire, se conduire: le modèle au Moyen Âge. XLVe Congrès de la SHMESP (Nancy-Metz, 22 mai–25 mai 2014)* (Paris: Éditions de la Sorbonne, 2015), 261–74.

Chazelle, Celia and Edwards, Burton van Name 'Introduction: The Study of the Bible and Carolingian Culture', in *The Study of the Bible in the Carolingian Era*, eds Celia Chazelle and Burton van Name Edwards, Medieval church Studies 3 (Turnhout: Brepols, 2003), 1–16.

Chesnut, Glen F., *The First Christian Histories: Eusebius, Socrates, Sozomen, Theodoret and Evagrius*, 2nd edn (Macon: Mercer University Press, 1986).

Chevalier-Royet, Caroline, 'Le commentaire de Raban Maur sur les *Livres des Rois*: manuel scolaire à l'usage des moines et guide pratique à l'usage des rois', in *Raban Maur et son temps*, eds Philippe Depreux, Stéphane Lebecq, Michel J.-L. Perrin and Olivier Szerwiniak (Turnhout: Brepols, 2010), 293–303.

Chevalier-Royet, Caroline, 'Entre tradition et innovation: Raban Maur, un érudit carolingien face à ses sources', in *Érudition et culture savante: de l'Antiquité à l'époque modern*, eds François Brizay and Véronique Sarrazin (Rennes: Presses Universitaires de Rennes, 2015), 53–70.

Choy, Renie S., *Intercessory Prayer and the Monastic Ideal in the Time of the Carolingian Reforms* (Oxford: OUP, 2016).

Clark, Frederic N., *The First Pagan Historian: The Fortunes of a Fraud from Antiquity to the Enlightenment* (Oxford: OUP, 2020).

Claussen, M. A., 'Benedict of Aniane as Teacher', in *Discovery and Distinction in the Early Middle Ages: Studies in Honour of John J. Contreni*, eds Cullen J. Chandler and Steven A. Stofferahn (Kalamazoo, MI: Western Michigan University Press, 2013), 73–87.

Claussen, M. A., 'Reims, Bibliotèque Carnegie, 806: A Little-known Manuscript of Benedict of Aniane's *Concordia Regularum*', *EME*, 23(1) (2015): 1–42.

Conant, Jonathan P., 'Louis the Pious and the Contours of Empire', *EME*, 22(3) (2014): 336–60.

Contreni, John J., 'Carolingian Biblical Studies', in *Carolingian Essays: Andrew W. Mellon Lectures in Early Christian Studies*, ed. U.-R. Blumenthal (Washington, DC: CUA Press, 1983), 71–98; repr. in his *Carolingian Learning, Masters and Manuscripts* (Aldershot: Variorum, 1992), item V.

Contreni, John J., 'Carolingian Biblical Culture', in *Iohannes Scottus Eriugena: The Bible and Hermeneutics*, eds Gerd Van Riel, Carlos Steel and James McEvoy (Leuven: Leuven University Press, 1996), 1–23; repr. in his *Learning and Culture in Carolingian Europe: Letters, Numbers, Exegesis, and Manuscripts* (Farnham: Ashgate Variorum, 2011).

Contreni, John J., 'The Carolingian Renaissance: Education and Literary Culture', in *The New Cambridge Medieval History, Vol. II, c.700–c.900*, ed. Rosamond McKitterick (Cambridge: CUP, 1995), 709–57.

Contreni, John J., 'The Patristic Legacy to c. 1000', in *The New Cambridge History of the Bible: From 600 to 1450*, eds Richard Marsden and E. Ann Matter (Cambridge: CUP, 2012), 505–35.

Contreni, John J., 'Learning for God: Education in the Carolingian Age', *The Journal of Medieval Latin*, 24 (2014): 89–130.

Coogan, Jeremiah, 'Transforming Textuality: Porphyry, Eusebius, and Late Ancient Tables of Contents', *Studies in Late Antiquity*, 5(1) (2021): 6–27.

Coogan, Michael D., *The Old Testament: A Historical and Literary Introduction to the Hebrew Scriptures* (Oxford: OUP, 2006).

Corke-Webster, James, *Eusebius and Empire: Constructing Church and Rome in the Ecclesiastical History* (Cambridge: CUP, 2019).

Corradini, Richard, 'Approaches to History: Walahfrid's Parallel Universe', in *Historiography and Identity III: Carolingian Approaches*, eds Rutger Kramer, Helmut Reimitz and Graeme Ward (Turnhout: Brepols, 2021), 155–97.

Costambeys, Marios J., *Power and Patronage in Early Medieval Italy: Local Society, Italian Politics, and the Abbey of Farfa, c. 700–900* (Cambridge: CUP, 2007).

Costambeys, Marios, Innes, Matthew and MacLean, Simon, *The Carolingian World* (Cambridge: CUP, 2011).

Coumert, Magali, 'Raban Maur et les Germains', in *Raban Maur et son temps*, eds Philippe Depreux, Stéphane Lebecq, Michel J.-L. Perrin and Olivier Szerwiniak (Turnhout: Brepols, 2010), 137–53.

Coutray, Régis, 'La réception du "Commentaire sur Daniel" de Jérôme dans l'Occident médiéval chrétien (VII–XII siècle), *Sacris Erudiri*, 44 (2005): 117–87.

Coutray, Régis, *Prophète des temps derniers: Jérôme commente Daniel* (Paris: Beauchesne, 2009).

Coz, Yann, 'Quelques interprétations des *Historiae adversus paganos* d'Orose au IXème siècle', *The Journal of Medieval Latin*, 17 (2007): 286–99.

Crawford, Matthew R., *The Eusebian Canon Tables: Ordering Textual Knowledge in Late Antiquity* (Oxford: OUP, 2019).

Croke, Brian, 'A.D. 476: The Manufacture of a Turning Point', *Chiron*, 13 (1983): 81–119.

Croke, Brian, 'Origins of the Christian World Chronicle', in *History and Historians in Late Antiquity*, eds Brian Croke and Alanna M. Emmett (Oxford: Pergamon, 1983), 116–31.

Cross, J. E., '"Legimus in ecclesiasticis historiis": A Sermon for All Saints, and its Use in Old English Prose', *Traditio*, 33 (1977): 101–35.

Curtius, Ernst Robert, *European Literature and the Latin Middle Ages*, trans. Willard R. Trask (Princeton, NJ: Princeton University Press, 1953).

Dal Santo, Matthew, 'Gregory the Great, the Empire and the Emperor', in *A Companion to Gregory the Great*, eds Bronwen Neil and Matthew Dal Santo (Leiden and Boston, MA: Brill, 2013), 57–82.

Delacenserie, Emerance, 'Beyond the Compilation: The Two *Historiae tripartitae* of Theodore Lector and Cassiodorus', *Sacris Erudiri*, 56 (2017): 415–44.

Deliyannis, Deborah Mauskopf, 'Introduction', in *Historiography in the Middle Ages*, ed. Deborah Mauskopf Deliyannis (Leiden: Brill, 2003), 1–13.

Deniaux, Elisabeth, Lorren, Claude, Bauduin, Pierre and Jarry, Thomas (eds), *La Normandie avant les Normands de la conquête romaine à l'arrivée des Vikings* (Rennes: Ouest-France, 2002).

Depreux, Philippe, 'Büchersuche und Büchertausch im Zeitalter der karolingischen Renaissance am Beispiel des Briefwechsels des Lupus von Ferriès', *Archiv für Kulturgeschichte*, 76 (1994): 267–84.

Depreux, Philippe, *Prosopographie de l'entourage de Louis le Pieux (781–840)*, Instrumenta I (Sigmaringen: Thorbecke, 1997).

Depreux, Philippe, 'Ambitions et limites des réformes culturelles à l'époque Carolingienne', *Revue historique*, 307 (2002): 721–53.

Depreux, Philippe, 'L'actualité de Fréculf de Lisieux: à propos de l'edition critique de son œvre', *Tabularia*, 4 (2004): 53–60.

Depreux, Philippe, 'Raban, l'abbé, l'archevêque. Le champ d'action d'un grand ecclésiastique dans la société carolingienne', in *Raban Maur et son temps*, eds Philippe Depreux, Stéphane Lebecq, Michel J.-L. Perrin and Olivier Szerwiniack (Turnhout: Brepols, 2010), 49–61.

Diebold, William, '*Nos quoque morem illius imitari cupientes*: Charles the Bald's Evocation and Imitation of Charlemagne', *Archiv für Kulturgeschichte*, 75 (1993): 271–300.

Diem, Albrect, 'The Carolingians and the *Regula Benedicti*', in *Religious Franks: Religion and Power in the Frankish Kingdoms: Studies in Honour of Mayke de Jong*, eds Rob Meens, Dorine van Espelo, Bram van den Hoven dan Genderen, Janneke Raajimakers, Irene van Renswoude, and Carine van Rhijn (Manchester: MUP, 2016), 243–61.

Diesenberger, Maximilian, Yitzhak Hen and Marianne Pollheimer (eds), *Sermo doctorum: Compilers, Preachers, and their Audiences in the Early Medieval West* (Turnhout: Brepols, 2013).

Dolbeau, François, *Prophètes, apôtres et disciples dans les traditions chrétiennes d'Occident. Vies brèves et listes en latin* (Brussels: Société des Bollandistes, 2012).

Dolbeau, François, 'La formation du Canon des Pères, du IVᵉ au VIᵉ siècle', in *Les réceptions des Pères de l'Église au Moyen Âge: le devenir de la tradition ecclésiale*, eds Nicole Bériou, Rainer Berndt and Michel Fédou, Archa verbi. Subsidia 10, 2 vols (Münster: Aschendorff, 2013), vol. 1, 17–39.

Dorofeeva, Anna, 'Miscellanies, Christian Reform and Early Medieval Encyclopaedism: A Re-consideration of the Pre-bestiary Latin *Physiologus* Manuscripts', *Historical Research*, 90 (2017): 665–82.

Dorofeeva, Anna, 'Reading Early Medieval Miscellanies', in *Scribes and the Presentation of Texts (From Antiquity to c. 1550). Proceedings of the 20th Colloquium of the Comité international de paléographie latine, Beinecke Rare Book & Manuscript Library, Yale University (New Haven, September 6–8, 2017)*, eds C.W. Dutschke and B.A. Shailor, Bibliologia 65 (Turnhout: Brepols, forthcoming 2021).

Dorofeeva, Anna, 'What is a Vademecum? The Social Logic of Early Medieval Compilation', in *The Art of Compilation: Manuscripts and Networks in the Early Medieval Latin West*, eds Anna Dorofeeva and Michael Kelly (Binghamton, NY: Gracchi Books, forthcoming 2022).

Dubois, Jacques, 'Les listes épiscopales témoins de l'organisation ecclésiastique', *Revue d'histoire de l'église de France*, 62 (1976): 9–23.

Dubreucq, Alain, 'La littérature des "Specula": Délimitation du genre, contenu, destinataires et réception', in *Guerriers et moines. Conversion et sainteté aristocratiques dans l'Occident médiéval (IXᵉ–XIIᵉ siècle)*, ed. Michel Lauwers (Turnhout: Brepols, 2002), 17–39.

Duchesne, Louis, *Fastes épiscopaux de l'ancienne Gaule*, 3 vols (Paris: Thorin & fils, 1894–1915).

Dummer, Jürgen, 'Frechulf von Lisieux und die *Historia ecclesiastica tripartita*', *Philologus*, 115 (1971): 58–70.

Dümmler, Ernst, 'Karolingische Miscellen', *Forschungen zur Deutschen Geschichte*, 6 (1866): 115–29.

Dümmler, Ernst, 'De procinctu Romanae miliciae', *Zeitschrift für deutsches Alterthum*, 15 (1872): 443–51.

Dusil, Stephan, Schwedler, Gerald and Schwitter, Raphael (eds), *Exzerpieren – Kompilieren – Tradieren: Transformationen des Wissens zwischen Spätantike und Frühmittelalter* (Berlin: De Gruyter, 2016).

Eckhardt, Willhelm Alfred, 'Die *Capitularia missorum specialia* von 802', *DA*, 12 (1956): 498–516.

Edwards, Mark, 'The First Council of Nicaea' in *The Cambridge History of Christianity, vol. 1: Origins to Constantine*, eds Margaret M. Mitchell and Frances M. Young (Cambridge: CUP, 2006), 552–67.

Eisenhut, Heidi, *Die Glossen Ekkeharts IV. von St. Gallen im Codex Sangallensis 621* (St. Gallen: Verlag am Klosterhof, 2009).

Emerick, Judson, 'Charlemagne: A New Constantine?', in *The Life and Legacy of Constantine: Traditions through the Ages*, ed. M. Shane Bjornlie (London: Routledge, 2017), 133–61.

Engen, Jan van, 'Letters, the Lettered Voice and Public Culture in the Carolingian Era', *Scrivere e leggere nell'alto Medioevo*, Settimane 59 (Spoleto: Centro italiano di studi sull'alto Medioevo, 2012), 403–26.

Epp, Verena, 'Von Spurensuchern und Zeichendeutern. Zum selbstverstännis mittelalterlicher Geschichtsschreiber', in *Von Fakten und Fiktionen: mittelalterliche Geschichtsdarstellungen und ihre kritische Aufarbeitung*, ed. Johannes Laudage (Cologne: Böhlau, 2003), 43–62.

Evans, Robert A. H., 'God's Judgment in Carolingian Law and History Writing', in *The Church and the Law*, eds Rosamond McKitterick, Charlotte Methuen and Andrew Spicer, *Studies in Church History*, 56 (2020): 60–77.

Evans, Robert A. H., '"Instructing readers' Minds in Heavenly Matters": Carolingian History Writing and Christian Education', in *Churches and Education*, eds Morwenna Ludlow, Charlotte Methuen and Andrew Spicer, *Studies in Church History*, 55 (2019): 56–71.

Evans, Robert and Rosamond McKitterick, 'A Carolingian Epitome of Orosius from Tours: Leiden VLQ 20', in *Historiography and Identity III: Carolingian Approaches*, eds Rutger Kramer, Helmut Reimitz and Graeme Ward (Turnhout: Brepols, 2021), 123–53.

Ewig, Eugen 'Das Bild Constantins des Großen in den ersten Jahrhunderten des abendländischen Mittelalters', *Historisches Jahrbuch*, 75 (1955): 1–46.

Faitini, Tiziana, 'Towards a Spiritual Empire: Christian Exegesis of the Universal Census at the Time of Jesus's Birth', in *The Church and Empire*, eds Stewart J. Brown, Charlotte Methuen and Andrew Spicer, *Studies in Church History*, 54 (2018): 16–30.

Ferrari, Mirela, 'Mira Brevitate: Orosio e il Decretum Gelasianum', in *Roma, magistra mundi. Itineraria culturae medievalis. Mélanges offerts au Père L. E. Boyle à l'occasion de son 75ᵉ anniversaire*, ed. Jacqueline Hamesse, Textes et études du Moyen Âge, 3 vols (Louvain-la-Neuve: F.I.D.E.M., Collège Mercier, 1998), vol. 1, 225–31.

Fitzgerald, Allan and Cavadini, John C. (eds), *Augustine through the Ages: An Encyclopedia* (Grand Rapids, MI: William. B. Eerdmans, 1999).

Formisano, Marco, 'Towards an Aesthetic Paradigm of Late Antiquity', *Antiquité tardive*, 15 (2007): 277–84.

Fouracre, Paul, *The Age of Charles Martel* (Harlow: Longman, 2000).

Fox, Michael, 'Alcuin the Exegete: The Evidence of the *Quaestiones in Genesim*', in Celia Chazelle and Burton van Name Edwards (eds.), *The Study of the Bible in the Carolingian Era*, Medieval Church Studies 3 (Turnhout: Brepols, 2003), 39–60.

Fransen, Paul-Iréné, 'Le dossier patristique d'Helisachar: le manuscript Paris BNF lat. 11574 et l'une de ses sources', *Revue bénédictine*, 111 (2001): 464–82.

Freise, Eckhard, 'Zum Geburtsjahr des Hrabanus Maurus', in *Hrabanus Maurus: Lehrer, Abt und Bischof*, eds Raymund Kottje and Harald Zimmermann (Wiesbaden: Steiner, 1982), 18–74.

Frend, W. H. C., 'Augustine and Orosius on the End of the Ancient World', *Augustinian Studies*, 20 (1989): 1–38.

Freund, Stephan, *Von Agilolfingern zu den Karolingern: Bayerns Bischöfe zwischen Kirchenorganisation, Reichsintegration und karolingischer Reform (700–847)* (Munich: Beck, 2004).

Fried, Johannes, 'Ludwig der Fromme, das Papsttum und die fränkische Kirche', in *Charlemagne's Heir: New Perspectives on the Reign of Louis the Pious (814–840)*, eds Peter Godman and Roger Collins (Oxford: Clarendon Press, 1990), 231–73.

Fried, Johannes, *Donation of Constantine and Constitutum Constantini: The Misinterpretation of a Fiction and its Original Meaning. With a Contribution by Wolfram Brandes: 'The Satraps of Constantine'* (Berlin: De Gruyter, 2007).

Führer, Julian, 'Hugues de Fleury: l'histoire et la typologie', in *La typologie biblique comme forme de pensée dans l'historiographie médiévale*, ed. Marek Thue Kretschmer (Turnhout: Brepols, 2015), 97–118.

Ganshof, Frans Louis, 'L'Historiographie dans la monarchie franque sous les Merovingiens et les Carolingiens', in *La Storiografia Altomedievale*, Settimane 17 (Spoleto: Centro italiano di studi sull'alto Medioevo, 1970), 631–85.

Ganz, David, 'The Preface to Einhard's *Vita Karoli*', in *Einhard: Studien zu Leben und Werk*, eds Hermann Schefers (Darmstadt: Hessische Historische Kommission, 1997), 299–310.

Ganz, David, 'Einhard's Charlemagne: The Characterisation of Greatness' in *Charlemagne: Empire and Society*, ed. Joanna Story (Manchester: MUP, 2005), 38–51.

Ganz, David, *Two Lives of Charlemagne* (London: Penguin, 2008).

Ganz, David, 'The Astronomer's Life of Louis the Pious', in *Rome and Religion in the Medieval World: Studies in Honour of Thomas F. X. Noble*, eds Valerie L. Garver and Owen M. Phelan (Farnham: Ashgate, 2014), 129–48.

Ganz, David, 'Historia: Some Lexicographical Considerations', in *Medieval Cantors and their Craft: Music, Liturgy and the Shaping of History, 800–1500*, eds Katie Anne-Marie Bugyis, A. B. Kraebel and Margot E. Fassler (York: York Medieval Press, 2017), 8–22.

Ganz, David, 'Early Caroline: France and Germany', in *The Oxford Handbook of Latin Palaeography*, eds Frank T. Coulson and Robert G. Babcock (Oxford: OUP, 2020), 237–61.

Garipzanov, Ildar H., 'The Carolingian Abbreviation of Bede's World Chronicle and Carolingian Imperial "Genealogy"', *Hortus Artium Medievalium*, 11 (2005), 291–8.

Garipzanov, Ildar H., 'The Communication of Authority in Carolingian Titles', *Viator*, 36 (2005): 41–82.

Garipzanov, Ildar H., *The Symbolic Language of Authority in the Carolingian World (c. 751–877)*, Brill Series on the Early Middle Ages 16 (Leiden: Brill, 2008).

Garipzanov, Ildar H., *Graphic Signs of Authority in Late Antiquity and the Early Middle Ages* (Oxford: OUP, 2018).

Garrison, Mary, 'The Collectanea and Medieval Florilegia', in *Collectanea Pseudo-Bedae*, eds Martha Bayless and Michael Lapidge (Dublin: Dublin Institute for Advanced Studies 1998), 42–83.

Gera, Dov, 'Unity and Chronology in the *Jewish Antiquities*', in *Flavius Josephus: Interpretation and History*, eds Jack Pastor, Pnina Stern and Menahem Mor, Supplement to the Journal for the Study of Judaism (Leiden: Brill, 2011), 125–47.

Geuenich, Dieter, 'Gebetsgedenken und anianische Reform: Beobachtungen zu den Verbrüdersbeziehungen der Äbte im Reich Ludwigs des Frommen', in *Monastische Reformen im 9. und 10. Jahrhundert*, eds Raymund Kottje and Helmut Maurer (Sigmaringen: Thorbecke, 1989), 79–106.

Geuenich, Dieter, 'Benedikt von Aniane, Helisachar und Einhard im St Galler Verbrüderungsbuch', in *Schatzkammer Stiftsarchiv St. Gallen. Miscellanea Lorenz Hollenstein*, eds Peter Erhart and Klaus Amann (Dietikon: Graf, 2009), 27–9.

Geuenich, Dieter and Ludwig, Uwe (eds), *Die St. Galler Verbrüderungsbücher*, MGH *Libri memoriales, nova series* 9 (Wiesbaden: Harrassowitz Verlag, 2019).

Gillis, Matthew Bryan, *Heresy and Dissent in the Carolingian Empire: The Case of Gottschalk of Orbais* (Oxford: OUP, 2017).

Gioanni, Stéphane 'Les listes d'auteurs «à recevoir» et «à ne pas recevoir» dans la formation du canon patristique: le *decretum gelasianum* et les origines de la «censure» ecclésiastique', in *Compétition et sacré au haut Moyen Âge: entre mediation et exclusion*, eds Philippe Depreux, François Bourgard and Régine le Jan (Turnhout: Brepols, 2015), 17–28.

Goetz, Hans-Werner, *Die Geschichtstheologie des Orosius* (Darmstadt: Wissenschaftliche Buchgesellschaft, 1980).

Goetz, Hans-Werner, 'Die "Geschichte" im Wissenschaftssytem des Mittelalters', in Franz-Joseph Schmale, *Funktion und Formen mittelalterlicher Geschichtsschreibung: Eine Einführung* (Darmstadt: Wissenschaftliche Buchgesellschaft, 1985), 165–213.

Goetz, Hans-Werner, 'On the Universality of Universal History', in *L'historiographie médiévale en Europe: actes du colloque organisé par la Fondation européenne de la science au Centre de recherches historiques et juridiques de l'Université Paris I du 29 mars au 1er avril 1989*, ed. Jean-Philippe Genet (Paris: Presses du CNRS, 1991), 247–61.

Goetz, Hans-Werner, 'Historiographisches Zeitbewußtsein im frühen Mittelalter: Zum Umgang mit der Zeit in der karolingischen Geschichtsschreibung', in *Historiographie im frühen Mittelalter*, eds Anton Scharer and Georg Scheibelreiter Veröffentlichen des Instituts für Österreichishe Geschichtsforschung 32 (Vienna: Oldenbourg, 1994), 158–78.

Goetz, Hans-Werner, 'Vergangenheitswahrnehmung, Vergangenheitsgebrauch und Geschichtssymbolismus in der Geschichtsschreibung der Karolingerzeit', in *Ideologie e pratiche del reimpiego nell'alto medioevo*, Settimane 46 (Spoleto: Centro italiano di studi sull'alto Medioevo, 1999), 177–225.

Goetz, Hans-Werner, *Vorstellungsgeschichte: gesammelte Schriften zu Wahrnehmungen, Deutungen und Vorstellungen im Mittelalter* (Bochum: Dieter Winkler, 2007).

Goetz, Hans-Werner, 'Historical Writing, Historical Thinking and Historical Consciousness in the Middle Ages', *Revista Dialogos Mediterrânicos*, 2 (2012): 110–28.

Goez, Werner, *Translatio Imperii: Ein Beitrag zur Geschichte des Geschichtsdenkens und der Politischen Theorien im Mittelalter und in der Fruhen Neuzeit* (Tübingen: Mohr, 1958).

Goez, Werner, 'Zur Weltchronik des Bischofs Frechulf von Lisieux', in *Festgabe für Paul Kirn zum 70. Geburtstag, dargebracht von Freunden und Schülern*, ed. Ekkehard Kaufmann (Berlin: E. Schmidt, 1961), 93–110.

Goffart, Walter, 'Bede's *Vera lex historiae* Explained', *Anglo-Saxon England*, 34 (2005): 111–16; repr. in his *Barbarians, Maps, and Historiography* (Ashgate: Farnham, 2009), item VII.

Gómez, César Chaparro, 'El *De ortu et obitu patrum* de Isidoro de Sevilla. El problema de su composición y transmisión', in *L'édition critique des oeuvres d'Isidore de Séville: les recensions multiples: actes du collque organise à la Casa de Velázquez et à l'Université Rey Juan Carlos de Madrid (14–15 janvier 2002)*, eds Ma A. Andrés Sanz, J. Elfassi and J. C. Martín (Paris, 2008), 49–62.

Goodson, Caroline J. and Nelson, Janet L., 'The Roman Contexts of the "Donation of Constantine"', *EME*, 18(4) (2010): 446–67.

Gorman, Michael M., 'The Commentary on Genesis of Claudius of Turin and Biblical Studies under Louis the Pious', *Speculum*, 72(2) (1997): 279–329.

Gorman, Michael M., 'The Commentary on Genesis of Angelomus of Luxeuil and Biblical Studies under Lothar', *Studi medievali*, 40 (1999): 559–631.

Gorman, Michael M., 'Source Marks and Chapter Divisions in Bede's Commentary on Luke', *Revue bénédictine*, 112 (2002): 246–90.

Grafton, Anthony, *Joseph Scaliger: A Study in the History of Classical Scholarship, vol. 2: Historical Chronology* (Oxford: Clarendon Press, 1993).

Grafton, Anthony and Williams, Megan, *Christianity and the Transformation of the Book: Origen, Eusebius, and the Library of Caesarea* (Cambridge, MA: HUP, 2006).

Gravel, Martin, 'Les lettres de autres: correspondances et réseaux en filigrane des grandes collections carolingiennes', *Le Moyen Âge*, 126(2) (2020): 243–71.

Greer, Sarah, Hicklin, Alice and Esders, Stefan (eds), *Using and not Using the Past after the Carolingian Empire, c. 900–c.1050* (London: Routledge, 2020).

Grotans, Anna A., *Reading in Medieval St Gall* (Cambridge: CUP, 2006).

Grunauer, Emil, 'De fontibus historiae Freculpi episcopi lixoviensis' (doctoral dissertation, University of Zurich, 1864).

Grünewald, Thomas, '*Constantinus novus*: zum Constantin-Bild des Mittelalters', in *Costantino il Grande: dall'antichità all'umanesimo: Colloquio sul cristianesimo nel mondo antico, Macerata, 18–20 dicembre 1990*, eds Giorgio Bonamente and Franca Fusco, 2 vols (Macerata: Università degli studi, 1992), vol. 1, 461–85.

Guenée, Bernard, *Histoire et culture historique dans l'Occident médiéval* (Paris: Aubier, 1980).

Guenée, Bernard, 'L'historien et la compilation du XIIIᵉ siècle', *Journal des Savants*, (1985), 119–35.

Gwynn, David M., 'The Council of Chalcedon and the Definition of Christian Tradition', in *Chalcedon in Context: Church Councils 400–700*, eds Richard Price and Mary Whitby (Liverpool: LUP, 2009), 7–26.

Hahn, Johannes, 'The Conversion of the Cult Statues: The Destruction of the Serapeum 392 A.D. and the Transformation of Alexandria into the "Christ-loving" City', in *From Temple to Church: Destruction and Renewal of Local Cultic Topography in Late Antiquity*, ed. Johannes Hahn (Leiden: Brill, 2008), 335–66.

Halfond, Gregory I., *Archaeology of Frankish Church Councils, AD 511–768* (Leiden: Brill, 2010).

Hamesse, Jacqueline, 'La vocaubulaire des florilèges médiévaux', in *Méthodes et instruments du travail intellectuel au Moyen Âge. Etudes sur le vocabulaire*, ed. Olga Weijers (Turnhout: Brepols, 1990), 209–30.

Harries, Jill, 'Church and State in the Notitia Galliarum', *Journal of Roman Studies*, 68 (1978): 26–43.

Hartmann, Carmen Cardelle de, 'Überlieferungsprozesse: Sammeln, Auswählen, Kanonisieren: eine Einführung', *Mittellateinisches Jahrbuch*, 53 (2018): 1–10.

Hartmann, Florian, 'Auf dem Weg zur bischöflichen Dominanz? Entscheidungsfindung und leitende Akteure auf den Konzilien von Frankfurt 794 bis Paris 829', in *Konzilien und kanonisches Recht in Spätantike und frühem Mittelalter: Aspekte konziliarer Entscheidungsfindung*, eds Wolfram Brandes, Alexandra Hasse-Ungeheur and Hartmut Leppin (Berlin: De Gruyter, 2020), 169–90.

Häse, Angelika, *Mittelalterliche Bücherverzeichnisse aus Kloster Lorsch: Einleitung, Edition und Kommentar*, Beiträge zum Buch- und Bibliothekswesen 42 (Wiesbaden: Otto Harrassowitz, 2002).

Hathaway, Neil, '*Compilatio*: From Plagiarism to Compiling', *Viator*, 20 (1989): 19–44.

Heath, Christopher, *The Narrative Worlds of Paul the Deacon: Between Empires and Identities in Lombard Italy* (Amsterdam: Amsterdam University Press, 2018).

Hen, Yitzhak, 'Specula principum carolingi e l'immagine di Costantino', in *Constantino I. Enciclopedia Costantiniana sulla figura e l'immagine dell'imperatore del cosiddetto editto di Milano*, eds Peter Brown *et al.* (Rome: Istituto della enciclopedia italiana, 2013), online: https://www.treccani.it/enciclopedia/elenco-opere/Enciclopedia_Costantiniana [last accessed 25 March 2021].

Henderson, John, 'The Creation of Isidore's *Etymologies or Origins*', in *The Ordering of Knowledge in the Roman Empire*, eds Jason König and Tim Whitmarsh (Cambridge: CUP, 2007), 150–74.

Henderson John, *The Medieval World of Isidore of Seville: Truth from Words* (Cambridge: CUP, 2007).

Henten, Jan Willem van, 'Herod the Great in Josephus', in *A Companion to Josephus*, eds Honora Howell Chapman and Zuleika Rodgers (Chichester: Wiley Blackwell, 2016), 235–46.

Herzog, Reinhart and Koselleck, Reinhart (eds), *Epochenschwelle und Epochenbewußtsein* (Munich: Fink, 1987).

Hill, Joyce 'Carolingian Perspectives on the Authority of Bede', in *Innovation and Tradition in the Writings of Venerable Bede*, ed. Scott DeGregorio (Morgantown, WV: West Virginia University Press, 2006), 227–49.

Hillgarth, Jocelyn Nigel, 'The *Historiae* of Orosius in the Early Middle Ages', in *De Tertullien aux Mozarabes: mélanges offerts à Jacques Fontaine, à l'occasion de son 70ᵉ anniversaire, par ses élèves, amis et collègues*, eds Louis Holtz and Jean-Claude Fredouille, 3 vols (Paris: Institut d'Études Augustininennes, 1992), vol. 2, 157–70.

Holder, Arthur G., 'Bede and the New Testament', in *The Companion to Bede*, ed. Scott DeGregorio (Cambridge: CUP, 2010), 142–55.

Holloway, Paul A., 'Inconvenient Truths: Early Jewish and Christian History Writing and the Ending of Luke-Acts', in *Die Apostelgeschichte im Kontext antiker und frühchristlicher Historiographie*, eds Jörg Frey, Clare K. Rothschild, Jens Schröter and Bettina Rost (Berlin: De Gruyter, 2009), 418–33.

Holtz, Louis, 'Le ms. Lyon, B.M. 484 (414) et la méthode de travail de Florus', *Revue bénédictine*, 119 (2009): 270–315.

Horster, Marietta and Reitz, Christiane, 'Handbooks, Epitomes, and Florilegia', in *A Companion to Late Antique Literature*, eds Scott C. MacGill and Edward Jay Watts (New York: John Wiley, 2018), 431–50.

Howell Chapman, Honora and Rodgers, Zuleika (eds), *A Companion to Josephus in his World* (Chichester: Wiley Blackwell, 2016).

Huglo, Michel, 'Trois livres manuscrits présentés par Helisachar', *Revue bénédictine*, 99 (1989): 272–85.

Huglo, Michel, 'D'Helischar à Abbon de Fleury', *Revue bénédictine*, 104 (1994): 204–30.

Hummer, Hans J., *Politics and Power in Early Medieval Europe: Alsace and the Frankish Realm, 600–1000* (Cambridge: CUP, 2005).

Humphries, Mark, 'Chronicle and Chronology: Prosper of Aquitaine, his Methods and the Development of Early Medieval Chronography', *EME*, 5(2) (1996): 155–75.

Humphries, Mark, 'Rufinus's Eusebius: Translation, Continuation and Edition in the Latin *Ecclesiastical History*', *Journal of Early Christian Studies*, 16(2) (2008): 143–64.

Inglebert, Hervé, *Les Romains chrétiens face à l'histoire de Rome: histoire, christianisme et romanités en Occident dans l'Antiquité tardive (IIIᵉ–Vᵉ siècles)* (Paris: Institut d'études augustiniennes, 1996).

Inglebert, Hervé, 'Renommée et Sainteté: historiographie et hagiographie dans les chroniques tardo-antiques latines et dans le *De ortu et obitu patrum* d'Isidore de Séville', *Salesianum*, 67 (2005): 977–88.

Inglebert, Hervé, 'Les conceptions historiographiques de la totalité du passé à l'époque carolingienne (750–910)', in *Rerum gestarum scriptor: histoire et historiographie au Moyen Âge*, eds Magali Coumert, Marie-Céline Isaïa, Klaus Krönert and Sumi Shimahara (Paris: Presses de l'Université Paris-Sorbonne, 2012), 77–86.

Innes, Matthew, 'Charlemagne's Will: Piety, Politics and Imperial Succession', *English Historical Review*, 112 (1997): 833–55.

Innes, Matthew, 'The Classical Tradition in the Carolingian Renaissance: Ninth-Century Encounters with Suetonius', *International Journal of the Classical Tradition*, 3 (1997): 265–82.

Innes, Matthew, *State and Society in the Early Middle Ages: The Middle Rhein Valley, 400–1000* (Cambridge: CUP, 2000).

Innes, Matthew, 'Teutons or Trojans? The Carolingians and the Germanic Past', in *The Uses of the Past in the Early Middle Ages*, eds Yitzhak Hen and Matthew Innes (Cambridge: CUP, 2000), 227–49.

Innes, Matthew, '"He Never Even Allowed his White Teeth to be Bared in Laughter": The Politics of Humour in the Carolingian Renaissance', in *Humour, History and Politics in Late Antiquity and the Early Middle Ages*, ed. Guy Halsall (Cambridge: CUP, 2002), 131–56.

Innes, Matthew and McKitterick, Rosamond, 'The Writing of History', in *Carolingian Culture: Emulation and Innovation*, ed. Rosamond McKitterick (Cambridge: CUP, 1994), 193–220.

Jaeger, Stephen, 'Ernst Robert Curtius: A Medievalist's Contempt for the Middle Ages', *Viator*, 47(2) (2016): 367–80.

Janson, Tore, *Latin Prose Prefaces: Studies in Literary Conventions* (Stockholm: Almqvist & Wiksell, 1964).

Jay, Pierre, *L'exégèse de Saint Jérôme d'après son 'Commentaire sur Isaïe'* (Paris: Études augustiniennes, 1985).

Jebe, Johanna, 'Bücherverzeichnisse als Quellen der Wissensorganisation: Ordnungspraktiken und Wissenordungen in den karolingerzeitlichen Klöstern Lorsch und St Gallen', in Andreas Speer and Lars Reuke (eds), *Die Bibliothek – The Library – La Bibliothèque: Denkräume und Wissensordnungen*, Miscellanea Mediaevalia 41 (Berlin: De Gruyter, 2020), 3–28.

Johnson, Scott Fitzgerald, *Greek Literature in Late Antiquity: Dynamism, Didacticism, Classicism* (Aldershot: Ashgate, 2006).

Jones, Christopher A., *A Lost Work by Amalarius of Metz: Interpolations in Salisbury Cathedral Library MS 154* (Woodbridge: Boydell & Brewer, 2001).

Jong, Mayke de, 'Old Law and New-found Power: Hrabanus Maurus and the Old Testament', in *Centres of Learning: Learning and Location in Pre-Modern Europe and the Near East*, eds Jan Willem Drijvers and Alasdair A. MacDonald (Leiden: Brill, 1995), 161–76.

Jong, Mayke de, 'The Empire as *Ecclesia*: Hrabanus Maurus and Biblical *Historia* for Rulers', in *The Uses of the Past in the Early Middle Ages*, eds Yitzhak Hen and Matthew Innes (Cambridge: CUP, 2000), 191–226.

Jong, Mayke de, 'Exegesis for an Empress', in *Medieval Transformations: Texts, Power and Gifts in Context*, eds Esther Cohen and Mayke de Jong (Leiden: Brill, 2001), 69–100.

Jong, Mayke de, '*Sacrum palatium et ecclesia*: L'autorité religieuse royale sous les Carolingiens (790–840), *Annales*, 58 (2003), 1243–69; 'The Sacred Palace, Public Penance and the Carolingian Polity', in *Great Christian Jurists and Legal Collections in the First Millennium*, ed. Philip L. Reynolds (Cambridge: CUP, 2019), 155–81.

Jong, Mayke de, '*Ecclesia* and the Early Medieval Polity', in *Staat im Frühen Mittelalter*, eds Stuart Airlie, Walter Pohl and Helmut Reimitz (Vienna: Austrian Academy of Sciences Press, 2006), 113–32.

Jong, Mayke de, 'Queens and Beauty in the Early Medieval West: Balthild, Theodelinda, Judith', in *Agire da donna: Modelli e pratiche di rappresentazione (secoli VI–X); Atti del convegno (Padova, 18–19 febbraio 2005)*, ed. Cristina La Rocca (Turnhout: Brepols, 2007), 235–48.

Jong, Mayke de, *The Penitential State: Authority and Atonement in the Age of Louis the Pious, 814–840* (Cambridge: CUP, 2009).

Jong, Mayke de 'The State of the Church: *Ecclesia* and Early Medieval State Formation', in *Der frühmittelalterliche Staat—europäische Perspektiven*, eds Walter Pohl and Veronika Wieser (Vienna: Austrian Academy of Sciences Press, 2009), 241–54.

Jong, Mayke de, 'Carolingian Political Discourse and the Biblical Past: Hraban, Dhuoda, Radbert', in *The Resources of the Past in Early Medieval Europe*, eds Clemens Gantner, Rosamond McKitterick and Sven Meeder (Cambridge: CUP, 2015), 87–102.

Jong, Mayke de, 'Hraban as Mediator: *De Honore Parentum* (Autumn 834)', in *Splendor Reginae. Passions, genre et famille: Mélanges en l'honneur de Régine Le Jan*, eds Laurent Jégou, Sylvie Joye, Thomas Lienhard, and Jens Schneider (Turnhout: Brepols, 2015), 49–58.

Jong, Mayke de, 'The Empire That was Always Decaying: The Carolingians (800–888)', *Medieval Worlds*, 1(2) (2015): 6–25.

Jong, Mayke de, 'The Two Republics: Ecclesia and the Public Domain in the Carolingian World', in *Italy and Early Medieval Europe: Papers for Chris Wickham*, eds Ross Balzaretti, Julia Barrow and Patricia Skinner (Oxford: OUP, 2018), 486–500.

Jong, Mayke de, *Epitaph for an Era: Politics and Rhetoric in the Carolingian World* (Cambridge: CUP, 2019).

Jong, Mayke de, 'From the Order of the Franks to the World of Ambrose: the *Vita Adalhardi* and the *Epitaphium Arsenii* Compared', in *Historiography and Identity III: Carolingian Approaches*, eds Rutger Kramer, Helmut Reimitz and Graeme Ward (Turnhout: Brepols, 2021), 39–63.

Judic, Bruno, 'Grégoire le Grand, Alcuin, Raban et le surnom de Maur', in *Raban Maur et son temps*, eds Philippe Depreux, Stépane Lebecq, Michel Perrin and Olivier Szerwiniack (Turnhout: Brepols, 2010), 31–48.

Kaczynski, Bernice Martha, 'Editions, Translation and Exegesis: The Carolingians and the Bible', in *'The Gentle Voices of Teachers': Aspects of Learning in the Carolingian Age*, ed. Richard E. Sullivan (Columbus, OH: Ohio State University Press, 1995), 171–85.

Kaczynski, Bernice Martha, 'Bede's Commentaries on Luke and Mark and the Formation of a Patristic Canon', in *Latin and its Heritage: Essays in Honour of A. G. Rigg on his 64th birthday*, eds Siân Echard and Gernot R. Wieland, Publications of the Journal of Medieval Latin 4 (Turnhout: Brepols, 2001), 17–26.

Kaczynski, Bernice Martha, 'The Authority of the Fathers: Patristic Texts in Early Medieval Libraries and Scriptoria', *The Journal of Medieval Latin*, 16 (2006): 1–27.

Kaczynski, Bernice Martha, 'Reading and Writing Augustine in Medieval St Gall', in *Insignis sophiae arcator: Essays in Honour of Michael W. Herren on his 65th birthday*, eds Gernot R. Wieland, Carin Ruff and Ross G. Arthur, Publications of the Journal of Medieval Latin 6 (Turnhout: Brepols, 2006), 107–123.

Kany, Roland, 'Warum fand die Apostelgeschichte keine Fortsetzung in der Antike? Elf Thesen zu einem ungelösten Problem', in *Die Apostelgeschichte im Kontext antiker und frühchristlicher Historiographie*, eds Jörg Frey, Clare K. Rothschild and Jens Schröter (Berlin: De Gruyter, 2009), 327–48.

Kaschke, Sören, 'Die Teilungsprojekte der Zeit Ludwigs des Frommen', in *La productivité d'une crise: le règne de Louis le Pieux (814–840) et la transformation de l'Empire Carolingien = Produktivität einer Krise: die Regierungszeit Ludwigs des Frommen (814–840) und die Transformation des karolingischen Imperiums*, eds Philippe Depreux and Stefan Esders (Ostfildern: Thorbecke, 2018), 87–128.

Kaschke, Sören, 'Enhancing Bede: The *Chronicon universale* to 741', in *Historiography and Identity III: Carolingian Approaches*, eds Rutger Kramer, Helmut Reimitz and Graeme Ward (Turnhout: Brepols, 2021), 201–29.

Kelly, Christopher, 'The Shape of the Past: Eusebius of Caesarea and Old Testament History', in *Unclassical Traditions, Volume I: Alternatives to the Classical Past in Late Antiquity*, eds Christopher Kelly, Richard Flower and Michael Stuart Williams (Cambridge Classical Journal, Proceedings of the Cambridge Philological Society, Supplementary Volume 34, 2010), 13–27.

Kelly, J. N. D., *Jerome: His Life, Writings, and Controversies* (London: Duckworth, 1975).

Kempshall, Matthew S., 'Some Ciceronian Models for Einhard's Life of Charlemagne', *Viator*, 26 (1995): 11–37.

Kempshall, Matthew S., 'The Virtues of Rhetoric: Alcuin's *Disputatio de rhetorica et de virtutibus*', *Anglo-Saxon England*, 37 (2008): 7–30.

Kempshall, Matthew S., *Rhetoric and the Writing of History, 400–1500* (Manchester: MUP, 2011).

Kershaw, Paul J. E., 'Eberhard of Friuli, a Carolingian Lay Intellectual', in *Lay Intellectuals in the Carolingian World*, eds Patrick Wormald and Janet L. Nelson (Cambridge: CUP, 2007), 77–105.

Kershaw, Paul J. E., *Peaceful Kings: Peace, Power, and the Early Medieval Political Imagination* (Oxford: OUP, 2011).

Knape, Joachim, *Historie in Mittelalter und früher Neuzeit: Begriffs- und gattungsgeschichtliche Untersuchungen im interdisziplinären Kontext*, Saecula Spiritalia 10 (Baden-Baden: Valentin Koerner, 1984).

Knibbs, Erik, 'Ebo of Rheims, Pseudo-Isidore, and the Date of the False Decretals', *Speculum*, 92(1) (2017): 144–83.

Kölzer, Theo, *Die Urkunden der Karolinger. Zweiter Band, Die Urkunden Ludwigs des Frommen* (Wiesbaden: Harrassowitz, 2016).

König, Jason and Whitmarsh, Tim, 'Ordering Knowledge', in *Ordering Knowledge in the Roman Empire*, eds Jason König and Tim Whitmarsh (Cambridge: CUP, 2007), 3–39.

Kosto, Adam J., 'Statim invenire ante: Finding Aids and Research Tools in Pre-Scholastic Legal and Administrative Manuscripts', *Scriptorium*, 70(2) (2016): 285–309.

Koziol, Geoffrey, 'Christianizing Political Discourses', in *The Oxford Handbook of Medieval Christianity*, ed. John H. Arnold (Oxford: OUP, 2014), 473–89.

Koziol, Geoffrey, 'The Future of History after Empire', in *Using and Not Using the Past after the Carolingian Empire, c. 900–c.1050*, eds Sarah Greer, Alice Hicklin and Stefan Esders (London: Routledge, 2020), 15–35.

Kramer, Rutger, 'Adopt, Adapt and Improve: Dealing with the Adoptionist Controversy at the Court of Charlemagne', in *Religious Franks: Religion and Power in the Frankish Kingdoms: Studies in Honour of Mayke de Jong*, eds Dorine van Espelo, Bram van den Hoven van Genderen, Rob Meens, Janneke Raaijmakers, Irene van Renswoude and Carine van Rhijn (Manchester: MUP, 2016), 32–50.

Kramer, Rutger, *Rethinking Authority in the Carolingian Empire: Ideals and Expectations during the Reign of Louis the Pious* (Amsterdam: Amsterdam University Press, 2019).

Kramer, Rutger, 'The Bede Goes On: Pastoral Eschatology in the Prologue to the Chronicle of Moissac (Paris BN lat. 4886)', in *Cultures of Eschatology II: Time, Death and Afterlife in Medieval Christian, Islamic and Buddhist Communities*, eds Veronika Wieser, Vincent Eltschinger and Johann Heiss (Berlin: De Gruyter, 2020), 698–730.

Kramer, Rutger, 'A Crowing Achievement: Carolingian Imperial Identity in the *Chronicon Moisiacense*', in *Historiography and Identity III: Carolingian Approaches*, eds Rutger Kramer, Helmut Reimitz and Graeme Ward (Turnhout: Brepols, 2021), 231–69.

Krüger, Karl Heinrich, *Die Universalchroniken*, Typologie des sources du Moyen Âge occidental 16 (Turnhout: Brepols, 1976).

Lake, Justin, 'Truth, Plausibility, and the Virtues of Narrative at the Millennium', *Journal of Medieval History*, 35(3) (2009): 221–38.

Lake, Justin, *Richer of Saint-Rémi: The Methods and Mentality of a Tenth-Century Historian* (Washington, DC: CUA Press, 2013).

Lake, Justin, 'Authorial Intention in Medieval Historiography', *History Compass*, 12(4). (2014), 344–60.

Lake, Justin, 'Current Approaches to Medieval Historiography', *History Compass*, 13(3) (2015): 89–109.

Lake, Justin, 'Rethinking Fredegar's Prologue', *The Journal of Medieval Latin*, 25 (2015): 1–28.

Lake, Justin, 'Rewriting Merovingian History in the Tenth Century: Aimoin of Fleury's *Gesta Francorum*', *EME*, 25(4) (2017): 489–525.

Landberg, Fritz, *Das Bild der alten Geschichte in mittelalterlichen Weltchroniken* (Berlin: E. Steisand, 1934).

Landes, Richard, 'Lest the Millennium be Fulfilled: Apocalyptic Expectations and the Pattern of Western Chronography 100–800 CE', in *The Use and Abuse of Eschatology in the Middle Ages*, eds Werner Verbeke, D. Verhelst and Andries Welkenhuysen, Mediaevalia Lovaniensia Series 1, Studia 15 (Leuven: Leuven University Press, 1988), 137–211.

La Rocca, Cristina and Veronese, Francesco , 'Cultures of Unanimity in Carolingian Councils', in *Cultures of Voting in Pre-Modern Europe*, eds Serena Ferente, Lovro Kuncevic and Miles Pattenden (London: Routledge, 2018), 39–57.

Leclercq, Jean, *The Love of Learning and the Desire for God: A Study of Monastic Culture*, trans. Catharine Misrahi (New York: Fordham University Press, 1974).

Lehmann, Paul, *Mittelalterliche Bibliothekskataloge Deutschlands und der Schweiz* (Munich: C. H. Beck, 1918).

Le Jan, Regine, 'Aux frontières de l'idéel, le modèle familial en question?', in *La productivité d'une crise: le règne de Louis le Pieux (814–840) et la transformation de l'Empire Carolingien = Produktivität einer Krise: die Regierungszeit Ludwigs des Frommen (814–840) und die Transformation des karolingischen Imperiums*, eds Philippe Depreux and Stefan Esders (Ostfildern: Thorbecke, 2018), 273–88.

Le Maho, Jacques, 'Die erzbischöfliche Pfalz von Rouen', in *Splendor palatii: Neue Forschungen zu Paderborn und anderen Pfalzen der Karolingerzeit*, eds L. Fenske, J. Jarnut and M. Wemhoff, Deutsche Königspfalzen: Beiträge zu ihrer historischen und archäologischen Erforschung 5 (Göttingen: Vandenhoeck and Ruprecht, 2001), 193–210.

Le Maho, Jacques, 'Francs et Normands avant 911: es dessous d'une réécriture', *911–2011: penser les mondes normands médiévaux: actes du colloque international de Caen et Cerisy (29 septembre–2 octobre 2011)*, eds David Bates and Pierre Baudin (Caen: Presses Universitaires de Caen, 2016), 29–52.

Leng, Rainer, 'Ein Würzburger Necrolog aus dem 9. Jahrhundert', *DA*, 63 (2007): 1–40.

Leonard, Victoria, *In Defiance of History: Orosius and the Unimproved Past* (Abingdon: Routledge, 2022).

Levy, Kenneth, 'Abbot Helisachar's Antiphoner', *Journal of the American Musicological Society*, 48 (1995): 171–86.

Leyser, Conrad, 'Late Antiquity and the Medieval West', in *A Companion to Late Antiquity*, ed. Philip Rousseau (Chichester: John Wiley, 2009), 29–42.

Leyser, Conrad, 'From Maternal Kin to Jesus as Mother: Royal Genealogy and Marian Devotion in the Ninth-century West', in *Motherhood, Religion, and Society in Medieval Europe, 400–1400: Essays Presented to Henrietta Leyser*, eds Conrad Leyser and Lesley Smith (Farnham: Ashgate, 2011), 21–39.

Leyser, Conrad, 'Augustine in the Latin West, 430–ca. 900', in *A Companion to Augustine*, ed. Mark Vessey (Chichester: John Wiley, 2012), 450–64.

Leyser, Conrad, 'The Memory of Pope Gregory the Great in the Ninth Century: A Redating of the Interpolator's Vita Gregorii (BHL 3640)', in *Gregorio Magno e le origini dell'Europa: atti del Convegno internazionale, Firenze, 13–17 maggio 2006*, ed. Claudio Leonardi (Florence: Sismel, 2014), 449–62.

Leyser, Conrad, 'The Memory of Gregory the Great and the Making of Latin Europe, 600–1000', in *Making Early Medieval Societies: Conflict and Belonging in the Latin West, 300–1200*, eds Kate Copper and Conrad Leyser (Cambridge: CUP, 2016), 181–201.

Liebeschuetz, J. H. W. G., 'Ecclesiastical Historians on their Own Times', *Studia Patristica*, 24 (1993): 151–63.

Lifshitz, Felice, *The Norman Conquest of Pious Neustria: Historiographic Discourse and Saintly Relics, 684–1090* (Toronto: Pontifical Institute of Mediaeval Studies, 1995).

Lifshitz, Felice, *Religious Women in Early Carolingian Francia: A Study of Manuscript Transmission and Monastic Culture* (New York: Fordham University Press, 2014).

Lošek, Fritz, '*Non ignota canens*? Bemerkungen zur Chronik (*Historia*) des Frechulf von Lisieux', in *Ethnogenese und Uberlieferung: angewandte Methoden der Fruhmittelalterforschung*, eds Karl Brunner and Brigetta Merta, Veröffentlichungen des Instituts für Österreichische Geschichtsforschung 31 (Vienna: Oldenbourg, 1994), 223–31.

Lössl, Josef, 'A Shift in Patristic Exegesis: Hebrew Clarity and Historical Verity in Augustine, Jerome, Julian of Aeclanum and Theodore of Mopsuestia', *Augustinian Studies*, 32(2) (2001): 157–75.

Lößlein, Horst, 'Beobachtungen zur Arbeitsweise Frutolfs von Michelsberg', *DA*, 74 (2018): 585-638.

Lozovsky, Natalia, '*The Earth is Our Book*': *Geographical Knowledge in the Latin West, ca. 400–1000* (Ann Arbor, MI: University of Michigan Press, 2000).

Lubac, Henri de, *Medieval Exegesis: The Four Senses of Scripture*, 4 vols; vol 1, translated by Mark Sebanc (Grand Rapids, MI: William B. Eerdmans, 1999), vols 2–4 translated by E. M. Macierowski (Grand Rapids, MI: William B. Eerdmans, 2000).

Mabillon, Jean, *Annales ordinis s. Benedicti*, 6 vols (Paris: Charles Robustel, 1703–39).

MacLean, Simon, *History and Politics in Late Carolingian and Ottonian Europe: The Chronicle of Regino of Prüm and Adalbert of Magdeburg* (Manchester: MUP, 2009).

MacLean, Simon, 'Insinuation, Censorship and the Struggle for Late Carolingian Lotharingia in Regino of Prüm's *Chronicle*', *English Historical Review*, 124 (2009): 1–28.

MacLean, Simon, 'Recycling the Franks in Twelfth-Century England: Regino of Prüm, the Monks of Durham, and the Alexandrine Schism', *Speculum*, 87(3) (2012): 649–81.

Maître, Philippe le, 'Les méthodes exégétiques de Raban Maur', in *Haut Moyen-Age: culture, éducation et société. Études offertes à Pierre Riché*, eds Claude Lepelley and Michel Sot (Nanterre: Éditions Publidix, 1990), 343–52.

Maneuvrier, Christophe, 'Le récit de la translation des reliques de saint Regnobert: histoire d'une éphémère fondation monastique effectuée aux portes de Lisieux sous l'épiscopat de Fréculf', *Tabularia* 5 (2005): 1–11.

Manitius, Max, *Geschichte der lateinischen Literatur des Mittelalters, I: Von Justinian bis zur Mitte des 10. Jahrhunderts* (Munich: Beck, 1911).

Markauskas, Melissa, 'Rylands MS Latin 12: A Carolingian Example of Isidore's Reception into the Patristic Canon', in *Isidore of Seville and his Reception in the Early Middle Ages: Transmitting and Transforming Knowledge*, eds Andrew T. Fear and Jamie Wood (Amsterdam: Amsterdam University Press, 2016), 177–208.

Markus, Robert A., 'The Roman Empire in Early Christian Historiography', *Downside Review*, 81 (1963): 340–53.

Markus, Robert A., 'Church History and the Early Church Historians', in *The Materials, Sources and Methods of Ecclesiastical History*, ed. Derek Baker, Studies in Church History 11 (Oxford: Basil Blackwell, 1975), 1–17; repr. in his *From Augustine to Gregory the Great: History and Christianity in Late Antiquity* (London: Varorium Reprints, 1983), item II.

Markus, Robert A., 'Chronicle and Theology: Prosper of Aquitaine', in *The Inheritance of Historiography 350–900*, eds Christopher Holdsworth and T. P. Wiseman (Liverpool: LUP, 1986), 31–43.

Markus, Robert A., *Saeculum: History and Society in the Theology of St Augustine*, rev. edn (Cambridge: CUP, 1988).

Markus, Robert A., *Gregory the Great and his World* (Cambridge: CUP, 1997).

Markus, Robert A., '*Tempora christiana* Revisited', in *Augustine and his Critics. Essays in Honour of Gerald Bonner*, eds Robert Dodaro and George Lawless (London: Psychology Press, 2000), 201–13.

Marrou, Henri Irénée, 'Saint Augustin, Orose et l'augustinisme historique', *La storiografia altemedievale*, Settimane 17 (Spoleto: Centro italiano di studi sull'alto Medioevo, 1970): 59–87.

Marsham, Andrew, 'Universal Histories in Christendom and the Islamic World, c. 700– c.1400', in *The Oxford History of Historical Writing, Vol. 2: 400–1400*, eds Sarah Foot and Chase F. Robinson (Oxford: OUP, 2012), 431–56.

Martens, Peter, *Origen and Scripture: The Contours of the Exegetical Life* (Oxford, OUP, 2012).

Matthews, John, *The Roman Empire of Ammianus* (Baltimore, MD: Johns Hopkins University Press, 1989).

Mayr-Harting, Henry, 'Augustine of Hippo, Chelles, and the Carolingian Renaissance: Cologne Cathedral Manuscript 63', *Frühmittelalterliche Studien*, 45 (2011): 51–75.

McCarthy, T. J. H., 'Frutolf of Michelsberg's Chronicle, the Schools of Bamberg, and the Transmission of Imperial Polemic', *Haskins Society Journal*, 23 (2001): 51–70.

McCarthy, T. J. H., *Chronicles of the Investiture Contest: Frutolf of Michelsberg and his Continuators* (Manchester: MUP, 2014).

McKitterick, Rosamond, *The Frankish Church and the Carolingian Reforms, 789–895* (London: Royal Historical Society, 1977).

McKitterick, Rosamond, *The Carolingians and the Written Word* (Cambridge: CUP, 1989).

McKitterick, Rosamond, *The Frankish Kingdoms under the Carolingians, 751–987* (London: Longman, 1983).

McKitterick, Rosamond, 'Royal Patronage of Culture in the Frankish Kingdoms under the Carolingians: Motives and Consequences', in *Committenti e produzione aristico-*

letteraria nell'alto medioevo occidentale, Settimane 39 (Spoleto: Centro italiano di studi sull'alto Medioevo, 1992), vol. 2, 93–129.

McKitterick, Rosamond, *History and Memory in the Carolingian World* (Cambridge: CUP, 2004).

McKitterick, Rosamond, 'The Carolingian Renaissance and the Culture of Learning', in *Charlemagne: Empire and Society*, ed. Joanna Story (Manchester: MUP, 2005), 151–66.

McKitterick, Rosamond, *Perceptions of the Past in the Early Middle Ages* (Notre Dame, IL: University of Notre Dame Press, 2006).

McKitterick, Rosamond, *Charlemagne: The Formation of a European Identity* (Cambridge: CUP, 2008).

McKitterick, Rosamond, 'Carolingian Historiography', in *Wilhelm Levison (1876–1947): Ein jüdisches Forscherleben zwischen wissenschaftlicher Anerkennung und politischem Exil*, eds Matthias Becher and Yitzhak Hen, Bonner historische Forschungen 63 (Siegburg: Franz Schmitt, 2010), 93–112.

McKitterick, Rosamond, 'Glossaries and Other Innovations in Carolingian Book Production', in *Turning over a New Leaf: Change and Development in the Medieval Book* (Leiden: University of Leiden Press, 2012), 21–76.

McKitterick, Rosamond, 'Postérité et transmission des œvres historiographiques carolingiennes dans des mondes normands', in *L'Historiographie médiévale normande et ses sources antiques (X^e–XIIe siècle)*, eds Pierre Bauduin and Marie-Agnès Lucas-Avenel (Caen: Presses Universitaires de Caen, 2014), 25–39.

McKitterick, Rosamond, 'Transformations of the Roman Past and Roman Identity in the Early Middle Ages', in *The Resources of the Past in Early Medieval Europe*, eds Rosamond McKitterick, Sven Meeder and Clemens Gantner (Cambridge: CUP, 2015), 225–44.

McKitterick, Rosamond, *Rome and the Invention of the Papacy: The Liber Pontificalis* (Cambridge: CUP, 2020).

McKitterick, Rosamond and Ward, Graeme, 'Knowledge of the History of the Jews in the Early Middle Ages', in *Barbarians and Jews: Jews and Judaism in the Early Medieval West*, eds Yitzhak Hen and Thomas F.X. Noble (Turnhout: Brepols, 2018), 231–56.

McLynn, Neil B., *Ambrose of Milan: Church and Court in a Christian Capital* (Berkeley, CA: University of California Press, 1994).

McMahon, Madeline, 'Polemic in Translation: Jerome's Fashioning of History in the *Chronicle*', in *Historiography and Identity I: Ancient and Early Christian Narratives of Community*, eds Helmut Reimitz and Veronika Wieser (Turnhout: Brepols, 2019), 219–45.

Mégier, Elisabeth, 'Christian Historical Fulfilments of Old Testament Prophecies in Latin Commentaries on the Book of Isaiah (ca. 400 to ca. 1150)', *Journal of Medieval Latin*, 17 (2007): 87–100.

Mégier, Elisabeth, *Christliche Weltgeschichte im 12. Jahrhundert: Themen, Variationen und Kontraste: Untersuchungen zu Hugo von Fleury, Ordericus Vitalis und Otto von Freising* (Frankfurt am Main: Peter Lang, 2010).

Mégier, Elisabeth, '*Ecclesiae sacramenta*: The Spiritual Meaning of Old Testament History and the Foundation of the Church in Hugh of Fleury's *Historia ecclesiastica*', in *Christliche Weltgeschichte im 12. Jahrhundert: Themen, Variationen und Kontraste. Untersuchungen zu Hugo von Fleury, Ordericus Vitalis und Otto von Freising*, Beihefte zur Mediaevistik 13 (Frankfurt am Main: Peter Lang, 2010), 361–82.

Mégier, Elisabeth, 'L'histoire biblique pré-abrahamique est-elle un sujet pour les historiens? S. Jérôme, S. Augustin et les critères d'historicité dans les *historiae* de Fréculphe de Lisieux', in *Les réceptions des Pères de l'Église au Moyen Âge: le devenir de la tradition ecclésiale*, eds Rainer Berndt and Michel Fédou, Archa verbi: yearbook for the study of medieval theology 10 (Münster: Aschendorff, 2013), vol. 2, 1057–73.

Mégier, Elisabeth, 'Karolingische Weltchronistik zwischen Historiographie und Exegese: Frechulf von Lisieux und Ado von Vienne', in *Diligens scrutator sacri eloquii. Beiträge zur Exegese- und Theologiegeschichte des Mittelalters. Festgabe für Rainer Berndt SJ zum 65. Geburtstag*, eds Matthias M. Tischler, Hanns Peter Neuheuser and Ralf M. W. Stammberger (Münster: Aschendorff, 2016), 37–52.

Mégier, Elisabeth, '*Historia* and *Littera* in Carolingian Commentaries on St Matthew. Elements for an Inventory of Exegetical Vocabulary in the Medieval Latin Church', in *Producing Christian Culture: Medieval Exegesis and its Interpretative Genresi*, ed. Giles E. M. Gasper (Abingdon: Routledge, 2017), 89–113.

Mégier, Elisabeth, 'Le temps des Ages du monde, de saint Augustin a Hugues de Fleury (en passant par Isidore de Seville, Bede le Vénérable, Adon de Vienne et Fréculphe de Lisieux)', in *Le sens du temps: actes du VIIᵉ Congrès du Comité international de latin médiéval, Lyon, 10–13.09.2014*, eds Pascale Bourgain, Jean-Yves Tilliette and Jan M. Ziolkowski (Geneva: Droz, 2017), 581–600.

Melville, Gert, 'Zur *Flores-Metaphorik* in der mittelalterlichen Geschichsschreibung: Ausdruck eines Formungsprinzips', *Historisches Jahrbuch*, 90 (1970): 65–80.

Melville, Gert, 'Wozu Geschichte schreiben? Stellung und Funktion der Historie im Mittelalter', in *Formen der Geschichtsschreibung*, eds Reinhart Koselleck, Heinrich Lutz and Jörn Rüsen (Munich: Deutscher Taschenbuch Verlag, 1982), 86–146.

Melville, Gert, 'Le problème des connaisances historiques au Moyen Âge: compilation et transmission des textes', in *L'historiographie médiévale en Europe. Actes du colloque organisé par la Fondation Européenne de la Science au Centre de Recherches Historiques et Juridiques de l'Université Paris I du 29 mars au 1ᵉʳ avril 1989*, ed. Jean-Philippe Genet (Paris: Presses du CNRS, 1991), 21–41.

Ménager, Céline, 'Écrire l'histoire de Constantin à l'époque carolingienne. Valeur historique de la *Vita Helenae* d'Almanne d'Hautvillers', in *Rerum gestarum scriptor: histoire et historiographie au Moyen Âge*, eds Magali Coumert, Marie-Céline Isaïa, Klaus Krönert and Sumi Shimahara (Paris: Presses de l'Université Paris-Sorbonne, 2012), 303–12.

Merrills, Andrew H., *History and Geography in Late Antiquity* (Cambridge: CUP, 2005).

Meseguer Gil, Antonio José, 'La obra histórica de Paulo Orosio y sus diferencias con Agustín de Hipona: transmisión de conceptos historiográficos en la Antigüedad Tardía', *Onoba*, 5 (2017): 89–101.

Meyvaert, Paul, 'Bede's *Capitula lectionum* for the Old and New Testaments', *Revue bénédictine*, 105 (1995): 348–80.

Mommsen, Theodor E., 'Aponius and Orosius on the Significance of the Epiphany', in *Medieval and Renaissance Studies*, ed. Eugene F. Rice Jr. (Ithaca, NY: Cornell University Press, 1959), 299–324.

Mommsen, Theodor E., 'Orosius and Augustine', in *Medieval and Renaissance Studies*, ed. Eugene F. Rice Jr. (Ithaca, NY: Cornell University Press, 1959), 325–48.

Moore, Michael Edward, *A Sacred Kingdom: Bishops and the Rise of Frankish Kingship, 300–850* (Washington, DC: CUA Press, 2011).

Morrison, Karl F., *Tradition and Authority in the Western Church, 300–1140* (Princeton, NJ: Princeton University Press, 1969).

Morse, Ruth, *Truth and Convention in the Middle Ages: Rhetoric, Representation and Reality* (Cambridge: CUP, 1991).

Mortensen, Lars Boje, 'The Diffusion of Roman Histories in the Middle Ages. A List of Orosius, Eutropius, Paulus Diaconus, and Landolfus Sagax', *Filologia Mediolatina*, VI–VII (1999–2000): 101–200.

Mösch, Sophia, *Augustine and the Art of Ruling in the Carolingian Imperial Period: Political Discourse in Alcuin of York and Hincmar of Rheims* (Abingdon: Routledge, 2020).

Mosshammer, Alden A., 'Lucca Bibl. Capit. 490 and the Manuscript Tradition of Hieronymus' (Eusebius') Chronicle', *California Studies in Classical Antiquity*, 8 (1975): 203–40.

Mosshammer, Alden A., *The Chronicle of Eusebius and the Greek Chronographic Tradition* (Lewisburg, PA: Bucknell University Press, 1979).

Mosshammer, Alden A., 'Two Fragments of Jerome's Chronicle', *Rheinisches Museum für Philologie*, 124 (1981): 66–80.

Muhlberger, Steven, *The Fifth-century Chroniclers: Prosper, Hydatius, and the Gallic Chronicler of 452* (Leeds: F. Cairns, 1990).

Murphy, Francis X., 'St. Jerome as an Historian', in *A Monument to Saint Jerome: Essays on Some Aspects of his Life, Work and Influence*, ed. Francis X. Murphy (New York: Sheed & Ward, 1952), 115–41.

Natunewicz, Chester F., 'Freculphus of Lisieux, his *Chronicle* and a Mont St Michel Manuscript', *Sacris Erudiri*, 17 (1966): 90–134.

Nelson, Janet L., 'Public Histories and Private History in the Work of Nithard', *Speculum*, 60(2) (1985), 251–93; repr. in her *Politics and Ritual in Early Medieval Europe* (London: Hambledon Continuum, 1986), 196–237.

Nelson, Janet L., 'History-Writing at the Courts of Louis the Pious and Charles the Bald', in *Historiographie im frühen Mittelalter*, eds Anton Scharer and Georg Scheibelreiter (Vienna: Oldenbourg, 1994), 435–42.

Nelson, Janet L., 'Translating Images of Authority: The Christian Roman Emperors in the Carolingian World', in *The Frankish World, 750–900* (London: Hambledon Press, 1996), 89–98.

Nelson, Janet L., 'Making a Difference in Eighth-Century Politics: The Daughters of Desiderius', in *After Rome's Fall: Narrators and Sources of Early Medieval History. Essays Presented to Walter Goffart*, ed. Alexander Callander Murray (Toronto: University of Toronto Press, 1998), 171–90; repr. in her *Courts, Elites, and Gendered Power in the Early Middle Ages* (Aldershot: Ashgate, 2007).

Nelson, Janet L., 'Normandy's Early History since *Normandy Before 1066*', in *Normandy and its Neighbours, 900–1250: Essays for David Bates*, eds David Crouch and Kathleen Thompson (Turnhout: Brepols, 2011), 3–15.

Nelson, Janet L., 'Hincmar's Life in his Historical Writings', in *Hincmar of Rheims: Life and Work*, eds Rachel Stone and Charles West (Manchester: MUP, 2015), 44–59.

Nelson, Jinty, 'Charlemagne and the Bishops', in *Religious Franks: Religion and Power in the Frankish Kingdoms: Studies in Honour of Mayke de Jong*, eds Dorine van Espelo, Bram van den Hoven van Genderen, Rob Meens, Janneke Raaijmakers, Irene van Renswoude and Carine van Rhijn (Manchester: MUP, 2016), 350–69.

Németh, András, *The Excerpta Constantiniana and the Byzantine Appropriation of the Past* (Cambridge: CUP, 2018).

Niblaeus, Erik, 'Beautiful Power: Panegyric at the Court of Henry II (1039–56)', *Journal of Medieval History*, 47(1) (2021): 1–21.

Niermeyer, J. F. and van de Kieft, C. *Mediae Latinitatis lexicon minus* (Leiden: Brill, 2002).

Nimmegeers, Nathanaël, *Évêques entre Bourgogne et Provence (V^e–XIe siècle): la province ecclésiastique de Vienne au haut Moyen Âge* (Rennes: Presses Universitaires de Rennes, 2014).

Noble, Thomas F. X., 'Tradition and Learning in Search of Ideology: The *Libri Carolini*', in *'The Gentle Voices of Teachers': Aspects of Learning in the Carolingian Age*, ed. Richard E. Sullivan (Columbus, OH: Ohio State University Press, 1995), 227–60.

Noble, Thomas F. X., *Images, Iconoclasm and the Carolingians* (Philadelphia, PA: University of Pennsylvania Press, 2009).

Nothaft, C. Philipp E., 'Chronologically Confused: Claudius of Turin and the Date of Christ's Passion', in *Late Antique Calendrical Thought and its Reception in the Early Middle Ages*, eds Immo Warntjes and Dáibhí Ó Cróinín (Turnhout: Brepols, 2017), 265–92.

O'Brien, Conor, *Bede's Temple: An Image and its Interpretation* (Oxford: OUP, 2015).

O'Brien, Joshua M., 'Locating Authorities in Carolingian Debates on Image Veneration: The Case of Agobard of Lyon's *De picturis et imaginibus*', *Journal of Theological Studies*, 62(1) (2011): 176–206.

O'Daly, Gerard, *Augustine's City of God: A Readers Guide* (Oxford: Oxford University of Press, 1999).

O'Loughlin, Thomas, 'The Controversy over Methuselah's Death: Proto-Chronology and the Origins of the Western Concept of Inerrancy', *Recherches de théologie ancienne et médiévale*, 62 (1995): 182–225.

O'Loughlin, Thomas, *Teachers and Code-Breakers: The Latin Genesis Tradition, 430–800* (Turnhout: Brepols, 1998).

O'Loughlin, Thomas, 'Eusebius of Caesarea's Conceptions of the Persecutions as the Key to Reading his *Historia ecclesiastica*', in *The Great Persecution: Proceedings of the Fifth Patristic Conference, Maynooth, 2003*, eds D. Vincent Twomey and Mark Humphries (Dublin: Four Courts Press, 2009), 91–105.

Oort, Johannes van, *Jerusalem and Babylon: A Study into Augustine's City of God and the Sources of his Doctrine of the Two Cities* (Leiden: Brill, 1991).

Opelt, Ilona, 'Augustustheologie und Augustustypologie', *Jahrbuch für Antike und Christentum*, 4 (1961): 44–57.

O'Reilly, Jennifer, 'Islands and Idols at the Ends of the Earth: Exegesis and Conversion in Bede's *Historia ecclesiastica*', in *Bède le Vénérable: entre tradition et postérité*, eds Stéphane Lebecq, Michel Perrin and Olivier Szerwiniak (Villeneuve d'Ascq: Université Charles-de-Gaule-Lille, 2005), 119–45.

O'Sullivan, Sinéad, 'Glossing Vergil and Pagan Learning in the Carolingian Age', *Speculum*, 93(1) (2018): 132–165.

Otten, Willemien, 'The Texture of Tradition. The Role of the Church Fathers in Carolingian Theology', in *The Reception of the Church Fathers in the West: From the Carolingians to the Maurists*, ed. Irena Backus, 2 vols (Leiden: Brill, 2001), vol. I, 3–50.

Ottewill-Soulsby, Sam, '"Hunting Diligently through the Volumes of the Ancients": Frechulf of Lisieux on the First City and the End of Innocence', in *Remembering the Ancient City in the Post-Antique World*, eds Javier Martinez Jimenez and Sam Ottewill-Soulsby (Oxford: Oxbow Books, forthcoming 2022).

Pangerl, Daniel Carlo, *Die Metropolitanverfassung des karolingischen Frankenreiches* (Hanover: Hahnsche Buchhandlung, 2011).

Parkes, Malcolm, 'The Influence of the Concepts of *Ordinatio* and *Compilatio* on the Development of the Book', in *Medieval Learning and Literature: Essays Presented to*

Richard William Hunt, eds J. J. G. Alexander and M. T. Gibson (Oxford: Clarendon Press, 1976), 115–41.

Patt, Sarah, *Studien zu den "Formulae imperiales": Urkundenkonzeption und Formulargebrauch in der Kanzlei Kaiser Ludwigs des Frommen (814–840)* (Wiesbaden: Harrassowitz, 2016).

Patzold, Steffen, 'Eine "Loyale Palastrebellion" der "Reichseinheitspartei": Zur "Divisio imperii" von 817 und zu den Ursachen des Aufstandes gegen Ludwig den Frommen im Jahre 830', *Frühmittelalterliche Studien*, 40 (2006): 43–77.

Patzold, Steffen, 'Eine Hierarchie im Wandel: die Ausbildung einer Metropolitanordnung im Frankenreich des 8. und 9. Jahrhunderts', in *Hiérarchie et stratification sociale dans l'Occident médiéval 400–1100*, eds Dominique Iogna-Prat, François Bougard and Régine Le Jan (Turnhout: Brepols, 2008), 161–84.

Patzold, Steffen, *Episcopus: Wissen über Bischöfe im Frankenreich des späten 8. bis frühen 10. Jahrhunderts* (Ostfildern: Thorbecke, 2008).

Patzold, Steffen, 'Einhards erste Leser: zu Kontext und Darstellungsabsicht der *Vita Karoli*', *Viator*, 42 (2011): 33–55.

Patzold, Steffen, '"Einheit" versus "Fraktionierung"': zur symbolischen und institutionellen Integration des Frankenreichs im 8./9. Jahrhundert', in *Visions of Community in the Post-Roman World: The West, Byzantium and the Islamic world, 300–1100*, eds Walter Pohl, Clemens Gantner and Richard Payne (Farnham: Ashgate, 2012), 375–90.

Patzold, Steffen, 'Verortung in einer mobilen Welt: Zum Zusammenhang zwischen Kirchenzehnt und der Einhegung von Mobilität im Karolingerreich', *Historische Zeitschrift*, 308 (2019): 285–312.

Patzold, Steffen, 'Capitularies in the Ottonian Realm', *EME*, 27(1) (2019): 112–32.

Patzold, Steffen, *Presbyter: Moral, Mobilität und die Kirchenorganisation im Karolingerreich* (Stuttgart: Anton Hiersemann, 2020).

Patzold, Steffen and van Rhijn, Carine (eds), *Men in the Middle: Local Priests in Early Medieval Europe* (Berlin: De Gruyter, 2016).

Peters, Edward M., 'Transgressing the Limits Set by the Fathers: Authority and Impious Exegesis in Medieval Thought', in *Christendom and its Discontents: Exclusion, Persecution, and Rebellion, 1000–1500*, eds Scott L. Waugh and Peter D. Diehl (Cambridge: CUP, 1996), 338–62.

Petitmengin, Pierre, '*Capitula* païens et chrétiens', in *Titres et articulations du texte dans les oeuvres antiques: actes du colloque international de Chantilly, 13–15 décembre 1994*, eds Jean-Claude Fredouille, Marie-Odile Glouet-Cazé, Philippe Hoffman, Pierre Petitmengin and Simone Deléani (Paris: Institut d'études Augustiniennes, 1997), 491–507.

Pezé, Warren, *Le virus de l'erreur. La controverse carolingienne sur la double prédestination: essai d'histoire sociale* (Turnhout: Brepols, 2017).

Pezé, Warren (ed.), *Wissen und Bildung in einer Zeit bedrohter Ordnung: der Zerfall des Karolingerreiches um 900 = Knowledge and Culture in Times of Threat: The Fall of the Carolingian Empire (ca. 900)* (Stuttgart: Hiersemann, 2020).

Phelan, Owen M. *The Formation of Christian Europe: The Carolingians, Baptism, and the Imperium Christianum* (Oxford: OUP, 2014).

Phelan, Owen M., 'The Carolingian Renewal in Early Medieval Europe through Hrabanus Maurus's *Commentary on Matthew*', *Traditio*, 75 (2020): 143–75.

Pohl, Walter, 'History in Fragments: Montecassino's Politics of Memory', *EME*, 10(3) (2003): 343–74.

Pohl, Walter, and Wood, Ian W. 'Introduction: Cultural Memory and the Resources of the Past', in *The Resources of the Past in Early Medieval Europe*, eds Clemens Gantner, Rosamond McKitterick and Sven Meeder (Cambridge: CUP, 2015), 1–14.

Polanichka, Dana M. and Alex Cilley, 'The Very Personal History of Nithard: Family and Honour in the Carolingian world', *EME*, 22(2) (2014): 171–200.

Pollard, Richard Matthew, 'The *De Excidio* of "Hegesippus" and the Reception of Josephus in the Early Middle Ages', *Viator*, 46(2) (2015): 65–100.

Pollmann, Karla and Willemien Otten (eds), *The Oxford Guide to the Historical Reception of Augustine*, 3 vols (Oxford: OUP, 2013).

Ponesse, Matthew D., 'Standing Distant from the Fathers: Smaragdus of Saint-Mihiel and the Reception of Early Medieval Learning', *Traditio*, 67 (2012): 71–99.

Pontal, Odette, *Die Synoden im Merowingerreich* (Paderborn: Ferdinand Schöningh, 1986).

Pössel, Christina, 'The Consolation of Community: Innovation and Ideas of History in Ratpert's *Casus Sancti Galli*', *Journal of Ecclesiastical History*, 65(1) (2014): 1–24.

Raaijmakers, Janneke, *The Making of the Monastic Community of Fulda, c. 744– c.900* (Cambridge: CUP, 2012).

Raaijmakers, Janneke, 'Studying Jerome in a Carolingian Monastery', in *The Annotated Book in the Early Middle Ages: Practices of Reading and Writing*, eds Mariken Teeuwen and Irene van Renswoude (Turnhout: Brepols, 2018), 621–46.

Raaijmakers, Janneke and van Renswoude, Irene, 'The Ruler as Referee in Theological Debates: Reccared and Charlemagne', in *Religious Franks: Religion and Power in the Frankish Kingdoms: Studies in Honour of Mayke de Jong*, eds Dorine van Espelo, Bram van den Hoven van Genderen, Rob Meens, Janneke Raaijmakers, Irene van Renswoude and Carine van Rhijn (Manchester: MUP, 2016), 51–71.

Rädle, Fidel, *Studien zu Smaragd von Saint-Mihiel* (Munich: W. Fink, 1974).

Raisharma, Sukanya, 'Much Ado about Nothing: A Localizing Universal *Chronicon*', in *Historiography and Identity III: Carolingian Approaches*, eds Rutger Kramer, Helmut Reimitz and Graeme Ward (Turnhout: Brepols, 2021), 271–90.

Rankin, Susan, '*Terribilis est locus iste*: The Pantheon in 609', in *Rhetoric Beyond Words: Delight and Persuasion in the Arts of the Middle Ages*, ed. Mary Carruthers (Cambridge: CUP, 2010), 281–310.

Rauer, Christina, 'Female Hagiography in the Old English Martyrology', in *Writing Women Saints in Anglo-Saxon England* ed. Paul Szarmach (Toronto: University of Toronto Press, 2014), 13–29.

Ray, Roger, 'Bede, the Exegete, as Historian', in *Famulus Christi: Essays in Commemoration of the Thirteenth Centenary of the Birth of the Venerable Bede*, ed. Gerald Bonner (London: SPCK, 1976), 125–40.

Ray, Roger, 'Bede's *Vera lex historiae*', *Speculum*, 55(1) (1980): 1–21.

Ray, Roger, 'Who Did Bede Think He Was?', in *Innovation and Tradition in the Writings of the Venerable Bede*, ed. Scott DeGregorio (Morgantown, WV: West Virginia University Press, 2006), 11–35.

Reeve, Michael D., 'The Transmission of Vegetius' *Epitoma rei militaris*', *Aevum*, 74 (2000): 243–354.

Reimitz, Helmut, 'The Social Logic of Historiographical Compendia in the Carolingian Period', in *Configuration du texte en histoire*, ed. Osamu Kano (Nagoya: Graduate School of Letters, 2012), 17–28.

Reimitz, Helmut, *History, Frankish Identity and the Framing of Western Ethnicity, 550–850* (Cambridge: CUP, 2015).

Reimitz, Helmut, 'Histories of Carolingian Historiography: An Introduction', in *Historiography and Identity III: Carolingian Approaches*, eds Rutger Kramer, Helmut Reimitz and Graeme Ward (Turnhout: Brepols, 2021), 1–35.

Rembold, Ingrid, *Conquest and Christianization: Saxony and the Carolingian World, 772–888* (Cambridge: CUP, 2018).

Renswoude, Irene van, *The Rhetoric of Free Speech in Late Antiquity and the Early Middle Ages* (Cambridge: CUP, 2019).

Reuter, Timothy, 'Gifts and Simony', in *Medieval Transformations: Texts, Power and Gifts in Context*, eds Esther Cohen and Mayke de Jong (Leiden: Brill, 2001), 157–68.

Reynolds, L. D. (ed.), *Texts and Transmission: A Survey of the Latin Classics* (Oxford: Clarendon Press, 1983).

Reynolds, Roger, 'Liturgical Scholarship at the Time of the Investiture Controversy: Past Research and Future Opportunities', *The Harvard Theological Review*, 71 (1978): 109–24.

Rhijn, Carine van, 'Royal Politics in Small Worlds: Local Priests and the Implementation of Carolingian *Correctio*', in *Kleine Welten: Ländliche Gesellschaften im Karolingerreich*, eds Thomas Kohl, Steffen Patzold and Berhard Zeller (Ostfildern: Thorbecke, 2019), 237–53.

Ricci, Cristina, 'Claudius of Turin', in *The Oxford Guide to the Historical Reception of Augustine*, eds Karla Pollmann and Willemien Otten, 3 vols (Oxford: OUP, 2013), vol. 2, 798–800.

Riché, Pierre, 'Instruments de travail et méthodse de l'éxègete à l'époque carolingienne', in *Le Moyen Age et la Bible*, eds Pierre Riché and Guy Lobrichon (Paris: Éditions Beauchesne, 1984), 147–61.

Riess, Frank, 'From Aachen to Al-Andalus: The Journey of Deacon Bodo (823–76)', *EME*, 13(2) (2005): 131–57.

Riggsby, Andrew M., *Mosaics of Knowledge: Representing Information in the Roman World* (Oxford: OUP, 2019).

Rissel, Maria, *Rezeption antiker und patristischer Wissenschaft bei Hrabanus Maurus: Studien zur karolingischen Geistesgeschichte*, Lateinische Sprache und Literatur des Mittelalters 7 (Bern: Peter Lang, 1976).

Roberts, Edward, *Flodoard of Rheims and the Writing of History in the Tenth Century* (Cambridge: CUP, 2019).

Romig, Andrew J., 'In Praise of the Too-clement Emperor: The Problem of Forgiveness in the Astronomer's *Vita Hludowici Imperatoris*', *Speculum*, 89(2) (2014): 382–409.

Rose, Els, *Ritual Memory: The Apocryphal Acts and Liturgical Commemoration in the Early Medieval West (c. 500–1215)* (Leiden: Brill, 2009).

Rouse, Richard R. and Rouse, Mary A., '*Ordinatio* and *Compilatio* Revisited', in *Ad litteram: Authoritative Texts and their Medieval Readers*, eds Mark D. Jordan and Kent Emery Jr (Notre Dame, IL: University of Notre Dame Press, 1992), 113–34.

Sahner, Christian, 'From Augustine to Islam: Translation and History in the Arabic Orosius', *Speculum*, 88(4) (2013): 905–31.

Savigni, Raffaele, 'Storia universale e storia ecclesiastica nel *Chronicon* di Freculfo di Lisieux', *Studi medievali*, 28 (1987): 155–92.

Savigni, Raffaele, 'L'Eglise et l'épiscopat en tant que corps social', in *La productivité d'une crise: le règne de Louis le Pieux (814–840) et la transformation de l'Empire carolingien = Produktivität einer Krise: die Regierungszeit Ludwigs des Frommen (814–840) und die*

Transformation des karolingischen Imperiums, eds Philippe Depreux and Stefan Esders (Ostfildern: Thorbecke, 2018), 289–312.

Schaller, Dieter, 'Der junge *Rabe* am Hof Karls des Großen (Theodulf. Carm. 27)', in *Festschrift Bernhard Bischoff. Zu seinem 65. Geburtstag dargebracht von Freunden, Kollegen und Schülern*, eds Johanne Autenrieth and Franz Brunhölzl (Stuttgart: Hiersemann, 1971), 123–41.

Scheck, Thomas P., *St. Jerome: Commentary on Matthew* (Washington, DC: CUA Press, 2008).

Schelle, Bertha, 'Frechulf von Lisieux: Untersuchungen zu Leben und Werk' (PhD dissertation, University of Munich, 1952).

Schieffer, Rudolf, 'Karl der Große und die Einsetzung der Bischöfe im Frankenreich', *DA*, 63 (2007): 451–68.

Schleidgen, Wolf-Rüdiger, *Die Überlieferungsgeschichte der Chronik des Regino von Prüm* (Mainz: Selbstverlag der Gesellschaft für Mittelrheinische Kirchengeschichte, 1977).

Schmidt, Roderich, '*Aetates mundi*: die Weltalter als Gliederungsprinzip der Geschichte', *Zeitschrift für Kirchengeschichte*, 67 (1956): 288–317.

Scholten, Désirée, 'Cassiodorus' *Historia Tripartita* before the Earliest Extant Manuscripts', *The Resources of the Past in Early Medieval Europe*, eds Clemens Gantner, Rosamond McKitterick and Sven Meeder (Cambridge: CUP, 2015), 34–50.

Schöne, Alfred, *Die Weltchronik des Eusebius in ihrer Bearbeitung durch Hieronymus* (Berlin: Weidmann, 1900).

Schroeder, Joy A. (ed. and trans.), *The Book of Genesis*, The Bible in Medieval Tradition (Grand Rapids, MI: William B. Eerdmans, 2015).

Sessa, Kristina, 'Constantine and Silvester in the Actus Silvestri', in *The Life and Legacy of Constantine: Traditions through the Ages*, ed. M. Shane Bjornlie (London: Routledge, 2017), 77–91.

Seifert, Arno, '*Historia* im Mittelalter', *Archiv für Begriffsgeschichte*, 21 (1977): 226–84.

Sheerin, Daniel, 'Interpreting Scripture in and through Liturgy: Exegesis of Mass Propers in the Middle Ages', in *Jewish Biblical Interpretation and Cultural Exchange: Comparative Exegesis in Context*, eds Natalie B. Dohrmann and David Stern (Philadelphia, PA: University of Pennsylvania, 2008), 161–181 at 169–70.

Shimahara, Sumi, *Haymon d'Auxerre, exégète carolingien* (Turnhout: Brepols, 2013).

Shimahara, Sumi, 'L'exégèse biblique de la fin du IXᵉ siècle au milieu du XIᵉ siècle. État des lieux', in *Wissen und Bildung in einer Zeit bedrohter Ordnung: der Zerfall des Karolingerreiches um 900 = Knowledge and Culture in Times of Threat: The Fall of the Carolingian Empire (ca. 900)*, ed. Warren Pezé (Stuttgart: A. Hiersemann, 2020), 103–46.

Simon, Gertrud, 'Untersuchungen zur Topik der Widmungsbriefe mittelalterlicher Geschichtsschreiber bis zum Ende des 12. Jahrhunderts', Part I: *Archiv für Diplomatik*, 4 (1958): 52–119 and Part II: *Archiv für Diplomatik*, 5 (1959): 73–153.

Sloan, Michael C., 'Augustus, the Harbinger of Peace: Orosius' Reception of Augustus in *Historiae Adversus Paganos*', in *Afterlives of Augustus, AD 14–2014*, ed. Penelope J. Goodman (Cambridge: CUP, 2018), 103–21.

Smalley, Beryl, *The Study of the Bible in the Middle Ages*, 2nd edn (Oxford, Blackwell, 1983).

Smith, Julia M. H., *Province and Empire: Brittany and the Carolingians* (Cambridge: CUP, 1992).

Sode, Claudia, 'Der Briefe der Kaiser Michael II. und Theophilos an Kaiser Ludwig den Frommen', in *Zwischen Polis, Provinz und Peripherie: Beiträge zur byzantinischen*

Geschichte und Kultur, eds Anuscha Monchizadeh and Lars Martin Hoffmann (Wiesbaden: Harrassowitz, 2005), 141–58.

Sønnesyn, Sigbjørn, 'Eternity in Time, Unity in Particularity: The Theological Basis of Typological Interpretations in Twelfth-Century Historiography', in *La typologie biblique comme forme de pensée dans l'historiographie médiévale*, ed. Marek Thue Kretschmer (Turnhout: Brepols, 2014), 79–95.

Sot, Michel, 'Introduction', in *Raban Maur et son temps*, eds Philippe Depreux, Stéphane Lebecq, Michel J.-L. Perrin and Olivier Szerwiniak (Turnhout, Brepols, 2010), 9–17.

Stansbury, Mark, 'Early-Medieval Biblical Commentaries, their Writers and Readers', *Frühmittelalterliche Studien*, 33 (1999): 49–82.

Staubach, Nikolaus, *Das Herrscherbild Karls des Kahlen: Formen und Funktionen monarchischer Repräsentation im früheren Mittelalter*, Teil I (Münster: University of Münster, 1982).

Staubach, Nikolaus, '*Cultus Divinus* and karolingische Reform', *Frühmittelalterliche Studien*, 18 (1984): 546–81.

Staubach, Nikolaus, *Rex christianus: Hofkultur und Herrschaftspropaganda im Reich Karls des Kahlen, Teil II: Die Grundlegung der 'religion royale'*, Pictura et poesis 2 (Cologne: Böhlau, 1993).

Staubach, Nikolaus, '*Christiana tempora*: Augustin und das Ende der alten Geschichte in der Weltchronik Frechulfs von Lisieux', *Frühmittelalterliche Studien*, 29 (1995): 167–206.

Staubach, Nikolaus, 'Quattuor modis intellegi potest Hierusalem: Augustins *Civitas Dei* und der vierfache Schriftsinn', in *Alvarium: Festschrift für Christian Gnilka*, eds Wilhelm Blümer, Rainer Henke and Markus Mülke, Jahrbuch für Antike und Christentum Ergänzungsband 33 (Münster: Aschendorff, 2002), 345–58.

Steckel, Sita, *Kulturen des Lehrens im Früh- und Hochmittelalter. Autorität, Wissenskonzepte und Netzwerke von Gelehrten* (Cologne: Böhlau, 2011).

Steckel, Sita, 'Between Censorship and Patronage: Interaction between Bishops and Scholars in Carolingian Book Dedications', in *Envisioning the Bishop: Images and the Episcopacy in the Middle Ages*, eds Sigrid Danielson and Evan A. Gatti (Turnhout: Brepols, 2014), 103–26.

Steckel, Sita, 'Von Buchstaben und Geist: pragmatische und symbolische Dimensionen der Autorensiglen (*nomina auctorum*) bei Hrabanus Maurus', in *Karolingische Klöster: Wissenstransfer und kulturelle Innovation*, eds Julia Becker, Tino Licht and Stefan Weinfurter (Berlin: De Gruyter, 2015), 89–130.

Stevens, Wesley M., *Rhetoric and Reckoning in the Ninth Century: The Vademecum of Walahfrid Strabo* (Turnhout: Brepols, 2018).

Stone, Rachel, 'Kings are Different: Carolingian Mirrors for Princes and Lay Morality', in *Le prince au miroir de la literature politique de l'Antiquité aux Lumières*, eds Frédérique Lachaud and Lydwine Scordia (Mont-Saint-Aignan: Publications de Universités de Rouen et du Havre, 2007), 69–86.

Stone, Rachel, 'Translation of Alcuin's *De virtutibus et vitiis liber* (Book about the Virtues and Vices)', *The Heroic Age*, 16 (2015).

Suchan, Monika, 'Gerechtigkeit in christlicher Verantwortung: Neue Blicke in die Fürstenspiegel des Frühmittelalters', *Francia*, 41 (2014): 1–23.

Szerwiniack, Olivier, 'Un commentaire hiberno-latin', in *Archivum Latinitatis Medii Aevi*, 51 (1992/3): 5–137; 65 (2007), 165–208.

Tabbernee, William, 'Eusebius' "Theology of Persecution": As Seen in the Various Editions of his Church History', *Journal of Early Christian Studies*, 5 (1997): 319–34.

Tanz, Sabine, 'Orosius im Spannungsfeld zwischen Eusebius von Caesarea und Augustin', *Klio. Beiträge zur alten Geschichte*, 65 (1983): 337–46.

Teeuwen, Mariken and Van Renswoude, Irene (eds), *The Annotated Book in the Early Middle Ages: Practices of Reading and Writing* (Turnhout: Brepols, 2018).

Thelamon, Françoise, *Païens et chrétiens au IVe siècle: l'apport de l'Histoire ecclésiastique de Rufin d'Aquilée* (Paris: Études augustiniennes, 1981).

Thelamon, Françoise, 'Écrire l'histoire de l'Église: d'Eusèbe de Césarée à Rufin d'Aquilée', in *L'historiographie de L'église des premiers siècles*, eds Bernard Pouderon and Yves-Marie Duval, Théologie historique 114 (Paris: Éditions Beauchesne, 2001), 207–35.

Timmermann, Josh, 'Sharers in the Contemplative Virtue: Julianus Pomerius's Carolingian Audience', *Comitatus*, 45 (2014): 1–45.

Timmermann, Josh, 'An Authority among Authorities: Knowledge and Use of Augustine in the Wider Carolingian World', *EME*, 28(4) (2020): 532–59.

Tischler, Matthias M., *Einharts* Vita Karoli: *Studien zur Entstehung, überlieferung und Rezeption*, 2 vols (Hanover: Harrassowitz, 2001).

Trompf, G. W., *Early Christian Historiography: Narratives of Retributive Justice* (London: Continuum, 2000).

Tyler, Elizabeth M. and Balzaretti, Ross, 'Introduction', in *Narrative and History in the Early Medieval West*, eds Elizabeth M. Tyler and Ross Balzaretti (Turnhout: Brepols, 2006), 1–9.

Van Nuffelen, Peter, *Orosius and the Rhetoric of History* (Oxford: OUP, 2012).

Van Nuffelen, Peter, 'Not Much Happened: 410 and All That', *Journal of Roman Studies*, 105 (2015): 322–9.

Van Nuffelen, Peter, 'Ecclesiastical History', in *A Companion to Late Antique Literature*, eds Scott McGill and Edward J. Watts (Hoboken, NJ: John Wiley, 2018), 161–75.

Veronese, Francesco, 'Jonas of Orléans', in *Great Christian Jurists and Legal Collections in the First Millennium*, ed. Philip L. Reynolds (Cambridge: CUP, 2019), 413–28.

Vessey, Mark, 'Introduction', in *Cassiodorus: Institutions of Divine and Secular Learning and On the Soul* (Liverpool: LUP, 2004), 1–101.

Vessey, Mark, 'Reinventing History: Jerome's *Chronicle* and the Writing of the Post-Roman West', in *From the Tetrarchs to the Theodosians: Later Roman History and Culture, 284–450 CE*, eds Scott McGill, Cristiana Sogno and Edward Watts (Cambridge: CUP, 2010), 265–89.

Vocino, Giorgia, 'Framing Ambrose in the Resources of the Past: The Late Antique and Early Medieval Sources for a Carolingian Portrait of Ambrose', in *The Resources of the Past in Early Medieval Europe*, eds Clemens Gantner, Rosamond McKitterick and Sven Meeder (Cambridge: CUP, 2015), 133–54.

Wallis, Faith, *Bede: The Reckoning of Time* (Liverpool: LUP, 1999).

Ward, Elizabeth, 'Caesar's Wife: The Career of the Empress Judith', in *Charlemagne's Heir: New Perspectives on the Reign of Louis the Pious (814–840)*, eds Peter Godman and Roger Collins (Oxford: Clarendon Press, 1990), 205–27.

Ward, Graeme, 'All Roads Lead to Rome? Frechulf of Lisieux, Augustine and Orosius', *EME*, 22(4) (2014): 492–505.

Ward, Graeme, 'Lessons in Leadership: Constantine and Theodosius in Frechulf of Lisieux's Histories', in *The Resources of the Past in Early Medieval Europe*, eds Clemens Gantner, Rosamond McKitterick and Sven Meeder (Cambridge: CUP, 2015), 98–111.

Ward, Graeme, 'The Order of History: Liturgical Time and the Rhythms of the Past in Amalarius's *De Ordine Antiphonarii*', in *Writing the Early Middle Ages: Studies in*

Honour of Rosamond McKitterick, eds Elina Screen and Charles West (Cambridge: CUP, 2018), 98–111.

Ward, Graeme, 'Exegesis, Empire, and Eschatology: Reading Orosius' *Histories Against the Pagans* in the Carolingian World', in *Cultures of Eschatology II: Time, Death and Afterlife in Medieval Christian, Islamic and Buddhist Communities*, eds Veronika Wieser, Vincent Eltschinger and Johann Heiss (Berlin: De Gruyter, 2020), 674–97.

Ward, Graeme, 'The Sense of an Ending in the *Histories* of Frechulf of Lisieux', in *Historiography and Identity III: Carolingian Approaches*, eds Rutger Kramer, Helmut Reimitz and Graeme Ward (Turnhout: Brepols, 2021), 291–315.

Wattenbach, Willhelm, *Deutschlands Geschichtsquellen im Mittelalter bis zur Mitte des dreizehnten Jahrhunderts*, 2 vols (Berlin: W. Hertz, 1893–4), 6th edn.

Wattenbach, Wilhelm and Levison, Wilhelm *Deutschlands Geschichtsquellen im Mittelalter. Vorzeit und Karolinger*, Part 3: *Die Karolinger vom Tode Karls des Grossen bis zum Vertrag von Verdun*, revised by Heinz Löwe (Weimar: Hermann Böhlaus Nachfolger, 1957).

Werner, Karl Ferdinand, 'Die literarischen Vorbilder des Aimoin von Fleury und die Entstehung seiner *Gesta Francorum*', in *Medium Aevum Vivum: Festschrift für Walther Bulst*, eds H. R. Jauss and D. Schaller (Heidelberg: Winter, 1960), 69–103.

Werner, Karl Ferdinand, 'Gott, Herrscher und Historiograph: der Geschichtsschreiber als Interpret des Wirkens Gottes in der Welt und Ratgeber der Könige (4. Bis 12. Jahrhundert)', in *Deus qui mutat tempora: Menschen und Institutionen im Wandel des Mittelalters: Festschrift für Alfons Becker zu seinem fünfundsechzigsten Geburtstag*, eds Ernst-Dieter Hehl, Hubertus Seibert and Franz Staab (Sigmaringen: Thorbecke, 1987), 1–31.

Werner, Karl Ferdinand, 'L'*Historia* et les rois', in *Religion et culture autour de l'an mil: royaume capétien et Lotharingie: actes du colloque Hugues Capet 987-1987, la France de l'an mil, Auxerre, 26 et 27 juin 1987, Metz, 11 et 12 septembre 1987*, eds Dominique Iogna-Prat and Jean-Charles Picard (Paris: Picard, 1990), 135–43.

Werner, Karl Ferdinand, '*Hludowicus Augustus*: gouverner l'empire chrétien: idées at réalités', in *Charlemagne's Heir: New Perspectives on the Reign of Louis the Pious*, eds P. Godman and R. Collins (Oxford: Clarendon Press, 1990), 3–123.

West, Charles, *Reframing the Feudal Revolution: Political and Social Transformation between Marne and Moselle, c. 800–c. 1100* (Cambridge: CUP, 2013).

West, Charles, 'Knowledge of the Past and the Judgement of History in Tenth-Century Trier: Regino of Prüm and the Lost Manuscript of Bishop Adventius of Metz', *EME*, 24(2) (2016): 137–59.

Westgard, Joshua A., 'Bede and the Continent in the Carolingian Age and Beyond', in *The Cambridge Companion to Bede*, ed. Scott DeGregorio (Cambridge: CUP, 2010), 201–15.

Whelan, Robin, *Being Christian in Vandal Africa: The Politics of Orthodoxy in the Post-Imperial West* (Oakland, CA: University of California Press, 2018).

Whelan, Robin, 'After Augustine, after Markus: The Problem of the Secular at the End of Antiquity', *EME*, 29(1) (2021): 12–35.

Whitman, Jon, 'The Literal Sense of Christian Scripture: Redefinition and Revolution', in *Interpreting Scriptures in Judaism, Christianity, and Islam: Overlapping Inquiries*, eds by Mordechai Z. Cohen and Adele Berlin (Cambridge: CUP, 2016), 133-58.

Wilmart, André, 'Le couvent et la bibliothèque de Cluny vers le milieu du XIe siècle', *Revue Mabillon*, 11 (1921), 89–124.

Witakowski, Witold, 'The *Chronicle* of Eusebius: Its Type and Continuation in Syriac Historiography', *Aram*, 12 (2000): 419–37.

Wood, Ian N., 'Saint-Wandrille and its Hagiography', in *Church and Chronicle in the Middle Ages: Essays Presented to John Taylor*, eds Ian N. Wood and Graham A. Loud (London: Bloomsbury, 1991), 1–14.

Wood, Ian N., 'Chains of Chronicles: The Example of London, British Library ms. add. 16974', in *Zwischen Niederschrift und Wiederschrift: Hagiographie und Historiographie im Spannungsfeld von Kompendienüberlieferung und Editionstechnik*, eds Richard Corradini, Max Diesenberger and Meta Niederkorn-Bruck (Vienna: Austrian Academy of Sciences Press, 2010), 67–77.

Wood, Ian N., 'Universal Chronicles in the Early Medieval West', *Medieval Worlds*, 1 (2015): 47–60.

Wood, Ian, 'The Problem of Late Merovingian Culture', in *Exzerpieren – Kompilieren – Tradieren: Transformationen des Wissens zwischen Spätantike und Frühmittelalter*, eds Stephan Dusil, Gerald Schwedler and Raphael Schwitter (Berlin: De Gruyter, 2016), 199–222.

Wood, Jamie, *The Politics of Identity in Visigothic Spain: Religion and Power in the Histories of Isidore of Seville* (Leiden: Brill, 2012).

Young, Frances M., *Biblical Exegesis and the Formation of Christian Culture* (Cambridge: CUP, 1997).

Zecchini, Giuseppe, 'Latin Historiography: Jerome, Orosius and the Western Chronicles', in *Greek and Roman Historiography in Late Antiquity: Fourth to Sixth Century A.D.*, ed. Gabrielle Marasco (Leiden: Brill, 2003), 317–45.

Zechiel-Eckes, Klaus, 'Ein Blick in Pseudoisidors Werkstatt. Studien zum Entstehungsprozess der falschen Dekretalen: Mit einem exemplarischen editorischen Anhang (Pseudo-Julius an die orientalischen Bischöfe, JK †196)', *Francia*, 28(1) (2001): 37–90.

Zinn, Grover A., '*Historia fundamentum est*: The Role of History in the Contemplative Life according to Hugh of St. Victor', in *Contemporary Reflections on the Medieval Christian Tradition. Essays in Honor of Ray C. Petry*, ed. George H. Shriver (Durham, NC: Duke University Press, 1974), 135–58.

Index